AF772484

IN THE DEEDS WE TRUST

Percival P. Baxter displaying his eight pound trout, June 3, 1884. Money given him for his catch was saved and grew to fund fishery research. (Photo: Baxter Family Collection)

IN THE DEEDS WE TRUST

BAXTER STATE PARK 1970–1994

TRUDY IRENE SCEE, Ph.D

TOWER
PUBLISHING

Copyright © 1999 by Baxter State Park Authority, Maine.
Published by Tower Publishing, Standish, Maine.

All rights reserved including the right of reproduction in whole or in part in any form. Requests for permission or further information should be addressed to Baxter State Park Authority.

Cover Design: Edward Dwyer
Cover Photograph: Whidden Pond (Photographed by Edward Dwyer)

ISBN: 1-881758-60-5

Library of Congress Catalog Card Number: 94-12045

Printed in the United States of America

CONTENTS

FOREWORD

Percival Baxter passed away on June 13, 1969. During the preceding forty years, from the time he left politics, he devoted much of his energy and resources to the acquisition, bit by bit, of what was to become Baxter State Park. It was a difficult project, requiring utmost patience—a frustrating task which often necessitated diplomacy and compromise to attain his final goal. I recall a conversation with him at the time of the installation of the Togue Pond gate and the closure of the Abol Road: he said, "that, though an expensive undertaking, it was necessary because the Park had to gain control of its access." This was done during his lifetime. He further stated in a letter to Helon Taylor: "While I am living, I fear no encroachment on the Park, but as time passes and new men appear upon the scene there may be a tendency to overlook these restrictions and break the spirit of these gifts."

In the Deeds We Trust describes events which have occurred in the twenty-five years since the Governor's death. It is not a chronological record, but rather a discussion, subject by subject, of the many major issues that arose during the period. It further documents the evolution of the administration of the Park, the Authority and Advisory, and the public's perception of its role in determining Park policy.

Finally, the reader gains an appreciation of the challenges and demands realized by an administrator who consistently directed Baxter State Park within the spirit of the monumental gift. Among the growing lists of willing, dedicated persons who have given of their talents in support of Baxter's dream, one name, Irwin "Buzz" Caverly, Jr., stands tall. Buzz has devoted himself and his career to the uncompromising pursuit of Percival Baxter's vision. The Park and the people of Maine are indeed fortunate to be the beneficiaries of his guidance and enduring commitment.

Rupert White
Baxter Park Advisory Committee
and grandnephew of Governor Baxter

PREFACE

In 1993 the Park Use Committee of the Baxter State Park Advisory recommended to the Baxter State Park Authority that the Park hire an historian to write a history of Baxter State Park since 1970. The Authority approved the recommendation, and the Park, under Director Irvin C. Caverly, Jr., advertised for an historian. The Park received manuscript proposals in spring 1994, reviewed the competitive bids with the Authority and Advisory, and in late summer 1994 offered the author a contract for the project. Having recently finished a doctorate in history, and having an earlier background in forestry and engineering, the author was more than pleased to undertake a study which both embraced her academic and professional interests and offered her an opportunity to explore an absolutely wonderful wilderness area. While not strictly required for the project, visiting the Park on numerous occasions and hiking many of its trails—as well as attending several Authority and Advisory meetings and other Park related events—certainly added to the author's insight into and appreciation of Governor Percival Proctor Baxter's gift to the citizens of Maine.

The author was not the first person to undertake writing a history of Baxter State Park for the Authority. While researching *In The Deeds We Trust: Baxter State Park, 1970-1994*, the author learned that not only had an earlier work by Dr. John Hakola of the University of Maine at Orono been commissioned by the Park, two other persons had previously been engaged for the task. Both of the men initiated research, then asked the Authority to release them from their duties due to time and other constraints. The Park then contracted with Hakola for a manuscript in 1970. Hakola conducted exhaustive research and submitted his completed manuscript (he had submitted some of the chapters earlier) in late 1979. In 1980 the Park contracted with Thea Wheelwright of TBW Books of Maine for the editing and publication of Hakola's monograph. As published in 1981 and distributed by both the Park and, initially, TBW Books, *Legacy of A Lifetime, The Story of Baxter State Park* proved of interest to the general public and an invaluable administrative tool. Hakola's work established the value of keeping the Park's written history up-to-date, hence setting the background and in some ways the precedent for *In The Deeds We Trust*.

The following pages and chapters are not all-inclusive. Such a work would be prohibitive not only in length but in detail. Rather, the author has strived to make *In The Deeds We Trust* interesting and informative to the general reader through coverage of numerous issues and events which came to the public's attention during the twenty-five year period examined, as well as covering basic Park operations from 1970. At the same time, the author has examined controversial or critical policy issues (often one-and-the-same) which the Park is likely to encounter again in the future—or encounter in a different guise—as well as crucial Park events or developments in sufficient depth as to make *In The Deeds We Trust* an administrative resource. The general reader will hopefully come away from the book with an appreciation of the complexity of Park policy and administration, while those persons more acquainted or involved with Park operations might acquire a more thorough understanding of the Park's past and the development of current Authority and Park policy. The Endnotes provide further information on some topics as well as identifying pertinent documentation.

Early in the research of *In The Deeds We Trust*, the appropriate title for the manuscript became evident to the author. As the following pages illustrate time and time again, members of the Baxter State Park Authority, members of the Advisory, and Park Administrators consistently consulted Governor Baxter's Deeds of Trust regarding decisions concerning the best interests of the Park and about appropriate Park policy and operations. That those who disagreed with Park policy over various issues often refuted Park and Authority interpretations of the Deeds of Trust does not negate such consultations, but rather illustrates the often obscure or imprecise nature of the Trust Deeds and the difficulties the Authority and staff encountered in meeting the many demands placed on Park resources in the late twentieth century. The Deeds of Trust and other records left by Baxter served as the source of inspiration and legal guidance for the Park and Authority, and provided the basis for decisions of the Maine Attorney General's Office and Justices of the State of Maine when the Park, Authority, or members of the general public sought legal clarification of policy or operational issues.

The author would like to thank several individuals for their contributions. To start, the author would like to thank those persons most responsible for hiring her to write the history update: Park Director Irvin "Buzz" C. Caverly and Authority members Ray B. "Bucky" Owen, Susan J.

Bell, and Michael C. Carpenter. The author would also like to thank the members of the Authority seated since autumn 1994, Andrew Ketterer and Charles Gadzik, as well as continuing member and Chair Owen, for their support of the project. The author would also like to thank all those persons who answered her questions during the course of research—Authority and Advisory members as well as Park staff. Such information contributed to the project by increasing the author's insight into Park operations, or by simply keeping her from wandering off on the wrong Park trail. As Caverly reportedly told a friend who wanted to guide the author across the Park's famed Knife Edge, "just don't get the historian killed before she finishes the book."

The author would also like to thank Park staff, especially Director Caverly, for maintaining extensive files covering the 1970-1994 period which immeasurably aided the project. Along those lines the author would also like to thank Paul Stern and Alice Sproul of the Attorney General's Office for securing legal records for her use, as well as Advisory member Benjamin Townsend for providing personal records and papers as well as some Advisory minutes. Other persons offered similar assistance. Additional sources used during the research stage have been indicated in the Bibliography and Endnotes, and their availability is greatly appreciated.

Concerning the writing and review of the manuscript, the author wants to thank everyone forced to read the manuscript in its primitive stages, especially Buzz Caverly and his staff members Jensen Bissell, Chris Drew, and Jean Hoekwater. Caverly asked the three staff members to read the rough draft, in part or in its entirety, an undesirable task for anyone. The author would also like to thank the members of the Baxter State Park Advisory History Committee: Chair Edward Dwyer, John Howard, Jane Thomas, and Roy Farnsworth. The History Committee assisted Director Caverly and Park Naturalist Jean Hoekwater in reviewing a revised draft as submitted in late 1996, a long and no doubt painful process. Dorcas Miller assisted the committee in making revision recommendations. Roxanna McLean, Baxter State Park Secretary, participated in the History Committee and initiated the task of reformatting the manuscript to meet camera-ready publication specifications, and Dana Smith of the University of Maine completed the task. Although the History Committee did not agree with everything the author had written, they did not censor the work.

Furthermore, they made numerous suggestions which greatly improved the text. The group also aided in the selection of photographs during the publication process. As is true for any historical monograph, any errors or oversights remain the responsibility of the author.

ACKNOWLEDGMENT

Baxter State Park is sincerely thankful for the many people who were involved in bringing this history to life, but one BSP Advisory member and Park volunteer deserves special mention: Edward Dwyer has been with this project for its inception to its completion. Without his single-minded devotion to detail and extreme patience throughout the many stages of editing and publishing, an era of Baxter State Park history would have been forever lost and unavailable to the inquiring minds of future generations. For a true labor of love and a task well done, Ed...Many thanks and "Happy Trails."

Buzz Caverly
Director, Baxter State Park

Chimney Pond (Photo: *Bangor Daily News*)

Chapter One

An Introduction to Baxter State Park 1970–1994

Percival Proctor Baxter, Governor of the State of Maine from 1921 to 1924, died on June 12, 1969. Like other Governors he left behind a record of political prowess and legislative contribution. Unlike other Governors, Baxter left behind a personal triumph and a truly priceless gift: the establishment of a wilderness park of over 201,018 acres, left in trust to the people of Maine. Baxter had accumulated the land over the course of more than thirty years and deeded it to the State of Maine in twenty-eight separate deeds. The first deed, dated March 3, 1931, conveyed 5,960 acres, acres which included the highest mountain in Maine, Mount Katahdin, and territory which Baxter called "the most picturesque area of the State." The last deed, dated August 6, 1962, conveyed 7,764 acres in T2R9 in the southern portion of Baxter State Park—as the Maine State Legislature officially named the wilderness gifts in 1933—around Togue and Abol Ponds. Known collectively as the Deeds of Trust, the deeds became the guiding legal instruments and philosophical basis for the stewardship of Baxter State Park, arguably Percival Baxter's greatest gift to both humanity and the wilderness he loved.[1]

Baxter State Park was not the only legacy of Percival Baxter. Baxter also made substantial philanthropic contributions elsewhere. He made various donations to public and charitable works during his life time, including granting the city of Portland land for public parks and reserves and deeding Mackworth Island, a long-time family property in Portland Harbor, to the state to be used for public purposes, preferably those benefitting children. He initially provided a $10,000 maintenance fund for the island, and later donated $625,000 to the State for the purpose of moving the State School for the Deaf to the island. The State used a portion of the larger fund to construct a new bridge to the island and a greater share, augmented by state funds, to build the Governor Baxter School for the Deaf.[2]

Baxter's will bequeathed funds to various cities and several institutions for the benefit of both people and animals. Some of the bequests provided funding to support earlier endowments or land grants. Baxter also left a trust fund of over $5,000,000 for "the care, protection, and operation of the forest land known as Baxter State Park, and for other forest lands hereinafter acquired by the State of Maine ... for recreational or reforestation purposes." The trust granted the State of Maine "full power to harvest the crop" on any forest land purchased, or to reforest the land, as well as to protect it from insects, fire, or other damage. Proceeds from harvests would be used for the care, management, and extension of such lands. Baxter stated that he hoped some of the lands would become models of forest management, similar to forests he had seen in Germany, Scandinavia, and elsewhere. In 1970, the State Legislature acted to implement Baxter's long-time desire for forestry reform in Maine by establishing the Maine Forest Authority, funded primarily through Baxter's Trust Fund. The Maine Attorney General, the Forest Commissioner, the Maine State Park Commissioner, the Commissioner of Inland Fisheries and Game, and one member of the general public—appointed by the Governor—comprised the Maine Forest Authority. Hartley Baxter, grandnephew of Percival Baxter, served as the appointed member of the Maine Forest Authority during its brief existence in the 1970s.[3]

Essentially supplementing funds from the larger trust, most of which made its way to the Park, an earlier trust, the Baxter State Park Trust Fund, was used to finance Park operations, personnel additions, and capital improvement after Baxter's death. Established in 1961 and used sparingly through 1969, the Baxter State Park Trust Fund contained a principal of almost $1,600,000 at the time of Baxter's death. (A much smaller trust fund started in 1945 and theoretically used for Park operations, although in reality it seldom was, was closed out and its principal added to the Baxter State Park Trust Fund in 1970.) The Boston Safe Deposit and Trust Company managed the Trust Fund and would continue to do so in following years. A smaller trust was held by the State.[4]

In addition to granting Baxter State Park (BSP) to the people of Maine and providing funds for its operations and maintenance, Percival Baxter had made plans as to how the land should be administered and its policies formulated. In 1933, the State Legislature, in the absence of any other governing body and in accordance with federal law, created a five member Baxter State Park Commission comprised of the Governor, the Commissioner of Inland Fisheries and Game, the Forest Commissioner, and two appointed members of the general public. In 1939, at the request of Governor Baxter, the State Legislature repealed the 1933 act and created the Baxter State Park Authority. The State Forest Commissioner, the Commissioner of Inland Fisheries and Game, and the Attorney General served on the Authority. The Authority governed the policies and operations of Baxter State Park. Baxter did not agree with all Authority decisions, but he reiterated his confidence in the Authority and worked with the Authority until the year of his death. The Authority continued to govern the Park through 1970 to the close of 1994, the twenty-five year period herein examined. The Authority held responsibility for all policy issues concerning the Park, leaving day-to-day operations to the Park's chief administrator. Before 1975 the Park Supervisor held that position; after March 1975 a Park Director headed operations. For a majority of the period studied, Irvin C. Caverly, Jr. served as chief administrator. In 1970, the Authority appointed a seven person Advisory Committee. The Advisory, comprised of members of the general public, varied in membership numbers over the years, but made crucial contributions to the Park throughout the period studied. Over the course of time, the Advisory formed various subcommittees to address specific issues. The Advisory held no policy or administrative powers, yet it contributed significantly to Authority and staff decisions through its insights and advice.

The Authority in 1970 had more than 200,000 acres to manage under a multiple use mandate. The Deeds of Trust, although varied in specifics, established the Park as a wilderness area, one which would be open to the people of Maine, and visitors to the state, to enjoy through recreational pursuits. The vast majority of the Park's land was set aside as a wilderness preserve, later known as the Sanctuary, reflecting the love of animals Baxter exhibited throughout his life. In order to placate or cooperate with—depending on one's perspective—local citizens, and in consideration of their largely hunting based economy, Baxter agreed in the 1950s and early 1960s to allow hunting on some 51,500 acres in T6R9, T6R10, and T2R9.

Hunting regulations in the specified areas were the same as those governing hunting in the rest of the state. One exception, however, involved moose. The Authority in the early 1980s secured legislation outlawing moose hunting in BSP. The Park did experience problems with poaching and other hunting violations in the period studied, but for the most part hunters followed established regulations.

Another exception to provisions followed elsewhere in the Park involved forestry provisions for 28,594 acres in T6R9 and T6R10, the "northern two townships" or the "Scientific Forest Management Area" as the parcels were consecutively called. Here the Park was to create a productive model forest, one managed by scientific forestry which could serve as a showcase of the best of forest technology. Establishing such a model of forest management proved one of the greatest challenges the Authority and BSP personnel—State employees paid through trust fund income and other Park revenue—would face from 1970 to the end of the period.

All areas of Baxter State Park, including the forest management area, were open to public recreation. Yet, not all forms of recreation would be allowed in the Park or in all areas of the Park. A twenty-five year controversy over snowmobile use, and a less lengthy, or at least more intermittent, controversy over motorcycle use, occurred during the studied era. Use of all-terrain vehicles and all-terrain or mountain bicycles also became an issue during the final years of the period. The Authority ultimately banned the first and allowed the second only on the established Park road system. Likewise, the Authority limited the use of motor boats on bodies of water within the Park, and limited the size of any motor vehicle allowed within Park boundaries. The goal of BSP policy governing vehicle access was to make the Park as accessible to the public as possible without destroying the wilderness in general, harming flora or fauna, or damaging the wilderness experience as enjoyed by Park visitors. Baxter had stated more than once that he wanted the Park to be accessible to the people of Maine, but he stressed that the Park should be enjoyed in the right way, by those willing to make the effort to see nature on foot. In keeping with the wilderness aspect of the Park, the Authority also banned the use of televisions, radios, and similar electronic equipment. At the close of the period cellular telephones made their appearance in BSP, but, for the time being, no enforcement measures were taken except when telephones proved disruptive to other Park users.

Respecting Baxter's oft stated desire to protect wildlife, the Park maintained a ban on pets during the twenty-five year period. This does not mean that all pets stayed out of the Park. Park records reveal numerous instances of people attempting to smuggle in their favorite pet; sometimes dressing them as human babies, sometimes hiding them under blankets or in various containers, and sometimes bringing them in through unattended gates or across the Park's open boundaries. The Park also received special requests to allow pets, requests which they had to deny. Guide dogs for the blind did make occasional visits to the Park, the most celebrated and frequent of them during the period being the Seeing Eye dog Orient, who first went to the Park in 1990 as part of his hike along the entire Appalachian Trail—which has its northern terminal point on Katahdin—with his follower Bill Irwin. The two subsequently visited the Park numerous times. Mike Perry, another blind Appalachian Trail hiker, brought his dog, Tessy, to BSP in 1981.[5]

In order to control access to the Baxter State Park, the Park maintained gatehouses at key entrance points. In 1970 these included gatehouses at Matagamon, Nesowadnehunk, and Togue Pond, and the Telos Gatehouse. Late in the period the Authority, due to changing use patterns and changes in the neighboring Great Northern Company's road system, elected to close Telos Gatehouse. They also relocated, renamed, and eventually closed, the Nesowadnehunk Gatehouse. Another gatehouse change involved moving the Togue Pond Gatehouse further north to allow personnel to better control access to Roaring Brook when overuse of the area caused both parking difficulties and potential environmental damage.

Gatehouse attendants provided BSP users with information about the Park, checked to see that vehicles met Park regulations and that no pets were being smuggled in (although they could only do so in a unobtrusive manner—they did not search vehicles), maintained records of vehicle counts, and collected day use fees for non-residents of Maine. Gatehouse staffing changed over the years, in response to use patterns and to budgetary constraints.

With the exception of the Scientific Forest Management Area, road construction in Baxter State Park had essentially ended by 1970. The roads, in keeping with Baxter's visions for a wilderness park, remained primitive and unpaved. Originally wide enough for only one-way traffic with vehicles forced to move to the side to allow oncoming vehicles to pass, over the years the roads widened in places so as to allow for two-way—albeit it a tight squeeze—traffic. Some of the widening had occurred due to the simple process of drivers inadvertently clearing roadsides when they pulled over to allow another driver to pass. Much of the widening, however, occurred as a result of modern machinery being used to maintain Park roads. In the late 1980s, the Park relocated several miles of road along the western perimeter, bringing the entire road system within BSP boundaries.

The Maine Department of Transportation held responsibility for maintaining Park roads, although the amount of funding budgeted to BSP road work proved a subject of dispute during many years. In spite of being unpaved and unplowed, the roads still required grading, culvert work, gravel in some locations, and so forth. The goal of road maintenance, however, was not to create a pleasurable backwoods road but to make the Park accessible. Many of the complaints received about Baxter State Park over the years focused on road conditions. Depending upon the weather, Park roads could be slippery, pitted, rutted, muddy, or dusty. The Park contained roughly fifty miles of dirt road in 1994, most of it the Perimeter or Tote Road which traversed the Park from the Togue Pond entrance on the southeast, along a north westerly route to the Nesowadnehunk Gate location on the western boundary, then northeasterly to the Matagamon Gate on the northeastern border. Other Park roads were essentially spurs to various camping or recreational areas, the longest such road being the Roaring Brook Road leading to the Roaring Brook Campground and the several trails which started or ended, depending on one's perspective, at Roaring Brook. At the close of the period, the Park began to close access to Roaring Brook when its parking areas reached peak capacity on any given day. The Park Director also considered the possibility of closing the road on a permanent basis, making the Roaring Brook area accessible only by foot in summer or by snowshoe or cross-country skiing in winter. Roaring Brook Road issues, like virtually all others concerning access, proved controversial.

Uncountable issues proved controversial in the twenty-five year period, several of which are discussed in detail in following pages. The crucial issue for the Park centered on how to best protect the natural environment, in all its aspects, from overuse in an era of ever increasing demand. Baxter had made abundantly clear his desire that the Park remain a wilderness area, one in which people could view the beauty of Katahdin and the surrounding landscape. At the same time, he wanted the Park to remain wild and a haven for animals. Unfortunately, the greater the number of people visiting a wilderness area, the greater the potential for that wilderness area to lose its wildness. Erosion, the disposal of natural and unnatural waste products, noise and air pollution from motor vehicles, and a basic disruption of the wilderness experience from the simple fact of having to share it with too many other people, are only a few of the problems which Baxter State Park had to address in the late twentieth century. Baxter State Park remained committed to protecting the natural environment, or the "resource" as personnel and others frequently termed it at the end of the period. Many Park solutions, or anticipated solutions, proved unpopular with various sectors of the general population.

Visitor use did indeed increase from 1970 through 1994. Statistics were compiled in various ways, but total gatehouse counts between mid-May and mid-October, the standard summer season, showed a marked increase in BSP visitors. For example, in 1980, 70,486 people registered at the Park's gatehouses during the summer season. In 1986, gatekeepers tabulated 75,038 people entering BSP. In 1994, gatekeepers counted 80,537 people coming into the two gate-houses then staffed, Togue Pond and Matagamon, from May to October. Compared to reports of 68,490 visitors for 1970, and 64,365 for 1971, Park use greatly increased over the twenty-five year period. Winter and off-season visitors raised the numbers further, although not everyone registered.[6] Such increase intensified problems facing the Park such as visitor safety, environmental protection, campground availability, and trail maintenance.

The Kidney Pond Camps as they appeared in winter 1987-88 prior to operational management by the Authority. (Photo: Baxter State Park)

The demand on Park trails required extensive personnel attention to ensure that they remained passable and as safe as possible. Park staff designed trails with the aim of minimizing the impact of hikers on the environment, and rerouted trails as necessary. With roughly 180 miles of hiking trails extant at the close of the period, including the northern terminus of the interstate Appalachian Trail, Trail Crew members had their hands full. Volunteers aided staff efforts, especially after the mid-1980s.

The Park limited the number of visitors who could spend any given night in the Park. No person could camp outside a designated area without permission. Visitors also needed reservations to stay overnight within the designated areas and had to pay camping fees. The Park maintained eight campgrounds in 1970, nine in 1980, and ten in 1994. The Park also maintained four group areas during 1970-1994. Various outlying camp sites also existed. Camping reservations could be made for tent sites, lean-tos, bunkhouses, and individual cabins. Fees increased during the period, but from most perspectives—in terms of the quality of the sites and the beauty of the environment—fees remained reasonable. Changes in users fees, as true for other changes of Baxter State Park Rules and Regulations, were announced ahead of time, discussed by the Authority in a public setting (all Authority meetings were open to the public, save personnel matters discussed in Executive Session), and, depending on the specific rule, public hearings were held before the Authority reached a decision. As discussed in a later chapter, a significant challenge to BSP camping and user regulations in general occurred in 1976 when a group of Native Americans occupied Abol Campground without permission, a situation which came close to ending with a forced evacuation.[7]

While camping fees, as well as day use fees charged to out-of-state visitors, provided income, the Park financed its operations largely through trust fund revenue. After the Park received the larger endowment—hereafter referred to as the Baxter State Trust Fund or simply the Trust Fund—following Baxter's death, BSP began a period of internal expansion by hiring new personnel to meet staffing needs, making improvements in Park facilities and equipment, and purchasing leases. Baxter had agreed to honor certain pre-existing rights or leases when he made several of his land purchases over the years. These rights included permission to hunt in specified areas and, as discussed in following pages, cutting rights in T2R9. They also include a number of private leases.

In 1955 Percival Baxter had discussed the issue of private leases with the Authority. He stated that the lease holders had been leased only the use of specified structures; they did not possess title to the buildings. They could not, therefore, convey the structures or reassign their leases to any other parties. Baxter proposed that in the future all such leases in the Park be terminated. The Authority took little action in this regard until 1967, and even renewed or transferred some leases between 1955 and 1967. In 1967, however, upon learning that the Kidney Pond Camps sporting business was up for sale, Baxter asked the Authority to consider the matter carefully and not take any action which might infringe on the "deed of gift" of the property to the State.[8] The Authority thereafter moved to terminate private leases in the Park, voting to do so by January 1, 1970. They later revised the termination date to January 1, 1971. The process of ending the leasing system lasted four years, extending into the early 1970s, and, one might argue, in terms of its after effects it extended into the 1990s.

The first lease to revert to the Park[9] was that of Kidney Pond Camps, which had been transferred to a new lessee. The new lease holder, Charles J. Lipscomb, sold his personal property interests to the Authority in 1968 for $52,500. The Authority decided to lease the property on a concession basis for a period of five years, doing so largely to keep the camps open without having to immediately assume operational responsibilities. Ruth and Charles Norris leased the property, after participating in a public bid.[10]

Subsequent to completing transactions on the Kidney Pond Camps, in July 1967 the Authority notified the lessees of the York Twin Pine Camps, Jeannette and Earl W. York, Jr., that their lease would not be renewed. After having the personal property and improvements to the buildings appraised, the Authority and the Yorks, after considerable negotiations, agreed on a purchase price of $45,000 in late 1969. The title transfer to the Daicey Pond property occurred on June 30, 1970. The property remained vacant for one year, during which time Park Supervisor Irvin C. Caverly, Jr. and Park Business manager William E. Cross proposed that the buildings be converted to a single cabin rental facility. The Authority agreed to the suggestion, and in 1972 the Park began to rent the cabins on a daily basis.[11]

A few other leases were terminated and the lessees compensated for property (or given new short-term leases) during 1969 and 1970. These transpired without extensive bargaining and at much lower monetary prices than those paid for the larger sporting camp leases. One such lease was held by Priscilla L. Clark for a lot on Second Matagamon Lake; one was held by Victor W. Davignon, also on Second Matagamon Lake; and the third was held by Louis C. Martin on First Matagamon Lake.[12]

Three other leases underwent the termination process with different results. The first to be resolved was a lease held by the Boy Scouts of America at Abol Pond. After informing the organization that their lease would not be renewed and holding several discussions on the matter, the Authority informed the Boy Scouts that although they would not be given a lease or other property rights they could continue to use their former premises until such a time as they abused their privileges.[13]

The second lease involved land on Togue Stream originally leased to Ronald Budreau by Great Northern. In 1969, after termination procedures had begun, the current three lease holders—Budreau and his partners Daniel McQuarrie and Darrell F. Morrow—requested improvement compensation. The Authority rejected their request. The Authority eventually decided to meet the lessees' requests, but before they could do so an Assistant Attorney General reported that Budreau had a lifetime right to renew his lease unless he violated its conditions. No evidence of violations existed. Therefore, as historian John Hakola wrote in *Legacy of A Lifetime, The Story of Baxter State Park*, "unless it could be shown that the Park Authority lease violated the trust indenture, and unless it could be shown that Great Northern's lease with Budreau allowed for termination, the Authority had no legal right to terminate the lease.[14]

The holder of the third lease, the Fin and Feather Club of Millinocket, joined suit with Budreau and his partners. The club had had a number of disputes with Baxter State Park over access and other policies in previous years, and had held a lease on a portion of land fronting Abol Pond for eleven years before being informed in 1969 that their lease would not be renewed. The Authority and the club had performed restocking work on the pond to make it more conducive to fishing, and the club did not want to give up its interests in the waterfront property. The Authority extended to the Fin and Feather Club a use offer similar to that given the Boy Scouts, but the club elected to join with the Budreau lease holders in an action against the Authority for illegal lease cancellation. Before any legal action had transpired, the BSPA brought suit against the club and the others to have the legal status of the various parties determined. The Maine Supreme Court in March 1974 ruled that the Authority had the right to lease land, to negotiate new leases after gaining property, and to terminate leases after proper notification. The Court held the Budreau and Fin and Feather club leases terminated as of December 31, 1970. The Authority requested that the lease holders remove their property. After the lease holders failed to comply, the Authority had the property removed and the buildings demolished.[15]

After phasing out the various leases, the Park in some instances retained buildings for public and administrative purposes. In the cases of the Budreau and Fin and Feather Club leases, the Park destroyed existing buildings. In several instances the Park engaged in cleanup work. The phasing out of leases and the initial decisions on what to do with the various facilities did not permanently resolve all disputes, however. The former sporting camps on Daicey and Kidney Ponds soon became the focus of media attention and public controversy, especially Kidney Pond Camps.

Before putting the Kidney Pond Camps out to bid in the 1960s for a concession operation, the Authority had considered other options. The options included hiring new personnel specifically to operate the camps, abandoning some of the buildings (the "luxury" ones), and renting the guest cabins individually in a similar manner as BSP ran other campgrounds.[16] The camp contained twenty-one guest cabins, a main lodge for meals, laundry facilities, an owner or operator's cabin, staff quarters, and assorted other buildings for a total of thirty-eight existing buildings or structures, many of them made of hand-hewn logs. The guest cabins had electricity (produced by two generators which served the entire camping facility), running hot and cold water, showers, toilet facilities, iron stoves, porches, and a view of the pond. In late 1967, the Authority's appraiser identified the buildings as approximately forty years of age with roughly fifteen years of remaining economic life.[17]

The agreement signed with Ruth and Charles Norris in April 1968 granted them permission to run the 24.4 acre facility until the close of the 1972 season. The concession fee totaled $12,550, payable in annual increments of $2,510. The lease granted the Norrises permission to use all extant buildings and most of the personal property such as furniture and equipment. No alcoholic beverages could be sold, and Park permission had to be secured before any new buildings could be erected. The Norrises were responsible for any personal injuries on the premises and for maintaining the dirt access road and bridge from the Park's Perimeter Road. In January 1972, the Authority renegotiated the contract through 1977 for the same fee and basic terms, even though, as Park Business Manager William E. Cross pointed out, they were not recovering their costs in terms of the money put into maintaining the camps versus income from their lease with the Norrises. The Park had also experienced difficulties with oversize vehicles making deliveries to the camp, difficulties which then Supervisor Irvin C. Caverly, Jr. worked out with the Norrises. Otherwise, the arrangements seemed to be working well and Cross noted that many of the buildings were in better shape than they had been in 1967.[18]

Problems did arise with the bridge over Nesowadnehunk Stream in following years, repairs for which the Authority held the Norrises responsible under the terms of their lease. The bridge had washed out and been moved during the 1960s, and by the 1970s needed further attention.[19] Although the Authority considered other options for the future, in 1977 and in 1982 the Authority again negotiated five year leases with the Norrises. Under the terms of the newest lease, the fee increased to $9,500 and the Norrises were held responsible for maintaining all personal property including generators, which had cost BSP money in the past. The Park assumed responsibility for the access roads. The new lease allowed for termination of the lease by either party in the event of any major occurrence which might influence the running of the camps. The new lease was signed through the office of a new Business Manager, Robert Williams, and with much input by the Advisory.[20]

By 1984, the Norrises were both in their seventies. Although Park records state that overall the Norrises had done "an excellent job" managing Kidney Pond Camps, problems and concerns had arisen over the maintenance of roads, generators, and septic tanks. The Park had also experienced a low return on the operation in terms of the market value and income of the camps. Williams urged that a contingency plan be made in the event that the Norrises become ill or for other reasons unable to continue the operation, or should a major malfunctioning of the camp power or septic systems occur. The Park needed to budget for any anticipated changes. Williams and Caverly reviewed alternatives previously suggested. Such suggestions included continuing to lease the camps as in previous years; converting the buildings to wilderness cabins similar to those at Daicey Pond and operating them through the regular Park reservations system using either Park personnel or contract operators; or using a combination of options such as contracting for food and cleaning services and reserving the cabins under the Park reservations system with Park or contracted operators managing the operation. Specifics could be worked out, but a plan of action was necessary.[21]

The Norrises continued to operate Kidney Pond Camps under the terms of their lease until the close of the 1987 season. An Advisory subcommittee reviewed the Park's options in the meantime. Business records showed Kidney Pond Camps operating at a significantly higher cost to the Park than nearby Daicey Pond Camps.[22] The Norrises' lease would officially expire on January 1, 1988. Before it expired, a heated debate arose over the future of the camps.

In June 1987, Director Caverly, Attorney General James Tierney, Deputy Attorney General Philip Ahrens, attorney for the Park, and Harold Colt inspected Kidney Pond Camps. Due to the need for extensive maintenance work, and the need to make a decision quickly in the absence of the other members, Authority Chair Tierney decided to close the camps for the 1988 season. The other Authority members subsequently expressed their support for his decision. The Authority notified the Norrises of the decision soon thereafter, thus allowing adequate time for informing the public of the shutdown. The Norrises later indicated an interest in securing another lease if the Park paid for any maintenance work deemed necessary, but not if the lessee had to pay for the work.[23] The Authority then solicited public comments about the camps and the various options available.

Several people wrote to the Authority expressing their views, and numerous individuals spoke at a special meeting of the Authority in December 1987. Some people felt that the camps should be maintained as they were, that to change them would be to destroy a part of the Park's and the region's history. In some instances those who favored no change had personal memories of the camps which they valued, and a couple of people mentioned that Baxter had stayed there himself and had not terminated the leases. (The later argument, however, did not take into account Baxter's actions during the last years of his life.) One person voiced the possibility of having the camps placed on the National Historic Register, a possibility which would be raised again. Other people believed that the amenities offered at Kidney Pond Camps were not in keeping with Baxter's "forever wild" concept, and such things as indoor plumbing, electricity, food services, and so forth should be removed or terminated. Several people expressed concerns that the camps' clientele was a privileged one and that reservations should be available to everyone on a first come first served basis, and at more reasonable rates than those currently charged. Having the Park continue to run the camps as they were would be to place an unreasonable financial burden on BSP, a few people observed. No one who expressed a viewpoint at the December meeting wished to see the camps totally removed and a tent camping area put in its place, although privately some might have favored that option.[24]

The Authority ultimately voted to accept a number of proposals made by the Advisory in December 1987. The proposals recommended that the Park maintain tighter control over the camps' operations than it had in the past; that if anyone other than Park staff were to operate the camps it should be under a contract, not a lease basis; that access to the area be increased to the benefit of people visiting the Park but not staying at Kidney Pond, and that canoes rented there be available to the general public; that reservations for the camps be made through the regular Park system; and that all funding for improvements come from BSP revenue, not through outside donations or funding. After accepting the proposals and entertaining further discussion, the Authority voted to change the Kidney Pond Camps operation to one like that of Daicey Pond Camps. They also asked Caverly, now Park Director, to develop a plan for the conversion.[25]

Renovations at Kidney Pond, as approved by the Authority, monopolized the energies of several staff members and volunteers during portions of 1988. The plan draft called for the removal of 22 buildings, which would leave eleven camps for public rentals and four for service buildings. The main lodge would be retained as a library and meeting facility. Light poles,

Ice provided a convenient thoroughfare when Park staff moved cabins after concession leases for Kidney Pond Camps were terminated.
(Photo: Baxter State Park)

electrical wiring, plumbing, all toxic materials, and a dump would be removed. (During the 1980s the Park had removed all other dumps within its boundaries.) Septic tanks would be removed or filled. Some of the buildings to be removed would be sold at auction, some would be relocated within the Park. One of the cabins was moved and used for a new gatehouse at the West Gate. Basic repairs were made on the cabins retained, and various projects undertaken to make the area more accessible to the general public. Like Daicey Pond, canoe rentals would be on a first come first served basis. The Park projected a maximum day campground use of forty-four persons for Kidney Pond, in comparison with a seventy-five person average for previous years.[26]

The Park proceeded with repairs and renovations in good faith, but not everyone had been persuaded as to the sagacity of the Authority's decisions. Historical preservationists continued to argue that the camps should be preserved as architectural and cultural artifacts of Maine's sporting camps. In 1987, Winston Robbins of the Advisory had requested that the Maine Historic Preservation Commission evaluate the eligibility of Kidney Pond Camps and Daicey Pond Camps for nomination to the National Register of Historic Places. The commission determined that Kidney Pond Camps did meet the criteria for nomination, due in part to the survival not only of its housing facilities but also of its many ancillary buildings. The Commission expressed its hopes that the Authority elect to preserve the camp in its entirety, as all components of the camp were vital to understanding Maine's sporting camps. The Commission's architectural historian, Kirk P. Mahoney, would endeavor to prepare the necessary applications for nomination.[27]

The Authority had not desired to proceed with nomination to the National Register in 1987. In 1988, George Kerivan, a high school history teacher from Massachusetts, wrote to Park Director Caverly (as well as to the State Attorney General, the editor of *Yankee Magazine*, and possibly other persons) urging that the camp be maintained as it had existed, and that a museum be maintained in the camp, perhaps through the establishment of a trust fund devoted to that purpose. Plans had already begun on camp renovations, however, and as Caverly responded to Kerivan, the Authority had historically resisted accepting outside donations due to the expressed wishes of Baxter and his family. The library would be maintained, and room existed there for some displays. Baxter had not wanted a museum within the Park, therefore one would not be created. Kerivan wrote back to Caverly and reiterated the importance of saving as much of the history of the sporting camp as possible, and agreed to meet with Caverly or the new Park Naturalist, Jean Hoekwater, about the matter.[28]

The parties involved did not reach a mutual understanding in 1988 or 1989, nor would they by the close of 1994. In February 1991, Kerivan wrote to the Maine Historic Preservation Commission requesting that they once again consider Kidney Pond Camps for nomination to the National Historic Register, as well as Daicey Pond Camps. Daicey Pond, Mahoney reported, did not meet the criteria. Kidney Pond might well do so, but by 1991 changes had been made and the site would need to be re-evaluated. Mahoney spoke with Caverly via the telephone and wrote to him as well. The inclusion on the National Register did not, Mahoney wrote, "restrict a property owner's rights to the use and disposition of his property." The only exception would be if an owner "undertakes a federally funded or licensed activity," at which time the Commission would "comment upon the effect of such an undertaking on any historic resources in the project area." In general, "listing in the Register is merely a recognition of significance." The Commission would not proceed with nomination against the wishes of the Park Authority.[29]

The Authority did not wish to pursue the nomination. Caverly wrote to Mahoney regarding the Authority's position, stressing that the Park, based on Baxter's Deeds of Trust and other writings, aimed to protect natural, not cultural, resources. The Park would continue to preserve and protect the buildings at Daicey and Kidney Ponds "as time and budget constraints permit." Furthermore, the Park continued to guard against federal involvement in BSP, monetary or other, based on Baxter's long personal history of working to keep the federal government out of the Park and his actions in placing BSP under the jurisdiction of the Baxter State Park Authority.[30]

Architectural or historical preservationists continued to argue that inclusion in the National Register would have no negative impact on the Park and that the Park should do more to protect the area's material heritage than it indicated itself willing to undertake. The issue stayed in the public eye in 1992 as the local press gave it a fair amount of attention and Kerivan and others circulated a petition, which they later sent to State legislators, to have the matter brought before the Authority again. By 1992, nineteen of the buildings extant in 1987 had been removed from the Kidney Pond Camp locality. The Commission stated that the campgrounds might no longer qualify for nomination. Caverly stated to a *Katahdin Times* reporter in early March that " 'those camps have been run into the ground for the almighty dollar, and you can quote me on that.' " The cabins still remaining at the site had had to have new foundations and roofs constructed. Septic tanks removed had been "rotted-out," and the ancient electrical wiring had been dangerous. The Park was proud of the improvements made to the site, Caverly asserted, and had received numerous compliments on the renovations.[31] The controversy, however, did not die.

As submitted to Senator Charles Pray and Representative Herbert Clark, the aforementioned petition contained 286 signatures. It petitioned the State Legislature to recommend to the BSPA that the "Baxter Park Authority allow the request to have Daicey Pond Camps (formerly Twin Pine Camps) and Kidney Pond Camps be considered for recognition by the Maine and National Historical Preservation Society." The Legislature acted on the request and passed a joint resolution requesting the Authority "Allow Recognition of Daicey Pond Camps and Kidney Pond Camps as Historic Sites."[32] The resolution referred specifically to the Maine Historic Preservation Commission, potentially creating something of a conundrum as the Commission, through Mahoney, had already indicated more than once that Daicey Pond was not presently eligible for recognition and Kidney Pond might no longer be eligible. The Commission's Director, Earle G. Shettleworth, Jr., wrote to the Park Resource Manager Jensen Bissell following a telephone conversation between Bissell and Mahoney. Bissell had requested further information on the National Register's program guidelines. Shettleworth forwarded them to Bissell, and suggested that the Authority request a site visit and evaluation by the Commission. Failing such a request, the Commission would carry out its own review and determine Kidney Pond's eligibility—Daicey Pond he repeated was not eligible—and if warranted proceed with the nomination process. If the Authority still objected to a listing, the Commission would halt the process.

Federal regulations would, however, allow the Commission "to request a formal determination of eligibility from the National Register."[33]

The Park reiterated its stance, and requested that Legal Council Paul Stern prepare an overview of the issue. Stern, an Assistant Attorney General, reported that the attempts to place the former sporting camps on the National Register were in opposition to Baxter's desire to prevent federal involvement in BSP and "are an attempt to do exactly what Baxter demanded not be done: create a monument." Baxter had given the Park to the people of Maine in trust, to be governed according to his intent, and "if the Legislature or the Authority acts in a manner in contravention to Baxter's intent, it is a violation of the trust." Baxter had made clear his intentions that the Authority, not the State Legislature, manage the Park. The Authority was not bound by the Legislature's resolution. On June 2, 1992, the Authority voted not to have the two camps listed on the National Register.[34] After the close of the studied period, Kerivan and others would again bring the matter to public attention, arguing, as some did after the 1992 vote, that the reasons given by Park staff and the Authority did not justify the decisions made.[35] As with many other issues involving Park policy, the issue of cultural preservation versus Park autonomy had not been resolved by late 1994.

While the battle over historic preservationism was being waged, the Authority had developed new contracts. The Park reopened Kidney Pond Camps to the public in 1990, and in 1994 entered a three year agreement with Steve and Gladys Buzzell for the camps' operation. Both couples had served as operators or caretakers for a few years, and both campgrounds used the regular reservations system. Contracts were subject to cancellation by the Authority. After the close of the studied period, the Authority elected to cancel the Kidney Pond Camps contract, as well as that for Daicey Pond Camps, and run the operation with Park personnel.[36]

Camping, be it in the historic cabins at Kidney or Daicey Pond or in shelters or tent areas elsewhere in the Park, remained a strong interest of Park visitors from 1970 through 1994. So too did hiking, canoeing, cross-country skiing, technical climbing, and—as later discussed—in some places at some times, snowmobiling. Yet, some people came to the Park for a quite different reason. Throughout the twenty-five years, scientific research played a role in BSP operations. The most well known research project was the mid-1980s to 1990 attempt to reintroduce caribou to the state of Maine. The project directors used BSP as a release site. As discussed in following pages, the project became extremely controversial and its results debatable, depending upon one's criteria. Other research projects proved clearly successful, yielding new knowledge and sometimes helping maintain the health of plant and animal species in the wild, often in a broader context than Baxter State Park. One noted example of a successful research project, in terms of results as well as information gained, was that of the peregrine falcon project of the mid-1980s. Park staff worked with various organizations to reintroduce the birds to Maine and to BSP. As far as can be determined as of a decade later, the birds nested successfully and secured the beginnings of a falcon population.

Most research projects have been less glamorous than reintroduction attempts. Research in BSP has included numerous habitat studies for moss, shrubs, trees, insects, and various mammals, reptiles, and birds. The Park at times has had to take steps to prevent the removal of plant or animal species from the Park, as well as of rock and fossil specimens as not all research in the Park has involved plants or animals. The geology and geography of the region have created their own unique research possibilities. In some instances the Park has approved one aspect of a study but not another. At the close of the twenty-five year period, for example, the Authority decided to deny one portion of a study of the pine marten, a small mammal, due to the expected mortality of voles or shrews which would be briefly captured for study and number counts. The project had begun in the late 1980s and leaving a portion of it incomplete raised several questions. The decision, as discussed in later pages, helped open the door to a discussion some members of the public and scientific community had been urging for some time, that of criteria used to evaluate research applications to the Park.

Although most research applications during the period were accepted, some applicants resented what they considered unrealistic expectations or guidelines. In some cases the status of much of the Park as a wildlife refuge and wilderness area affected Park decisions. One area of contention in the mid-1990s and earlier, however, involved the issue of potential benefits to be derived from research. While the Park clearly decided against any proposal which would harm natural resources, the Park also tended to favor projects which would have a definite benefit, in terms of yielding usable information, to BSP. The issue remained to be resolved at the end of the period as to whether projects which might render benefits to Maine, the scientific community, or society in general, but not necessarily yield any direct benefit to BSP, should be given equal consideration.[37] In the meantime, as was true for earlier years, the Authority, Advisory, and Park staff worked to protect and preserve Baxter's gift to Maine, to wilderness, and to humanity, encountering both support and opposition along the way.

Chapter Two

Wood, Wind, and Fire: Challenges to Baxter State Park Forest Policy and Protection

Subsequent to Governor Baxter's death the first major issue to confront Baxter State Park, in terms of natural resource management, was the cutting rights controversy. The controversy surfaced in 1972 and 1973 and would, along with the handling of a major blowdown in 1974 and an extensive fire in 1977, influence future resource management methods. Several parcels of land which Baxter had acquired for the Park over the years carried various types of leases or legal rights, be they concerned with camps, hunting rights, access, or timber harvesting. Baxter acquired such parcels intending to allow the leases to run their stipulated terms, or to allow specific groups or individuals designated rights or privileges. This was true for land acquired in 1962 from the Great Northern Paper Company.

After protracted negotiations, Governor Baxter had purchased 7,764 acres in T2R9 from Great Northern Paper Company (GNP) in 1962. As part of the sale agreement, Great Northern retained the right to cut timber in T2R9 as well as access rights to T3R9 where GNP held cutting rights to land purchased in 1954. Access was to be gained via the Roaring Brook Road, and GNP would hold access and cutting rights until December 1, 1973.[1] Controversy over the company's cutting rights arose in 1972 when GNP indicated its intent to harvest timber in the two townships before the expiration of its contractual right.

Great Northern had previously exercised cutting options. However, when GNP decided to conduct further harvesting in the area, located in the southeast portion of the Park near Mount Katahdin, and when the Authority decided to investigate its options, the matter became one of public concern.[2] The company contacted the Park in September 1972 about its harvesting plans. On September 19, 1972, BSP Business Manager William Cross wrote to the Authority, then composed of Chair and Attorney General James S. Erwin, Commissioner of Inland Fisheries and Wildlife Maynard F. Marsh, and Forest Commissioner Austin H. Wilkins, stating the estimated value of the timber and outlining the options the Authority might consider.[3]

According to Cross, it had already been established that GNP had the right to cut timber in the two townships. However, the company could also decide to either give the timber rights away or to follow a combination of the two actions. The possibility had also been raised of the Authority paying the company the net value of the stumpage, $732,000, or of "swapping stumpage, namely the swapping of cutting rights between the south end (T2 and T3, R9) and the northwest corner (T6R10)."[4] Wilkins later stated that he himself had suggested some type of swap in order to keep GNP from harvesting wood in the more heavily used southern portion of the Park.[5] It was this last possibility, that of swapping cutting rights, which resulted in a public uproar.

Cross informed the Authority that the 1972 Sewall Company Report on T2R9 and T3R9 indicated that roughly 132,971 cords of pulpwood, 7,716 cords of boltwood, and 7,020 MBF of logs, with a gross value of $861,813, currently existed in the southern townships to which GNP held cutting rights. At the same time, the 1971 Sewall Company Report for T6R9 and T6R10 indicated that roughly $2,329,900 worth of stumpage existed in that locality, in the form of 477,175 cords of pulpwood (both hardwood and softwood) and 9,444 MBF of logs (possibly excluded from the assigned monetary value). Cross posed the question of whether the Authority should consider swapping cord-for-cord for volume, or swapping in terms of dollar-for-dollar value. Cross also included stumpage figures for T6R9.[6]

During following days, the Authority and GNP negotiated a trade. The Authority would extend the company's cutting rights until 1975 and at the same time exchange GNP's rights in the two southern townships for rights in the northern township, T6R10, located in the area of the Park set aside by Baxter for creating model forestry practices: the area later known as the Scientific Forest Management area or SFMA. The paper company would be responsible for building the roads necessary for harvesting the wood, some of it old-growth timber. The parties secured a timberland permit for the proposed harvesting on November 29, 1972. However, with the estimated stumpage value allegedly much greater in the northern region, with former GNP contractors stating that the company had essentially finished its cutting in the southern region, and with the suggestion that roads built by the company in the north would both afford BSP greater access to timber not included in the deal and provide a shorter transportation route to GNP's new sawmill north of the Park, the motives of the Authority and the company came under scrutiny and became the subject of a threatened law suit.[7]

Authority members Marsh and Erwin supported Wilkin's plan for the same reason Wilkins stated he had suggested it: to keep harvesting operations out of the southern end of BSP. They also stated that they had investigated the possibility of purchasing GNP's cutting rights, but legal council had determined that BSP Trust Funds could not be used for such transactions. In addition, Assistant Attorney General Lee M. Schepps later stated that he had advised Erwin and GNP attorney Don Perkins that although he did not believe that the Authority had the power to "allow a swap because there was no other lands [with] respect to which the Authority had power to grant cutting rights," he did believe, "that the Authority has the power to permit GNP to engage in the practice of scientific forestry" in the designated northern location and "to accept from GNP as consideration a relinquishment of GNP's cutting rights in the southern township."[8]

Other rationale for the cutting rights transaction surfaced. For example, at one point the ever controversial, but then allowed, use of snowmobiles in the Park became an issue, as Erwin stated that it was in the best interests of the Park and the other parties to keep cutting operations away from snowmobilers. At another point, Wilkins added that cutting in the northern part of the Park might be one way to help protect BSP from the spruce budworm epidemic then gathering force. When pressed further, Wilkins stated that the deal would help ensure the Park a steady flow of revenue for its various operations.[9]

Maine Governor Kenneth Curtis, after first requesting that the Authority take its time with the issue, announced publicly in mid-November that the proposed deal was "the best solution" for BSP.[10] In spite of such support and the various justifications offered by the Authority, the transaction remained the center of controversy. In late November 1972, the Natural Resources Council of Maine (NRCM), a non-profit environmental organization which would become involved in several BSP issues over the years, announced its plan to seek litigation over the cutting rights transaction. The NRCM, along with Stuart White, Charles Fitzgerald, David Flanagan, and Richard W. Smith, filed suit December 27, 1972, against the BSPA and

Great Northern Nekoosa Corporation. The impending litigation was one of the first issues the Authority had to address when it met in January 1973. Now composed of BSPA Chair Marsh, new Attorney General Jon Lund, and Acting Commissioner of Forestry Fred E. Holt, the Authority discussed the matter and voted to file an answer to NRCM's suit.[11]

The NRCM suit was not the only challenge to the timber swap. In early December 1972, the Chair of the Maine Land Use Regulation Commission (LURC), State Representative John Martin, posed the question of the necessity of GNP obtaining a LURC permit for the proposed cutting operation. Created by the State Legislature in 1969, LURC oversees the zoning, planning, and management of Maine's unorganized territories, and BSP is located in unorganized territory. The agency, under the terms of its establishment, seeks to protect the land's "natural" values as well as to preserve other ecological, scenic, or historic factors. The agency considers cutting timber a "development" requiring a LURC permit. In view of this, LURC asked the Attorney General's office for an opinion on the issue. The Attorney General's office, in an opinion rendered by Deputy Attorney General George C. West, responded on January 2, 1973. According to West, LURC did not have the authority to require GNP to receive a permit for the harvesting operation. Governor Baxter had conveyed the cutting rights in his Deeds of Gift or Trust, and for LURC to infringe upon these rights would be a violation of the Trust.[12]

In addition, and what would prove crucial in succeeding years, the 1973 Opinion asserted that "the Baxter State Park Authority has paramount control and management of the Park." Baxter State Park was not, the opinion stated, "administered by the Park Commission subject to the changing desires of the people ... the Authority has full power, not shared power, as to Park management and control." The Authority's power of control was subject only to "court review of the correctness of the Authority's action interpreted in light of the terms of the Deeds of Trust." The State Legislature fully intended for the Authority "to be a unique Authority managing and controlling a unique gift from Governor Baxter." The Authority's "important fiduciary responsibilities" were not "to be diluted by the encroachment of any State agency." The 1973 Opinion both ended the participation by LURC in the cutting rights controversy and effectively established the relationship between LURC and BSP through the early 1990s.[13]

Before receiving the January 2, 1973, decision, however, the Authority had proceeded with plans to make the timber swap. On the day NRCM filed its suit, the BSPA met and discussed the final draft to their Harvesting Plan for T6R10. The plan covered the first six months of the anticipated harvest. The plan had been developed by "twelve men representing the Attorney General, Inland Fisheries and Game, professional foresters, and the Great Northern Paper Company." The plan was thoroughly discussed among the Authority, the Advisory, and three GNP representatives, revisions made, and the revised plan approved.[14] In the center of public scrutiny, the Authority continued to stress its belief that it was acting in the Park's best interest.

The BSPA met again on January 23, 1973, the day after they determined how to respond to the NRCM suit, to discuss the cutting plan. The Authority adopted measures concerning road quality, stump disposal, and erosion control, and appointed Gary Morse of the Forestry Department to serve as a liaison with GNP. Francis Dunn, a past and future participant in caribou transplant activities, was to serve as an assistant and an advisor on wildlife issues. Both were to make written reports on a regular basis.[15]

Things did not proceed as planned. Weather conditions had delayed actual cutting in the northern township until late January, and in early February the Authority determined that the area marked to date for cutting did not meet "acceptable standards." Attorney General Lund motioned, and the Authority so voted, that Morse inform GNP of this fact and that Chair Marsh also write to the company and request that they refrain from cutting until BSPA standards were met. In addition, Commissioner Holt suggested that a revision of diameter limits on spruce might be desirable.[16]

Attorney General Lund did more than object to marking standards. His office filed a separate suit against the Authority after determining, among other things, that the cutting would not meet the definition of scientific forestry as mandated by the Deeds of Trust. Assistant Attorney General Schepps conveyed, in an inter-departmental memorandum to Lund dated January 12, 1973, that he had drawn up the first draft of the contract for the cutting transaction in November 1972 with a view to establishing the necessary framework for acceptable forestry practices for T6R10. The contract as signed, however, no longer contained the termination and liquidated damages provisions which he had outlined. The revised contract did not maintain for the Authority the same controls over the cutting and road plans as had the original contract. Schepps had secured the opinion of W. R. Dinneen, Director of the Maine Forest Service, and that of Cliff Swenson, Chief Forester for the Seven Islands Land Company. Although the two differed in respect to their opinions on some aspects of the signed BSP and GNP agreement, both expressed reservations about the existing cutting and road plans meeting the standards of scientific forestry as they understood the term. Schepps stated that other authorities might and probably should be consulted about the matter.[17]

Soon after Schepps wrote his memorandum, Lund's office obtained a temporary restraining order to stop the cutting. In early March, 1973, a Superior Court Justice granted a preliminary injunction to halt the cutting, after refusing to limit the issues in the NRCM suit. Lund's legal suit became part of the NRCM suit, and Lund advised the Authority to hire an independent attorney.[18]

Within weeks the controversy ended. Governor Curtis considered purchasing GNP's cutting rights with funds from the state's General Fund, but before any action along this line could transpire the Authority made a settlement with the company.[19] The Authority purchased all of GNP's cutting rights in BSP for $725,000 made in one full payment from the Baxter State Park Trust Fund on March 30, 1973, the arrangement having been made some days earlier. In mid-March the Authority also decided to close the logging road built into T6R10 and posted it for purposes of fire prevention. Approximately 180 cords of wood had already been cut by GNP, and the Authority voted to sell the wood to the company.[20]

The final decision to purchase GNP's rights was a swiftly made and executed one. Although the Authority had earlier been informed that Trust Fund money could not be used for such transactions, in March 1973 they learned otherwise. Deputy Attorney General John W. Benoit, Jr. researched the matter and determined—based largely on the Deeds of Trust and the legal definitions of the terms "care," "protection," and "operation," the purpose for which the Baxter State Trust Fund had been established—that Trust Fund money could indeed be spent to purchase GNP cutting rights.[21]

As noted in Benoit's memorandum, the 1961 and 1965 State Legislation which accepted the Trust Fund corporate stock had stipulated that income from the Trust Fund be used for " 'the care, protection, and operation'" of Baxter State Park. According to Benoit, "to purchase standing timber, otherwise scheduled to be cut, is to conserve it; to protect it." A purchase of timber cutting rights such as that contemplated would, by "foreclosing the cutting and removal of mature trees," have a positive "ecological result." The "preservation of sound timber, by purchase or otherwise, would guard against damage from erosion. Conservation would be realized; and to preserve is to protect." Some contemporary foresters might have argued with a few of the memorandum's premises, but it did establish the position that purchasing cutting rights did not constitute a violation of the Deeds of Trust. The Authority acted immediately on the matter, and reached a purchase agreement with GNP within a week of receiving Benoit's memorandum.[22] The decision served to end a situation which had few other prospects for a speedy or satisfactory resolution. The decision also brought an end to outstanding leases on BSP timber. In the future, the focus would center less on who might harvest stumpage, and instead focused on how, or if, timber was harvested. This shift had already become apparent during the cutting controversy.

Although not the first instance of a call for a management plan for the SFMA, as well as for the Park as a whole, the expressed desire and need for one during the cutting rights controversy brought a new level of attention to the lack of a written long-term master plan. Public criticism of the proposed timber swap, in particular Attorney General Jon Lund's suit, pinpointed the lack of a master plan as a critical weakness in BSP operations. Individual BSP staff and Authority members might well have had long-term goals in mind for the Park, along with specific operating plans for achieving them, but a comprehensive published plan remained a necessity.[23] The road to creating and initiating such a plan would prove lengthy.

In an April 1973 letter to Governor Kenneth M. Curtis, written after the cutting rights settlement, Attorney General Lund outlined some of his objectives in bringing suit against the Authority and GNP. Lund stated that his office had maintained that the "'Timberland Permit,' so-called, did not represent or contemplate the practice of 'scientific forestry and reforestation'" for which purposes T6R10 and "certain other lands in the northern end of Baxter State Park" were held by the State of Maine subject to the terms of Baxter's Deeds of Trust. The Attorney General's suit had been rendered moot before coming to trial, thus no judicial determination had been made concerning Baxter's use of the term scientific forestry, a determination which Lund believed still crucial. According to Lund's office, the "State in general," did not compare favorably with the federal government or "certain private companies" in its "forest management practices and procedures." The "power to authorize cutting in Baxter Park" remained, Lund argued, and interested parties still had "no court decision upon which to rely."[24]

The lands included in the SFMA were, Lund stated, left to the State "not only for 'scientific forestry and reforestation' but also for Park and recreational uses," falling as it were under the definition of the term "'multiple use.'" Under the principles of multiple use, the land would be managed for all of its resources, both ecological and recreational. Some areas might be managed for all such resources as timber production, watershed protection, wildlife management, and various forms of recreation; other areas might be managed for less than all resources. Management for the various resources needed to be "harmonious and coordinated," and must not "impair the productivity of the land." "The most sophisticated and highly developed techniques" available should be used in pursuit of these goals. Baxter had called for "'a continuing crop of timber,'" a goal similar to the principle of "sustained yield," and the SFMA should be managed to achieve sustained yields of the various "products and services obtainable from a forest." To this end, an in-depth, on the ground, and thorough inventory of all timber and other resources needed to be conducted. Soil conditions, timber growth rates, and other specifics needed to be measured and included in a "sophisticated and comprehensive" management plan which included principles of multiple use. Such a plan needed to be prepared prior to any cutting or harvesting so that tree species and sizes to be harvested, areas for cutting, and road design could be determined in a scientific manner and to the benefit of the forest as a whole. Furthermore, the Park had been remiss, according to Lund, in not having had such an inventory and plan made previously. In any future harvesting, all trees should be marked by Park personnel and other measures taken to ensure that decisions of import would be handled by the Park and the Authority.[25] Although a management plan of the scope envisioned by Lund would be some years in the making, subsequent events both highlighted the need for a comprehensive plan and contributed to the early versions of such a plan. Lund may or may not have been overzealous in his criticism of the State and the Authority. Either way, his opinions on several points were neither unique nor untimely.

The next major event or series of events to engage the Park in public controversy and internal review involved a large scale timber blowdown. In November 1974, severe wind conditions caused extensive blowdown in the southwest portion of BSP, affecting not only less frequented portions of the region but also shutting down the Katahdin Stream, Abol, and Daicey Pond Campgrounds for part of the following season, and presenting what Park personnel considered a potentially serious fire danger. Handling of the blowdown ultimately led to another suit against the Authority, and resulted in further demands for what the public considered a more cohesive management plan for the Park. As in other events during the 1970s through the mid-1990s, the blowdown involved close scrutiny of the wording of the Deeds of Trust and research into various Baxter communications for indications as to Baxter's views and intentions concerning the matter at hand.

The storm which began on November 21, 1974, brought extensive winds which lasted for over six hours and reached estimated velocities of over 100 miles per hour. The storm uprooted both hardwood and softwood trees, breaking many in two, causing an estimated blowdown of more than 100,000 cords of wood in roughly thirty-six square miles. In some areas entire acres were stripped of standing trees, in other places damage was less pervasive. Early reports listed the damage as extending from Rum Mountain to Abol Slide, to the timberline along Abol Trail, and along the sides of Owl, Barren,

OJI, and South Brother Mountains. Tree damage occurred around Lily Pad, Kidney, Daicey, Foss-Knowlton, and Lost Ponds. The damaged area reached from the top of Abol Hill northwest to Foster Field to the West Branch of the Penobscot River and beyond the Park boundaries, and extended along several miles of the Perimeter or Tote Road. Property damage was reported as minimal, although a number of stranded vehicles and a few hunters had to be plowed out. The last storm to have caused such extensive timber damage was that of 1963, a storm which claimed the lives of two persons. No solid figures on damage from the 1974 storm could be given until aerial photographs could be obtained. Park Supervisor Irvin C. Caverly, Jr. flew over the area at the end of November to make a preliminary assessment. At the time of the blowdown, Maynard Marsh of Inland Fisheries and Game served as BSPA Chair, while Fred Holt and Jon Lund continued to hold the two other Authority positions.[26]

Irvin C. Caverly, Sr., District Ranger for the Department of Conservation and father of BSP Supervisor Caverly, flew over the damaged area on December 12, 1974, and reported his observations. The flight was made at the request of the Park Supervisor. The elder Caverly reported that "if this could be observed and publicized as many storms are in populated areas it would be declared a natural disaster." Damage varied, but where heavy "gave the appearance from the air of trees being mowed, much the same as hay," the phenomena being true for "hardwood and softwood alike." After observing the damage from the air, District Ranger Caverly and Robert Applebee traveled by car as far along the perimeter road as possible—to just beyond the Abol camping area. From there westerly the road was impassable. As to his perceptions, Caverly wrote: "damage observed is beyond the ability of this writer to describe." The effects of the wind and snow storm would be visible for years to come, Caverly predicted.[27]

Ranger Caverly noted that although Park buildings seemed to have escaped extensive damage, "surrounding grounds are a shambles," and "lean-tos are living up to their name 'leaning.'" Caverly suspected that many hiking trails had been obliterated, and, above all, that the most threatening aspect of the blowdown in the future would be the resulting fire danger.[28] His son had expressed the same concern in previous days,[29] and the concern over

A large scale timber blowdown in November, 1974, precipitated lengthy discussions, legal challenges and close scrutiny of the Deeds of Trust before sustained clean-up operations commenced.
(Photo: Irvin Caverly Jr.)

fire danger would remain a focal point of Park and Authority plans and actions in following months. Ranger Caverly suggested that stringent smoking and other regulations be imposed in the heavily damaged areas, and wrote that "if salvage is carried out (as it should be) the situation can be eased as far as access is concerned." Caverly noted that he was not attempting to assess blowdown damage or acreage, as aerial photographs and various professionals would be involved in that process, but, hitting on what would become two controversial issues, stated that "it would appear that this storm and the spruce budworm are dealing a one-two punch. FIRE CAN BE THE KNOCKOUT."[30] Park and Authority attempts to address the fire danger and the danger posed by the spruce budworm, which was currently causing extensive damage in Maine and had been an issue raised during the cutting rights controversy, would cause both debate and criticism by certain sectors of the public during the 1970s.

In early December 1974, Authority member and Bureau of Forestry Director Fred E. Holt contacted the James W. Sewall Company of Old Town about obtaining aerial photographs of the blowdown area. At that time, most of the damage was known to be in T3R9, but photographs of any damage in T2R9 and T3R10 were also needed. Holt requested that the photographs be taken as soon as possible, before further snowfall couldobscure the blowdown area.[31] At the same time, Holt contacted Maine Helicopters, Incorporated, about the possibility of securing helicopter assistance in removing trees and slash from certain damaged areas of the Park as an alternative to conventional logging methods. The Authority and Park waited for the results of the aerial survey before making any firm decisions, but by mid-December anticipated that at least some cleanup would be necessary as a fire prevention measure. Otherwise, affected portions might need to be closed for several years. This would in turn affect the entire Park, as major hiking trails and the Perimeter Road traversed the blowdown area.[32]

In the meantime, BSP staff worked to clear the roads of timber and debris and to inspect the area by vehicle and on foot. Much of the road system was not deemed passable for vehicles until late April or early May 1975, however, and cleanup crews continued to work on campground areas until later in the year. Furthermore, many autumn work hours would be devoted to cleaning other areas in preparation for winter use.[33] In addition to the replacement of Lund on the Authority by new Attorney General Joseph E. Brennan in January, the Park acquired a new Director during March

1975, A. Lee Tibbs. Blowdown cleanup was one of the first issues to confront Tibbs, although Caverly, still serving as Park Supervisor, continued to handle much of the situation.

While BSP personnel and Authority members worked on keeping the Park operational and clearing the most intrusive blowdown damage, the public became increasingly interested in Park plans for salvaging, or not salvaging, blown down timber. The BSPA had approved the obtaining of aerial photographs in early December 1974, and had begun to study them for the best method of handling the blowdown area that same month. As soon as the Authority began to consider its options, suggestions began to come in from the public. Near the end of December the Natural Resources Council of Maine stated that the fallen timber should be left to decompose naturally, while other parties urged that the wood be salvaged and used to help the people of Maine.[34] The NRCM met in early January 1975, and resolved that they opposed "any effort to alter the natural processes of a wilderness park, including the removal of blown down trees," and therefore recommended that the BSPA "open trails for passage only, open campsites, and clear access roads back to a maximum of fifteen feet." Any further "activity," the NRCM argued, "would be in violation of Governor Baxter's intent and purpose and in violation of State statute." The Council wished to make it clear to the Authority that they were "categorically opposed to salvage operations" in BSP.[35]

The letter from NRCM Executive Director and Staff Attorney Clifford H. Goodall which conveyed these sentiments also stated that the NRCM was pleased that "an executive director" had been hired for BSP, and that "progress will finally begin on the development of a master plan which will answer some of the issues concerning the Park's future."[36] Such a plan, the NRCM anticipated, would "serve as a mechanism which will eliminate much of the confusion and controversy which has surrounded the Park." The master plan, when developed, no doubt did answer some of the questions some individuals had concerning BSP, but controversy, on the subject of blowdowns and other matters, continued to have a place in the Park's history. Immediately after receiving the letter from NRCM, the Authority responded that they anticipated at least some salvage work. In the Authority meeting held in January, however, Chair Holt stated that no operation would be carried out before proper plans had been made and "procedures established within a management plan to be approved by the full Authority."[37]

The Maine Appalachian Trail Club (MATC) also expressed an early interest in BSP cleanup or salvage plans. The club wrote to the Authority in January, and MATC Trail Overseer John Neff and three other interested persons hiked into parts of the blowdown area to review the damage that same month. In February, the club suggested that as much cleanup as was practical be done in heavily used areas, but that conditions might be left as they were in less accessible regions.[38]

The Authority's January decision to conduct a salvage operation came at the same time as early reservations arrived at the Millinocket Park office for the upcoming summer season. Supervisor Caverly and Park staff expressed concerns about which camping areas would remain open; the amount, if any, of day use which would be curtailed; the best methods of informing the public of the increased fire hazard presented by the current conditions; the need for a written fire plan; and about the danger of campers or other BSP users inadvertently starting a major conflagration. In March, BSP personnel and Maine Forest Service District Rangers would meet at the Forest Service office in Old Town to work on fire plans for the following seasons.[39] In the meantime, the Authority considered how to best employ a contractor for the salvage operation.

The Authority secured guidance from the Maine Department of Conservation on finding a contractor and related matters. Aerial photographs indicated that blowdown damage extended over some 2900 acres, presenting several questions about operations beyond the need for fire prevention and public access. Such issues as road conditions and suitability, erosion control, stumpage rates, handling of unmerchantable wood and slash, types and size of harvesting equipment, supervision, liability insurance, operator housing, target dates for conducting and concluding harvesting, and public relations all needed careful consideration. Preliminary maps were being made and communications conducted with GNP regarding Park trees which had fallen on GNP land and vice versa. The Authority determined that the consultant and the salvage operator should not be one and the same person; planning and salvage should be two separate operations.[40]

At the end of January 1975, the Authority decided to conduct salvage operations in T3R10 with an expected end date of June 1976. Abol and Katahdin Stream Campgrounds would be open on a day-to-day basis, depending on weather conditions. No advance reservations would be accepted. A forest consultant would be hired to help formulate and oversee the salvage operation, and persons interested in contracting for the salvage operation could submit bids to Park Business Manager William Cross. The consultant, when hired, would review any bids received. The Park would also try to recruit roughly a dozen persons from the federally funded Comprehensive Employment Training Act (CETA) program to help clear slash one-hundred feet back from roadsides, and help would be obtained from the MATC for clearing the BSP portion of the Appalachian Trail. If the Appalachian and Abol trails were cleared to a distance of twenty feet on each side by June, they would be opened for use. If not, they would remain closed. Weather conditions would also play a part in deciding when and if to open the trails.[41] The decisions made in January 1975, as well as those made the previous month and in succeeding months, would all become part of a lengthy court record the following year.

Yet, even after January 1975, assessment of damages and future Park needs continued. The Authority eventually elected to hire Vladek "Kim" Kolman of Kolman Land Consultants of Brewer as consulting forester, after first assembling a list of twenty-six possible consultants, notifying them of the opening, and advertising the position in newspapers in the event that any interested and qualified party had been overlooked. The Authority initially received eight bids, then determined that additional information and factors needed consideration and called for a second set of bids. The Authority's search for a consultant forester under the current conditions was the first of its kind in Maine, and the need for redrafts of contract specifications were not deemed surprising or unwarranted.[42] After receiving the second bids, the Authority and Park Director Tibbs ranked the six according to several criteria, predominantly in consideration of who best met the concerns of the Park for "reducing the fire hazard, restoring full use of the campgrounds and trails as soon as possible, and salvaging the wood with a minimum of damage to Baxter Park." Kolman did not submit the lowest bid, but the quality of the bid he submitted and his firmer grasp of the situation and Park needs gave him the advantage over the forester with the lowest bid.[43]

The Authority issued a purchase order to Kolman in late June. Kolman submitted his proposal for a salvage operation in early September at an Authority meeting, and again the following week at a public hearing at Kidney Pond Camps. At the Kidney Pond hearing the only real challenge to the plan came from Christian Herter of the NRCM. Herter questioned how Kolman's plan fit into the wilderness aspect of the Park. Herter also inquired about the existence of a written fire plan for the Park, asked that the public be given more time to examine Kolman's plan, and requested that additional hearings be held in a location such as Augusta or Portland so that more people might attend. The Authority voted to approve Kolman's proposal during their regular meeting that same day, September 9, 1975.[44]

Kolman initiated an inspection and mapping program soon after the Authority hired him. He inspected most of the blowdown area personally, and his company's staff traversed the perimeter of the major areas of damage. They also studied the aerial photographs previously obtained by the Authority, and finding it "extremely time consuming and almost humanly impossible to penetrate into the central parts of the blowdown," completed much of the classification of various sections of the wind damage by helicopter. The helicopter they employed hovered for extended periods of time so that visual observations could be made and "low, oblique photographs" taken. All data obtained from the various sources and methods were used in preparing maps and formulating salvage plans.[45]

Kolman determined that approximately 5,000 acres of forest land, some of it owned by GNP, had been damaged or destroyed by the November 1974 storm. The excessive winds, accompanied by heavy wet snows falling on already saturated but largely unfrozen ground and on the timber, had created such intense pressure on the stands that massive blowdown had resulted. The damage had occurred to varying degrees at various places, spreading from the lowlands near the west branch of the Penobscot River to the high slopes of Katahdin. In some places old growth pines, extending fifty to sixty feet above the main forest canopy, had been broken "eight to ten feet above the ground and thrown a considerable distance." In some areas, composed primarily of uniform age spruce mixed with some balsam fir, the wind had blown over entire stands. Birch trees on ridges were also heavily damaged or destroyed.[46]

The storm resulted in more than the direct destruction of timber. Although the losses of wildlife were unknown, dense softwood stands which generally provided winter shelter had been demolished. In some areas large sections of the forest floor had been uplifted, exposing seedling root systems and jeopardizing the chance of rapid regeneration. The presence of the large quantity of blown down trees might lead to large-scale insect infestation which might in turn spread to still healthy stands. The excess timber on the ground after drying could also, Kolman concluded, endanger not only the blowdown area to fire but all of Baxter State Park. Fire erupting in the damaged area would be likely to spread quickly and possibly cut off the escape routes of people camping at the Abol, Katahdin Stream, and Daicey and Kidney Pond camping areas. Unless measures were taken to eliminate the hazards created by the blowdown, the entire southwest section of the Park might have to be "closed for an extended period of time." Because of BSP's topography, however, only areas near roads and campsites, and those on flatlands and low ridges, could undergo salvage operations. Two entirely separate operations would be used for the two types of areas. In addition, the areas on flatlands and ridges would be divided in five sections, each with its own salvage plan.[47]

The four campgrounds in the blowdown vicinity operated on a day-to-day basis during the summer of 1975. All of the camps, and some nearby areas such as the Abol and Appalachian trails and parts of the Tote Road, were closed at one time or another due to hazardous fire conditions. The Park hired a private citizen to help clear the Daicey Pond road on a week-to-week basis in early July to try to reduce fire danger, and had two BSP crews working on the east and west sides of Kidney Pond, but still had to close the area when conditions warranted. After the Authority approved Kolman's salvage plan in September, they had him proceed with bid preparations for the roadside clearing operation. Assistant Attorney General Sarah Redfield drafted the contract, but later, when only one contractor submitted a bid, the Authority decided to include it as part of the contract for the salvage of the other five areas. To enable salvage operations to proceed, the Authority agreed in September to have the Nesowadnehunk Stream and Kidney Pond bridges repaired and replaced, respectively, with the costs to be recovered through a road haul fee levied on salvage operators.[48]

At the September 29, 1975, meeting of the Authority, Sam Butcher and Chris Herter of the NRCM restated NRCM's concerns about the need for a management plan for BSP. Park Director Tibbs informed them that he understood the need for such a plan, but that he had spent the summer familiarizing himself with the Park. He expected the preparation of a management plan to take about two years as he intended to prepare it piecemeal, gaining approval for each portion as the plan progressed. The NRCM members present offered to assist in preparing the plan, even to the point of helping financially. They also indicated that the plan should include factors such as blowdowns and sprayings. In this they identified two major concerns of both the Park and the NRCM. The NRCM would soon challenge BSP on both issues. In the meantime, due largely to a freeze on new positions, Chairman Marsh, in late November, suggested that Kolman submit an estimate of costs for preparing a management plan for the Park.[49]

The new call for salvage bids drew no bids. The BSPA responded by calling a meeting of interested parties to discuss the contract and to provide further information. They held the meeting in early December 1975, and Kolman assisted them in the task. Another bid then opened in late December, two bids were received, and on January 7, 1976, a contract for one part of the salvage operation—that identified as "Area Five"—was awarded to Stanley Sproul of Augusta. His competitor's bid was rejected as being too high and subject to changes in the salvage agreement which the Authority was unwilling to make. Area Five comprised 510 acres west of Nesowadnehunk Stream at the base of Doubletop Mountain. Expected yields of merchantable wood for the area were 9,546 cords of spruce and fir; 530 cords of hardwood pulp; 1,000 MBF of white pine; and lesser amounts of hemlock, white and yellow birch, red pine, and cedar. Estimated yields for this and other areas came from Kolman's salvage plan and calculations.[50]

Before the Stanley Sproul Company could begin salvage operations, however, concerns over the entire salvage operation plan, concerns which had been in existence since the previous year, erupted in a legal battle. The NRCM had made its opposition to a general salvage plan known as early as December 1974. Correspondence between Park personnel, Authority members, members of the Bureau of Forestry, and other persons associated with the Park and the project indicated that they knew that certain sectors of the population might take issue with a salvage plan, and they knew it even before such a plan had been developed. Public relations needed to be given due consideration, and the Authority had voiced this opinion as early as December 1974. Furthermore, Kolman was informed in early July 1975 that "special interest groups" might take legal action.[51]

In mid-July, Attorney General Joseph E. Brennan wrote to the other Authority members, Marsh and Holt, that he dissented from the decision to award the contract to Kolman Timberland Consultants. He dissented not because of any objection to the corporation or to a salvage operation, but because he believed that "the State should not contract out to private consultants work State agencies can do as well or better and at less cost." The talents of State workers were not sufficiently recognized by the Maine government in general. In addition, Brennan thought that State foresters were "more likely to be sensitive to the special statutes and Baxter State Park," and that they were "likely to be more responsive to the direction of the Authority" during the salvage operation. The range of bids received also indicated that uncertainty existed among the bidders as to what their responsibilities were under the contract. The entire blowdown problem, Brennan asserted, "illustrates the compelling need for a competent forester to be assigned to Baxter State Park." A continuing need existed "to provide for scientific forestry in T6R10 and T6R9 in accordance with the terms of the Trust created by Governor Percival Baxter." Mirroring other concerns of the NRCM, Brennan stated that "continuation of a crisis-by-crisis approach to forest management in the Park serves neither the terms of the Trust nor the interest of the people of Maine." Brennan urged the Authority to begin long-term planning under the principles of scientific forestry for the "appropriate sections of the Park."[52]

Former Attorney General Jon Lund also had problems with the salvage operation's progression, although for different reasons. Lund wrote to Holt about the salvage plan in mid-September, after the Authority had approved the plan. Lund had read the plan and, like the NRCM, argued that a written statement of policy or a management plan had to be prepared before planning a salvage operation. Lund objected, as had Herter at the earlier public hearing, to Kolman not having been given a written policy statement–including a statement of BSP's wilderness concept–before preparing his plan. (Park representatives had, however, discussed Park policies orally with Kolman.)[53] Certain aspects of the salvage plan concerned Lund, such as the omission of any concerted effort to determine how wildlife habitat truly had been affected by the 1974 blowdown. The blowdown might have made some areas inaccessible, but it might also have provided excellent habitat for certain species. In view of the wildlife sanctuary status of most of BSP, such studies were imperative. Furthermore, Kolman had written that no "'virgin stands of timber'" remained in BSP. That might be true, Lund acknowledged, but the Park still needed to allow its forested land to "resemble as much as possible a virgin forest." The salvage plan seemed to be based on the assumption that "'continuous enjoyment of Park facilities' is of paramount importance in management decisions," whereas Lund believed that Governor Baxter had at no time established such a priority. In sum, Lund argued, he didn't believe that "Baxter ever intended that the results of acts of nature, even violent acts of nature, should be prettified to fit man's puritan concepts of nature." The Authority simply had to establish a management plan to deal with the blowdown situation and with future problems.[54]

The Authority had also received a letter from Attorney Steven Murray dated September 4, 1975, concerning the proposed salvage plan. Murray wrote that he represented "several citizens, property owners, and tax payers in the State of Maine who make frequent use of Baxter State Park and consider themselves beneficiaries of the Baxter Trust." Murray did not identify these persons, but stated that they wished to review the salvage proposal and perhaps provide commentary on it. The plan was not being prepared for consideration far enough in advance for their review, however, so they would not attend the public hearing. Instead they wished for a proposal to be sent to Murray as soon as possible and requested that the hearing scheduled for September 9, 1975, be postponed for thirty days after the plan first became available for public review. Doing so, Murray asserted, "would lend credence to the Authority avowed policy of seeking public input into this issue."[55]

Chairman Marsh had responded to Murray's letter twelve days later and had stated that although he had been out of town most of the previous week, he had learned of Murray's letter at the hearing. He thought that Murray had already been sent a copy of the plan and that there was therefore no urgency. Marsh sent the attorney a copy of the salvage plan, informed him of what had transpired at the public hearing, and stated that he would welcome Murray's comments on the plan.[56] Murray did indeed have commentary to offer. Among other things, he filed an injunction to stop the salvage operation and served as the plaintiff's legal representative in the case of *Charles Fitzgerald v. Baxter State Park Authority.*

Assistant Attorney General Sarah Redfield accepted service on behalf of the Summons and Complaint filed by Charles Fitzgerald against the Baxter State Park Authority in late November 1975. With Assistant Attorney General John M. R. Paterson, Redfield prepared an answer to the complaint and submitted it to the Maine Superior Court in Augusta on December 9, 1975. Fitzgerald was not alone in filing the lawsuit against the Authority. Bethane Ragaglia, who owned a business with Fitzgerald and who, like Fitzgerald, lived in Atkinson; Edward Danforth of Orono, a *Bangor Daily News* nature columnist; Ronald Davis of Orono, a University of Maine biology professor; and Aime Gauvin of Kenduskeag, a freelance writer, joined Fitzgerald in the suit.[57]

Steven Murray's firm of Murray, Plumb, and Murray represented the five Maine residents. Of the five, Fitzgerald had earlier been involved in the cutting rights controversy and had opposed the BSPA's having the Forestry Bureau spray Park lands in an attempt to deal with spruce budworm; Ragaglia had been involved with the spraying controversy; Davis had helped start the Baxter State Park Subcommittee of the NRCM in 1960; and Gauvin, like Davis, had belonged to the NRCM's subcommittee since 1960.

The five plaintiffs sought temporary and permanent injunctive relief ordering the BSPA to refrain from engaging in a harvesting operation of the blown down trees or allowing anyone else to harvest the wood. The Authority had not yet started the planned salvage operation, so no injunction was issued in 1975. The plaintiffs sought to halt the operation because, they charged, it violated the Deeds of Trust and the implied and expressed intent of Governor Baxter. They also asserted that not enough time had been given for the public to review the salvage proposal, and reiterated other points Murray had made in his letter to Holt earlier that autumn.[58]

Redfield and Patterson responded by acknowledging basic facts about the establishment of the Park and about the blowdown itself as contained in the complaint, but contested other charges. They referred the Court to the texts of the invitations to bid, to the provisions of the Authority's contract with Kolman, to Kolman's report on the blowdown, and to Kolman's salvage plan to answer allegations made by the plaintiffs as to how the blowdown and considerations as to a salvage operation had been handled. Kolman had been "orally instructed by the Authority that no damage was to occur in the Park as a result of any actions undertaken in relation to the blowdown," the attorneys asserted. Kolman was familiar with the Deeds of Trust and with previous salvage operations in BSP. The defendants admitted that Murray had not received a copy of the proposed salvage plan until about December 8, 1975 (the day the Authority Chair received Murray's letter), but alleged that the complete text had been available for public review on December 5, 1975. Furthermore, in regards to the scheduling of the public hearing, notice of the hearing had been published in the *Bangor Daily News* on September 2 and 8, 1975, and in the *Katahdin Journal* on September 3, 1975. The Authority had also acted within the terms of the Deeds of Trust, and within the laws of Maine which authorized the State to restore areas of forest growth damaged by blowdown. The defendant's attorneys denied several allegations made by the plaintiffs, argued that the complaint was not ripe for judicial review as no contract had been signed or salvage operation commenced, and asked the Court to dismiss the complaint.[59]

News of the complaint spurred numerous editorials and letters to the editor in Maine newspapers. Some persons sided with the plaintiffs, while others expressed indignation that five individuals could interfere with what they considered a justified and necessary salvage operation. Aime Gauvin had earlier published a guest column describing and criticizing the public hearing. (Despite Murray's letter stating that his clients would not attend the hearing due to the short lead-in time, Gauvin had indeed made it to the blowdown tour provided by the Park and to Kidney Pond for the hearing.) In the days following the filing of the complaint, Gauvin stated and defended his opinions in the press. Likewise, Davis wrote a guest column for the *BDN* in early December criticizing the salvage proposal and arguing that it was largely unnecessary.[60]

In a similar manner, Fitzgerald, in an interview with the *Maine Times* in early 1976, stated that he was prepared to take the case to the Maine Supreme Court or higher if need be, no matter the financial cost. If the Court did not render a "modern-day" interpretation of Baxter's intents, Fitzgerald argued, and the Authority was not prevented from proceeding with the salvage operation, "'they will have set the grounds for lumbering the entire Park.'" Natural occurrences such as spruce budworm infestations and blowdowns would provide an endless supply of excuses for harvesting Park trees.[61]

Christian Herter of the NRCM expressed his organization's views on the issue. Herter wrote to the editor of the *BDN* in December 1975 that the NRCM had not changed its position since the previous year. The issue as it stood currently, however, was becoming "muddled." The NRCM wanted any salvage operations to be restricted to trails, campgrounds, and roads, but "whether one believes that the salvage plan itself is consistent with Governor Baxter's wishes, it really doesn't focus on the bigger issue." The bigger issue, according to Herter, was that a comprehensive management plan be "formulated and implemented as soon as possible." Salvage and other issues would then be determined on the basis of the plan. The Park needed to define the term "wilderness" in its plan, and this in turn would "affect the overall Park policy." The NRCM, Herter stated, had pushed for such a management plan since 1969, and the management plan continued to be the first priority of the NRCM. No salvage operation should be undertaken until the plan was in place.[62]

Herter continued to stress the importance of a management plan in 1976, but he did so as a BSP Advisory member. Herter joined the Advisory early in the year and was able to aid the planning process along with other Advisory members, the Authority, and BSP staff. Ronald B. Davis requested, but due to a full Advisory did not receive, an appointment to the Advisory, while Aime Gauvin attended several meetings in 1976.[63] Davis and Gauvin continued to oppose the salvage operation, but like Herter tried to influence the Authority from within as well as through their legal suit. Meanwhile, the salvage operation proceeded. After contracting with Sproul in early January for the Area Five salvage operation, and with no injunction barring the way, road work and the salvage operation commenced in the first two months of the year.[64]

By early February 1976 a road had been completed to Draper Pond, but progress in general seemed slow, in part because of the uncertainties over legal matters. The Park plowed part of the perimeter road system during the winter of 1975-1976 to enable the company to harvest blowdown timber, a decision which proved costly in the short-run and was not repeated the following winter. Preparation of legal briefs continued early in 1976, and Charles Fitzgerald expressed his concerns personally to Redfield, while the Authority continued to grapple with questions about spruce budworm and the need for a full time forester to carry out management decisions in the northern townships.[65]

At the same time as the Authority, Park staff, and Advisory tried to deal with the above issues, the issues of spruce budworm protection and the salvage operation became linked in a campaign against both which Ronald Davis helped initiate. The Park had engaged in a spruce budworm spraying operation in the late spring of 1975 which drew some criticism.[66] In late 1975, after filing as a plaintiff in *Fitzgerald v. BSPA*, Davis sent a letter requesting financial and, in essence, political support, for the "Baxter Park Defense Fund." Davis sent the letter to members of the Ecological Society of America, and possibly to other persons whom he thought would be interested in his new organization. Davis gave his audience some Park history, noted the existence of the "scientific forestry" region of BSP, then stated that the remainder of his letter would refer "to the other 85 percent of the Park where commercial logging is illegal."[67]

Davis stated in his letter that "after many years of urging, the Baxter Park administrators have failed to develop a serious wilderness management plan," thus the Defense Fund had "decided to use the courts." Two suits were currently pending according to Davis, "one to prevent future budworm spraying and the other to prevent a commercial 'salvage' operation in a large ... irregular area of blowdown." Davis stated that the salvage operation constituted "a large-scale, mechanized clear-cut operation with both aesthetic and ecologic implications." A closer reading of Kolman's proposal might have convinced Davis that the Authority did not intend to engage in a clear-cut operation, but, nevertheless, Davis was apparently convinced of the strength of his position. He asked that his addressees respond to his letter with "a check [made] out to the Baxter Park Defense Fund," and that they send a letter to the BSPA "explaining as an ecologist your objections to blowdown salvage and budworm spraying in an area intended as wilderness, and also indicating the importance of wilderness preservation." A copy sent to Davis of any letters mailed would be appreciated.[68]

Numerous letters arrived in Augusta addressed to Maynard Marsh or simply to the BSPA from mid December 1975 into January and February of 1976. Davis had asked that letters be mailed to Marsh and the Authority in Augusta, and letters did arrive—from throughout the nation. Over 120 letters from at least twenty-eight states made their way to BSP, with Maine and New England accounting for just over one half of the letters. Faculty members from numerous colleges and universities nationwide wrote letters protesting both spraying and salvaging, as did ecologists and other persons outside academia. Several of the letters followed the format suggested by Davis. A few persons indicated that they had heard about the salvage operation through other channels, primarily the media. Many of the writers stated that they believed the blowdown area in general should be left to natural forces to undergo the process of decay and to help rejuvenate the forest, while in regard to the spraying of insecticides they thought spraying would cause more harm than good and quite likely negatively impact the forest for years to come. Baxter State Park offered a unique opportunity to study forest communities where relatively little influence was exerted by man, and the opportunity should be realized.[69]

Copies of some letters protesting salvage operations reached Maine Governor James B. Longely. Copies of many letters, judging by notations on them, reached Davis in Orono. Eventually most if not all of the letters reached Park Director Lee Tibbs. To Tibbs went the job of responding to the correspondence. Unfortunately, Tibbs proved less than subtle in doing so. Although Tibbs modified his tone for a few of his responses, a copy of his basic form letter exists, and it is by no means a letter likely to pacify its recipients.[70]

In addition to stating that "wilderness" meant different things to different people, Tibbs stated in his form letter that " 'wilderness' as defined in the Federal Wilderness Act of 1964 cannot accurately be applied to Baxter State Park." His inference seems to have been that the letter writers were wrong in calling BSP a wilderness area. A few persons responded that BSP did not fit the 1964 criteria simply because it did not belong to the federal government. Tibbs went on to devote a paragraph to the Deeds of Trust and the scientific forestry area of BSP. This paragraph drew little response, or at least, little aggressive response. His next paragraph, however, did. Tibbs stressed the difficulty in managing land "in these difficult times" and stated that the many separate Trust Deeds made BSP administration "extremely complex." "Until one has read and studied the documents applicable to the administration of Baxter State Park," Tibbs stated, "and has actually spent considerable time in the Park itself, I submit that an accurate and meaningful recommendation cannot be made." Had Tibbs stopped at this point his audience might have simply found him a bit difficult to endure, but Tibbs went further. "Therefore," he wrote:

> I urge you to consider your original letter on this matter and honestly consider whether or not you are actually qualified to submit a recommendation to the Baxter State Park Authority. If you decide you are not it would seem appropriate to write a second letter indicating your decision.[71]

Instead of placating the opposition, Tibbs had issued a battle cry. Seemingly no one wrote back to Tibbs admitting their credentials were insignificant or their views transformed. Numerous people, however, wrote stating that they were indeed qualified to offer suggestions to the Authority—often citing professional credentials, although a few persons simply stated their "rights" as citizens of America or Maine, or as members of humanity—and asserted that they had no intention of retracting their original letters. In addition, in mid-January 1976, Davis sent a second letter to interested parties refuting the content of Tibb's letter and stating that at least thirty members of the Ecological Society had already sent initial letters to BSP. Most written responses to Tibbs' letter arrived at Park Headquarters by late February 1976, but a new batch of letters protesting spraying and harvesting arrived in late spring 1976.[72] Meanwhile and thereafter, the legal suit against BSP occupied the attention of Davis and the other plaintiffs.

Kolman continued in his position as consulting forester in 1976 and indicated that, along with many other persons involved with BSP, he believed a plan for the northern townships was long overdue. He had read the plan prepared during 1971-1972 for the timber swap with GNP and felt that the plan was essentially a sound one but needed revisions. An immediate inventory was also in order to establish a revised plan which would fit into the overall management plan for BSP. The Authority considered the possibility of having Kolman prepare a plan for the area without first sending a contract out for bid. Redfield looked into the legality of the possibility, and at the March meeting recommended that any proposed management plan go out to bid. The Authority then voted to go to bid in seeking a consulting forester to prepare a ten year management plan for the SFMA.[73]

By February 1976, the spruce budworm problem seemed to be in need of immediate attention if not immediate action. Fred Holt stated at the February Authority meeting that roughly 28,000 acres in the "management area" had been affected thus far, along with some 26,000 acres in the rest of the Park. He recommended that all affected areas be sprayed during the upcoming summer. A map of the proposed spray project was circulated before the March meeting, and Nancy Ross of the Department of Conservation discussed options with the Authority before they met.

Commissioner of Conservation Richard Barringer described a proposed State spraying project to the Authority during the meeting. Under the proposed State project the State would pay 7 percent of the expense and landowners and the federal government would split the balance. Ross added that any spraying in BSP would be paid for by the State. John Chadwick, also of the Department of Conservation, recommended that all affected areas of BSP, not just the SFMA area, be sprayed. Should no spraying be done, the Authority could expect a 90 percent mortality rate of fir. John S. Walker, recently appointed Director of the Bureau of Forestry, made a motion that the affected SFMA acreage be sprayed, Brennan seconded the motion, and the following vote was unanimous in favor of the motion.[74]

The proposed management plan for the northern townships also commanded Authority and Advisory attention on March 2, 1976. Christian Herter had objected to the spraying project that day, arguing once again that a management plan had to be prepared and approved by the Authority before any such spraying be done. Other persons at the March 1976 meeting agreed that the SFMA management plan was a priority, even if they did not agree with Herter's assertion that the plan had to precede spraying. The Authority and other persons present held some discussion as to availability of funds for the project, but decided that BSP had no other option than to proceed with the SFMA plan, which would become part of the general Park management plan. Any costs associated with the project "would be recovered through future management operations." At a special Authority meeting later that month, Redfield presented contract specifications for a consulting forester to prepare the proposed SFMA plan, and the Authority revised them as necessary. The Authority decided to advertise the contract bid in Bangor, Augusta, and Portland newspapers, in addition to following the regular bid procedures of the Bureau of Purchases.[75]

The Authority also, at the second March meeting, approved a special roadside clearance or restoration project to help eliminate the fire danger for the upcoming summer. They endorsed the project on a three week trial basis, and allowed for different methods and clearance distances to be tried. The following month Sproul, who was to have the trial project added to his contract, would submit a report giving the amount of wood cut, the area covered, and the costs incurred. Based on Sproul's work the Authority would determine future measures. When the Authority met again in April they decided unanimously to continue the project using in-house personnel for the time being. Kolman had estimated from Sproul's work that it would take thirteen workers about thirty-six days, at a cost of $28,000 plus chipping expenses, to complete the roadside clearing. Fire danger reduction was to remain the first priority and salvage the second.[76]

Roadside clearance continued in the spring, but not as quickly as anticipated due to poor working conditions and difficulties with slash disposal. Clearing had been limited to fifty feet with only the heavy blowdown areas being cleared, the remainder being left to a future date depending upon time constraints and worker availability. In regards to the regular salvage operation, by early June about 25 percent of the operation in Area Five had been completed, with "quite a bit of wood ready for haul." By early March, 160 cords had been removed and an undetermined footage of saw logs prepared for removal.[77] Natural regeneration, according to Kolman, appeared to have good potential in the area as most of the stumps were falling back into place relieving, it seems, the ground upheaval which had occurred during the 1974 storm. In addition, providing the Authority gave approval and the necessary performance bonds were obtained, two operators were ready to begin work in areas Three and Four. The Authority agreed at the June meeting to begin contract preparations for Carl Preble for Area Three.[78]

Spruce, pine, and fir were holding up well where connected to the ground, but by late spring 1976 birch was "going by fast," Kolman reported, and would soon "be good only for pulp." If it continued to deteriorate over the next year, GNP, the primary market for the salvage operation wood, might not accept it. Another problem, according to Tibbs in June, was that although income had started to come in from the roadside and Area Five projects, the overall project was presently a "losing proposition." He hoped that salvage operations in areas Three and Four would help reduce the anticipated loss for the entire salvage operation. During the upcoming winter, if work was to continue, contractors would have to finance any snow plowing themselves.[79] Finances for the project remained a problem through the summer, and by early September the project had a $9,000 deficit, including a $17,000 bridge cost. Yet, financially things were expected to improve as income continued to come in to Park coffers.[80]

Income could not, however, be expected to flow into BSP coffers indefinitely. On August 24, 1976, Superior Court Justice Lewis I. Naiman granted the plaintiffs in *Fitzgerald v. Baxter State Park Authority* a permanent injunction. The Court based its decision primarily upon the Private and Special Laws of 1955 expressing Governor Baxter's intent for the Park which authorized the State to "'clear, protect, and restore areas of forest growth damaged by acts of nature such as blowdowns,'" but required the State "'to subordinate recreational values to wilderness values and to act in accordance with the best forestry practices.'" The Court did not agree with all of the plaintiffs' contentions. It determined that the Deeds of Trust "speak for both recreational purpose and preserving a natural state," and the Court could not help "but find some ambiguity and inconsistency on the face of the deeds." The Court did, nevertheless, find the Authority in violation of the Baxter Trust in "several" "significant" aspects.[81]

Justice Naiman identified three significant violations. The first violation involved "the size and nature of the equipment being used to harvest the fallen trees." The Court found the skidder in use to be "extremely large," such that it necessitated a widening of Park roads, crushed undergrowth in off-road use, and, the Court stated, evidence existed that the skidder had been "actually moved through the blowdown area rather than positioned at the outskirts." Restrictions not common with commercial operations had been included in the salvage contract, but these were not sufficient "to counter the extensive environmental impact of the use of such equipment."[82]

The second violation concerned the location of much of the salvage operation. The current operation involved "clearing of areas least likely to be visited by campers and hikers." Witnesses for both the plaintiffs and the defendants had asserted that humanity "presented the greatest forest fire hazard in the Park." That being so, "the benefit of clearing blowdown in such an area [one not frequented by campers and hikers] appears to be minimal when compared to the impact upon the wilderness."[83]

The final significant violation of the Baxter Trust which the Court identified was "the fact that only the trunks of the fallen trees are being removed and that highly flammable slash material will be left to decompose." This it seemed, as with the previous "violation," would undercut the argument that the danger of forest fire would be reduced by harvesting." However, testimony on this issue was, the Court recognized, contradictory.[84]

In sum, the Court decided that "the type of operation presently being carried out" was "of minimal protective value when compared to the environmental impact and the effect upon the nature of wilderness envisioned by Governor Baxter." Merit did exist in the suggestion that harvesting "be permitted in those areas immediately adjacent to the roads and campgrounds where due to man's presence the danger of forest fires is greatest." The Court thereby prohibited the Authority from "continuing to harvest blowdown in the manner in which the present operation is being conducted, to wit: with the use of heavy equipment." The Authority could continue some salvage operations with other equipment, "in such a manner as will not unduly disturb the terrain and natural environment." Plans could continue, but only in a manner "which would more closely follow the terms of the Trust Deeds" as the Court had therein interpreted them.[85] The problem, one might argue, was that in some ways the instructions given by the Court contained vagaries similar to those found in the Deeds of Trust. However, the fact that the Authority had to halt operations using the indicated skidder (Park records suggest that more than one skidder was in use, with variations in size among them) was clear.

The Court's decision was not a foregone one to many persons interested in the case. Referring to a major blowdown which occurred in October 1963, in an April 1964 letter to Helon Taylor, Percival Baxter had stated that "I think the best practice to pursue is to leave them [blowdowns] where they fall and let nature do its worst." The exception to this was when leaving the trees "is dangerous to human life."[86] Timber had been harvested in affected areas following the 1963 blowdown, and those who favored salvaging after the 1974 blowdown certainly stressed fire prevention and the possible loss of human life as the most important reason for a salvage operation. However, varying interpretations of the Deeds of Trust and related Baxter correspondence, and often opposing theories of how to best balance the interests of the Park's natural resources with an increasing demand for use by the public, played a role in the 1974 blowdown and its cleanup—just as they did in other major issues the Park confronted between 1970 and 1994. If some Authority members felt less than pleased with the injunction granted, so too did the plaintiffs. The plaintiffs felt that the injunction did not go far enough. The decision as rendered limited the type of equipment to be used and set some guidelines for blowdown salvage operations, but recognized the basic right of the Authority to authorize such operations. The plaintiffs filed an appeal on September 21, 1976, and the Authority filed a cross-appeal on October 6, 1976. The Superior Court's decision was ultimately upheld. In the meantime, the Authority, Park staff, and salvage operators remained in limbo regarding the project.[87]

Sales of already salvaged wood had continued after the August injunction, including an arrangement to have an operator saw some of the salvaged timber for Park use. By late August, all five areas had been contracted for salvage. When contacted in October, the contractors indicated that they were interested in continuing work provided they could use trucks for hauling and small skidders for yarding. Park staff still believed that fire remained a serious threat, and expressed particular concern about Area Two. Hiking trails in Area Two included parts of the Perimeter Road, the Appalachian Trail, and the Katahdin Stream Campground area.[88] After filing their cross-appeal, the Authority decided to cease salvage operations for the winter. If no word was received from the Court by spring, they would request a stay in order to continue operations. In November 1976, Sproul requested a release from his bond. The Authority agreed to the request, providing his work was checked to ascertain that all terms of his contract had been met.[89]

While waiting to hear from the Court about the salvage operation, or the Restoration Plan as it was now frequently called, the Authority and staff proceeded with plans to hire a permanent forester and to develop plans for the northern townships and for the Park in general. In autumn 1976, the Authority awarded Sewall Company a contract to take aerial photographs of the 28,000 acre scientific forestry area and to prepare a type map. The company flew one set of photographs during the fall and a second set the following spring. The Soil Conservation Service also conducted field work during autumn 1976, and during the late winter worked on a soil interpretation report. The Soil Conservation Service planned to work with the Sewall Company on the proposed scientific forestry management plan, and the Park planned to use forestry students from the University of Maine to do some basic forest inventory work during summer 1977. Advisory member and UM professor Fred Knight worked on both the overall plan strategy and on hiring the students. The Soil Conservation Service completed its report in April. The report included aerial photographs, soil classification maps and overlays, and a report on soils within the scientific management area.[90]

Likewise, work on the master plan continued. By early February 1977, three of the plan's anticipated nine sections had been completed in rough draft form. Six additional sections were in progress. The entire first draft was scheduled for submission in April or May that year. After the Authority tentatively approved the plan they anticipated holding a number of informational meetings to inform the public of the plan's contents and solicit public response. Hopefully, a final draft would be submitted for approval in late autumn 1977.[91]

To aid in formulating both plans as well as providing needed help on a day-to-day basis, the Park sought to create and fill a permanent professional forester's position. The intended classification, Forester II, did not have a register with the State Personnel Department, which slowed the hiring process. Finally, in the spring of 1977, Personnel approved the position as a ninety-day appointment so that plans could proceed and forestry students hired for summer inventory work. The Authority granted Kolman the temporary forester's position in May. Kolman had the necessary qualifications and had been working on a preliminary plan since the previous year. In early April, with a $15,000 balance remaining on Kolman's consulting forester's contract, the Authority had, with Kolman's agreement, terminated the contract so that the funds could be used elsewhere. Kolman intended to take the exam for the permanent position when it was later given.[92]

Kolman started work as temporary staff forester in May 1977, and immediately began work in the SFMA area. By early July he had surveyed the area and developed an inventory plan which student foresters used that summer. At the same time, the Sewall Company submitted a type map of the area and planned to submit a complete report by late summer which would be used in the final SFMA management plan. The first draft of the master Park management plan was submitted late in the spring, and by July had been reviewed by the Authority and circulated among various State agencies. Comments had been submitted and were under consideration. Additions and revisions would be made, but advertising and circulating the rough draft would begin as soon as possible and initial informational meetings scheduled for mid-September. Millinocket, Orono, Augusta, and Portland would serve as locations for the September meetings.[93] Thus, although the Authority still waited in the summer of 1977 for the Court to make a final decision on the restoration project, work had proceeded on crucial issues, issues related in numerous ways to the salvage operation. Before plans could progress further, however, something happened, something which proponents of harvesting the blowdown area had stressed and feared, and which salvage proponents and opponents alike had discussed and debated: fire.

Forest fire had long been a concern of the Baxter State Park Authority and Park staff. Following the 1974 blowdown, questions about the possible fire danger presented by having tens of thousands of cords of blowdown wood drying on the forest floor had been voiced immediately. Concerns that fire might start in the affected southwestern portion of the Park, spread rapidly, destroy flora and fauna, and threaten human life had been a—if not *the*—major impetus for the controversial salvage plan. When fire broke out along the Park border on July 17, 1977, the worst fears of many people seemed about to be realized.

Firefighters worked from July 17 to July 31, 1977, to contain and suppress the fire which burned roughly 3,500 acres, some 1,900 of them within BSP. Lightning had started the fire in the vicinity of Lost Pond, and the fire had spread rapidly. High winds, hot weather, and blowdown spruce and fir created difficult conditions during several days. Much of the fire work ended by July 26, but the most pressing of the cleanup work took sev-

The 1977 fire burned across Park and paper company land.
(Photo: *Bangor Daily News*)

The intense smoke from the 1977 fire was visible for many miles.
(Photo: Maine Dept. of Inland Fisheries and Wildlife)

Next Page:

(Top) The forested slopes at higher elevations on Katahdin were spared by the 1977 conflagration. The West Branch of the Penobscot River can be seen in the lower right.

(Below) Fire generated wind blows through foliage adjacent to a wall of flame.

(Both photos: Maine Dept. of Inland Fisheries and Wildlife)

eral more days to complete. In BSP the fire area covered the area west of Abol Campground south to the West Branch of the Penobscot River. At the height of the blaze, two shifts of over one hundred firefighters each worked daily. They did so for almost three days. In addition, skidders, bulldozers, and several aircraft were employed. Firefighters within the Park concentrated on keeping the fire from going up the mountain near Abol. If they failed to keep the fire from reaching high ground, it seemed that there would be no stopping the conflagration. Earle S. Williams, Acting Supervisor of the State Forest Fire Control Division of the Department of Conservation, stated afterwards that the fire had been practically impossible to stop in the blowdown area due to a lack of roads and the heavy volume of fuel on the ground. Luckily, the direction of the fire was against the prevailing winds, which, along with the fire work along Abol Stream, kept much more land within BSP from being burned than might otherwise have been true.[94]

Baxter employees evacuated 406 people as a precautionary measure. The fire had been detected at 8:45 p.m. Evacuation procedures began one hour later for the Park's Abol, Daicey Pond, Katahdin Stream, and Roaring Brook campgrounds, and for the then privately operated Kidney Pond Camps as well as the Youth Conservation Corps camp. By 10:45 all campers had safely left the area. Chimney and Russell Pond campgrounds were first alerted about possible evacuation, then later evacuated. Chimney Pond campers were led by the Campground Attendant to the Roaring Brook parking area, and all left the Park by 3:05 a.m. Campers at Russell Pond were allowed to spend the night there, then hiked the 9.5 miles to South Branch Pond when the sun rose. Those persons evacuated in the night from the various campgrounds found shelter or sleeping space at area motels, campgrounds, and in the BSP headquarters' parking lot. The Town of Millinocket also opened the Jerry Pond recreation area for people in need of a place to stay.[95]

In addition to the camps and campgrounds, all trails in the southern half of the Park were closed during the fire. The trails stayed closed for two to three or more weeks, as did the campgrounds. After August 9—twenty-three days after the fire started—only the area inside the fire perimeter remained closed. Within this area mop-up operations continued and several ground fires still burned. Three BSP campgrounds in the northern half of the Park had remained open during the fire. However, with most of the campgrounds having closed, roughly 7,500 camper days were lost to the fire as well as an additional 10,000 day use visits. Although many persons' vacation plans were interrupted, none of their lives were lost.[96]

Park personnel did more than evacuate most of the Park. Baxter State Park staff worked with members of other agencies in fighting the fire. The staff worked in a variety of areas, from helping to coordinate fire activities to front line fire fighting, to purchasing food, running radios, and keeping unauthorized vehicles safely out of the fire area. From July 17 until at least July 20, 1977, BSP personnel mobilized and coordinated feeding units for all workers from all involved agencies, and operated a field kitchen twenty-four hours a day. The Maine Forest Service, to whom BSP paid $32,000 a year for fire protection, agreed to reimburse the Park for the time worked by twenty-nine Park women and men during the "incident period" of July 20 until the fire was declared under control on July 28. The Forest Service also agreed to pay the salaries for Janice Caverly, Virginia McKenna, and Gerald Merry for July 17 through July 19 for their work on the feeding unit, which lasted until the National Guard assumed the work July 22. Director Tibbs later asked the Forest Service to supply additional funds for overtime salaries for July 17 through July 19. The Department of Conservation eventually reimbursed most of the money requested. The Park also applied for funding from the Federal Disaster Assistance Administration. The Park had been experiencing a financial strain before the fire, and the cost of the fire in such measurable things as supplies, equipment, and labor proved extensive. As of noon July 25, the estimated cost of the fire had reached $483,355; mop-up and cleanup costs had yet to be determined; and the fire was not entirely extinguished.[97]

Fortunately, the 1977 fire did not destroy Park buildings. Total fire damage might have been worse. Soon after the fire, Supervisor Caverly sent a memo to all BSP employees and family members thanking them for their hard work. Caverly wrote that although reminders of the fire would exist for many years, and although the cost to wildlife was as yet unknown, thanks to them and to other workers the Park still had "approximately 196,500 acres ... untouched by the fire." Erosion control and rehabilitation needed to be done in parts of the Park that fire had traversed, however, and planning for this occurred almost simultaneously with the mop-up phase of the fire, when the most critical of the cleanup operations were also conducted.[98]

Kim Kolman reported on the "firebreak reclamation project" in early August. As numerous individuals had realized during the blaze, firebreaks bulldozed to contain the fire created their own environmental impacts. Kolman discussed steps which still needed to be taken to correct the situation. According to Kolman, in some areas firebreaks could be left to regenerate naturally through reseeding by neighboring stands—although streams might need to be protected from the effects of erosion and siltation by the construction of water bars or sedimentation pools. Other areas required water bars plus grading, seeding, and mulching, and might require stream bank restoration, reinforcement, or planting. In addition, arrangements had to be made with GNP to help keep unauthorized vehicles from crossing now unprotected southern Park boundaries. Park Director Tibbs agreed that the work needed to be done as soon as possible, but due to a shortage in Park employees, crews would have to be hired from elsewhere. Hopefully, crews could be hired to begin work after Kolman completed taking inventory in the Scientific Forest Management Area, and the project completed by late September. Tibbs also sought to secure funding from other State agencies for the project.[99]

The fire, as might be expected, drew inquiries from the public and from various State agencies. The Bureau of Forestry and the Department of Conservation held public reviews of the fire and its suppression, reviews held in August and September respectively. Following a visit to the fire site, the later meeting examined the environmental aspects of the fire as well as the technical ones. A six person board was established to review the fire in a professional capacity. The three major agencies involved in the fire's suppression, the Maine Forest Service (MFS), GNP, and BSP, presented information on fire fighting techniques and policies.[100]

Baxter State Park's representative at the September meeting, Director A. Lee Tibbs, stated that in spite of a few problems, problems one might expect in any large evacuation and fire, he felt that BSP staff did an excellent job. Under the existing plan, the Park aimed first to prevent fires, but worked to extinguish any wildfires that did occur. Visitor safety comprised the first priority during a fire, and evacuation procedures were an important part of the Park's fire plan. Once the Forest Service arrived at a fire, the Park relinquished authority for directing fire fighting activities.[101]

The September meeting also saw review of the Park's fire restoration plan. Kolman's proposal was ultimately, with a few modifications, approved and funded as Emergency Watershed Protection under the Federal Flood Control Act of 1950. Several members of BSP's seasonal staff had their dates of service extended and worked under Kolman on the designated fourteen acres. They completed the operation at the end of October 1977. During the fire, a section of Abol Pond had been restored to its original channel and a steep slope along Abol Stream contoured as both bodies of water had faced immediate threats to water quality and fish resources. Five waterbars had also been installed and some seeding done near Abol Pond. After receiving approval and funding for the additional restoration work, BSP staff completed the remainder of the project, leaving only seeding of steep slopes near the Abol Stream and Abol Field firebreaks until the following spring.[102]

The financial cost of the restoration project, including estimated work hours for the spring seeding and the work conducted during the fire—as well as the price of aerial photographs, soil grading, tree planting, liming, fertilization, chipping, mulching, waterbar installation, and administrative expenses—totaled $7,339. A representative from LURC, and its Executive Director, Kenneth Stratton, toured the fire area and apparently expressed approval for the completed project, even though it was and is generally acceded that BSP lies outside LURC jurisdiction.[103]

Although the restoration project generally earned favorable responses, the fire and the restoration project raised new questions concerning BSP fire plans and slowed progress on the Park's master and SFMA plans. Revisions and additions to BSP fire plans had been under consideration since 1975 as part of the Park's developing its policy and concept, or master, plan. A fire plan had been written in 1975 and a few revisions made to it in

1977—seemingly just after the fire—while planning in general continued. Following the 1977 fire, the Baxter Park Fire Review Board recommended that the BSP fire plan be updated prior to the 1978 fire season. To this end, in April 1978, Tibbs contacted eight persons whom he felt had an interest in BSP fire plans: three members of the MFS; one person each from UM, the Bureau of Public Lands, and GNP; plus Kim Kolman and Fred Holt. Tibbs asked the men to review the existing plan and submit any recommendations they might have. Tibbs expressed particular interest in suggestions concerning the concepts of fire control and fire management. The inference was that the existing plan included primarily information on how to stop fires, and did not discuss any benefits of allowing fires to burn when possible or mention other approaches to managing forest fires. According to Tibbs, one criticism of the existing plan was that it was a fire control not a fire management plan.[104]

Tibbs received written comments and called a May meeting to discuss the proposed changes. Written comments included a variety of suggestions. For example, Charlie Williams of UM's School of Forest Resources emphasized that BSP personnel should be trained in "crew units," each unit rotating through the various fire fighting jobs. In addition to making for faster organization in the event of fire, closer teamwork and coordination would result from the emphasis on working as crews and not responding as individuals, as Williams argued that "*individually* trained men behave like *individuals* when forced to take action in suppressing a fire." Williams also suggested yearly unannounced simulated fires in each district to evaluate personnel skills, equipment, and communications. Another suggestion from Williams was that the Park consider "intensive fuel management through thinnings, prunings, and cleanings in buffer zones around high value facilities and campgrounds."[105]

Fred Holt, currently serving as a BSP Advisory member, expressed a desire that a revised or perhaps additional plan be written, one which would include more policy statements. Holt took a different stance on fuel or hazard reduction than did Williams. Holt stated that he would downplay the subject of firebreaks and, it seems, other measures currently included in the relevant section of the fire plan. "Modification of fuel bed–hazard reduction—around campgrounds—yes, but with all the other objections the public has to 'management,' I'd forget about this measure of questionable practical use." Instead he suggested that personnel "just be knowledgeable about existing barriers and use them." Expecting staff to be aware of barriers and to use them without mentioning them in the fire plan, one modified or not to meet public concerns, might itself have been "of questionable practical use." Although Holt did make other suggestions concerning practical or direct matters, he expressed as much concern about public relations as about making the fire plan a working manual.[106]

According to Holt, a separate statement or pamphlet "for public consumption," might be advisable "with all the discussion about the broad area of fire management." Holt indicated that this document would "contain more on B[S]PA policy views-funding, coordination of agency personnel, and communication equipment." For example, for the time being, the Park should suppress all fires. However, the Authority might eventually establish some "let burn" areas. That this might one day occur should be stressed in the new or revised document, but with a clear statement to the effect that more study needed to take place so that the Park would "really know what will happen before instituting" a let burn policy in designated areas.[107]

Bart Harvey, GNP Management Forester, found the existing fire plan "quite adequate," and simply suggested that a few more specifics be added—such as a Park personnel organization chart, additional maps, and a plan for fire suppression in remote areas. Harvey did make one major policy statement. Although his company realized that BSP had some different management goals than GNP, in regard to fire management in the Park, "Great Northern's position is *that all unplanned fire should be suppressed.*" The Authority had to recognize "the fact that fire represents a very real threat to the adjacent property owners," and BSP and GNP shared "some fifty miles of common boundary." The company would keep an open mind about the use of controlled burning in BSP as a possible method of reducing fire hazard, but only on a "limited scale and applied only after careful planning."[108]

"The Baxter State Park Fire Plan," as revised in June 1978, incorporated many of the written suggestions Tibbs had received. The plan opened with two pages of BSP fire management policies. After noting the process of reviewing the fire plan and recognizing both the sixteen member task force that had worked on the fire plan as part of the general Park management plan, and the eight member Fire Plan Review Committee, the opening page indicated that Park policy had to include statutory requirements. Under Maine law, the Maine Forest Service was "'responsible for the prevention, control, and extinguishment of forest fires in all areas of the state,'" its Director being responsible for emergency planning which included plans for securing "manpower," equipment, transportation, communications, and feeding facilities. State law likewise governed the amount of money BSP paid each year for this service.[109]

Baxter State Park terrain, the inaccessibility of much of BSP, Park visitors, the existence of forest blowdown and of trees killed by spruce budworm, weather conditions, and "the uniqueness of Baxter Park" also influenced the formulation of Park fire management policy. For the immediate future, BSP's present "knowledge of conditions and technical capabilities" necessitated that the overall policy must be one of control. Annual reviews would, however, consider the need for any changes, and "long range" fire management studies were "being actively considered." Until such a time that changes in policy transpired, the Park would conduct a "vigorous fire prevention campaign," control fires as they occurred, and when possible use methods with the least impact on Park resources. When feasible, restoration might be made after fires to remove "the evidence of man's activities."[110]

The fire plan as revised in 1978 contained other new sections. Although many pages in the body of the plan were revised, most additions were made to the appendices. New appendices were added on personnel organization and skills, and concerning monthly check lists. Members of the two review committees were also identified in the end material.[111] The fire plan underwent various modifications in succeeding years, but the 1978 revision contained what would continue to be the core of BSP fire management.

Much of the BSP fire management policy as stated in the 1978 revision appeared in the Park management plan presented in August 1978. As previously indicated, work on the SFMA and Master Plan continued during the period of the 1977 fire, although progress did slow on the two projects. The Park had written a revised general plan in June 1976 which listed the primary goals and objectives of BSP. The 1976 plan was clearly written and easy to follow, but read much like an outline and specified neither the Park's status in reaching its goals nor the specific steps planned for attaining Park goals. The five page 1976 plan did add to the criteria for Park management stated in the earlier and shorter version, but still required much more information before attaining the status of a "comprehensive" management plan. Those who worked on the plan realized that the 1976 plan was only a temporary plan or draft, and work continued.[112]

As indicated earlier, staff, Authority, and Advisory members had worked on the management plan and had had a draft ready for public review just before the outbreak of the 1977 fire. Plans to distribute the plan on August 15 with an accompanying news release, and to schedule five public hearings by mid-September of 1977, were made before the fire and carried out in the following weeks. By late December 1977, the management plan had evolved, but the need for additions remained. Kenneth Fink of the NRCM attended the regularly scheduled December Authority meeting and discussed the Council's opinion of the plan. Overall, the NRCM approved of the new plan, but had two major areas of conflict. The first of these was that the plan should include a fire management plan rather than just a fire control plan. This issue was later addressed in the 1978 fire plan. The second concern of the NRCM was that there be a separate and more detailed plan for the scientific forestry area. This was still being worked on, as Tibbs stated at the meeting,[113] and would ultimately be resolved by the 1978 general management plan and later revisions.

The Authority and Park continued to seek a full time forester in early 1978, and to work on the SFMA and Park master plans. In the meantime, on April 6, 1978, the Maine Supreme Court delivered its decision to uphold the Superior Court blowdown decision of August 24, 1976. Sarah Redfield reported that the decision might help guide the Authority in the future, in that the decision did not define such terms as "heavy equipment" (the use of which the Court had generally forbidden in the blowdown area), "public park," or "natural wild state," and thus, one might infer from the discussion, placed few overall restrictions on the Authority. The decision, Redfield pointed out, also reiterated the status of the Park as a charitable trust, and recognized the 1955 Interpretation Act as an interpretation, not a modification, of the Baxter Trust. Furthermore, Redfield thought the decision did not affect the scientific forest management section of BSP. At the same time as the Supreme Court rendered this decision, the Authority faced a suit concerning the 1977 fire, the suit concerning the approach of BSP to firefighting or management. Although the suit was expected to be dismissed, it, along with the blowdown suits, did indicate public concerns—concerns which the Authority and Advisory considered in formulating its written plans. The BSP planning task force had earlier reviewed some 170 pages of material received from the public concerning various sections of the Park plan.[114]

The Authority devoted most of its May 1978 meeting to a discussion of the Park plan. The complete year-round BSP staff attended part of the meeting. Their input was both requested and considered. Negative criticism had been received during the earlier public discussions concerning public relations, and in May several persons discussed public relations and educating Park visitors about BSP policies. Yet, although public relations were deemed important, Robert Ohler of the Advisory made a valid observation in stating that the Authority and Advisory would not want to be compelled to hold a public hearing on every decision the Park Director or the Authority made. Nor, Ohler stated, should the Authority have to hold hearings on every management plan. The management plan, as the current thought ran, would be revised at least every five years.[115]

The management plan of 1978 was viewed as a working, operational, and somewhat preliminary plan. As Winston Robbins of the Advisory described it, the plan would guide both Park staff and the ever-changing membership of the Authority in making decisions, yet would not be an "iron clad" document. All anticipated goals, operating procedures, and so forth could not be implemented in one plan. As another Advisory member pointed out, the current draft was basically a policy plan from which more detailed strategies for securing specific objectives could be developed. Park Ranger Chris Drew indicated that a plan for the scientific forestry area had been in the works for five years, but meanwhile an increasing number of trees were being harvested each year. Drew expressed a desire to harvest more mature trees and to have the SFMA earn additional money for the Park. Although not a popular idea with everyone, monetary problems were apparent at the time and Drew's opinion was an understandable if not widely embraced one. Tibbs stated, in answer to Drew's urging for an SFMA plan, that the information provided by Kolman provided a foundation for the SFMA plan. Robbins asserted that once a well documented SFMA plan had been established and undergone public hearings and input, the plan would help support the Authority in any relevant future court cases. Ranger Charlie Kenney pointed out that, outside the SFMA, what was included in the policy or management plan was basically what was already being carried out in the Park. Much of it had simply not been written down previously.[116]

Park staff and others in attendance discussed other aspects of the plan at the May meeting, revisions were duly made, and in September the Authority—then composed of Chair Maynard Marsh, Attorney General Joseph Brennan, and Bureau of Forestry Director John Walker—voted unanimously to accept the "Baxter State Park Plan, Section I, Policies and Concepts" as submitted in August. Other unit management plans would later be submitted and voted upon. In the meantime, the press was notified and copies of the plan made available to the public.[117]

The BSP "Policies and Concepts Plan" as presented in August 1978 represented a major advance over earlier plans. As compared to the five-page 1976 plan, the 1978 plan included a thirty-one page body, a glossary, a bibliography, and six appendices. The 1978 introduction stated that the plan would be reviewed annually and updated or revised as necessary. The Statement of Purpose as adopted by the State Legislature in 1971, including several often quoted Baxter statements, followed the brief introduction and set the tone for much of what followed.[118]

The 1978 plan identified two major Park goals: "to manage Baxter State Park so as to maintain its natural wild state in accordance with Percival Proctor Baxter's deeds of gifts and conveyances," and "to secondarily provide for recreational use and enjoyment of the Park by people in a manner consistent with the Park's natural character." These two goals provided the basis for the major objectives listed thereafter. The four major objectives listed included policies or approaches for preserving natural resources, providing yet controlling public use, providing for visitor safety and emergency assistance, and providing user education. The two primary goals as well as the given objectives pinpointed the great dichotomy of the Park: the continuing need to balance the sometimes conflicting interests of wilderness and public use. As stated, however, protecting the "natural wild state" of BSP received top priority, at least as far as designated by the Deeds of Trust.[119] This might have satisfied those contemporary naturalists and ecologists who had long wanted to see wilderness protection specifically designated as the Park's primary goal, but may also have worried those persons concerned about any possible reductions of or restrictions on public access.

The 1978 plan divided the Park into five management zones, each with its own policy statement. Zone One included roads and roadsides; Zone Two included camping areas, developed day use areas, and administrative structures; Zone Three contained the bulk of Park land, land managed to meet Baxter's concepts of "forever wild" and the "natural wild state;" Zone Four encompassed the SFMA; and Zone Five was "established to allow for management and harvesting of wildlife as provided for in the Deeds of Trust," and was included in the other four zones. Zone four, the SFMA, was to be "governed by a special unit management plan." A later section of the general plan specified that the area would be managed for multiple use with forestry practices "harmoniously coordinated" with such other uses as "fisheries and wildlife, recreation, unique natural characteristics, and watershed values with a view toward effecting a proper balance among all uses." An included map identified the five management zones.[120]

The Park plan of 1978 provided specific plans for management, or steps to be taken in formulating management plans, for the five zones as well as guidelines for fish and wildlife management, public use, administration, and other aspects such as communications and public relations, adjacent lands, and economics. The plan noted that more detailed unit management plans would be forthcoming for implementing the policies enumerated, the policies to be put into practice as soon as possible. "Multidisciplinary task forces" would develop a unit plan for each management zone. Provisions would be made for public involvement in the planning process. Appendices to the 1978 plan included mention of, or citations for, Baxter communications, the Deeds of Trust, significant legislative acts regarding BSP, a list of the planning task force members and their occupations, a short historical sketch of the Park, and quotations from the Deeds of Trust and Baxter communications used in formulating Park policies and concepts.[121] With the 1978 "Baxter State Park Policies and Concepts" plan in place, attention turned once more to the SFMA.

Chapter Three

The Scientific Forest Management Area: Development and Progress in the "Northern Townships"

With the first substantial Park Management Plan written and accepted, and with a newly revised Fire Plan in place, the focus of Park planning fell on the Scientific Forest Management Area in late 1978. The SFMA had been a central concern of the Park and the public for several years, and after the completion of the 1978 "Baxter State Park Policies and Concepts," work on the SFMA plan progressed steadily. Forest management practices, both in and outside of the SFMA, had been an important issue at least since the 1972 proposed timber swap with Great Northern Paper Company. This concern over forest practices was evidenced in the content of Authority and Advisory meetings, in Director and Supervisor's reports, and in various legal suits. Even in matters not directly related to the SFMA, the SFMA—or what would become known as the SFMA—was used as a comparison or point of reference. When discussing what might or might not be appropriate in other areas of the Park, what might or might not be appropriate in the SFMA was frequently discussed or debated. Planning for the SFMA was an integral part of developing the BSP "Policies and Concepts," but the need to develop a separate plan for the northern townships had long been recognized. Initial SFMA planning had begun in the early 1970s, and formal steps were taken to secure necessary data in the aftermath of the 1974 blowdown. The 1978 general plan identified major objectives to be pursued and policies to be followed in the SFMA.[1]

While SFMA planning continued, other problems concerning the area demanded staff and Authority attention. The 1978 Park Management Plan did not deny the possible use of pesticides or other methods for controlling insect infestations and timber diseases in the Park, either in the SFMA or elsewhere, although the plan did specify that appropriate State authorities would be asked to give advice in the event of such infestation. Spruce-budworm damage remained a problem in some sections of BSP in 1979, and in the opinion of many people warranted control measures. Sections of the Park had been sprayed in previous years, resulting in both public protest and public support. The Authority and Park personnel had tried to keep the use of pesticides to what they considered acceptable minimums, and had not sprayed all affected areas all years when the spruce budworm posed problems during the 1970s.[2]

In early 1979, the Authority voted unanimously to spray for spruce budworm using thoricide R or Bt, a biological control agent, wherever possible and as needed in the SFMA, and "to leave it to the discretion of the Bureau of Forestry to use the least harmful chemical [of those available] in other areas." The Authority made this decision in April 1979, by which time the Park had finally been able to hire a full-time forester, George Ruopp. Ruopp had overseen the preparation of an SFMA and budworm report that year which recommended a salvage harvest operation and spraying due to a "high spruce budworm population and poor tree vigor." The Natural Resource Council of Maine, the Maine Bureau of Forestry, and the United States Forest Service had all been consulted regarding the recommendation, and had indicated basic approval for limited spraying in the SFMA. The Maine Bureau of Forestry would administer the actual spraying. The 1979 budworm control operation, as with previous sprayings, was undertaken as a means to protect softwood stands from further infestation and disease, and "to keep the fir component alive until it can be harvested." Harvest operations in turn would provide an access system for managing future stands, stands brought about through natural regeneration. The 1979 spraying was effective as far as could be determined, and the Authority voted not to spray in the SFMA or elsewhere the following year.[3]

By early September 1979, Ruopp had completed an inventory of the SFMA. The Park had sent the data obtained to the University of Maine in Orono for computer processing, Ruopp had submitted a general SFMA report, and Park officials anticipated completion of a comprehensive SFMA plan draft in January 1980. Work proceeded during the fall and winter, and the Authority reviewed the draft in the summer of 1980.[4]

The Authority—then composed of Chair and Attorney General Richard S. Cohen, Commissioner of Inland Fisheries and Wildlife Glenn H. Manuel, and Bureau of Forestry Director Kenneth G. Stratton—held special meetings in July and August 1979 to discuss the plan, and duly considered both verbal and written comments from interested parties. Jon Lund, then NRCM president, expressed concern in July that the SFMA "be operated consistent with the guidelines applicable to the whole Park," and stated that "it is optional for the Authority to be conducting forestry practices" in the SFMA. The theory that forestry was optional in an area established for scientific forestry was perhaps an intriguing one, but either way, Lund raised additional and arguably more germane points. Lund questioned whether recreational and scenic values were adequately addressed in the plan, arguing that walk-in camping areas could be established in the SFMA, and stated that other issues concerning public use needed further attention, such as the possible use of snowmobiles in the area. Other concerns raised in July involved the use of the Perimeter Road to transport timber, supplies, and machinery. Such questions had not yet been resolved, and Ruopp and others stressed that the plan could not address all possible issues nor was it necessarily complete at that point. Even after the Authority might accept the plan, future revisions and additions would still be necessary.[5]

At the meeting held on August 20, 1980, Park staff and the Authority addressed further concerns. Chair Cohen stated that he had reviewed certain letters written by Governor Baxter as well as the Deeds of Trust, then initiated a discussion of forestry practices in Europe as referred to by Baxter. Such practices had been considered in developing the SFMA plan, but, as Ruopp and others indicated, due to variations in ratios of foresters to technicians and other workers, variations in standards of wood utilization and in leaving ground cover for wildlife and forest rejuvenation, and due to variations in market conditions and other factors, silvicultural practices in the SFMA could not be patterned exactly after those of Europe. The effect of spruce budworm in BSP also warranted consideration. Money likewise posed a problem, and the methods for funding road building and initial projects remained unresolved. Stratton expressed concern over the emphasis on stumpage revenue for financing SFMA management, an issue the Authority decided to address further at their next meeting. Those assembled on August 20, 1980, generally felt that setting up a road system comprised the first priority in getting SFMA operations underway.[6]

The Authority met again the following day. Some of the same issues were raised. However, a consensus was reached on several matters by the close of the second August meeting. The Great Northern Paper Company had initiated road building or right-of-way clearing in the Southwest corner of the SFMA in 1972 after agreeing to the timber swap. New road building and forestry work would begin in that same area under the proposed plan. This would take advantage of existing roads or cleared areas, and allow harvesting in that portion of the SFMA most heavily affected by the spruce budworm. The general feeling was that work should begin as soon as possible to avoid further infestation problems and to prepare the area for future operations. The Authority therefore voted to authorize construction of the first mile of SFMA access road. The construction would be financed by Trust Fund reserves, dependent upon approval by legal counsel. Park Director Tibbs recommended that Winston Robbins, an engineer and Advisory member, be asked to supervise the construction. Robbins subsequently did so, with the help of other people.[7]

Questions about funding dominated part of the discussion on the second day. Concerns over recovering money for road construction were addressed, as some persons wondered if the price of the road should be recovered through the first harvest contract or be spread over harvesting contracts or timber sales over a set number of years. Ruopp responded that the road system was crucial to the SFMA, for the present and for the future. The road system, if it was to be of lasting value, needed to be viewed as a long-term investment. To set a specific time period for recovering costs would result in a need to over-harvest trees—to cut more timber in the near future than should be cut in terms of maintaining a satisfactory spruce and fir forest with a view to increasing the percentage of spruce. Roads built in the near future should be able to provide access one hundred years into the future. Eventually SFMA forestry operations would recover road costs, most of it within ten years, although Park money might be needed for such other operations as spruce budworm protection. Such considerations were part of the decision to fund the road system with Trust Fund money. The Authority agreed with Ruopp in several matters and did not request a specific time be set for recovering road construction funds, but did wish to see a tentative

Log transport on the Webster Ledge Road in the Scientific Forest Management Area. (Photo: Jensen Bissell)

budget for the next five years submitted, one which would cover personnel costs as well as road work and other expenses.[8]

Those present at the SFMA review meetings recognized the amount of work and careful consideration staff members and others had invested in the plan. Although some additions would be made, the plan was well received and eventual official approval was expected. In the meantime, the Authority hoped to secure more input from the public and such organizations as the NRCM. The degree of interest voiced in the past had led the Authority to expect greater attendance at the review meetings and more correspondence concerning the plan.[9] Other issues, such as that of snowmobile access changes, had captured public attention during 1980, and perhaps explained why the SFMA plan draft received less attention than the Authority had anticipated.

The plan sections on SFMA objectives, wildlife, recreation, critical areas, and transportation were expanded by late October, and Park Forester Ruopp reported that he expected the plan to be completed by the end of November. General discussions with contractors had been held during the summer, but the contractors had expressed a desire to read an approved plan before committing further time or effort to harvesting considerations. In response to questions concerning operational time frames, Ruopp stated that at the earliest operations might begin the following autumn, but the summer of 1982 seemed a more probable date. The Authority hoped to see a complete draft prepared in time for approval at the December meeting. The long awaited SFMA management plan was indeed submitted in December, although it did not receive immediate approval.[10]

The "Baxter State Park Authority Scientific Forest Management Area, A Forest Management Plan for the Initial Ten-Year Operational Period" consisted of an eighty-four page body plus bibliography and appendices. In some ways its scope and content exceeded those of the 1978 general Park plan, as it focused on one specific area and contained more detail as to how Park policies and objectives would be achieved, or strived for, within a specified time period. The plan did not attempt, however, to specify all measures to be considered or actions to be taken. The SFMA would be managed, and necessary intervention into natural processes undertaken,

> to develop the area into a showplace for those interested in forestry ... to provide for optimum levels of recreational use and enjoyment, fisheries and wildlife populations, aesthetics, unique characteristics, and watershed values, while practicing timber management; to provide for protection and restoration of forest resources that may be susceptible to damage by acts of nature; and to actively and consistently improve management of the area.[11]

The "most approved practices of scientific forestry" would be utilized in this "multiple use management," and sections on each of the objectives were included in the plan.[12]

The SFMA, according to the plan and expressed in terminology from Baxter's Deeds and Communications, was to be a "showplace" and an "inspiration." The plan's preface included excerpts from Baxter's 1955 Communications to Governor Edmund Muskie and the Maine Senate and House of Representatives, as well as excerpts from the 1955 Special Laws and Communications. The Park Forester would be responsible for "all approved practices," and supervised by the Park Director. Forest management would be of the highest standards currently in use or as documented by forest management research. Sustained yields of products and services, including but not limited to wood products or services, constituted a major objective, and the SFMA would be self-supporting in the long-term. Research compatible with scientific forestry would be allowed, as would insect, disease, and fire control. Management of the area would be coordinated with adjacent landowners, and no permanent structures would be erected in the SFMA. In the event that any person reading the plan missed its main tenet, the plan's introduction clearly stated that "the forever wild concept does not prevail in the SFMA." [13]

At the cost of being redundant, the SFMA plan reiterated major goals and objectives, as well as some anticipated operations, in the body of the report. The plan quoted extensively from a 1975 address by Swiss forester Hans Leibundgut on experimental forests, apparently to support SFMA objectives although no interpretive passages were provided. The plan identified the production of a "crop of high quality saw and veneer logs" as being a major objective; stated that the demand for saw and stud logs had decreased; then stated that "over the next fifty years, however, various forecasts [not identified] predict the use of timber products to double."[14] In the meantime, the plan emphasized the need to respond to the spruce budworm epidemic.

Roughly 70 percent of the SFMA's "productive forest land" comprised softwood stands, and about 66 percent of the area's mixed wood stands (23 percent of the total) had a high softwood component. The plan identified an overall 6 percent mortality rate from spruce budworm, but did not identify the softwoods so affected by percentages or by other units of measure. Fir apparently had sustained the greatest damage. The emphasis for the next few years would be to harvest as much fir as possible, both to salvage already damaged trees and to halt the spread of the infestation. Aside from the initial harvesting, stand rotations would average sixty-five years with wildlife habitat, water protection, and other factors taken into consideration.[15]

After careful consideration, an access plan calling for the construction of 27.2 miles of primary road and 50.8 miles of secondary roads had been decided upon. Harvested products would be transported westerly "through provided access points to private roads." For administrative and forest protection (primarily fire protection) purposes, an access route connecting with the Perimeter Road would be built. Road financing would be considered a long-term investment, but the access system would be completed within ten years. Stumpage revenues would eventually recover initial start-up costs as well as SFMA management expenses. Four full-time employees and five seasonal workers would allow for effective SFMA management. Cooperation with other public agencies would continue in the future, including the international, CANUSA funded, Green Woods Project for spruce budworm management; the Bureau of Public Lands of the Maine Department of Conservation, which had tentatively agreed to supply road surfacing material and possibly a site for housing harvesting crews; and the Maine Forest Service which, in addition to providing fire protection (at State determined annual fees) and aid in evaluating insect and disease problems, had already assisted in the SFMA inventory data processing.[16]

In January 1981, the BSPA voted to apply Bt to 7,000 acres of the SFMA, via helicopter, contingent upon tentative approval of the SFMA Management Plan. The Authority then granted tentative approval and scheduled a vote on final approval for their next meeting. They elected to delay the final vote to provide interested parties additional time to read the plan and submit any comments that they might have. The following month the Authority voted unanimously to adopt and proceed with the plan. Director Tibbs emphasized his desire to see road building and harvesting begin as soon as possible, sentiments which Chair Manuel echoed.[17]

In March 1981, former Park Business Manager William Cross submitted a revised SFMA economic analysis which incorporated expenses back to September 1978. The new analysis projected an $8,000 net income from the SFMA for the first five years, as opposed to the original projection of $400,000. At the same Advisory meeting, those in attendance discussed broadening the base of technical expertise for securing input into SFMA management, setting up "working groups" composed of individuals with interests in and knowledge of specific relevant fields. Kim Kolman, then a member of the Advisory, and George Ruopp agreed to develop a questionnaire and a proposal and to contact potentially interested parties.[18]

In spite of a desire to implement parts of the management plan as soon as possible, the Authority had difficulty securing bids for an initial cutting operation. No bids were received after two attempts in 1981 to secure a contractor. Reasons given or considered likely included the road specifications being too complicated and costly to meet, the term of the contract being too brief, GNP road use fees being too high, and current market conditions being too poor. The Park ultimately contracted with Sheridan Smith, Incorporated, for the first 3,400 feet of the access road at a cost of no more than $12,945. An additional $8,200 was spent on related expenses. Road work started in early August, and in late October the Authority, after receiving approval to negotiate a contract from the Maine Bureau of Purchases, voted to contract with Grant Forest Products, Incorporated, for a three year period. The stumpage proposal and price bid included road construction and maintenance along with stumpage rights for eleven tree species.[19]

In November, Ruopp reviewed the bidding process with those in attendance at the Authority meeting and discussed how the SFMA had been divided into "management districts" since he had started work in 1978. The Park currently intended to begin cutting operations in roughly 19,000 acres of mature age spruce-fir, an area with continuing budworm caused mortality. Although Quentin Smart of Grant Forest Products had planned to begin cutting that winter, in January 1982 the Authority learned that he had decided to delay operations due to heavy snowfall and poor market conditions. Commercial cutting in the SFMA was thus delayed yet again. Park staff had, however, continued working on various projects in the SFMA, including research, sign making, and cutting 11,000 feet of lumber. Road work had also started to a limited extent. Having another contractor begin work remained a possibility, but the situation did not look favorable for a spring or summer cutting operation. The Park had elected not to spray for budworm the previous year in anticipation of a cutting operation. No cutting operation had been conducted, and the SFMA Advisory Board recommended spraying 2,700 acres in the southwest corner of the SFMA in 1982. Timber there was in the critical stage, and, as Kenneth Stratton stated, unless it was cut it would need protection via spraying. Ruopp hoped that effects of a 1982 spraying would last for three years, as cutting in the area might take up to two years. The Authority voted unanimously in March to spray, with the understanding that the Park would be liable for costs. During this time, the SFMA also faced a substantial loss in funding and technical aid from the Green Woods Project, resulting in yet another challenge to be met.[20]

In autumn 1982, the long anticipated harvest operation in the SFMA finally began. Park staff marked trees in early fall, having done some related work earlier, and primarily selected spruce showing signs of deterioration due to budworm depredation. Harvesting started soon thereafter, and by November 22, 1982, the contractor had harvested 1,375 cords of wood, 967 cords for which the Park received payment as agreed, the remaining 378 cords being taken from the right-of-way with no fees levied on the contractor. The operation thus far had netted a little over $5,000. In addition, some

13,000 feet of road had been constructed, bringing the total road construction to roughly 16,500 feet. The Park had also acquired a house trailer at no cost from the Allagash Wilderness Waterway. After being moved to the Coffeelos Campsite on the Bureau of Public Lands property in T6R11 and undergoing a few renovations, the trailer provided winter housing for the SFMA crew. In spite of such progress, market conditions remained grim.[21]

Spruce budworm also continued to present a source of concern in late 1982, but one that did not require immediate action. Samples taken in September showed budworm populations to be moderate and affected trees were expected to withstand existing infestation levels. The recently established SFMA Advisory Group—composed of Winston Robbins, Robert Ohler, Brownie Carson, and Robert Gardiner—and the MFS had agreed that spraying be foregone in the spring of 1983 while they waited to see if an expected substantial budworm population increase did indeed occur. The majority of the timber in the area was considered too old and too heavily stocked, in terms of protecting the stands for optimum growth, to justify spraying costs at the present time. Nevertheless, if the anticipated "in-flight" from regions outside BSP occurred in 1983, spraying would be imperative in 1984.[22]

Irvin Caverly, after serving as Acting BSP Director, had become Director in the summer of 1982 and remained in charge of day-to-day operations during initial harvesting under the SFMA Management Plan. Caverly would stay at the helm of the Park through the close of the studied period, and thus proved instrumental in the development of the SFMA from a plan of what might be into a working, and eventually profitable, managed forest. Although Caverly provided continuity, the SFMA eventually employed a manager responsible for its operations. The addition of a Park Forester, or Park Resource Manager as the position eventually became entitled, to the Park staff helped negate any administrative conflicts of interest and permitted the Director and Forester to focus a majority of their time on their respective duties.[23]

George Roupp resigned from his position as Park Forester in 1983. Ruopp had earlier applied for the Director's position, and after leaving BSP entered the private business sector. Kim Kolman, who had initiated SFMA inventory and planning in the wake of the 1974 blowdown, had meanwhile re-entered the business world. Later, during Stratton's tenure as Director of the Maine Forest Service, Kolman served as a forester with responsibilities in Northern Maine, and to some extent BSP, once again. Meanwhile, after Ruopp's departure from the Park, Fred Rooney served as interim Park Forester with Paul Rumney working as a forest technician, and for a short time Dennis Brennan served as BSP Forester while the MFS—including Forester Kolman—guided operations. Ultimately, events leading to new controversy and the continuing need for a full-time professional SFMA manager led to a nation-wide search which resulted in the 1987 hiring of Jensen Bissell as Park Resource Manager.[24] Bissell would remain Resource Manager through the mid-1990s. Thus the SFMA, although it experienced a long period of relative disorganization before the late 1970s and a period of delay before official harvesting began in 1982, had relatively few managers between the 1970s and the 1990s. Management under Bissell became more intensive, and eventually more profitable, than it had been earlier.

The SFMA was not yet out of the red in 1983, however. Once more spruce-budworm spraying became a consideration. Costs for spraying were expected to decrease that year throughout Maine as a new and less expensive chemical, Matacil, would be used on many projects, and small airplanes would be used in most places instead of helicopters. Where the State continued to use Bt, lower volumes would be used. Although the Park planned not to spray in 1983, it would be responsible for some spraying costs. Prior to 1981, the State General Fund had financed spraying on State lands. That arrangement had recently changed, with current legislation making public agencies liable for costs. Although 90 percent of costs for any given year would be born by those agencies whose land was sprayed that year, 10 percent would be paid by a charge on lands included in a particular district but not sprayed that year. All lands entered in the program had to remain in it for a minimum of five years. The Park had entered 2,800 acres in the program in 1982, and would thereby be charged an estimated $1,600 in 1983 even though it would not have lands sprayed in 1983.[25]

The BSPA expressed confidence in 1983 that the areas of the SFMA most affected by the budworm had been "cleaned out." Chair Manual pointed out in June, however, that once SFMA operations had finally begun the forest products industry had fallen to its lowest point in several years. The situation warranted professional evaluation. He recommended that the Authority negotiate with the UM Forestry Department to have them conduct a study in the SFMA and use the SFMA essentially as a laboratory—to engage, it seems, in some aspect of scientific forestry as envisioned by Baxter. When the market reached a certain point, operators might be engaged for harvesting operations. The present contract could, it seems, be completed without further ado. The contract would expire at the close of 1984.[26]

The SFMA Advisory Group met with UM personnel and with employees of United States Forest Service (USFS) and the MFS during the summer to discuss possible options for the SFMA and various forestry issues. Cutting continued in the SFMA, even after Ruopp's departure. By August 16, 1983, when Ruopp left, 1,165 cords had been cut. By October 28, another 3,106 cords were cut and an additional harvest of 300 cords was expected for a total 1983 monetary yield of $35,000. Ultimate cordage was 5,160 cords—close to the year's target of 6,000—with an estimated yield of $30,000, depending on market conditions. The SFMA still presented a financial problem, however, and the committee advised contracting with the MFS to have them work as consultants. Fred Rooney of MFS had been serving as an SFMA interim forester since Roupp's departure. Stratton had requested that Rooney take over the SFMA program until the Authority determined how to best provide for the SFMA's management and future direction. Although the arrangement worked out on a day-to-day basis, it did raise policy questions.[27]

In November 1983, while the Authority considered its options, Rooney delivered a report recommending that cutting be at least doubled in 1984. He also recommended that the Authority retain Quentin Smart in the southern portion of the SFMA and employ another contractor in the northern portion, as wood in the northern section needed harvesting. Smart, however, according to his contract with the Park, would be granted the cutting rights in the northern portion if he bid within 10 percent of any other bidders for the wood. The market continued to be poor, Rooney reported, but showed signs of improvement. The Authority, Rooney maintained, had to demonstrate that it intended to be a "dedicated supplier of wood" and "show the local contractors we are serious about selling this wood." Director Caverly stated that due to Rooney's initiative, the Park had experienced progress in its SFMA operations. Smart agreed in 1984 to increase his operation for the year to 10,000 to 12,000 cords, and Rooney reported an estimated net income of $6,000, after all expenses, for the year of July 1, 1983, to June 30, 1984.[28]

Prior to Rooney's assuming responsibilities in the SFMA, some 16,500 feet of SFMA road had been completed, and an additional 10,000 feet of road was planned, at contractor expense, for the balance of 1983 and for 1984. New road construction was expected to be more efficient as non-commercial wood from the road-way would be used to fill in low parts of the road or would be leveled out, covered, and seeded instead of being bulldozed into stump piles. No new stump piles were anticipated and existing ones would be removed.[29]

Although it would soon become obvious that many individuals and some organizations disagreed with current SFMA operations, Authority members were able to express pleasure at the status of SFMA operations in early 1984. Rooney recommended spraying parts of the SFMA with Bt that year, and after some discussion the Authority accepted the recommendation. Rooney stressed, however, that silvicultural methods could address some problems and should be used in conjunction with the spraying program. The SFMA Advisory Group had earlier recommended that Rooney's interim plan of the previous year be reviewed in 1984, that more attention be paid to recreation in the SFMA, and that more emphasis be placed on the experimental aspect of the SFMA. Rooney agreed with the group's recommendations and suggested a tentative list of people who might serve on a committee to address these and related issues. Chair Manuel pointed out, however, that at the present time the SFMA operation was a salvage one, an experimental one might possibly be undertaken in the future.[30] Future events would show that portions of the general public would have preferred that the

SFMA Advisory Group's recommendations, as well as some of Rooney's, had been implemented as soon as they had been made, if not sooner.

The BSP Authority and Advisory discussed a recreational plan creating buffer zones around potential areas of conflict between forestry and recreation use in the SFMA, as well as the use of logging roads, at their 1984 April and June meetings. At the June Advisory meeting, the Advisory approved closing primary roads during spring and fall to prevent damage to the road system and possibly during high fire hazard times. The Advisory also recommended that secondary roads be blocked following completion of harvesting in a given area; that the Webster Lake Trail (which encompassed much of the recreational use in the SFMA) be permanently closed to vehicles; and that metal culverts be removed from secondary roads in favor of wooden ones, but that they continue to be used on primary roads. The Authority later voted to accept the proposals.[31]

The SFMA seemed to be on the right course, in terms of harvesting wood and generating income, by late summer 1984. By that time the Park had begun to "realiz[e] some significant income" from SFMA cutting operations. Kenneth Stratton stated in September that Fred Rooney had "done an excellent job of turning the whole operation around." The Authority approved extending the contract with Grant Forest Products into early 1985, and in general, with the SFMA financially and otherwise ahead of schedule, things seemed far more positive than they had a few years previously.[32]

Kim Kolman, now working for the MFS, delivered a report to the Authority in December 1984. He reported that he had visited the SFMA, reviewed operations there, discussed harvesting with Park employees, and voiced a few reservations. In general he believed the operation to be proceeding quite well. Five skidders were currently operating and would be doing so for most of the winter. Stumpage rates had been renegotiated, bringing them up to "a more reasonable level." Some problems had been experienced with the roads and with "manpower," however, and Kolman expressed his desire to become more involved with the SFMA. Attorney General Tierney stated his desire to see Kolman involved with the project, but reminded those attending the meeting that the SFMA's purpose was not to make money for the Authority but to engage in "the very best possible forestry practices." Director Caverly discussed the possibility of setting up a SFMA showcase along the Black Brook Trail. The public had shown a great deal of interest in the SFMA, and the possibility of developing a show area had been voiced for some time. Although Manuel felt that the Park should proceed with the idea, Tierney and Kolman suggested that the Park hold off opening such an area until more progress had been made. Discussion would continue on the matter in the near future.[33]

Fred Rooney raised the issue of a demonstration area near the junction of the primary SFMA road and the Webster Trail in January 1985. The SFMA was on schedule for all its objectives except for establishing demonstration areas, Rooney reported, and he hoped to see the indicated area opened by the following fall. The demonstration area would allow people to view examples of different types of harvesting, including clear-cut, selective, salvage, seed tree, and shelter wood systems. Concerning other issues, Rooney reported that he expected harvesting goals to be met for the year, that approximately 42 percent of the present harvest comprised saw logs, and that he anticipated additional increases in the already negotiated stumpage prices with new contracts. The most rewarding advances in the SFMA to date were improved forestry and road-construction practices. Sensitive-area surveys for certain sections of the SFMA had also been completed, so those sections could be entered beginning that summer and timber harvested without endangering any rare plant or habitat areas. Based on MFS data, the decision had been made not to do any further spruce-budworm spraying. Rooney concluded that the long process of "establishing the highly improved forests that Governor Baxter envisioned" was now beginning. The goal was an achievable one, but would take time to realize.[34]

Irvin Caverly had initiated the Park practice of preparing annual reports after he became Director in 1982. The reports included operational highlights for the entire Park, including the SFMA. According to the "Baxter State Park 1984 Annual Report," part of the reasoning behind the extension of Grant Forest Product's contract was that the operator had come to appreciate the objectives of the SFMA. The contractor had gone beyond the terms of his contract and donated extra time and funding, and used extra equipment, to perform work beneficial to the SFMA but not specified in his contract. Timber harvesting in general had improved, and the SFMA had benefitted from Rooney's and his technician's trip to Germany's Black Forest as well as their work in correcting "past problems." In particular, according to the report, practices in marking trees for removal had improved. The recreational zone plan and a majority of the sensitive area inventory under recently appointed Park Naturalist Gerald Merry had been completed, and, as road access to the Trout Brook Trail area had also been finished, plans for establishing demonstration areas there were to reach partial fruition by June 1985.[35]

Tierney reiterated his concern at the January meeting that the focus of the SFMA remain that of meeting Baxter's vision and using the best forestry practices, not making a profit. Stratton related that the MFS would, as the best way to handle the SFMA situation, provide an individual to "service the Park's needs in terms of forest management, in forestry related issues." The Park would pay for those services, and Stratton had already had a position transferred to Millinocket for filling. The filling could take place immediately upon an agreement being signed. Kolman discussed the highlights of the agreement, which he had prepared and the Authority had read, which would make the Park responsible for paying the salary and benefits of a Forester I, an employee of the MFS who would work as a BSP Forester. The MFS would supervise the forester, and, in the event of forest disease eruptions, pathologists would be provided at no extra cost. No decisions made by the MFS would be binding until agreed to by the Authority, and consistent contact would be maintained between the MFS, the BSPA, and the Park Director. The forester would also be encouraged to work with the Park Director on forestry issues outside the SFMA. According to Kolman, both the Park and the general public would benefit from the arrangement as the Park would receive the services of an entire group of professionals, not just the expertise of the particular forester assigned to the Park.[36]

Attorney General Tierney pointed out a rather obvious fact: the Park had already been receiving such advice without paying for it. Discussion along that line of reasoning did not ensue, but the qualifications of a forester assigned by the MFS were discussed. Stratton stated that Rooney would initially work with the person hired to ensure a smooth transition. Winston Robbins, Advisory chair, and Director Caverly stated that their concerns had been addressed during the discussions. The Authority then voted unanimously to accept the MFS agreement.[37]

In early March 1985, Kim Kolman introduced Dennis Brennan to those attending the regularly scheduled Authority meeting. Brennan had been hired as Park Forester, as defined by the MFS and BSP agreement. Brennan had already toured the SFMA and reported that he had found no serious problems. The existing contract was about to expire and all cutting was complete. About 70 percent of stumpage due to date had been received, and after the current contract ended Grant Forest Products would have ninety days to complete payments. Harvesting for the year had been somewhat less than anticipated. Cutting had stopped earlier than usual, due primarily, it seems, to high deer activity on some of the marked land and in order to shift emphasis to transporting wood already cut. Two new and separate bid packages were presently being mailed out, one for acreage south of Webster Lake and one for land north of the lake. Bid requests had already been published in Maine papers. Any bids received would be opened at the end of the month and contracts awarded in mid-May 1985.[38]

Forester Brennan reported to the Authority again in September. Operations had progressed smoothly. Some 9,111 cords of wood had been harvested during the 1985 fiscal year, and the 1986 fiscal year had started off with two operations in progress: Grant Forest Products, south of Webster Lake, and Merle York, Incorporated, north of the lake. The northern district was producing roughly 390 cords each week and the southern operation cutting 585 cords per week. Rates for the wood varied, but thus far totaled $10,822 per week for the SFMA and Brennan expected the rate of production to remain steady throughout the autumn. Concerns over disturbing deer yards, which had halted cutting early in the year, had been resolved as well as Brennan and the Department of Inland Fisheries and Wildlife considered possible through an agreement on the amount of timber to be harvested in or around the yards. As to concerns over whether Baxter's intentions were being met, Kolman stated that he had inspected the SFMA, that only diseased and damaged trees were being marked, that skidders were being used only where necessary, and that erosion control was "excellent and all slopes ha[d] been seeded." Some problems did exist with slash piles, some of which would need to be burned in a controlled fire. An "unsightly" pile of unmarketable cedar might be moved to BSP campgrounds and used as kindling.[39]

In spite of Park and Authority optimism over progress being made in the SFMA, and their attempts to address any problems that still existed, opposition to SFMA operations did arise. On November 21, 1985, Everett Carson, Executive Director of the Natural Resources Council of Maine, addressed the BSPA concerning the SFMA. Jerry Bley of NRCM and Gordon Mott had earlier toured the SFMA, expressed their concerns over cutting practices to Caverly in a letter, and had received an answer indicating that the Authority had been consulted and would contact the Council regarding the matter. This had apparently not happened, according to statements made at the Authority meeting, and after NRCM's November meeting, at which the issue had been discussed, the press had become involved.[40]

Actually, the press had published information concerning criticism of SFMA operations previous to November. Phyllis Austin of the *Maine Times* wrote a feature article on the SFMA in early October, just after Mott and Bley had toured the area. Photographs of the operations showed the cutting in what many people would deem a less than flattering perspective. Taken by Scott Perry, the cover photograph of the October issue pictured a Mack logging truck on an SFMA road accompanied by the title: "Cutting at Baxter Park; It looks like a Commercial Harvest. Why Isn't it Better?" The photograph and title set the tone for the article. Perry and Austin had seen the operations, and Austin reported the opinions of Mott and Bley, as well as responses by Stratton.[41]

According to Austin's article, Mott had stated that his first impressions were that high grading—removing the most valuable trees and not necessarily those in need of salvaging—was occurring and that economic gain motivated the Park in its cutting operations. The Park had spent too much money on pre-harvesting work thus far, in terms of capital return. His major concern involved a lack of attention being paid forest regeneration such that "'the land is restocking to weed species and raspberries.'" He did add, however, that he would need to do further investigating before drawing firm conclusions. Mott did not think that a salvage operation was needed as he believed that spraying with Bt had stopped budworm infestation in the SFMA after 1979. Mott had witnessed problems concerning water quality and a lack of wildlife habitat protection on his SFMA visit. Based on his observations, Mott asserted that contractor work being performed in the SFMA required closer supervision by the Park and Authority.[42]

Bley, according to the *Maine Times* article, agreed with Mott that the situation in the SFMA necessitated "an immediate review by outsiders." The Park had not followed through on several aspects of its own management plan for the SFMA. As things were, the cutting operation warranted "'an evaluation to see if there's a public consensus of the type of management being used.'"[43]

Austin quoted extensively from Kenneth Stratton as well as stating observations about the SFMA and Mott's and Bley's opinions. Much of the information provided by Stratton would be repeated at subsequent Authority meetings, however, Austin included some commentary which did not make its way into Park minutes. Stratton stated that conditions had indeed been grim in 1981 during initial operations. The Park had had to instruct Quentin Smart to clean up the areas he had worked in as he had previously failed to clean up logging debris, stumps, and so forth, and had not seeded "landing yards" with grass as required. Nevertheless, the situation had improved substantially and Stratton expected further improvements. He and Kolman agreed, according the article, that the public had no cause for concern even though the cutting might appear "no different than regular commercial operations." The Park faced the same conditions confronting the pulp and paper companies: the need to salvage wood from the effects of spruce budworm. Earlier spraying had not ended the budworm threat to SFMA stands. The Park was conducting salvage work, no matter any arguments to the contrary, as well as taking other steps toward stand improvement. Realistically, money did play a role in forest management, but money was not the Park or the Authority's motivating factor. Work done at the current time, he asserted, might well be judged "scientific" in later years.[44]

In the days following publication of the Austin article, other papers and media forums covered at least portions of the SFMA debate. Then, two days before the November BSPA meeting, Charles Fitzgerald, who had engaged in various legal suits against the Authority and had recently served on the Advisory Committee, announced that he and William Butler of Friends of the Maine Woods intended to sue the BSPA to stop the cutting operation. "'We're going to argue on Governor Baxter's intent,'" Fitzgerald said. Everett Carson reported that NRCM was considering joining the suit as the Council agreed with Mott that SFMA operations did not meet Baxter's intents. "The present cutting operation is 'out of kilter with Baxter's Deeds,'" according to Carson[45]

At the November 21, 1985, BSPA meeting, Carson stated that he thought that hard feelings existed over the course events had taken, but NRCM's concern rested with how the SFMA was being cared for, not with public relations. Mott had written an "extensive evaluation" of SFMA operations which had been distributed to the Authority and which Carson wished to review.[46]

The NRCM report addressed five major concerns. The concerns were:

> First, the current management approach is based upon the assumption that timber must be salvaged from death due to spruce budworm damage. Second, the highest value trees in the SFMA are being cut and sold on a poor market. Third, there are reasons to question whether adequate controls are being employed to guide the harvest. Fourth, there is serious question as to whether the long term economic return from the SFMA is being maximized by current management practices. Fifth, the broader range of established forest practice could be employed to better protect the non-timber values of the area including wildlife, recreation, water quality, and esthetics.[47]

Jerry Bley had also prepared and distributed a review of the SFMA management practices as Bley and Mott had witnessed them, in comparison with the Park Management Plan. Some of these comparisons included Park specified marking standards and an absence of tree markings in the SFMA; a Park stated intent to provide for softwood regeneration and an absence in the field of the same; and a statement in the 1984 SFMA Policy Statement that "the State Forester shall appoint an Advisory Committee including a representative of the University of Maine and persons with land management experience,'" a group which to the NRCM's knowledge had never met. According to Carson, NRCM's "on-the-ground observations simply don't measure up to Governor Baxter's intent." The NRCM therefore wanted SFMA harvesting, as currently conducted, to stop. The NRCM requested an immediate evaluation of current practices and necessary alterations made to meet Baxter's intentions. To that end, the Authority should convene a committee, an independent group that would make appropriate recommendations to the Authority.[48]

Kenneth Stratton responded by stating that the Authority and SFMA continually sought the advice of wildlife biologists concerning harvesting practices, civil engineers about road systems, and education specialists about recreation. To this Carson simply replied that, "input was not the issue; execution was the issue." Park Legal Counsel Paul Stern stated that NRCM had been kept informed of events and "asked to participate in all phases of the SFMA." In response to a question from Tierney, Carson stated that NRCM's position was based on Mott's report and his two visits to the SFMA. Stratton questioned why the NRCM had waited so long to make its statements, to which Carson gave a rather lengthy answer including the fact that the basic SFMA plan was a fine one but that recent visits to the SFMA, where harvesting was progressing "at a tremendous rate," made the Council decide that matters needed to be brought to the Authority's attention. Caverly stated that he had done everything possible to keep everyone informed of SFMA operations.[49]

Stratton, in response to NRCM's position on SFMA operations, revoiced statements made at numerous recent Authority meetings. He asserted that everyone involved with BSP and the SFMA had worked hard to try to meet Baxter's wishes, that current harvesting represented only the first step in a long process of creating such a forest, that the budworm problem had substantially complicated matters, and that the Authority had sought advice from professionals during the preceding years. Stratton saw no reason why the Authority should halt harvesting operations. Different experts might have differing opinions, but this did not negate SFMA work done thus far. The new policy statement adopted by the Authority did call for the creation of a review board, steps had been taken to that end, and the process of assembling such a board would continue. Stratton then asked Kim Kolman to update everyone present on SFMA matters.[50]

Kolman stated that he had the responsibility, with approval from the Authority, for managing the SFMA. He worked in conjunction with several people overseeing the SFMA. He wanted to clear up one major misunderstanding about the SFMA: the belief held by many people that harvesting operations in the SFMA were aimed at salvaging dead and dying fir. The Park salvaged what fir it could, but some of it was beyond salvaging. The major aim of SFMA operations was, as called for by the Management Plan, to rejuvenate and reestablish healthy new stands, and to ultimately prepare the SFMA to silviculturally resemble European forests—bearing in mind that some differences would always exist due to different forest conditions. Most SFMA stands were overstocked and needed harvesting. Stands of various aged trees remained an SFMA objective, stands which the Park would manage for sixty to seventy year rotations. Only outlying strips of trees were marked for cutting, not all trees in an area. Only those pines obstructing road building or suffering from disease had been cut. In sum, current practices were silviculturally correct as far as possible, no forestry operations being 100 percent correct. The only improvement he would suggest would be to increase personnel supervision.[51]

The Authority and those attending the November 21, 1985, meeting—some thirty members of the general public in addition to those who spoke were in attendance that day—laid aside discussion for a short time to view slides featuring SFMA cutting operations. Following the slide presentation, Eric Baxter stated that his family had remained involved in Park affairs and that they had supported Authority actions concerning the SFMA in past years. What bothered the Baxter family was "the circus-like atmosphere that sometimes happens within the media" concerning various issues, brought on it seems by certain "interested parties." Eric Baxter thought such an atmosphere would not have pleased the Governor. Instead he, Eric Baxter, and seemingly his family as well, expected "people who have concerns to come forward and air them so that they can be discussed by the Advisory Committee and acted upon and investigated and dealt with in a rational and timely manner." The fact that that had not happened in the present instance was "of great concern to the family."[52]

At this point Tierney, perhaps wishing to avoid having the meeting take on any more of an antagonistic tone than it already had, stated that he was "not at all pleased with the process that the Natural Resources Council of Maine has used to bring this matter to the public's attention," but that he did recognize that they had some concerns which should be further addressed. To that end, he suggested the immediate formation of a committee composed partially of NRCM representatives, and possibly Mott, and to have them report to the Authority. William Butler spoke briefly, suggesting that Baxter's intents be re-examined. Charles Fitzgerald voiced essentially the same sentiments. Fitzgerald, when queried, stated that he would like to be involved in the proposed committee, and Carson stated that such a group was basically what the NRCM wanted. With Eric Baxter and Kim Kolman supporting the formation of such a committee, and with Kolman reporting that members of the UM faculty had already been contacted about such a committee, the Authority moved on to other matters. Subsequent to the meeting, the *Bangor Daily News* announced that Fitzgerald continued preparations to sue the Authority and that NRCM and "others" reserved the right to join the suit should it prove necessary. According to the *Portland Press Herald*, Carson believed that "'courts should be the place of last resort for resolving disputes such as this,'" but the NRCM had been "spurred to action by increasing criticism from its members" and by the threatened lawsuit.[53]

Five days later, on November 26, 1985, the Authority convened a special meeting to discuss the SFMA situation. Commissioner Manuel called the meeting to order and stated that due to the seriousness of the situation the proposed committee should be unbiased. In contrast to the proposal made a few days earlier, Manuel stated that no one from BSP, IFW, the MFS, the NRCM or the current SFMA Advisory Group or Sub-committee should be on the committee to review SFMA operations. No attempt "to whitewash what has been done" should be made, Manuel stated, and the committee should be "composed of the best professional people" available. The committee's goal should be to obtain the "absolute truth." He suggested a seven member committee and indicated some organizations or specialties which should be represented on the committee.[54]

Authority members and those interested parties in attendance—essentially the same individuals who had spoken at the previous meeting—suggested people who might serve on the committee. After some discussion, the names of nine people who might comprise the committee were listed and the Authority voted to establish the committee as recommended. Although names had been added by those attending the meeting, not everyone was entirely pleased with the list. The list included seven men and one woman, Jane Arbuckle of the Maine Audubon Society. One of the men listed, Charles Gadzik, would later serve on the Authority and was currently managing 100,000 acres of land as Chief Forester for Baskahegan. Arbuckle had been recommended by another future Authority member, Professor Ray B. Owen. The NRCM had recommended Owen but he had been unable to serve and had instead suggested that Arbuckle be considered. The other persons listed were Professors Robert Seymour, John Diamond, and Gregory Brown of UM; Robert Frank of the USFS; Thomas Cieslinski of the Bureau of Parks and Recreation; and foresters Theodore Tryon and Michael Dann of the James W. Sewall Company and Seven Islands Land Company respectively.[55]

Charles Fitzgerald voiced displeasure at the approved list as he believed it contained too many people from the University of Maine; did not include the persons he had recommended (he had included himself, as a source of information on Baxter's intentions); and primarily, he asserted, because he and others were questioning the Authority thus the Authority should not be choosing who would serve on the committee. The Authority should have left the organizing of the committee to Fitzgerald and his unidentified "we"—seemingly William Butler, the NRCM, and other interested parties.

Butler, whom both Fitzgerald and Everett Carson had wished to see appointed, stated that "the committee was comprised of probably the best people available." However, Butler did not think that those selected would give the Authority a realistic evaluation of SFMA practices as such practices were probably too much like their own, practices which they would feel a need to defend. Butler had stated earlier that day that he had initially favored seeking court action to stop the cutting, and he still felt that cutting operations should cease until the situation had been evaluated. To Butler, the current cutting was "a savage brutal attack on the forest." Everett Carson stated that the committee was a good one and that he would be happy to work with it. Gordon Mott, who thought both Butler and Fitzgerald should have been selected, stated that he would still be happy to work with the committee as selected.[56]

When the Authority met again on January 21, 1986, they decided to defer discussion on the SFMA Committee until Brown submitted the committee's report. The report was expected to be ready by the end of the month, in time for a special meeting. At the regular January meeting, however, Jeffery Smith, attorney for Fitzgerald and Butler, submitted a request for one hour during the next meeting to present information about the SFMA. Smith's clients had filed a suit against the Authority concerning the SFMA. Tierney assured Smith that time would be ample enough for everyone to present their views, and suggested that written materials would be helpful.[57] Both Butler and Fitzgerald attended the January 21, 1986, meeting, and they attended the one held eight days later at the Augusta Civic Center.[58]

The January 29, 1986, BSPA special meeting was attended by at least four members of the press as well as six members of the new SFMA Advisory Committee and several persons either present or discussed at the November 1985 meeting as possible committee candidates. The meeting started with a brief update by Director Caverly on a recent search and rescue operation, then quickly moved to the matter at hand: the SFMA. The SFMA Advisory Committee reported that they had met on December 9, 1985, and several times thereafter, and had visited the SFMA once. The committee then presented both short-term—those to be implemented by or until February 1, 1986—and long-term recommendations. The committee had made copies of their written recommendations available before the meeting.[59]

The first long-term recommendation of the committee was that management of the SFMA be returned to the Authority and be a direct responsibility of the Authority. A separate budget for the SFMA should be maintained. Secondly, the committee recommended that a Standing Advisory Committee of eight to twelve members be appointed to advise the Natural Resource Manager, a position the committee, as its third recommendation, stated should be established. The Natural Resource Manager would be responsible for SFMA management and would work with both the Standing Advisory Committee and the Park Director. The Advisory Committee would be involved in the hiring process. The Resource Manager would be assisted by a team of professionals, the size of the staff depending on available funding. As their fourth long-term recommendation, the committee recommended that the current ten-year management plan be revised and updated by the Resource Manager and SFMA staff after their appointments and in conjunction with the Advisory Committee. The fifth recommendation involved deadlines for implementing the other four recommendations. The committee suggested a deadline of March 15 for appointing the Advisory Committee, May 31 for hiring the Natural Resource Manager, and December 31, 1986, for completion of the reviewed and revised SFMA Management Plan.[60]

The Authority and others attending the special meeting discussed the long-term recommendations, especially the qualifications of the Resource Manager and whether the recommended Advisory Committee would be composed of the same individuals as was the SFMA Advisory Group as formed in 1983 or on the new ad hoc committee, then listened to the short-term recommendations. Those present focused on the major short-term recommendation, that "no more than 3,000 cord equivalents ... be harvested after December 16, 1985." The committee had recommended the limit on harvesting a short time previously and the Authority had agreed to abide by it while the SFMA issue was being addressed. The committee recommended the limit largely because they believed that some guidelines established in the 1980 SFMA Management Plan were not being followed. The two major concerns involved a lack of detailed pre-operational planning for each SFMA compartment and a lack of detailed prescriptions for each stand. According to the committee, three foresters should be assigned to the SFMA for the remainder of the operating period, one to supervise the cutting crews and two to conduct pre-operational analysis and marking on a stand-to-stand basis. The committee also recommended that the 3,000 cords be allocated to right-of-way timber and poor quality fir stands.[61]

The Authority had already agreed to a 3,000 cord harvesting limit and had informed the Kennebec County Superior Court, in response to the Fitzgerald and Butler suit as filed on behalf of the Friends of the Maine Woods, that it would be harvested by February 1, 1986. Concerns surfaced at the January meeting about the fairness of the time limitation to the current contractor should weather and staff limitations prevent the removal of the wood before February 1, a date which the committee indicated was acceptable as long as the contractor did not exceed the 3,000 cord limit. Legal Counsel Paul Stern stated that operations could legitimately be stopped to protect the resource, as such a clause appeared in the contract. A decision to halt the operation had "to be based upon some reasonable grounds," however. Commissioner Manuel expressed his concerns over setting a precedent that might prove harmful to Maine contractors, as well as to the Park at some future date.[62]

In general, the recommendations presented by the committee were well received. The most serious reservations which the Authority expressed concerned money. The Authority realized that valid points had been raised, some of which could be immediately addressed, but others required funding of which the Park simply had little. Committee members stressed that they believed that money was available or obtainable for hiring at least one full-time person, and Brown stated that "the main concern from the beginning was the obvious under-staffing in management in the SFMA." After prolonged discussion of both the committee's five long-term recommendations and the suggestions presented by other individuals, the Authority decided to hold the vote on recommendation one—that concerning Authority direction over the SFMA—which in part the Authority felt it already met and in part would meet by following recommendation three: hiring a Natural Resource Manager. The Authority voted unanimously to accept recommendation three. The Authority also voted in favor of recommendation two: appointing a standing SFMA Advisory Committee—something which Park personnel and the Authority had, in a somewhat different manner, done in the past. The Authority likewise voted unanimously to accept recommendation four: having the SFMA Management Plan revised—something which the Authority had intended all along. The Authority decided not to vote on the fifth recommendation, that concerning time limits. Finally, regarding the February 1, 1986, date for ceasing harvesting operations, Tierney motioned to honor the cut-off date, Stratton seconded the motion, and Manuel abstained from voting.[63]

The Authority did not reach the voting stage of the meeting without considering extended commentary from a number of people. Charles Fitzgerald showed a film of SFMA operations taken from the ground and from a helicopter on December 8, 1985, illustrating numerous practices he and others found reprehensible—including large scale clearing of areas the Authority had identified as "patches" versus the asserted appellation, or practice, of clear cutting. Fitzgerald then presented oral testimony. Fitzgerald stated that he believed that the committee had done a good job except for omitting some critical observations of, and reservations about, SFMA operations. As such, he believed the final statement of long-term recommendations to be "tainted" and "white washed." Fitzgerald had, he stated, objected to the 1980 SFMA Management Plan and he still objected to it. The "entire plan" should be "scrapped." It remained commercial in its orientation and could not result in the type of showplace forestry envisioned by Baxter. There was no need for the Park to rush to initiate cutting or other operations, "there is no hurry at all," Fitzgerald argued.[64]

Mel Ames, William Butler, and Eberhard Thiele likewise presented testimony on the SFMA. They related what they had seen in visits to the cutting and other SFMA areas, and in general commented that too much haste was being used and not enough long-term planning being made. They also stated that the spruce-budworm problem had essentially ended, indicating, therefore, that the time for a new approach had arrived. Thiele gave a lengthy presentation of an eleven page paper he had written comparing SFMA and Maine forest operations to those of German forests, as well as showing slides, and was rewarded with a lengthy cross examination by Stratton and Kolman. Butler suggested that the Authority was not taking the suggestions of the committee seriously enough, which Stratton and Manuel assured him was not the case at all: the SFMA was indeed a serious matter to the Authority.[65]

Jerry Bley presented a letter from the Natural Resources Council of Maine. The NRCM congratulated the committee on the excellent work they had accomplished, and commended the Authority for setting up the independent committee and for selecting "qualified and committed individuals" to serve on the committee. The NRCM recommended that the Authority adopt all of the committee's recommendations. The Council had originally advocated an immediate end to cutting operations, but believed that the 3,000 cord and February 1, 1986, limits, as well as the new restrictions on harvesting practices, presented a "reasonable compromise." Improved silvicultural and management practices could be instituted for the SFMA's future. A Natural Resource Manager and a revised Management Plan, one into which the public had input, could resolve some past difficulties. However, no further timber harvesting should proceed until the Park fully implemented the committee's recommendations.[66]

As to the criticism that parts of the original committee draft had been deleted from the final version, Gordon Mott stated that he had recommended that they be omitted as they might "inject the committee into the legal proceeding," and the recommendations were more "palatable and easily acted upon by the Authority" without them. He did not feel that the recommendations were tainted by the exclusion. Mott endorsed the recommendations as submitted and urged that "we put the past behind us and join together to bring this matter to a positive conclusion." That being said, the Authority voted and the meeting adjourned.[67]

The Park and Authority worked to move the process along in subsequent months. In the weeks following the special January BSPA meeting, Fitzgerald, Butler, and Ames wrote to the Authority requesting membership in the SFMA Advisory Committee. The Authority voted in

March to appoint Fitzgerald and Ames. Harvesting operations ceased at the beginning of February as agreed, and the Park developed silvicultural prescriptions for each stand. In order to avoid having two advisory committees working on SFMA matters, at Caverly's suggestion members of the old SFMA Advisory Group were consulted as to whether one or more of them would like to join the new committee. Ohler joined the new group, as did Robbins at a later date.[68]

Budgeting for the upcoming fiscal year for BSP proved difficult with the changes in the SFMA already made and with those still to be implemented. When the original budget had been drawn, the Park had expected a more than $100,000 surplus of income over expenses for the SFMA. With the changes in harvesting, that no longer held true. Indeed, with the changes suggested by the new SFMA Advisory Committee, the Park expected a $146,000 deficit. The Trust Fund could be used to make up for some of it, but would thereby be drawn upon more heavily than planned or desired. The Park had managed to decrease its reliance on Trust Fund revenues during the past few years, but the coming year would see a high increase once again. However, changes involving the SFMA did not account for all budgeting problems. After considering its options, the Authority decided in May to approve the budget as previously submitted. The original budget did not provide for hiring a Natural Resource Manager, or for some of the other plans the SFMA Advisory Committee had hoped to implement that year. Attorney General Tierney stated that the passage of the original budget did not mean "that the Authority was walking away from their commitment to hiring a manager for the SFMA." Robert Gardiner of the BSP Finance Committee explained that a manager could still be hired through an amendment to the budget, and revenues increased through stumpage sales. In the meantime, the Authority needed a working budget for the new fiscal year.[69]

When the Authority, in the person of Kenneth Stratton—the other members being unable to attend—met in June to discuss the SFMA Advisory Committee's recommendations, the committee emphasized the need for a Resource Manager. The committee had submitted new recommendations in late May after discovering at the May BSPA meeting that it had had certain misunderstandings about the SFMA's financial workings. The committee had evolved somewhat during 1986, with Jerry Bley and Robert Ohler having joined the committee established at the close of 1985 and with Charles Gadzik serving as Chair.[70]

The committee communicated in June that it did not want to run the SFMA: it wanted to interact with an SFMA manager. The committee wanted to see a working forest established, the silvicultural methods employed to be worked out with the Resource Manager. Although the committee realized that the manager would help determine staffing needs, the committee found it reasonable to anticipate hiring a full-time technician as well as summer staff to help collect data and prepare and supervise SFMA operations. The committee stated in its report that it strongly believed that "timber harvesting operations in the SFMA should not resume until a Resource Manager is hired and the management plan is revised." They expected that it would take a manager six to eight months to become familiar with the SFMA and to "coordinate the review of the management plan." Anticipating that a manager would not be hired until the autumn, allowing for the indicated period for planning, and considering that it usually took until mid-June for the area to dry sufficiently for summer operations to begin, the committee did not project any SFMA income for the 1986-87 fiscal year.[71]

Park Naturalist Gerald Merry had become ill and retired from the Park some months previously, and, upon the recommendation of Caverly and Finance Committee Chair Gardiner, the SFMA Advisory Committee suggested using the Park Naturalist position to fund hiring a Resource Manager for the upcoming fiscal year. Part of the Resource Manager's time the first year would then be devoted to some of the Park Naturalist's duties. Thereafter, with the SFMA theoretically paying its own way, a full-time Park Naturalist would once again be employed by BSP. Also in consideration of Park budgeting problems, the committee acknowledged a need to wait until the 1987-88 fiscal year to hire other recommended SFMA personnel. Using conservative wood values (an $11.00 per cord average), and conservative cutting rates (1/3 cord per acre per year for stands that averaged growth and yield rates of 1/2 cord per acre per year), for the 1987-

88 fiscal year—and allowing for no harvesting for the upcoming 1986-87 year—the committee projected a $4,000 deficit for the upcoming year and an $11,000 profit—basic income over expenses—for the following year. Caverly and Stratton tentatively approved the plan at the June meeting, and stated that they would report the results of the meeting to the rest of the Authority and do what they could to move things along on the SFMA project.[72]

The Authority met again less than two weeks later, on June 18, 1986. The Authority agreed at the second June meeting to accept the SFMA Advisory Committee's report and to have Caverly proceed with the paperwork necessary to hire a Natural Resource Manager. Stratton, however, opposed accepting the report and requested that the record show his opposition.[73]

Stratton stated that at the last meeting he had expressed his concerns about the plan to delay harvesting operations for another year. He believed that as the committee had indicated its non-interest in formulating silvicultural prescriptions, as an existing plan was already in place "which is the product of input from a number of people and a lot of deliberation by this Authority over the last few years," as the Park had already "gathered considerable detailed information on the ground in preparation of silvicultural prescriptions," as work had already been established which "would cover the next two years," and as "a delay in getting operations started certainly makes a big difference in finances," the Authority should make a decision at the next meeting as to whether to proceed with harvesting. Two ongoing contracts existed and the Authority had not given the contractors any final word. Stratton had reconsidered his earlier decision to defer harvesting until an SFMA Resource Manager had been hired in light of the work accomplished thus far in SFMA policy and planning. No SFMA plan would define exactly the detailed work to be done on the ground, and as the committee had shown an unwillingness to undertake the problem, Stratton believed that cutting should proceed, or at least a decision be made.[74]

The committee made its opposition to Stratton's line of reasoning known, and Bley stated furthermore that had the Authority considered the recommendations earlier, a Resource Manager might already have been hired. Butler stated that the reasons he had helped seek an injunction against the SFMA cutting operation the preceding year were still valid. Bley asserted that the NRCM would reconsider its present approach of working through the system instead of going to court should cutting resume prior to the hiring of a manager and a review of the existing SFMA Management Plan. The committee expressed its interest in consulting with the Resource Manager about specific silvicultural methods in the future, and Gadzik stated that although the committee did not place a high priority on the remaining slash clean-up from the previous cutting operations, but rather on preventing new operations at the current time, the committee would accept Tierney's suggestion that clean-up proceed under Caverly's direction. At a later meeting they suggested that clean-up, specifically chipping slash, be held off due to a chipper not being readily available and the lack of a market for chips.[75]

With full Authority approval, in spite of differences over the cutting operation issue, Caverly and the SFMA Advisory Committee proceeded with hiring an SFMA Resource Manager. The process was a long and involved one, from drawing up a job description to establishing a hiring procedure, holding public meetings, advertising the position nationally, screening applicants, conducting in-depth interviews, and making a final recommendation. The Maine Department of Personnel ultimately received thirty-nine applications. Of these, a five person screening committee composed of Jerry Bley, Robert Seymour, Chris Drew, Kim Kolman, and Fred Hurley narrowed the list to six applicants. Five of the six accepted interview appointments which were held on December 1 and 2, 1986. The Interview Board consisted of Charles Gadzik, Charles Fitzgerald, Chris Drew, Walter Birt, Robert Frank, and Irvin Caverly. The candidates were then narrowed to two. But just when the position seemed about to be filled, another hurdle appeared.[76]

On December 11, 1986, at the regularly scheduled Authority meeting, Caverly introduced the subject of the SFMA Manager's position, and stated the fact that he had sent the Authority his recommendation the previous week. Immediately following Caverly's introduction, Walter Birt of the BSP Advisory Committee advised those in attendance that the Authority had just received a letter from his committee that day, a letter stating that due to financial concerns and possible violations of the Deeds of Trust the Authority should delay hiring a Resource Manager.[77]

Several persons expressed surprise that hiring a manager was even a question at that point. Bley stated that he strongly disagreed with the Advisory's letter and that the SFMA Committee had had no warning that the issue would be discussed. Hundreds of hours had been put into the process, and to hold off hiring a manager for the SFMA would be a disservice to both the process and to all the people who had worked on the project. Gadzik likewise stated that to postpone hiring a manager would be inappropriate and would "put the entire SFMA ... in limbo." Tierney humorously commented that "the letter was very good in terms of clearly stating a position which the Authority rejected some time ago." Even if he had agreed with much of the letter's contents a year before, he thought it would "be wrong to turn the whole process on its head." The policy decision had been made long before, and nothing had changed to justify changing the policy. Caverly expressed his appreciation for all the work the SFMA Advisory Committee had given him in the hiring process, stated that he had been given the assignment to hire a Resource Manager and had worked "with full vigor" to fulfill that assignment. He was convinced that "you couldn't find a better candidate than the two we have recommended." He, too, expressed surprise that the matter had come up at that late date, and said that to put the hiring on hold "could expose the entire process to a long period of controversy before we [will have] moved on with our responsibilities."[78]

Commissioner Manuel reviewed the history of the SFMA briefly and stated that, overall, cutting operations conducted thus far had been good ones. Timber had been salvaged which would otherwise have become unsalvageable by the present date. Other stands not part of the harvesting process were currently unsalvageable. The Park, in spite of certain claims to the contrary, had not engaged in clear cutting operations, but had done its best to salvage what could be salvaged in 28,000 acres "being devastated by spruce budworm." The project had been put on hold and to delay hiring a Resource Manager would be to delay SFMA work even further. He felt concerned about Park finances, but, weighing the options, he believed that the best thing to do would be to proceed with the hiring process and get "the project back on course."[79]

The third Authority member, MFS Director Stratton, disagreed. Stratton said that he shared some of the concerns expressed in the BSP Advisory Committee's letter. Issues had been raised that needed to be addressed whether or not a manager was hired in the near future. He felt the Authority should have discussed those issues at greater length than they had in the past. Winston Robbins of the Advisory Committee agreed that some of the concerns had not been addressed properly in the past, and stated that to hire a manager at the present time would just be taking money away from Park operating expenses which could be better utilized elsewhere. Robbins believed that with the combined efforts of SFMA Advisory Committee, the MFS, and the UM College of Forestry the necessary prescriptions for managing the SFMA could be arrived at without the additional cost of hiring a Natural Resource Manager within the next year or two. Robbins, after inquiring whether Fitzgerald's suit was still on the docket and being informed by Legal Counsel Paul Stern that it was, questioned whether the Authority should make a decision while "under the threat of litigation." Attorney General Tierney dismissed Robbin's question and moved the meeting on to other issues with the simple but forceful statement: "there [is] an adequate supply of lawyers to handle any suit and a decision [will] be made in executive session concerning the Resource Manager."[80]

The Authority apparently did decide the issue in executive session, as records show that the Authority hired Donald Jensen Bissell of Salem, Oregon, as BSP Natural Resource Manager that same day, December 11, 1986. Bissell began work at BSP on February 2, 1987. His employment culminated more than a year of reform effort and in some ways silenced over fifteen years of controversy surrounding forestry practices in Baxter State Park, both inside and outside the Scientific Forest Management Area.[81]

Bissell quickly began work on revising the existing SFMA Management Plan. He worked with the SFMA Advisory Committee to that end, and in

May 1987 both Bissell and Fitzgerald submitted tentative or partial plans at the SFMA Advisory meeting. Bissell also suggested that planning for operations proceed even though the management plan had not yet been revised. Some members present disagreed with Bissell's suggestion. As both Gadzik and Bissell pointed out, however, actual operations, as previously agreed, would not begin until the necessary plan revisions had been made, but planning for operations could commence, thus preparing the SFMA to move ahead with operations once an agreed upon revised management plan was in place.[82]

In following months, contractor H. O. Bouchard chipped remaining debris piles in the SFMA and transported the chips to GNP. Park personnel burned remaining slash piles during the first snowfall of the year. One of two computers purchased by the Park went primarily to Bissell for SFMA use, and in May Bissell completed a timber supply analysis based on a computer model developed in New Brunswick and adopted throughout Maine. Bissell used information gathered during the 1979 to 1980 SFMA inventory to simulate SFMA resources and to evaluate possible long-term management approaches. Although not an exact information source, the model did provide guidelines for developing harvesting operations aimed at creating a sustained yield forest.[83]

By late spring 1988, the SFMA Advisory Committee had tentatively approved the revised SFMA Management Plan. The time had come, according to Bissell and, seemingly, the committee, to resume operations in the SFMA. To that end, Bissell had advertised for possible contractors in April and received over twenty responses by early May. Bissell then sent informational packets to the contractors, explaining the purpose of the SFMA and requesting information about the contractors and their companies. Bissell evaluated the information received and compiled a list of contractors deemed qualified to work on the SFMA. The first project to be undertaken would be road construction on the north side of the SFMA, and Randy Cyr, Incorporated, of Sherman Mills was awarded the contract. In September 1987 the Authority had approved a $50,000 increase to the SFMA budget to begin construction.[84]

Bissell explained certain SFMA Management Plan revisions at the May 11, 1988, BSPA meeting. He anticipated the plan being approved as part of the new revision of the Baxter State Park Management Plan, as one of the Park's unit management plans. Bissell explained that the major difference in the 1988 SFMA plan from the 1981 SFMA plan was basically one of focus: the old plan had focused on addressing the ongoing spruce-budworm problem, the new one focused on establishing and initiating, "step by step," acceptable SFMA operations. At the present time, Bissell and the SFMA Advisory Committee concentrated on developing suitable SFMA operational methods, labor, and lodging. The Authority approved the Revised SFMA Management Plan that day, subject to some "technical changes in wording."[85] Additions would be made the following year concerning silviculture.

Although the SFMA Advisory Committee remained active throughout the year, and would continue to do so in the future, some changes did take place. Winston Robbins had joined the committee since its formation. Jane Arbuckle and John Diamond retired from the committee. Joseph Wiley, an IFW biologist, filled one of the two vacated positions while the second remained unfilled. Charles Gadzik would step down the next year as Committee Chair, but remain on the Advisory for some time. Roy Farnsworth, a Bates College geology professor, actively participated in SFMA work in 1988 by investigating–but not locating–possible gravel deposits in the SFMA for road construction. Although other membership changes would occur in coming years in the SFMA Advisory bringing both new expertise and points of view to the committee, a basic level of continuity would remain in effect as some members stayed on the committee for long periods of time and some members left then returned in one guise or another.[86]

Construction of new SFMA road began by early September 1988. The contract with Cyr called for 17,000 feet of eighteen-foot wide road. Cyr completed roughly 8,000 feet by the close of the year. By mid-September the SFMA had also secured a consulting forester, John Mills of Brewer, who would begin work in the next few weeks. The consulting forester would do field work to help prepare a contract for harvesting and also help

The Swedish Rottne single grip at work in the SFMA.
(Photo: Jensen Bissell)

Harvested land in the SFMA. Percival Baxter wanted Park forest operations to demonstrate "show place" standards.
(Photo: Jensen Bissell)

prepare plans for any additional road construction for 1989. In addition to other projects undertaken, the SFMA also initiated a more intensive two-way educational "program" than seen in previous years: Bissell, and to some extent others involved in the SFMA, attended educational public programs and forums as both students and educators. Through this practice SFMA personnel became more knowledgeable about programs or information outside the SFMA, and the public became more knowledgeable about the SFMA. This two-way process was seen elsewhere in the Park during the same period, and in some areas of Park operations and management the process had started years earlier.[87]

Cutting operations commenced in the SFMA once again in June 1989 after timber cruising had been completed. The trees to be harvested–and the harvesting methods employed–had been selected with the intention of maximizing regeneration potentials, increasing timber values, maintaining wildlife habitats and "aesthetic" qualities, and minimizing stand damage. Previous operations had purportedly aimed toward many of these same goals, but the 1989 and ensuing harvests no doubt benefitted from the preceding years of research and controversy concerning the best approach to SFMA operations, from new forms of forest modeling, and, it would seem, from closer supervision. Stands were also cruised after harvesting to ensure that harvesting had progressed as specified. Only two crews–each with a skidder–simultaneously engaged in the harvesting operations in 1989, a marked drop from harvesting during the mid-1980s. Two professional foresters, John Mills and George Ritz, had contracted with the Park for SFMA field work.[88]

Road construction continued in the SFMA in 1989 as it would in succeeding years as deemed necessary. In 1989 the SFMA had roughly 12,000 feet of all-weather road constructed, as well as some 7,500 feet of winter road. In addition, the Park constructed log camps to house contract personnel on land provided by the Bureau of Public Lands of the Department of Conservation at their Coffeelos Camps site in T7R11, accessed via the Great Northern Company's Telos Road. The Park would continue to use the site through the mid-1990s. With increased access to the SFMA, the issue of public access became increasing important, the issue having surfaced during the previous year or two. The Authority ultimately, after holding public discussions and after receiving input from other agencies and Advisory and staff members, initiated an access policy for the SFMA. In order to protect the SFMA and SFMA roads, the Authority elected to restrict vehicle access to the SFMA during times of high fire danger, as determined by a MFS Build-Up Index of 40 or higher; during heavy rains, for specified roads; and during "dangerous conditions" such as periods of heavy blowdowns and logging truck traffic.[89] The reasoning behind the policy had changed little from that evidenced years earlier.

Much of the hard work and planning initiated in and for the SFMA during the 1970s and 1980s began to come to fruition after the 1987 hiring of a permanent full-time Resource Manager and the 1988 approval of a revised SFMA Management Plan. In 1989 and following years that fruition progressed substantially. This does not mean that the late 1980s and the early 1990s saw the culmination of Baxter's visions for the SFMA, or those of other persons who maintained a strong interest in the Park's forestry operations, but that the Park made significant progress in forest management and silvicultural operations in the context of developing stands with sustained yields while at the same time providing for recreational and other uses of the area. The progress made during the late 1980s and the early 1990s was based in large part on the work of many individuals over many years. Much of the earlier controversy had ultimately proved invaluable to establishing a more scientific and more intensively managed forest. Perhaps indicative of progress being made, after a motion filed by BSP legal counsel, the Court ruled the 1986 suit filed against the Park by Fitzgerald dismissed. The Court did so on May 3, 1989, by which time many of the points raised had been rendered moot by changing SFMA practices. Years later, Fitzgerald recalled that what still rankled about the case was that no restitution had been made for previous SFMA operations.[90]

This does not mean that controversy regarding the SFMA ended for the short run or for the long run. As with the rest of the Park, the SFMA would not, and could not, meet the demands or the desires of all people. The managers of the SFMA, the various Advisory and Authority members, and numerous members of the general public—even those who had gone as far as to institute legal proceedings against the Park and the Authority–had strived to protect and develop, or not develop as the case might be, the SFMA in the manner they felt most conducive to sound forest management and in accordance with Percival Proctor Baxter's wishes. The Deeds of Trust provided major guidelines in determining the positions people assumed and the theories behind developing the SFMA, but could not provide the absolutes some people sought. Indeed, here as elsewhere people argued opposing viewpoints using the same documentation.

In the opinion of many people, including the Park Natural Resources Manager, mistakes had indeed transpired in the cutting operations of the early 1980s. Too many skidders removed too much wood in some stands and Baxter State Park subsequently lost certain management options. The SFMA operations of the early 1980s in several aspects resembled contemporary commercial cuttings more than they did the ideal forestry envisioned by Baxter. Yet, although the situation certainly could have been better, it also might have been worse. The Park ultimately learned from its mistakes. The Maine Superior and Supreme Courts established certain parameters or limitations for forestry operations during the 1970s through the 1980s, and even when cases stretched out for so long a time as to be rendered moot, or threatened suits did not get filed, Maine citizens affected the BSP forestry process–if only to ensure that certain issues received consideration. With closer supervision of operations and numerous changes in policy and practices, by virtually all relevant standards the SFMA entered the 1990s much closer to achieving the ideals embraced by Baxter than had been true for the earlier years of SFMA operations.

Chapter Four

Native Americans: A Demand for Unequal Access

In the spring of 1976, while Baxter State Park struggled to clean up the effects of the November 1974 blowdown, a series of events unfolded that would have lasting repercussions. Native American demands across the nation for unregulated access to lands considered traditional religious or cultural grounds came to Maine and to BSP in an abrupt confrontation of perceptions and interpretations involving Mount Katahdin and Park operations. The entire Park staff as well as the Baxter State Park Authority became involved in what began as an open controversy and evolved into a matter of diplomacy and pragmatism.

On April 15, 1976, BSP Supervisor Irvin C. Caverly, Jr. received a telephone call from Warden Supervisor Leonard Richie advising Caverly of a report he had received from Indian Wardens. According to Caverly's report of the conversation, Richie informed him that "some militant Indians were on their way" to Baxter State Park. Early the following morning, Friday, April 16, 1976, a group of about twenty-eight Native Americans arrived at the Park and traveled to Abol Campground where they set up a base of operations. The Native Americans did not have permission to do so, nor did they display a willingness to vacate the premises. The Park had not yet opened for the year for camping, and Park personnel wanted to keep vehicular and other traffic at an absolute minimum due to rain, mud, and run-off problems. The Park had been closed to the public since April 1, and was not scheduled to reopen until May 15. Access had not been totally closed, however, as restoration operations were in progress.[1]

To add to an already tense situation, according to a spokesperson from the Penobscot Indian Reservation in Old Town, the Native Americans intended to remain in BSP permanently. The group, which included some women and children, indicated that they intended to clear the area of trees and other growth in order to build a settlement. Preparing the ground for crops would soon commence; indeed, the group had entered the Park at the time of year that they had for that very purpose. The Native Americans, in context essentially squatters, would also climb Katahdin for ceremonial reasons.[2]

Park staff, under the supervision of Director A. Lee Tibbs, immediately contacted the Baxter State Park Authority—then composed of Maynard F. Marsh of Inland Fisheries and Game, Fred E. Holt of the Bureau of Forestry, and Attorney General Joseph E. Brennan. Assistant Attorney General David Flannagan was assigned to handle the situation, in terms of legal negotiations, for the Authority. According to Tibbs, the Native Americans had presented him with a fourteen page document outlining Indian claims to State land both inside and outside BSP. The group's arguments were heavily tied to a pending federal case involving tribal land claims and possible monetary and other compensation for treaty violations dating back to 1820. The group at Abol laid claim to the entire Park.[3]

On April 17, Saturday, Tibbs briefed Caverly on the situation, Caverly having been off duty the previous day. Tibbs and Caverly then traveled to Pamola Lodge in Millinocket where Tibbs introduced Caverly to Allen Sockabasin, Governor of the Passamaquoddy Indian Tribe or Council Chief, and Thomas Tureen, Indian Counsel retained by the Office of Native American Indian Rights of Washington, D.C. Caverly would drive the two Native American representatives to Abol Campground to meet with the Native Americans encamped there, while Tibbs, to honor previous commitments, would leave Maine at noon.[4]

Caverly, Tureen, and Sockabasin drove to Abol where Tureen and Sockabasin spoke with the campers. Tibbs had instructed Caverly to allow the two representatives to enter BSP and meet with the Native American group, composed primarily of Passamaquoddy and Penobscot Indians, whenever they desired. The understanding of Park staff was that the two men would help keep the situation under control until the Authority and the Indian Government could determine a solution to the problem.[5] However, this did not transpire in following days.

The Native Americans made several requests of Park personnel. Caverly and Assistant Attorney General Flannagan met and worked out answers to the requests as well as a few basic rules for the duration of the tribal members' stay. The Indians could use most of the lean-tos in the camping area, they would be allowed to make one trip to the lean-tos with all but one of their vehicles, a young child would be allowed to join his or her mother in the Park, and two members would be granted permission to leave the Park to visit Mount Chase accompanied by Park personnel. Park personnel would also document any questions or requests made by the Native Americans. Attorney Tureen and Governor Sockabasin would be the only visitors allowed into the area to meet with the group, and no additional tribal members—with the exception of the designated child—would be allowed to enter BSP to join the group. Several of the group's requests were denied in that the Native Americans would be held responsible for any damage they inflicted on the campground, they would not be allowed to use BSP gear, BSP personnel would not provide transportation except in an emergency situation or to escort Native Americans from the Park, and as the activities of the group remained illegal the Park would not grant them permission to resupply food.[6]

The press of course took an active interest in the latest events at BSP. The Native American campers communicated to Park staff that they did not desire press involvement and the Park denied press access to BSP. The press repeatedly attempted to gather information about the situation, and Caverly simply issued a statement to the effect that the Authority would be meeting with the Tribal Council early the following week and would make a statement at that time. State newspapers carried the story just the same, obtaining information from Indian spokespersons as well as from Tibbs, other BSP Personnel, Authority members, and law enforcement officers as the days progressed. The press ran editorials and printed letters from readers voicing opinions on the "occupation," opinions which ranged from "the Indians must go" to "the Indians should be allowed to stay." The *Bangor Daily News* obtained photographs taken within the Park, printing a photograph of part of the group gathered at a picnic area the day after the Native Americans arrived at BSP. The *BDN* and other papers also quoted State Police as having stated that no laws had as yet been broken as far as they could determine. Park Rules and Regulations had, however, certainly been violated.[7]

Caverly returned Tureen and Sockabasin to Millinocket on Saturday, April 17, following their meeting with the squatters. On Sunday the two representatives flew out of the area, to New York and Princeton, Maine, respectively. The following day the campers requested Park supplies which staff refused on the grounds of Park shortages. One or more of the group, in violation of their verbal agreement, left the camping area in a panel truck and proceeded north for some distance on the Perimeter Road. Park personnel also reported unauthorized tents and an illegal fireplace.[8]

Caverly, along with Assistant Supervisor Philip McGlauflin and Campground Ranger Donald McKenna, met with a number of the Native Americans on April 18, Easter Sunday. The campers voiced their objections to BSP personnel walking through the camping area as they believed it invaded their privacy. They were informed that the men in question were simply conducting their official duties. The group also discussed other problems, and Caverly reported that, in addition to their being "quite overbearing and rude," several of the Native Americans "gave the impression ... that they would become militant with the slightest provocation." "Several members," Caverly continued, had "continuously worn knives, tomahawks, [and] had been seen walking [the] road with bows and arrows."[9] At least part of the group was armed if not immediately dangerous.

After prolonged discussion, BSP staff and the Native Americans reached a peaceful conclusion to the meeting and adjourned for the day. Park staff addressed other problems as they arose, however, including campers carving on a birch tree, removing bark from a birch tree, allowing a dog to run loose, and various activities or actions the staff found rude or obnoxious. Meanwhile, Sockabasin returned to the Park, received transportation to the camping area by Park staff, escorted one camper out of BSP, and was then transported once again to Abol Campground by BSP personnel. At some point during this time period Sockabasin also communicated to the *BDN* that the three Tribal Governors in Maine had not heard of the group's plans before they moved into Baxter, and so the Governors had not voted on it. But he personally favored it, just as he approved "'any other Indian in any cause where he is fighting for his rights.'" Although Maine's tribes claimed much of northern and eastern Maine as theirs under new federal decisions, Sockabasin said he had heard of no plans to move into other areas. The Katahdin area was special as it represented a spiritual place to Maine Indians, a place where they had gone in the past to cleanse themselves and it remained a "'source of spiritual help for them.'" Furthermore, as the *BDN* reported on April 20, according to Sockabasin "since the [federal] court case, the land belongs to us. It's a legal question, not one of politics.'" The Office of the Attorney General disagreed, but stated that "'there is no immediate crisis." The Office had not yet determined if the Native Americans had violated any State statutes.[10]

Monday, April 19, 1976, things were relatively peaceful with no new infractions of Park rules discovered. The gates to the Park had been locked to prevent additional tribal members from joining the party at Abol Campground without the express permission of the Authority or Park personnel. Nearby Rangers would open the gates for any squatters who wished to leave the Park. Caverly remained in close contact with the Authority and legal counsel. In the evening Sockabasin returned to the Park once again and Ranger Barry MacArthur escorted Sockabasin, a woman, and a two year old child to Abol Campground. Sockabasin stated that he would leave the Park promptly but failed to do so. Meanwhile, Caverly had received a report that "three or four carloads of Indians would be arriving early the next morning to join the Indians at Abol." In response Caverly contacted all BSP commissioned Rangers he could reach and requested they report to Togue Pond. Caverly spent the rest of the night discussing the situation with staff and formulating strategy to be employed should a large group of Native Americans attempt to enter BSP. Apparently wanting to take all available precautions, the Park evacuated all women living in Park quarters.[11]

Although violence against women or men did not transpire, the night's efforts in preparing to meet a new group of what would be illegal campers should they remain in the Park, and who would certainly violate the agreement reached with those Native Americans already illegally encamped in BSP, did have its intended results. During the early hours of Tuesday, April 20, 1976, Park Rangers made nine arrests of Native Americans using the old entrance behind Abol Pond to enter the Park. Rangers found the individuals hiding in the woods. Upon being spotted the individuals attempted to flee, but they eventually submitted to arrest without incident. The nine arrested included eight men and one woman. They carried food, beer, and cigarettes as well as aspirin, two hunting knives, and a hunting bow complete with arrows. At least one of the nine came from Pleasant Point Indian reservation in Princeton.[12]

Tribal Governor Sockabasin appeared on the scene during the arrests, at which point Caverly determined that Sockabasin had not left the Park as he had stated he would, had not been helping to resolve the situation, and had instead "been using his visitation rights as leverage in stirring up the Indians both inside and outside of Baxter Park." According to Caverly, "one of his own people reported he had made arrangements for the nine who were arrested to be brought in the back way when he himself was aware no new Indians would be allowed to enter the Park." Sockabasin attempted to interfere with the arrests, and Caverly told him that he was "surprised that a man in his position would pull the stunts he had pulled," and that he was "completely disappointed in him and certainly lost what respect I have for him." Sockabasin then, in Caverly's words, "made it very clear ... he could care less what I thought." Staff members in the meantime completed the arrests and began transporting the prisoners to Togue Pond. Piscataquis County Deputies picked the individuals up at Togue Pond and transported them to the county jail in Dover-Foxcroft. The nine were later released on personal recognizance pending arraignment that Thursday on trespassing charges. Although staff members reported feeling tension in the air for the rest of the day, no new problems arose in BSP. Sockabasin left the Park after Deputies transported the prisoners to jail, but not without becoming involved in a mild verbal altercation with BSP personnel.[13]

Native Americans occupying Abol Campground in support of their 1976 land claim challenge. (Photo: *Bangor Daily News*)

Caverly met Indian Affairs Commissioner George Mitchell at the Millinocket Airport in the afternoon of the same day and drove him to Abol Campground. Mitchell met with the campers, then he and Caverly returned to Millinocket at 11:00 p.m. At this point the plan was for the three Tribal Governors to arrive at BSP the following morning and meet with the campers. Mitchell and Caverly stayed at the Millinocket office until 1:00 a.m. making telephone calls pertaining to the situation. Through the calls Mitchell learned that the Tribal Governors would not be coming to BSP after all, but would meet in Old Town to discuss the situation with tribal council. Caverly and Mitchell then retired for the balance of the night, or so they thought.[14]

At roughly 4:00 a.m. on April 21, Caverly received a telephone call from the Maine State Police in Orono advising Caverly that Mitchell's mother-in-law had died. Mitchell left Millinocket. He planned to attend the tribal meeting in Old Town that day as well as attending to his personal affairs. Caverly drove to Abol Campground and informed the squatters that there was no morning meeting with the Tribal governors scheduled for the Park. Caverly then updated the group on the Governors' meeting plans. The three Governors, their attorneys, and Mitchell did decide at their afternoon meeting, however, to meet with the campers in the Park that night and did so for several hours.[15]

During the afternoon and evening hours of April 20, the Attorney General's Office had made several statements to the public. Attorney General Brennan, who had requested Mitchell's assistance with the situation, stated that the Native Americans were being urged to leave the Park immediately. He also said that "the people now in the Park are there illegally and in violation of Park regulations." He said that the Authority was willing to meet with Indian leaders and their legal council that Friday, but that the Authority "'would not entertain claims under duress and accompanied by threats.'" Assistant Attorney General Flannagan had stated that following Caverly and Mitchell's five hour conference with the Indians at Abol the Authority's position remained "to make every possible effort to get a peaceful resolution to the situation," and that they believed "tomorrow will be the culmination of those efforts." He did not identify what action the State would take if the Native Americans did not leave.[16]

On Wednesday, April 21, 1976, the Maine Governor's Office released a number of statements. Governor James B. Longley, during his weekly news conference, said that "the State had been fair and patient" during the encampment period and that the Native Americans in the Park did not have the support of their tribal leaders. He said that he hoped "'that the Indians will leave peacefully and as good citizens of Maine. If they do not, we intend to remove them.'" The Governor did not specify a date by which the group had to leave BSP, but did say that he would give full support to law enforcement agencies should they be needed. The Governor's Press Secretary stated later in the day that he did not think that the Authority and the Governor would allow the situation to continue much longer, and could decide as early as Thursday to have the Native Americans removed from the Park. "'This is going to be a state operated under the laws of the State of Maine,'" Press Secretary Ralph Lowe said. "'And no individual is going to take the law into their own hands.'"[17]

The result of the meeting on April 21, 1976, was that the Native American campers agreed to leave Baxter State Park on three conditions. First, they wanted the Park to convey property rights to land on Chesuncook Lake. Second, they wanted yearly visitation rights granted them so that they might hold spiritual ceremonies in BSP. Third, they wanted charges against the nine arrested persons dropped or no charges filed. Attorney Thomas Tureen, who had participated in the meeting, made several phone calls from Park Headquarters later that night including calls to Maine Governor Longley, Attorney General Brennan, and Assistant Attorney General Flannagan. Caverly also talked to numerous persons via the telephone. In addition, State Police Sergeant Larry Gross and Warden Supervisor Richie spent time at BSP Headquarters that night helping with the problem.[18]

At roughly 2:00 a.m., April 22, Attorney Tureen, according to Caverly's report, "finally realized the Baxter State Park Authority was not going to concede to the Indians' stipulations." He was advised to return to Abol Campground to inform the group that they would have to depart BSP by 8:00 a.m. that day. Tureen wanted to wait several hours before making the trip, but was advised that he should go immediately so that the campers would have time to pack their gear. Caverly and Warden Supervisor Richie transported Tureen to the Park and to Abol Campground. Tureen wanted to stay in the Park for the remainder of the night, but Caverly and Richie insisted that he return to Millinocket with them. He reluctantly complied.[19]

After returning to Millinocket, Sergeant Gross, Warden Supervisor Richie, and BSP Supervisor Caverly recruited personnel to help BSP Rangers should it prove necessary to force the campers to leave after the established time limit. Force proved unnecessary. At 8:00 a.m. the Native American group arrived at Togue Pond, held a brief ceremony, and departed the Park by 8:15 without incident. Caverly informed the press that "we didn't make any threats" during or after the negotiation process, "and we didn't elaborate. They left without issue." Furthermore, Caverly stated that the Park would not file charges against the Native Americans who had occupied Abol Campground. Although the group left without altercation, they did state that they would be back.[20]

Those involved in the six day ordeal expected that the Native Americans would indeed be back. But they anticipated at least a short respite. They did not get one.

The following afternoon, April 23, the Maine State Police telephoned Caverly to report that they had received a tip that Native Americans were moving in from out-of-state and that a total of five hundred might be expected. Preparations commenced immediately.[21]

Caverly notified all personnel to be on alert. He received a telephone call from Sergeant Gross at 11:00 p.m. conveying the message that the Native Americans were en route from Princeton to Old Town. Caverly waited until 8:00 a.m., Saturday, April 24, then contacted the Millinocket Police Department and asked to be notified if "an unusual amount of Indians showed up in town." Caverly drove through town a number of times and "spotted several vehicles that looked of suspicious nature."[22]

Caverly discussed the situation with Sergeant Gross early in the afternoon and the two decided to accept a Great Northern offer of an airplane for the purpose of checking Park access points. This saved a great deal of time over driving the route, thus leading to a fairly quick assurance that so far no new intrusion had begun. However, while returning to the airport Caverly received a radio call informing him that he was to contact the Millinocket Police as soon as possible. A patrolman met Caverly at the airport before he could return the call, and informed him that thirty to forty Native Americans would arrive at Togue Pond early the next morning.[23]

According to Caverly, "Sergeant Gross and I immediately started to prepare for what seemed the inevitable." Gross contacted the State Police for reinforcements. Caverly contacted Warden Richie, and Warden Inspector Eric Wight arranged for Wardens to assemble at Togue Pond. Caverly likewise telephoned Sheriff Frank Murch of the Piscataquis County Sheriff's Department, and Murch volunteered five Deputies to assist. Caverly also instructed BSP Rangers to report to Togue. In addition to making security arrangements, Caverly contacted Attorney General Brennan, Assistant Attorney General Flannagan and Deputy Attorney General Richard S. Cohen.[24]

Late in the evening, Victor Slich of WGAN telephoned Caverly and told him that the station had been advised that thirty to forty native Americans would arrive at Togue Pond the following morning accompanied by an NBC television crew. Meanwhile, planning and preparations for the coming day continued.[25]

By 2:00 a.m. April 25, roughly twenty State Troopers, five Deputy Sheriffs, twelve Game Wardens, and eleven Commissioned BSP Rangers had assembled at Togue Pond. They waited. Nothing happened. No word arrived. After several hours Assistant Attorney General Charles Ledbetter arrived, and Lieutenant Rupert Johnson of the Maine State Police joined the waiting group. Still nothing happened. Lieutenant Johnson and Sergeant Gross left for Millinocket to check on any developments. There were none, and the two arrived back at Togue Pond at roughly 10:30 a.m. At this point Caverly and those assembled at Togue Pond decided that the Native Americans were not coming. All law enforcement officers were dismissed. As Caverly later reported, "either we were set up by the Indians or they fund out we were there and waiting for them. The latter is more likely, ... as we know they had scanners and were probably tuned to our activities.[26]

A spoof on the Park and the authorities or an aborted mission, the Park had been prepared to meet and fend off any new violations of Park Rules and Regulations by Native Americans. As for the future, the decision was made to wait until Park rules or State laws had been violated before mobilizing. The Park and the Authority knew where to acquire reinforcement if necessary and would call for it "without question or hesitation."[27] Although no repeats of the long encampment of Native Americans occurred in following months, the issue of Native American rights or requests concerning Baxter State Park had not ended.

Governor Longley had lauded the peaceful end to the "Indian situation" after they left the Park on April 23. The fact that it almost came to a show of force did not negate the success realized by the Park, Authority, and those who assisted in bringing about a nonviolent close to the Abol Campground intrusion. Although after negotiations had failed the night before the exodus Longley had stated that State Troopers would be called upon if necessary, he stated on Thursday that the Native Americans having left of their own volition was "a fine example of how reasonable people can accommodate what is right without needless conflict." He also said that "this inspiring piece of Maine land belongs to all of us now to share together in friendship."[28] Clearly such an ideal, the ideal Baxter had made a reality when he gave Baxter State Park to all the people of Maine, was what the Park and Authority had been defending all along. To give part of BSP to one group, no matter the specific group, runs contrary to Park policy as evinced from the earliest years of the Park's history through the 1990s, even if officially Park policy was less clearly stated in its earlier than its later years. The Deeds of Trust were always clear on the subject of Baxter's wanting all of the citizens of the state of Maine to share in the natural beauty and wealth of Katahdin and the surrounding area. Park personnel and the Authority would continue to defend the Park against special interests—even if they felt sympathetic to them—in following years.

Members of the group which had vacated the Park also made statements about the situation's conclusion. Stanley Neptune, who had spent the six days in BSP, stated that the group had left not because of Park or State pressure, but because they had accomplished what they set out to accomplish. "Everything that happened was good," he told the press. "It [the Park] was a place to go to get answers ... we left because it was time to leave." The group which had camped in BSP, along with others, wanted to have a new reservation set up, one where members of the Penobscot, Passamaquoddy, Micmac, and Maliseet tribes could reestablish older Indian ways. The traditional Native American culture was being lost on the existing reservations. Under the new Wabanaki Federation members of the various tribes hoped to secure State lands on which to settle. The group had hoped to acquire part of BSP, but it had become obvious that that would not come to pass. Another person who had stayed at Abol, Sam Sapio, stated that the group had gone to Baxter to do some of their "traditional things." They had, Sapio stated, engaged in "spiritual events," but he declined to give further information on the subject. Throughout the six day intrusion, Native American spokespersons had stated that the group just wanted a place to live "away from white society." Indian Commissioner Mitchell reiterated this assessment just after the group left the Park.[29]

While Native Americans continued to seek land in the Katahdin area to use as a possible settlement site, the Park maintained that the group could request non-seasonal Park use through the same procedures as did everyone else. The same held true for seasonal use of BSP.[30] Over the next two years requests for special permits and other privileges would be made by various tribal members.

Attorney General Brennan stated in May 1976 that the charges against the arrested Native Americans would be dismissed based on the rational that those who had stayed in the Park in violation of Park rules had not been charged, and most people involved with the issue felt that they had been more in violation than those arrested near the entrance to BSP. Park rules, in terms of enforceability, did warrant further attention, however.[31]

While the enforceability of Park rules did not meet further challenges by Native Americans during the ensuing year, the issue of Indian requests did. Members of the Penobscot Indian Reservation presented oral requests to the Authority in August 1977, following previous verbal contacts on the issue. John Sapiel, Donald Francis, and Stanley Neptune presented the Native American requests on behalf of the Wabanaki Nation or Federation.

They stated that the Governor and Council of the Passamaquoddy tribes supported their current activities. The three men stated that the Indians would eventually get the land back through the courts and thereafter settle on Katahdin, but in the meantime they wanted special permission for Park use without fees for durations of two to three or more days, with the mountain or any other area used by their people closed to non-Indians. The Authority asked that the requests and all necessary specifics be presented in writing and that the Authority would then take the matter into consideration, an item by item consideration. The Authority gave the men copies of the Park Rules and Regulations to aid them in writing their requests. The men were instructed to specify how their requests varied from rules governing Park use by the general public.[32]

The Native Americans did not respond in writing as requested and the Authority shelved the subject until such time as a written request might be received. In October 1978, twenty-five to thirty Native Americans attended the regular Authority meeting and restated requests for special permission. The Authority had expected members of the group to attend the previous meeting, but when they did not appear—nor send in the requested written information—the Authority had sent them an invitation to the October meeting. George Mitchell, himself a Native American, came with the group and did some of the speaking for the delegation. The delegation had previously met in Old Town and selected various persons to speak at the Authority meeting. One spokesperson, Dana Mitchell, asked that any members of the press leave. Another spokesperson then addressed the Authority in an Indian language, without benefit of translation. A member of the groups' Council of Elders then presented a short declaration reaffirming the Wabanaki peoples' alliance to one another and their determination to "walk freely on Mother Earth and on the spiritual mountain, K'tahdin." The forty-eight word declaration did not make any requests of the Authority or Park staff. The group did not want to entertain questions or to offer any specifics. Nor did they offer any written materials with, perhaps, the exception of a copy of the declaration. The delegation did agree to try and set up a meeting at their "home" in about a month's time.[33]

At the November 1978 Authority meeting Dana Mitchell stated that the group as a whole had not been prepared to attend the meeting and thus had not done so. They would not submit written information that day. The Native Americans still wanted the Authority to attend a meeting at the Indians' "home." Sarah Redfield of the Attorney General's Office then reviewed the past two years concerning the Indian requests and told those assembled that the "Authority has legitimately asked for specific information so they can specifically answer. Is that type of cooperation forthcoming," Redfield asked, "or are we going to have to go [on] with th[ese] noncommunicative meetings for much longer?" Thereafter followed a lengthy exchange in which Redfield tried to obtain detailed information and Mitchell answered in a less than direct manner, in terms of providing the specific kinds of information the Authority sought.[34]

Mitchell communicated to Redfield and the Authority that although some things had been decided upon by the Native American group other things remained undetermined. Defining numbers of tribal members seeking entrance to BSP might be a problem for the Nation or Confederation, and privacy would be required. Mitchell stated also that "basically what the people feel, from what I understand, [is that] they do not want to define some of the spiritual or religious aspects of traditional ways within the confine[s] that the Park might want. They do wish to use the Park and would like to use it without any restrictions from the Park Authority." Remote areas might prove desirable. Redfield repeated that the group would have to define certain parameters or specifics or the Authority would not be able to grant any special permission for Park use. The written transcript of the meeting reveals frustration on both of the speakers' parts. Redfield stated that the State of Maine had clearly decided that Baxter State Park did not belong to the Native Americans. Mitchell pointed out recent federal laws aimed at securing Indian rights involving federal land. Redfield pointed out that BSP was not federal land. In Mitchell's opinion, however, "Federal Law supersedes State Law." The discussion progressed no further.[35]

The Baxter State Park Authority did not elect to change Park Rules and Regulations to meet Native American requests. Native Americans remained subject to the same regulations governing the general public, in spite of any desire for the opposite. The issue did not disappear after autumn 1978, but it occupied less and less Authority and staff attention. This occurred largely because tribal members requesting changes failed to present their position in a manner which the Authority deemed sufficient for making an informed, responsible exception to Park policy and operations. The Authority would not grant unequal access to Baxter State Park without justifiable cause.

Katahdin's Knife Edge has inspired many Park visitors. Chimney Peak is at the left and Katahdin Lake can be seen in the distance.
(Photo: Edward Dwyer)

Chapter Five

Search And Rescue: Visitor Protection in Baxter State Park

In his 1982 *Legacy of a Lifetime*, John Hakola, referring primarily to the formative period of Baxter State Park to 1969 and the Katahdin area, stated:

> looking at photographs of the Knife Edge; of forbidding, steep slopes down Mt. Katahdin itself; dizzying views from it and surrounding peaks of the chasms below, one is astonished that there have not been many more serious or fatal accidents.[1]

Climbing and scrambling to and across the Knife Edge; ascending and descending Katahdin; hiking and viewing surrounding peaks and chasms, one might easily concur with Hakola's conclusion. With a two thousand foot sheer drop into the Great Basin along much of Katahdin's north face, and numerous drops to the south, the arc or horseshoe shaped cirque of Katahdin —from Hamlin Ridge on the northeast to Chimney Peak on the southeast— offers both unparalleled vistas and uncountable hazards. The mile long Knife Edge ridge or arete in particular presents a celebrated, and sometimes underestimated, challenge to Park visitors. Technical climbing routes on Katahdin present unique experiences along granite cliffs in summer and ice walls in winter, but also present a continual potential for errors.[2]

The Katahdin area may be no more dangerous than other alpine areas, but its risks remain abundant. Hakola asserted of the decades before 1970 that "the fact that so few [fatalities or serious accidents] have occurred is a tribute to Park rangers and their supervisors through the years."[3] This remained as true, if not more so, for the period of 1970 through 1994.

Yet, Park rangers and other BSP personnel have had more than the potential dangers of Katahdin with which to contend. The Katahdin area comprises a relatively small portion of Baxter State Park in terms of Park geography. The Park contains a myriad of trails, numerous bodies of water, and other features which can also present dangers to the unwary visitor.

Protecting Park visitors over some 200,000 acres during an era of ever increasing use has not proved an easy task. Between 1970 and 1994, eighteen persons died in Baxter State Park. Numerous others sustained injuries. Seven of the Park deaths were direct results of health conditions, conditions which Park staff could not realistically have been expected to anticipate or successfully treat under Park conditions. Yet, Park staff attempted to safeguard all visitors, and to that end developed an extensive search and rescue program which saved the lives of several individuals, minimized injuries to others, and, in some cases, made it possible for the remains of Park fatalities to be recovered for loved ones.[4] Many issues concerning Baxter State Park have proved controversial, but the dedication of BSP personnel, organized search and rescue teams, State and municipal organizations, and volunteers from the general public—all of whom have worked together to aid Park visitors—has not been one of them.

No one incident or fatality resulted in the formation of the search and rescue program as it existed in the mid-1990s. Rather, the program developed in response to numerous factors and developments, most, but not all, directly related to the Park. A number of Park incidents did receive more public attention than others, and led to new insights on how to best protect the public from various dangers. As with other issues concerning Baxter State Park, pertinent search and rescue events transpired before 1970, claiming the lives of ten Park visitors in the 1960s through falls, exposure to the elements, drowning, and lightening. In addition, one Park Ranger, Ralph Heath, died in 1963 while attempting to rescue a woman caught in a snowstorm on Katahdin after leaving the trail. The woman also perished.[5]

By 1970, Park Rules and Regulations necessitated for safety reasons that all Park visitors register at gatehouse checkpoints. Visitors could register at Togue Pond, Matagamon Lake, or Nesowadnehunk Field, depending on their point of entry. Park visitors also had to secure a permit in order to camp, ski, or snowshoe, or to climb any mountain in BSP between mid-October and mid-May. In order to secure a permit they had to prove competency for their chosen activity. No permission to climb or ski any peak in the Park would be granted "under hazardous conditions or without adequate equipment and proper wearing apparel." The Park provided guidelines for alpine skiing and winter climbing equipment and apparel, and considered them part of an individual's qualifications to engage in these activities. The Park Supervisor or a designated member of the staff would make final determination on winter activities.[6]

In addition to the above regulations, many of which developed from 1960s incidents, and as a direct result of a 1969 incident in which a teenage Boy Scout left the Cathedral Trail on Katahdin and fell to his death, by 1970 boys and girls' groups were required to have at least one "competent twenty year old counselor or leader for every five campers whether for a day's hike or overnight." Regulations later stipulated that one leader at least eighteen years of age accompany every five minors of under sixteen years of age. These leaders were to maintain discipline while on the trail and see that Park regulations were followed. By 1973, Park regulations also forbid children under the age of six from above the timberline.[7]

Although no guarantee of visitor safety, such requirements highlighted the Park's concern with visitor safety and reflected measures taken where possible to help avoid repetitions of the accidents and fatalities of the 1960s. In addition, by 1970 the Park had spent $31,000 on a new radio system for the Park, a system which would make communications among staff during search and rescue operations more efficient,[8] and rangers had acquired some formal search and rescue training. Staff education in search and rescue methods would continue in following years. For example, a few rangers participated in the Adirondack Winter Mountain Training School held in BSP during December 1969 and January 1970, based at Chimney Pond campground and focused on training climbing instructors.[9] In 1970, two staff members attended Mountain Rescue Training School in North Conway, New Hampshire, and three rangers received training there in 1971. Also in 1971, two Park rangers attended the annual AMC Winter Mountaineering School in Acton, Massachusetts.[10] Climbing instructor and Department of Transportation Personnel Officer George L. Smith and Harold Taylor, also an experienced climber, held a mountain training program at Chimney Pond in 1972, providing Park staff with additional training,[11] and succeeding years would see the further education of Park personnel in various types of search and rescue skills and operations.

Many of the changes initiated in search and rescue operations and regulations from the late 1960s to the close of the studied period were initiated by Irvin C. Caverly during his lengthy tenure as chief Park administrator. Even during A. Lee Tibbs' years as Park Director, Caverly, as Park Supervisor, continued to oversee most day-to-day operations. Caverly, like the people he worked with and for, remained dedicated to keeping visitors as safe in Baxter State Park as possible. Fatalities occurred, but not because Park staff overlooked visitor safety issues.

In May 1971 one of the first search and rescue missions of the 1970s transpired. This time the ending was more gratifying for all persons concerned than many 1960s incidents had been, and demonstrates advances in communications and search methods. Events following the incident illustrate both the intent of Park personnel to make Park visits as safe as possible and the inability of Park personnel to safeguard all Park visitors.

Late in the afternoon of May 20, 1971, Ida Damon, wife of Park Ranger Ellsworth Damon, notified Acting Supervisor Irvin C. Caverly that a young man, Tom Forbes–roughly twenty years of age–was believed lost on North Traveler Mountain. Caverly engaged an Inland Fish and Game Department (IFG, later Inland Fisheries and Wildlife or IFW) pilot who flew Ranger Damon over the area until dark. Due to an impending storm, Caverly decided to wait until dawn to initiate a foot search of the mountain, and requested that the IFG rescue team remain on standby in the event they were needed. At 4:30 a.m. the following morning, Rangers Daniel Watson, Thomas Chase, and Michael Porter started up North Traveler to try to pick up Forbes' trail. Rangers Loren Goode, Charles Kenny, and Harold Bossie, Jr. started toward Fowler Pond and thence up the east side of Traveler Mountain. Caverly and Ranger Damon stayed at South Branch Pond to be ready to lend assistance to either search party as needed, and Caverly assigned Damon to participate in another air search if weather permitted. At 6:30 a.m. Ranger Chase radioed Caverly that his team had spotted Forbes roughly one-quarter mile off the trail on the east side of Traveler Mountain. He appeared to be in good condition. Caverly radioed the second team to return to South Branch Pond, then left to meet the first team. Caverly met the group about one mile from the peak of North Traveler Mountain. Forbes had already received first aid, and the Forbes and the search team continued on toward the campground. They arrived at 8:45 a.m. Caverly congratulated all parties involved in the mission for the way they had performed their duties, and stated that, "each time one of these incidents take place, we hope that it won't happen again, but we know it's going to."[12]

It did indeed happen again—three days later. On May 29, 1971, Ernest Burhoe of the Matagamon gate house radioed headquarters that a nine year-old boy was lost in the Fowler Pond area. No further information was available. Caverly received the call at 6:22 p.m., and had Ranger Earl York, Jr., flown to the area. At 7:31 York radioed that the boy, Ronald Flannery, had wandered off at 9:00 that morning from where he, his father, and his uncle had been fishing. The boy's father and uncle and several fishermen had looked for the boy throughout the day. The boy had reportedly been sighted at Fowler Brook late in the afternoon. Caverly had Park rangers form teams and begin a search. Two IFG wardens at the scene headed the teams. Meanwhile, various parties on the Russell Pond Trail, the Appalachian Trail, and the Roaring Brook-Chimney Pond Trail had been reported missing. By 10:15 p.m., those persons had all been accounted for. Ronald Flannery, however, was still missing. The night being a relatively mild one, Caverly called off the search until daylight. By sunrise search parties departed, a temporary search headquarters was set up at South Branch Pond, and IFG pilots had initiated an aerial search. At roughly 7:15 a.m., the pilots reported that they believed they had sighted the Flannery party and the boy on the shore of Long Pond. Caverly made arrangements with Shin Pond Flying Service to be flown into the area so that he could interview the boy and family members. As it turned out, Flannery had spent the night in a lean-to he had constructed after becoming disoriented in the woods. In his report on the incident, Caverly thanked not only those persons involved in the search but also the Boy Scouts of America for the training they had given Ronald Flannery.[13]

A few days later, yet another search operation was necessary. On June 4, 1971, twenty year-old Penny Lowe separated from a friend of hers after the two lost the trail between Lily Pad Pond and Windy Pitch Pond at about 10:00 a.m. The two were staying at Kidney Pond Camps, and when one returned without the other and reported her friend lost, Charlie Norris, camp operator, went in search of Lowe. Norris encountered Caverly and Ranger Chase on foot patrol at 3:50 p.m. and the two likewise began to look for the young woman, along with three other rangers. The searchers split into three groups to cover the area, then regrouped into two parties. Shortly after five o'clock, Caverly radioed for an IFG airplane. Park Ranger Kenney accompanied the pilot. At 7:20 p.m. ground searchers located Lowe roughly one-half mile west of Windy Pitch Pond. Lowe had not been happy about the prospect of spending the night in the woods alone, but had built two fires and gathered a sufficient amount of wood to see her through the night if need be. Once again, Caverly extended "thank-yous" to all involved in the effort.[14]

Less than a month later, BSP conducted another search and rescue operation. This time a party of nine persons was reported missing. The group, composed of fifteen and sixteen year-old students and their twenty-one and twenty-nine year-old instructors, had disappeared after leaving Katahdin Stream Campground for Katahdin along the Appalachian Trail. Caverly received news of their status at 6:10 p.m., June 26. In view of the warm weather and the size of the party, Caverly decided to wait until morning to begin a search. At 5:00 a.m. the following day, Caverly flew over Katahdin with a Katahdin Flying Service pilot. They did not see the group. Rangers Howard York and Greg Hanrahan left Roaring Brook at 5:30 a.m. to check the Basin Pond area, and Caverly returned to Millinocket to organize a search operation. At 7:30 a.m., however, Russell Pond rangers radioed that the missing party had arrived there tired and hungry but in good health. Due to their weary condition, the party was flown to Wassataquoik Lake then Togue Pond. The group had, Park staff learned, left Baxter Peak at about 1:15 p.m. the previous day and missed their intended trail, Saddle, due to a snow patch obscuring their view of markers. The group had continued on to Caribou Spring, stayed at Davis Pond overnight, then hiked to Russell Pond.[15]

Things slowed down in the Park after the latest search, in terms of accidents and missing persons, but the events of late May to late June 1971 demonstrated the need for continual vigilance. Many similar types of operations, operations without fatalities or serious injuries, would be enacted in following years—operations too numerous to discuss individually. In 1971 alone, Park personnel conducted ten "successful" search and rescue operations by early December, and in later years upwards of twenty operations per year were not unusual.[16] Some years witnessed more search and rescue operations than others, and some of these were only "routine missions," missions which Director Tibbs described in 1976 as "helping a person injured or sick along a trail ... or searching for someone who is reported overdue." Most of these incidents, Tibbs reported, "are not of a life and death nature but require considerable staff time."[17] Collectively, such operations demonstrated the constant need for Park staff to be prepared for all contingencies, and portrayed successful results from prompt and well managed search and rescue missions.

With a view to meeting several requirements of mountain search and rescue operations, six BSP rangers formed the Baxter State Park Alpine Mountain Rescue Team in early 1973. The initial members were Rangers Chase (team leader), Porter (second team leader), Pingree (secretary and public relations person), Kenney, York, and Drew. The Park issued necessary equipment and required staff to keep it in optimum condition and prepared for use at a moment's notice. Members agreed to yearly physical exams and to attending any scheduled training in search and rescue work. The team underwent winter training during March 30 to April 2, 1973, under the instruction of George Smith and Harold Taylor. The training included individual climbing and rescue skills as well as avalanche hazard recognition education and methods of evacuating injured victims on steep ice and snow. The BSP team finished the program with technical climbs to Katahdin's summit along two different routes.[18]

Yet, all the efforts put into protecting Park visitors could not totally safeguard human life. The first accidental death in BSP in the twenty-five year period under study was that of John Holis, who died from a gunshot wound, apparently self-inflicted, at Abol Stream in 1972. The man's remains were discovered later that year.[19]

Two incidents transpired in 1974 which resulted in extended search and rescue operations. The first of these, the Thomas Keddy tragedy, called into action the services of the new BSP Mountain Search and Rescue Team and generated extensive publicity and a lengthy review. It also resulted in the second death in Baxter State Park between January 1970 and December 1994, and the thirty-sixth known death—of any cause—in BSP or what would become BSP.[20] Six men, all experienced summer and winter hikers, and all but one of them experienced winter technical climbers, left Chimney Pond campground on the morning of January 31, 1974, a Thursday. All either worked for the Appalachian Mountain Club or had done so in the past. Three of the men had made previous winter trips to Baxter, had engaged in several technical climbs to the ridge of Katahdin, and had "came to love deeply the climbing opportunities in South Basin" as Katahdin was "free of the overcrowding" found "on the limited ice of the White Mountains" of New Hampshire. Two of the men arrived in BSP on January 22, 1974, to help Park staff work on a cross country ski trail. The others arrived on Friday, January 25. Between that Friday and the following Thursday, the day of the fatal climb, the men packed their supplies to Chimney Pond, collected wood and settled in, and made practice climbs above Chimney Pond on the Pamola Cliffs. The men informed Ranger Loren Goode of their climbing intentions, or at least some of them, although Goode, not a technical climber, was to leave Chimney Pond on Thursday morning.[21]

Thursday morning the six climbers formed two teams. The two most experienced technical climbers, Robert Proudman and Paul DiBello, served as team leaders. The sky appeared ominous that morning, but the climbers thought that they would have twelve to eighteen hours before an impending storm might hit the area, ample time they thought to make their climb. The men did not carry overnight gear as they intended to return to camp for the night. They all wore the same basic clothing, including wool shirts and windbreakers, but left the choice of additional clothing to each party member. They began their climbs at 9:30 and 10:00 a.m.—a late start for a winter journey up Katahdin.[22]

The climb seemed to go well for most of the day. However, when the day began to fade the teams had not yet completed their climb, and they were still separate. Proudman reached what proved to be the men's overnight site—a small ledge—first, and the two other members of his team soon thereafter established verbal contact with the second team. The team lead by DiBello asked Proudman's team to wait for them as they had only one headlamp for the three of them. DiBello's group had encountered more difficult climbing conditions than Proudman's team. They thought it would take twenty minutes to reach Proudman's team. Instead it took them roughly three hours—a crucial three hours. Proudman, still alone, tried to prepare a place for the men to spend the night.[23]

As Proudman later described it, "the storm hit with a suddenness that was awesome. Five minutes after I'd been standing smoking a leisurely cigarette, I was scrunched into a corner of the ledge with my hood up and my face between my knees." He could not look up or snow falling from both the sky and the slopes above would quickly fill his face. Snow piled up around and upon him. The snow abated after a time, but then "the temperature dropped and the wind picked up to gale force." Communication with the other men remained impossible. After some time, it seemed like a long time to Proudman, the other five men managed to reach the ledge. Page Dinsmore, Mike Cohen, Paul DiBello, and Tom Keddy all needed assistance making the climb, especially Keddy, who fell five or six times. The time was then perhaps midnight.[24]

Being unable to find a more sheltered place to await dawn, the men huddled together on the three by five foot ledge, placing DiBello—who seemed to be in the worst condition—in the center. It had taken Keddy about one-half hour to get his dacron parka on, and that with Proudman's help. The men called roll to make sure that they remained conscious, sang songs, did isometrics, and exchanged back rubs. The temperature was estimated at -15 degrees Fahrenheit with winds of forty to fifty or more miles per hour and gusts of up to one hundred miles per hour. Midway through the night the men stood up to check on each other's conditions. DiBello could not stand up. The others lifted him: his legs seemed limp and nonfunctional. Songs and back rubs decreased as the night wore on. At dawn those who could stand did so. Dinsmore told Proudman that he had to leave, that he was freezing to death. As Proudman described it, "his face was white from frostbite with splotches of red where the blood vessels in the skin had broken." Dinsmore's skin shocked Proudman. As Proudman described it, "he *was* freezing to death. We all were."[25]

Dinsmore left the ledge, climbing without a rope. Proudman and Michael Cohen attempted to untangle some of the frozen ropes. The two decided to have Proudman walk out with the first disentangled rope, then have Cohen attach a second rope, and when that had been pulled out add the third rope, and so forth. Proudman would hopefully have enough line to connect the ledge with the mountain ridge above. The remaining four men would then hopefully be able to leave the technical climbing area and find an easier, non-technical, descent. Proudman made it to the ridge and secured his end of the rope. He then started back down to the bivouac site or ledge "en rappel," only to discover that he had only the one rope to work with, the second rope had come untied. Thus physically cut off from the other men, and unable to establish verbal contact with them, Proudman decided to set off on his own. He thought that there was still some possibility of a rescue attempt (whether one initiated after he reached help, or one already in progress, he did not say). As he later stated about his decision, "I wish now that I could have told them that it was probably, here on in, every man for himself."[26]

After three hours of trying to keep Keddy and DiBello conscious and warm, Cohen and George determined that they could no longer stay with the two man as "they had no more heat to give." Keddy had deteriorated and was semi-conscious. Cohen and George arranged the two men in the position they determined most protected, tried to insulate them with the remaining ropes and packs, then climbed to the ridge. They soon separated. Cohen followed an erroneous route for a short distance then backtracked and started down the Dudley Trail. George reached Chimney Pond at 1:30 p.m. Cohen arrived ten minutes later.[27]

In the meantime, Proudman had found Dinsmore and the two had taken a wrong turn at the Helon Taylor Trail junction, descending the Keep Ridge instead of the Dudley Ridge, then eventually had just headed *down*. Proudman's eyes had become frostbitten, and he had to take bearings from the sun and the rough shapes and colors which he could still see. At about

2:30 they intersected the Chimney Pond Trail below Basin Pond. Dinsmore headed to Roaring Brook in search of a radio and Proudman headed back to Chimney Pond. Proudman encountered BSP Ranger Arthur York on the trail and learned that George and Cohen had made it back to camp, and that a search and rescue mission had started.[28]

After the third and fourth men had left the bivouac site, DiBello roused himself to try to aid Keddy. Keddy's condition continued to deteriorate. Four times DiBello pulled Keddy back onto the ledge after Keddy slipped into unconsciousness and began to slide off the ledge. DiBello eventually decided to try to reach safety himself. He started off with some rope, hoping to pull Keddy up to the ridge, but after the rope snagged thirty feet up from the bivouac site DiBello cut himself free. The time was then about 3:30 p.m. He made it to the ridge and began to descend, making it to the Dudley Trail near timberline by dark. Suffering from some degree of blindness, DiBello lost the trail, then fell sixty feet. Lying in the snow, he heard a helicopter. He thought that the helicopter was coming to rescue him, but upon realizing that this was not true, he managed to get to his feet and continue walking. He made it back to camp at about 6:30 p.m. The helicopter DiBello had heard had carried his friends Proudman, George, and Cohen out of BSP.[29]

Thomas Keddy did not make it out alive. He died sometime that night without having moved from the ledge. Searchers found his body the following morning, Saturday, February 2, 1974. He had been twenty-six years old at the time of his death. Members of the rescue team indicated that had they thought that there was any chance that Keddy was alive late Friday night, they would probably have risked a night-time rescue attempt. As it was, with a doctor present at Chimney Pond late Friday stating that there was no chance that Keddy could still be alive, authorities decided not to risk the lives of search members in what seemed certain to prove a doomed attempt. The weather had remained deadly with gusting winds and roughly -25 degree Fahrenheit temperatures. Even when searchers located Keddy's body Saturday morning they were unable to move it due to the extreme weather conditions.[30]

Search and Rescue team members place an accident victim aboard a hovering National Guard helicopter atop Pamola Peak.
(Photo: Baxter State Park)

Park and State authorities had initiated a search and rescue mission immediately after Doug George reached Chimney Pond at 1:30 (or 12:30 with change in time) Friday afternoon. Ranger York and his wife Elaine administered first aid to George, and later Cohen and DiBello when they arrived, and radioed BSP headquarters alerting them of the situation. The Park immediately contacted necessary parties for the search, including the recently formed BSP Mountain Search and Rescue Team, the IFG rescue team, the Appalachian Mountain Club (AMC) rescue team (which included members of the Central Maine Climbing team), and the Eastern Mountain Sport (EMS) rescue team. The Army National Guard also lent crucial assistance to the operation, and George L. Smith of the AMC contacted mountaineering physician Laurier E. Nolin to enlist his aid.[31]

Immediately after receiving York's message, Park Supervisor Caverly had dispatched assistant BSP team leader Pingree and Ranger Barry MacArthur to Chimney Pond, and sent Ranger York to Roaring Brook to ascertain if Proudman and Dinsmore had inadvertently gone there. Before York could reach Roaring Brook, Dinsmore reached the camping area and radioed headquarters. Caverly told him to stay where he was as help was on the way. Caverly had already contacted the Maine National Guard Rescue Unit in Bangor and they were en route. They picked up Dinsmore first.[32]

Members of the various rescue teams arrived at Roaring Brook and Chimney Pond during the late hours of February 1, including Dr. Nolin. In the meantime, the first four survivors to reach safety had been flown by helicopter (Dinsmore had first been transported to Avalanche Field by snowmobile) to the Millinocket Hospital during the afternoon. DiBello had been carried to Pamola Brook by BSP Rangers and IFG wardens (Ranger and team member Kenney had also arrived at Chimney Pond by this time to lend assistance, as had Warden Inspector Eric Wight and Warden Dan Watson), and from there to Roaring Brook by Park staff and rescue volunteers. From Roaring Brook DiBello was transported by snowmobile to Togue Pond, then carried by National Guard helicopter to Millinocket. No helicopters could reach Chimney Pond after nightfall that day, and Major Eugene Richardson of the Army National Guard estimated wind chill temperatures to be one hundred degrees below zero. Earlier in the day the Guard had been able to drop some rescue members at Chimney Pond.[33]

Various parties arrived in Millinocket by car and plane from throughout Maine and from New Hampshire during the evening and night of February 1 and 2. Park staff as well as snowmobilers from the Millinocket area helped transport people and supplies to Chimney Pond throughout the night. Before reaching the campground, a decision was made that George Smith, Dr. Nolin, Paul Ross, and Rick Wilcox would attempt a night ascent up Katahdin.[34] However, when leaders of the various teams met after 11:00 p.m. February 1, at Chimney Pond they determined that no rescue operation would be attempted until morning. As Smith later testified,

> the weather was too severe at midnight on Friday to jeopardize the lives of the searchers when the possibility of Keddy's survival was zero due to two nights and one day of exposure, [and] with [the] first hand report of his condition when last observed by DiBello, plus other information of the extent of cold injury to the five survivors.[35]

Smith then notified BSP Supervisor Caverly of the decision, Caverly having earlier requested that Smith take charge of field operations on upper Katahdin.[36]

Additional members of the IFG team arrived at Chimney Pond by helicopter early Saturday morning. Four teams were then sent up to Pamola Peak: three teams comprised of BSP, EMS, IFG, and AMC searchers headed up the Dudley Trail, and a fourth, EMS, team started up the Helon Taylor Trail. Weather conditions remained severe with gusting winds and -20 degree Fahrenheit temperatures. In addition, some of the men had had little to eat in the previous twelve or more hours and had had insufficient sleeping gear.[37]

The five member EMS climbing team ultimately made it to the scene of the tragedy before the other searchers. Three of the men descended by rope to the bivouac site where, as Wilcox later stated, "we found Tom Keddy frozen solid in a hanging position approximately eight feet below where he was tied into two rock pitons." The ropes at the scene, Wilcox reported, "were twisted and frozen and would have taken hours to untangle even under good conditions. With frozen hands it was out of the question." Wilcox also noted that Keddy was wearing good double boots and that, "except for the lack of a good heavy down parka," "the rest of his equipment was of good quality." After roughly ten minutes the team decided not to try to move Keddy's body due to still hazardous weather conditions. The team secured the body to the cliff, then ascended three hundred feet of technical climbing and another three hundred feet of non-technical (ropes not necessary) terrain to reach the ridge. After walking down to Index Rock on the Dudley Trail, the team reached the BSP team and informed them of what they had encountered. Both teams agreed to await improved weather before attempting to recover the body.[38]

Supervisor Caverly requested that Smith aid in a recovery expedition when weather conditions improved, as they were expected to do in then next few days. The operation ultimately transpired on Wednesday, February 6, 1974. Ten members of the AMC Central Maine Climbing Group (including Smith and his son) and five BSP rescue team members (Drew, Chase, York, Kenney, and Pingree) participated in the recovery on upper Katahdin. The men climbed to Pamola Peak early that morning. They had hiked to Chimney Pond from Roaring Brook the preceding day. The team set up a "body recovery system," then belayed AMC's David H. Smith and BSP's Tom Chase down three hundred feet to the bivouac site. By noon the men had transported the body on a litter to the top of the ridge and carried it to an open area where an Army National Guard helicopter could land. Caverly and Assistant Supervisor Philip McGlauflin were standing by at Chimney Pond, and realizing that it would take another day to remove the body to Togue Pond and that forecasters predicted snowstorms for Thursday, Caverly had radioed Millinocket to request National Guard assistance. The Guard complied, and its helicopter transported Keddy's body to Millinocket while the recovery team hiked down to Chimney Pond and then to Roaring Brook. At Roaring Brook the recovery team was fed and met by snowmobile operators for transportation out of the Park. The week long operation had finally ended.[39]

Following the tragedy and the retrieval of Keddy's body, the Baxter State Park Authority decided to hold a hearing on the accident to review events of the incident and operation and to obtain comments and recommendations on how to help prevent a similar incident from happening in the future. Maine newspapers announced and covered the hearing. The Authority convened the meeting in Orono on March 5, 1974, by which time three of the survivors had recovered sufficiently to attend. Proudman, age twenty-five, Cohen, age twenty-nine, and George, age twenty-one, attended the hearing. DiBello, age twenty-three, sustained the most serious injuries, and in early March had his right foot and part of his left foot amputated. Dinsmore, age nineteen, was also still in the hospital in March and unable to either attend the hearing or to write, but his father had sent a letter to the Authority for him.[40]

The Authority heard and accepted written testimony from a number of individuals at the hearing, both rescue participants and the survivors. A number of persons stated that like it or not, an increasing number of persons would seek to climb Katahdin in winter. According to EMS climber Rick Wilcox, Baxter State Park offered some of the best ice climbing conditions in the United States, and, as he stated in his written report, "you must adapt and I believe get used to the idea that a lot of climbers will be visiting the area." He suggested BSP contact other public parks to see how they had handled the influx of climbers.[41]

Several persons noted that accidents were bound to happen in technical mountain climbing. As IFG Warden Eric Wight stated in his written testimony,

> throughout the world there are those who for some reason, known only to themselves and others like them, find pleasure in placing themselves next to the very extremes of nature. Whether it be very deep in the ocean, very high in an airplane with a parachute, or going fast in a racing car, there is a very basic similarity. Unfortunately, someone occasionally loses the game.[42]

William Kitterage, an experienced climber and climbing instructor who had participated in the recovery operation, likewise stated that,

> the principals involved were experienced and skilled climbers, ... we have to admit that, given the circumstances, there is probably no way that any climber would have done things much differently. In other words, we are face-to-face with a situation where men were aware of a danger (in as much as they knew how fast the weather could change on Katahdin), were aware of their limitations in coping with that danger, took the chance ... and did not come out of it easily. ... There is just no way that this sort of accident can be prevented from happening to experienced climbers.[43]

Other individuals expressed similar sentiments.

Still, these attending the meeting did make suggestions about how to reduce the likelihood of such accidents, and testimony presented to the Authority noted some of the errors which had been made in the Keddy tragedy. Perhaps the most telling testimony of the latter type was submitted by the survivors in their written report, written by Proudman with the aid of the others. Misjudgments made before the climb, according to the report, "were small and harmless in themselves, but when taken cumulatively they cut the total safety margin below an acceptable level." These errors in judgment were as follows: underestimating the seriousness of the approaching storm; deciding not to take overnight gear as they planned to return to Chimney Pond for the night, thereby sacrificing safety to speed; and allowing each person to make his own choice as to what extra clothing to bring rather than insisting, for example, that each man bring an "expedition weight down parka." As a result of the latter misjudgment, "Paul and Tom were the most poorly equipped of the six of us and this now shows with Paul's poor condition and Tom's death." As to the events of Friday, the day after the climb, Proudman and the survivors addressed perhaps the most difficult issue:

> We each abandoned our partner(s), partially on the slim hope that some rescue was in the works or that a rescue could at least start in time to save the boy(s) from death. And there was always that deepest instinct in the background to save oneself, if and when the terms made this final choice necessary. Looking back, the rescue hope is transparent. There was no way a team could, in those conditions, reach the fellows in time. The rescue hope was partially an excuse to leave. Frost-fogged minds made this decision to leave for a direct, deep reason: the strong and simple will to live. There was no alternative. We each decided to save ourselves."[44]

The survivors acknowledged in their report that they had begun the climb without any expectation of a rescue operation should an accident occur. Yet, the report continued, "from the Park Manager's perspective... there is an obvious responsibility to protect the public health, safety, and welfare." The survivors thereby made several recommendations to the Authority.[45]

First of all, the survivors' report stated that had there been communication between Rangers York and Goode, or a sign-out sheet at Chimney Pond, Park staff would have been aware that the climbers had run into difficulty. As it was, the group had earlier requested and, they asserted, received permission from the Park Supervisor to spend one or more nights away from the campground. Park staff, the survivors stated, had then thought that the men were doing just that—camping out for the night. Because of their persistence in seeking permission for an overnight bivouac, Park staff did indeed think that the men had elected to camp out. However, Caverly later stated that no permission had been granted for an overnight expedition. The group had repeatedly revised their itinerary and then requested camping permission for one site or another, but Caverly stated that he had never agreed with their proposals. Either way, when Ranger York radioed Caverly Friday morning to report that the group had not returned, Caverly advised York not to be concerned yet as "the party was well equipped, very knowledgeable," and had stated their intent to spend a night on the mountain. Caverly spoke to Ranger Goode Friday morning, contrary to the implications of Proudman's report, and Goode had the impression, after having spent several days at Chimney Pond with the climbers, that the group might have decided to sleep out on Thursday night. Therefore, permission granted or not, Caverly decided to give the men time to return to camp (most people who spent the night on the mountain would return by noon of the following day) before organizing a search party. The survivors raised the possibility in their report, however, that York might have, or did, check the cabin and ascertained that their warm gear was still there and, considering the weather, should have concluded Thursday night that the climbers were in trouble. Proudman thought that Caverly and the rangers had judged the climbers more competent than they themselves in evaluating climbing conditions.[46] Quite likely, a misunderstanding over the issue of the group's right to be on the mountain or elsewhere away from Chimney Pond overnight obscured the reality of the climbers' plight for several hours. The breakdown in communications seems largely to have occurred not between BSP staff members as the survivors implied, but between BSP personnel and the climbers.

The survivors commended everyone involved in the rescue operation, which they acknowledged had saved their lives. They especially commended Caverly and the BSP staff. However, they suggested that "modern technical climbers" be "available to the climbing public as watchdogs at Chimney Pond." According to their report, "it was easy for Loren Goode to let the complicated details of our party's discussions go without being understood. If he were a climber then he and the rest of Buzz's staff might have had a better understanding of our plight that night."[47]

No evidence exists that Goode's understanding, or lack of it, of technical climbing ultimately influenced the outcome of events. More pertinent was the simple misunderstanding as to the party's plans to return that night. Yet, even if the alarm had been sounded by late Thursday night, given the weather conditions a search party might not have been assembled and able to reach and transport the climbers before Keddy's death on

Friday. To avoid future accidents, however, several persons did recommend that one or more persons trained in technical climbing be employed at Chimney Pond to evaluate equipment, climbing plans, and climbers; organize rescue parties (perhaps using other climbers already in the area); and so forth. The three survivors present at the March hearing, as well as three other persons—at least two of them climbers—made this recommendation. In a somewhat related measure, climber and trainer George Smith asserted that one back-up team was not enough, five should be the minimum, while survivor George indicated that a back-up team was insignificant. The Park currently required each group of climbers to have a back-up team for assistance in case of emergency.[48]

A number of persons, climbers and others, suggested that sign-out sheets and weather conditions be posted at Chimney Pond, or suggested one or the other. Several persons suggested that climbers carry radios. The climbers present had varying views on the subject. Interestingly, of the three survivors present, one thought radios would be helpful, but many climbers would not want to carry them; one thought that radios would intrude on the wilderness, but could himself accept their use; and one did not support the idea of radios being required. Several members of the Park staff favored measures to increase communication, from the use of sign-out sheets to twenty-four hour radio contact between Chimney Pond and Millinocket, to improved communications between BSP and the National Guard in Augusta. Caverly had already taken action on the last measure before the meeting, and staff members had previously discussed some of the other suggestions. Staff members present also stated that existing Rules and Regulations had to be followed, and Caverly stated that probably they also needed additions. Caverly had stated after the tragedy that probably all climbers and winter parties should be required to spend all nights at Chimney Pond. In addition to these suggestions, Major Richardson and Supervisor Caverly asserted that helicopter landing areas should be enlarged and that the Park Director be given the decision on when to proceed with a rescue. Dr. Nolin stated that a doctor should be included in, seemingly, all rescue teams.[49]

Those present at the March hearing, as well as those who had sent reports to the Authority earlier, apparently all appreciated the way the rescue and recovery operations had progressed. The efforts of Park staff, the various rescue teams, the public, and the Army Air National Guard were all commended. In ensuing weeks and months the Authority and Park staff would work to implement some of the recommendations, including obtaining daily weather reports for posting at campgrounds, hiring a ranger with technical climbing skill for stationing at Chimney Pond during both the summer and winter seasons, expanding the list of equipment requirements and recommendations, posting sign-out sheets, and taking various other measures, a number of which would require time to enact.[50]

By the start of the following winter season, Park Winter Rules and Regulations had been revised to include most of the changes. As previously, winter parties had to demonstrate experience and qualification for their chosen activity. In addition, they had to prove possession of more items of equipment and clothing than previously listed in Park regulations, sign in and out for day trips, and spend all nights in camp. They were also warned that they could be charged for any air searches undertaken in their behalf. The Park posted weather conditions at campsites and stationed a ranger trained in technical climbing at Chimney Pond.[51]

While the Park staff and the Authority continued to review and respond to the Keddy tragedy, the second major operation of 1974 occurred. This time the operation centered around an eighty-six year old man, Augustus Aldrich, and lasted eight days. Aldrich hiked into Chimney Pond from Roaring Brook on July 4, 1974. His friend, Rachael Charland, fifty-six years old, accompanied him. They made very slow progress, causing Park rangers concern due to the lateness of the day. Aldrich at one point tried to convince Charland to go on without him, stating that he would sleep along the trail. The two finally made it to Chimney Pond after a ranger met them en route and carried their packs the rest of the way.[52]

The following morning Aldrich informed Charland that he intended to climb to Baxter Peak and appeared upset that she did not want to accompany him. She was tired, fog was setting in, and it was raining. Aldrich said that he was going just the same. Aldrich told Park visitors that he planned to go to Blueberry Knoll, hike from there to Hamlin Ridge and Baxter Peak, then return to camp by way of the Saddle Trail. He did not register before leaving. He left Chimney Pond at 7:30 a.m. No one saw Aldrich again.[53]

Rangers Goode and MacArthur left Chimney Pond at 8:00 a.m. to hike, and radioed the camp to close the Knife Edge due to weather conditions. The two men then proceeded to the North Peaks by way of Caribou Spring, then returned to Caribou Spring. At that time, 10:30, they received a call informing them of Aldrich's plans. The rangers had already closed all trails in the upper Katahdin area due to fog and heavy clouds. They did not want Aldrich to proceed. Goode hiked to the Saddle, while MacArthur returned to the North Peaks to retrieve binoculars the men had inadvertently left there. Neither ranger saw any sign of Aldrich, although Goode did encounter two people heading for the summit and had them return to Chimney Pond. The two hikers had not seen anyone matching Aldrich's description, nor had two men Goode encountered coming from Hamlin Ridge seen Aldrich. There was no real problem at this point, the rangers simply did not want Aldrich to climb in such inclement weather. Goode radioed to Chimney Pond, however, and asked Ranger Dave Caret to walk to Blueberry Knoll to look for Aldrich. The three rangers returned to Chimney Pond without having encountered Aldrich. They were not yet overly concerned, as Aldrich was known to wander off while on a day hike.[54]

Goode and MacArthur left Chimney Pond for supplies and on their return trip learned that Aldrich had still not returned. The two rangers searched around Basin Ponds and Blueberry Knoll while Caret checked the trails down to Basin Ponds. They searched until 11:00 p.m. The search resumed at 6:15 the following morning, with IFG wardens, additional Park staff, and volunteers searching. Caverly requested National Guard helicopter assistance but their arrival was delayed. Meanwhile, a Maine Warden Service plane was called in, and Al Averill of Northeast Helicopter provided transportation for Officer George Leighton of the Brewer Police Department and his search dog to Chimney Pond. The trainer and his dog were able to follow Aldrich's scent for some time that evening, but then, perhaps due to the continuing rain, lost it.[55]

The search for Augustus Aldrich continued through July 12, 1974. Park staff, volunteers, and members of the IFG Warden Service, the Bureau of Forestry, the Department of Conservation, the Piscataquis County Sheriff's Department, the Piscataquis County Civil Defense, the Dirigo Search and Rescue Association, and of the Brewer Police Department participated in the search. Aldrich was not located nor were his remains. A further loss to his family occurred when his nephew, Hollister Kent, died of an apparent heart attack near Dry Pond while hiking to Chimney Pond to aid in the search.[56]

The BSP Mountain Rescue Team continued undergoing training sessions in the mid-1970s, but due to a shortage of incoming younger rangers the group disbanded in 1979. Caverly then contacted various volunteer rescue groups, held lengthy discussions with them, and issued contracts for any additional aid that might be needed in operations requiring technical climbers. Search and rescue missions continued to be one focus of Park operations throughout the 1970s. Financing the operations remained a problem, and the Park struggled to find ways to obtain reimbursements for portions of the funds spent on search and rescue activities. Theories of charging individual Park users for any operations undertaken on their behalf proved unfeasible. Most Authority members and others involved with Park operations looked to the State Legislature for reimbursements (on the grounds that the State and the IFG were responsible for wilderness rescue operations), or argued that the Park needed to budget for such expenses and keep them as low as possible.[57]

While funding search and rescue missions remained problematic, the need for them by no means decreased. In 1975, for example, Park personnel worked to evacuate the body of Glen English, who fell roughly 150 feet to an instant death on Horse Mountain. Park records indicate that English had not done any planning for the summer climb, and that he had had no climbing equipment with him.[58] In early 1980, Katahdin claimed another life. The 1980 case differed from previous Katahdin fatalities in that it resulted directly from a fall, not from exposure or from taking a wrong path or becoming lost. On February 26, 1980, Victor J. Pavidis, Jr., age thirty-two, perished attempting to climb "the False Chimney." The medical examiner in charge of determining cause of death, H. C. Gilman stated that "it is felt that the subject died accidentally after a fall from the ice face, which resulted in sufficient tangle of his climbing ropes and webbing to result in asphyxiation."[59]

Although requirements for winter climbing had increased by 1980, such restrictions could not have prevented accidents such as that suffered by Pavidis. Pavidis and five other men had formed two teams to ascend the False Chimney Trail, an ice climbing route, early on February 19. They planned to climb to the Knife Edge then return to camp via the Dudley or Saddle Trails. Pavidis climbed with his close friend, Paul Grossman. The other team had climbed first, and Pavidis had requested that they remove their pitons as he wanted to make the ascent on his own, without the use of the other team's equipment. All the pitons had thus been removed with the exception of one. At the time of his fall, Pavidis had reached an outcropping of ice. He chose not to go around it, and proceeded to climb using two ice axes. One of the axes he had attached to his belt with safety line, the other he had not. At about 1:00 p.m., Grossman, responding to a noise from above, looked up and saw his friend hanging with his right arm raised, and his arm, head, and neck entangled with rope and webbing. Pavidis had fallen four or five feet.[60]

Grossman climbed as quickly as he could to Pavidis and in the process fell roughly one hundred feet. He landed in a snow field and was not seriously injured. Meanwhile, James Butler, a member of the other team, rappelled down to Pavidis, stabilized his own position, and cut Pavidis free. Butler later reported that before he had cut the webbing and ropes that Pavidis "had made a gurgling noise but was not speaking." Butler lowered Pavidis to a safer location. Butler and Grossman then attempted for roughly thirty minutes to revive Pavidis through mouth to mouth resuscitation and cardio-pulmonary resuscitation (CPR). At 2:00 the men decided to remove Pavidis' body to the base of the day's climb. This took them until dark to accomplish. At 8:15 p.m. the climbers reached Chimney Pond where they reported the accident to Ranger Tom Chase.[61]

After receiving word of the accident late that night, Supervisor Caverly organized an evacuation operation to remove the body. By 5:00 a.m. the following morning, February 20, BSP rangers were en route to Chimney Pond. By 8:30 a.m., Rangers Robert Howes and Barry MacArthur had returned to Chimney Pond from the bottom of South Basin with Pavidis's body. With Ranger Chase, they started toward Roaring Brook with the body. Caverly, Park Naturalist Gerald Merry, intern student Keith Smith, and BSP Maintenance Supervisor Philip McGlauflin met them at Basin Pond and provided assistance. From Roaring Brook, Caverly and Merry transported the body by ambulance sled, lent by the Millinocket Fire Department, to the Golden Road south of the Park boundary from where the body was taken to the Millinocket Hospital.[62]

Pavidis had had previous winter climbing experience. The weather conditions the day of his accident were good for the area at that time of year: temperatures of 18 to 20 degrees Fahrenheit, and winds of roughly 20 to 30 miles per hour. His crew had come to the Park with the necessary equipment. He might have made one or two different choices on February 19, 1980, but his fall was an accident, one it would have been difficult for a climber to anticipate. As Supervisor Caverly's report of the incident and evacuation stated, all fatalities were difficult to deal with, but in terms of Park usage—roughly twenty thousand people climbed Katahdin each year during those years and seven hundred to one thousand of them did so in the winter—the Park's operation "was a good one." Park personnel would continue to educate visitors about the dangers presented by Katahdin and the area, and would "hope for a minimum of occurrences" such as that which had just happened. Staff would "continue to prepare and deal with each the most effective way possible when it arises."[63]

The BSP staff dealt with a different set of circumstances in 1982 which led to a change in day-to-day winter operations. This time the problem involved three different parties in three areas of the Park, and could potentially have involved more people. The Park had continued throughout the 1970s and early 1980s to register winter parties differently than they did summer visitors, in terms of having them meet more stringent criteria in order to engage in certain activities. The Park registered most winter visitors in the early 1980s as either technical climbers or winter campers. During the third week of January 1982, severe winter weather conditions set in, conditions which posed a threat to both categories of Park users.[64]

At 8:00 a.m. on January 18, 1982, Ranger Chris Drew radioed headquarters and informed Director Caverly that on the camp thermometer, which measured as low as -40 degrees Fahrenheit, the mercury "was out of sight." Wind chill charts available reached -120 degrees, but with winds gusting at Chimney Pond at 50 to 90 miles per hour, Caverly and Drew believed the actual wind chill temperature at Chimney Pond to be below -120 degrees. Temperatures would have been even lower on the peak of Katahdin, and basically frigid throughout the Park. A winter party was staying at the camp at Chimney Pond, but staff had advised them not to venture out for climbing. Drew was scheduled to leave the camp, and another ranger to take his place, but weather no longer made such a transfer an option. For the time being no major problem existed as everyone had enough food and fuel to last a number of days. Just the same, with a window having blown out in the rangers camp and a bucket of water freezing in the floor not far from the camp woodstove, as Caverly reported to the Authority, "gentlemen, it was cold!"[65]

A more pressing situation existed elsewhere in the Park, but no one knew exactly where. A local sporting camp owner had transported a group of nine people to the vicinity of Nesowadnehunk Lake two days earlier, and the camp owner notified Caverly of the party and his concerns about them on January 18, soon after Caverly had spoken with Drew. Caverly decided that an immediate search operation was in order, and contacted a local pilot to fly over the area. High winds forced the pilot, Robby Robinson, to turn back. Caverly then contacted Colonel White of the National Guard in Bangor. White agreed to have a helicopter and crew of the 112th Medivac Unit prepared for flight when wind conditions improved. The Medivac personnel arrived in Millinocket at 2:15 with two helicopters. After an extended search, in which Caverly flew with one crew and Ranger MacArthur with the other, the searchers located the missing party at Russell Pond Campground. The helicopter crew which had located the group evacuated three of them, the three persons being severely frostbitten and requiring hospital care. The second helicopter evacuated the remaining four people. Caverly had to order the party onto the helicopters as they had already become hypothermic but did not want to leave. They insisted that they had food and fire to sustain themselves, when in reality they had neither. The individuals had to board without their camping gear, as approaching darkness made it necessary for them to leave immediately.[66]

As the Medivac and Park staff were completing the Russell Pond evacuation, word arrived that an individual at Katahdin Stream Campground had gone hiking and returned with severe frostbite on one foot. Because night had fallen, and no landing field existed at Katahdin Stream, the 112th Unit could not fly to the camp. The Northern Timber Cruisers Snowmobile Club, upon Caverly's request, transported the frostbite victim eight miles to Togue Pond using the East Millinocket Fire Department ambulance sled. One of the National Guard helicopters was able to land at Togue, and transported the victim from there to the Millinocket Community Hospital. Park staff closed BSP for recreational use and evacuated the remaining parties from Chimney Pond and Katahdin Stream the following day. The first group received snowsled transport from Roaring Brook, the second skied out of the Park. The Park reopened for recreational purposes when the weather improved on January 20. Due to the emergency situation, the National Guard did not charge the Park for their assistance.[67]

Following the incident, Caverly and District Rangers Drew and Howes reviewed the situation. They determined that part of the current problem related to changes in staffing and winter camping accommodations. In the 1970s enough rangers had been available for stationing in the Park in winter to oversee activities at the five campgrounds open for the season. Since then, all nine campgrounds in the Park had been opened for winter use, as well as the outlying facilities, while on most winter nights only two rangers stayed in the Park. Roughly half the number of personnel were attempting to oversee operations and winter parties at twice the number of campgrounds, plus they had to check the other locations. Due to the greater risk generally posed in technical climbing, and the greater interest currently shown in the sport, staff energies often centered on climbing parties. All winter parties in BSP could not be checked on every night. The time had come to evaluate the situation and determine which locations should remain open in the future if staffing remained at current levels. In the meantime, the Park initiated a class-day weather rating system similar to that already in use in BSP during the summer season. When temperatures dropped to -30 degrees or -50 with wind chill factors included, or when rain or sleet conditions existed, recreational entrance to the Park would be restricted or halted. Those persons already in the Park would be confined to camp. The winter-use coding system was incorporated in the "'1982 Winter Activities Rules Revision."[68]

In August 1983, Baxter State Park personnel participated in yet another type of search and rescue operation, one which no class-day system could have prevented: they searched for an airplane reported to have crashed within Park boundaries. Theoretically both people and debris needed to be removed from the wilderness, but not all of this proved feasible. This was not the first airplane accident in the Park. In the 1940s a military plane had crashed into Fort Mountain killing six people, and in the 1970s two planes had crashed in BSP. Both of the 1970s incidents, one in 1975 and the other in 1978, involved small planes and neither resulted in fatalities.[69]

At about 9:30 p.m., on Friday, August 5, 1983, Park personnel reported hearing a low flying aircraft near Nesowadnehunk Field. They had no evidence that an aircraft had landed or crashed. The following morning, however, at 6:15 a.m., Park Naturalist Gerald Merry received a telephone call from the Penobscot County Sheriff's Department informing him that a plane had crashed in BSP. The plane, a Canadian airplane carrying Canadian residents, had been headed to Fredericton, New Brunswick. Canadian aircraft had started a search for the plane soon after it crashed. A Soviet-French satellite had reported a downed airplane and pinpointed it to BSP. The Canadian search team might have located the plane before BSP was even notified of the crash, but adverse weather conditions complicated the search.[70]

On Saturday, BSP personnel joined the search effort as did members of the Army Air National Guard from Bangor, the Maine Warden Service, the Piscataquis as well as the Penobscot County Sheriff's Office, the Dirigo Rescue Unit of Orono, the Wilderness Rescue Unit of Waterville, the

Millinocket Fire, Police, and Ambulance Units, the Millinocket Airport, the Maine State Police, and members of the general public. Standing by to aid if necessary were members of the Camden Mountain Rescue Team and the Piscataquis and Aroostook County Civil Defense teams. Over fifty people directly participated in the search and evacuation. At certain points in the operation communication problems developed, problems later addressed at a review of the incident held in Orono and presided over by Allen Martin of the Dirigo Rescue Unit, as well as in correspondence. Some concern was expressed over BSP's not having been informed earlier that an airplane had crashed in the Park, as well as over a few inter-agency or inter-organizational matters. Communication problems, along with continuing adverse weather conditions, hampered both ground and air rescue teams. In addition, during part of the day there was little if any air to ground communication.[71]

Park Ranger Chase flew with Canadian military personnel during air searches Saturday morning and afternoon, while other rangers aided the ground search. The Emergency Locator Transmitter (ELT) attached to the downed four-seater plane identified its general location as the Klondike, a remote and largely inaccessible portion of BSP. Tree cover is dense in the Klondike, and Caverly expressed some surprise that a plane had been able to break through the tree canopy. Ranger Chase helped serve as a guide and was the first person to sight the crash area. This occurred at approximately 3:00 p.m.[72]

Helicopters from the National Guard and the Canadian unit received a report of the sighting and flew to the scene. The airplane had been demolished by the crash, but, amazingly, both the pilot and the two passengers were alive and had sustained no major injuries. They had been thrown from the plane on impact and all three had been unconscious at one point. Newspapers quoted BSP Director Caverly as stating, "considering the plane was totaled, there is no rhyme nor reason as to why they are alive." Pilot Bernie Poulin of the National Guard added that "if it weren't for the ELT, we never would have found them."[73]

Helicopters lowered rescuers to the site and, after receiving first aid, the three young Canadian men were hoisted to the Canadian helicopter and transported to the Millinocket Hospital. The evacuation from BSP was complete by approximately 4:15 p.m. Although problems had arisen during the operation, the crash victims were rescued and safely removed to Millinocket. After the operation, communication failures among and between agencies, as well as some which arose between searchers during the afternoon and morning of the evacuation, were discussed among the agencies and recommendations made. Review meetings were held in September and October. Baxter State Park revised its recently released Standard Operating Procedure to include the lessons learned during the operation. Although U. S. Aviation Underwriters, Incorporated, requested that the wreckage be removed, and although the Park would have liked it removed, BSP denied the request on the grounds that such an operation would pose dangers to anyone involved in the mission, dangers which outweighed the potential benefits. The Park did permit Dirigo Search and Rescue to visit the site on foot and retrieve the plane's radio equipment. At the end of 1983, one of the crash victims wrote to BSP thanking Park personnel for all that they had done, said it was a "'camping trip'" he would never forget, and requested photographs of the crash site, seemingly so that he could never forget.[74]

The following year, Katahdin gave three other men an experience that they would never forget. Sadly, two of their friends died in the course of events. On February 8, 1984, five young men left Chimney Pond to climb the Chimney (a technical climbing route) in what they planned to be a warm-up for four more days of climbing in the area. All five had previous winter climbing experience. Two of the men had visited BSP four years previously and done extensive technical climbing on the mountain. Their experience on the Chimney led them to believe that snow conditions on Katahdin were stable. They returned to camp and three of the men—Ken Levanway, Bob Esser, and Rick Cumm—prepared to make a second climb, one on the Pamola ice cliff, the next day. The others, Steve Hilt and Pete Cochetti, decided to follow the Cathedral Trail to Baxter Peak. The next morning Levanway, Esser, and Cumm started on their planned climb and discovered conditions to be too harsh, in terms of winds and temperatures, to continue, and returned to Chimney Pond by 8:00 a.m. They decided to climb with Hilt and Cochetti. The five men left Chimney Pond together. Fifteen to twenty minutes later an avalanche swept them downhill.[75]

Cochetti later reported that the men had all been wearing face masks and goggles and had not seen the avalanche approaching. Snow knocked Cochetti on his back and carried him downhill. When the avalanche stopped carrying him, Cochetti was completely buried in snow and could neither see nor breathe. He managed to work his arms free and clear an air passage. Eventually he dug himself out. He had been buried under a foot and a half of hard-packed snow.[76]

Cochetti shouted, heard a response, and located Cumm. Cumm yelled repeatedly that someone was buried underneath him. Cochetti removed the snow around Cumm's face to enable him to breathe, then started to dig for the other person. The snow was hard-packed, and after digging frantically for about five minutes Cochetti realized that he had to have a shovel. He looked at his watch. The time was 9:56. Cochetti ran to the ranger's cabin at Chimney Pond, burst in, and informed Ranger Charles Kenny of the emergency. Kenney gave Cochetti a shovel, and Cochetti returned to his comrades.[77]

Kenney radioed Park headquarters then donned his winter gear, grabbed an ice axe and a shovel, and hurried to the scene. Cochetti had managed to locate the three other men and to clear the snow from their heads. Levanway and Hilt appeared to be dead. Cochetti and Kenney focused on digging out these two, and administering CPR to them. Neither Levanway nor Hilt responded to CPR. Cochetti and Kenney then concentrated on freeing Cumm and Esser. The avalanche had set up quickly, making all digging difficult. Cochetti and Kenney managed, however, to free Cumm and Esser from the snow, provide first aid, and place extra clothing around them in an attempt to circumvent hypothermia. It was obvious that Cumm and Esser had suffered serious injuries.[78]

In the meantime, Park staff had radioed and telephoned for assistance. Headquarters requested aid from Al Cooper, owner of the relatively nearby Katahdin Lake Camps, and he and Paul Rumney, BSP Forest Technician, started toward Chimney Pond. Ranger Howes, who had been doing trail work in the area, arrived at the avalanche scene first, where Cochetti and

Kenney were digging out the deceased while awaiting help to evacuate the two injured men. By 11:04 a.m. all the men had been freed. Soon thereafter, enough people had arrived on the scene to transport the two injured men to Chimney Pond where they received medical attention. Chimney Pond radioed Millinocket at 1:25 p.m. that the two injured men were in camp and needed to be flown out of the Park.[79]

Ranger MacArthur, serving as Duty Officer, followed the revised Park guidelines in handling much of the early operation, Caverly being in the field when the avalanche occurred. MacArthur requested aircraft assistance from the National Guard in Bangor and learned that they had been grounded for three days. The Brunswick Naval Station offered to assist, but they estimated that it would take three hours for their helicopter to arrive. The Maine Forest Service likewise offered assistance, and two of their helicopters arrived at the Millinocket Airport just before 1:30 p.m. By this time Director Caverly had reached Millinocket, as had several members of the press. During the course of the day, at least twenty calls would arrive from the press inquiring about the status of the avalanche survivors and the evacuation operation.[80]

Ranger Chase and a medical team flew with the MFS crew to Chimney Pond, after first ascertaining that flight and weather conditions would permit them to do so. Winds were high, but the helicopters arrived at Chimney Pond, picked up Esser and Cumm, and headed back to Millinocket at approximately 2:40 p.m. The Navy helicopter had arrived in Millinocket in the meantime, but returned to Brunswick once the survivors had been successfully evacuated.[81]

The bodies of the deceased still needed to be removed from the scene of the avalanche. MacArthur had acquired permission from the medical examiner in Millinocket to move the bodies. One of the MFS helicopters therefore returned to Chimney Pond with the necessary equipment but, with the other helicopter, had to return to base due to fading daylight. Assisted by several volunteers, Rangers Howes, Kenney, and Drew (who had snowsledded to Chimney Pond) moved the bodies to Chimney Pond. From there they were transported to the road at Abol Bridge, some fifteen miles,

The climber is standing at the northern terminus of the Appalachian Trail atop Katahdin. Persons visiting the Park in winter must comply with special requirements which promote group and personal safety.
(Photo: Edward Dwyer)

by snowsleds, arriving at about 6:30 p.m. In addition to the helicopter crews and various volunteers, the Northern Timber Cruisers, Dirigo Search and Rescue, Katahdin Lake Camps, and the Millinocket Fire Department, Hospital, and Sheriff's Department lent assistance to BSP staff and the operation. In late June, the three survivors were reportedly doing well and expecting complete recoveries.[82]

As with other extended search and rescue operations during the period, the Park and Authority reviewed the operation. The operation had proceeded smoothly and the work of Cochetti and Kenney was deemed responsible for saving the lives of the two injured men. According to Park records, the tragedy probably could not have been anticipated by the climbers. Kevin Slater of the University of Maine, an experienced climber and trainer, went to the Park on February 8 with Dirigo Search and Rescue, flew into Chimney Pond, and examined the avalanche. The following day he conducted further tests with Ranger Kenney. Based on his tests, Slater concluded that the snowpack which the five climbers had ventured on to had been extremely unstable, with a dense slab of snow roughly twenty-six inches thick and about seventy-five feet square above the climbers just waiting to be released—which their climbing onto the snow had done. According to Slater, neither the climbers nor Park rangers could have known the imminence of danger. Slater also reported that several other avalanche potentials existed in the area. In light of this, the Park issued a news release to inform the general public of the danger and restricted climbing routes until conditions improved. Park staff also contacted already registered winter parties and informed them of the situation.[83]

The following year, 1985, two persons died as a result of accidents in Baxter State Park. The first of these, seventy-two year old Stanley Sinclair, died as a result of a snowmobile accident near Nesowadnehunk lake on January 31. The second, thirty-six year old Wilbur Rand, died from a fall on South Brother Mountain on August 4.[84] Park personnel engaged in evacuation operations in both incidents.

Park personnel conducted another evacuation in August 1986. Sixteen year-old Derek Quiet fell off the Knife Edge. Quiet had been part of a thirteen person group hiking Katahdin. The group planned to hike from

Roaring Brook to Chimney Pond, then to Baxter Peak via the Cathedral Trail. From Baxter Peak they planned to cross the Knife Edge and follow the Dudley Trail down to Chimney Pond. The first part of the trip proceeded as planned. Then Quiet and two friends, Lance Johnson, age eighteen, and Wayne Grant, age seventeen, went ahead of the rest of the party. They passed the South Peak of Katahdin and continued along the Knife Edge. They then ran into difficulty managing the terrain, and Johnson and Grant turned back. Quiet left the trail and attempted a descent of the South Basin side of Katahdin. He was progressing downward, negotiating an area through which the Cilley-Barber climbing route passes, when he slipped and fell. He landed in water flowing over the Cilley-Barber climbing route.[85]

Johnson and Grant returned to Baxter Peak in search of help and reached Park Mountain Patrol Ranger Jason Kay. Kay radioed Ranger Esther Hendrickson at Chimney Pond at 1:50 p.m. informing her that a male hiker had fallen off the Knife Edge near South Peak, the exact location unknown. The two young men displayed confusion, and Hendrickson later stated that even after they reached Chimney Pond at 4:00, "they seemed to be in a state of shock." They could provide neither Kay nor Hendrickson with information about just where the accident had occurred. A hiker, Chris Ernst, reported to Hendrickson that he had encountered two boys climbing up the Knife Edge, off the marked trail, and that they had said that their friend had fallen "'all the way to the bottom.'" Hendrickson was able to spot Quiet with binoculars. In the meantime, South District Ranger Howes contacted the Army National Guard In Bangor, the Brunswick Naval Station, Dirigo Search and Rescue, the Wilderness Search and Rescue Team, the Camden Mountain Search and Rescue Team, and the Lincoln Search and Rescue Team. Howes would coordinate much of the field activity in the following days, while Chief Ranger Chris Drew managed much of the operation's overall coordination.[86]

While awaiting the rescue units' arrival, Chris Ernst secured permission to walk as far into the basin as possible, without necessitating any climbing, to try to establish voice contact with Quiet. Ernst did not establish any such contact. When the 112th Medivac Unit of the National Guard arrived with rescue team members, Hendrickson pointed out Quiet's location. More rescue members arrived with a Navy helicopter. One helicopter was able to get close enough to Quiet to ascertain that he was "obviously deceased." By this time, roughly 6:45 p.m., a rescue team had started up the cliffs, and other members and volunteers began to carry a litter into the basin. They soon had to turn back due to darkness. The lead team, however, was able to move Quiet's body out of the water and secure it for the night. The team included Ernst. They returned to camp at 10:00 p.m.[87]

Seven rescue team members commenced the evacuation operation at 5:45 the following morning. Hard rainfall made for dangerous hiking and retrieval conditions. Rescuers managed to reach the body and lower it six hundred feet, closer to the reach of non-technical climbers. Park personnel and members of various teams headed into the basin, but the operation had to be terminated due to worsening weather. Rescuers developed a plan for the next day and built a raft to transport the body across Chimney Pond if need be.[88]

At 6:30 a.m. the next day, August 12, 1986, workers headed into the basin with axes to clear a trail. Footing was poor and conditions in general remained difficult. Workers lowered the body further and attached the litter to a line to ensure that it would hold in place if rescuers lost their footing. By roughly 2:00 p.m. the body, with some difficulty, had been transported to Chimney Pond Camp. The Army National Guard had earlier agreed to transport the body, even though they normally only transported living persons in attempts to preserve life. By this time personnel, volunteers, and rescue team members alike were exhausted from their labors. The Guard's transport of the body saved many hours of hand carrying it to Roaring Brook in wet slippery conditions and during what would become nighttime hours, and possibly saved injuries to an already weary group.[89]

At a review session on the operation held in Bangor on January 14, 1987, Park staff and other persons made several suggestions for improving missions on Katahdin. A few of the issues raised involved the need for additional training for summer search and rescue operations. Several of the issues discussed had risen in recent operations, including the need for continually improving communication between various agencies and among search and rescue teams. Communications overall seem to have been smoother than in years previous, however, especially those during the airplane search incident of 1983. Although not discussed at the review, the Park a few years previously had updated its radio system, switching to sixteen frequency radios which allowed them direct contact with all State agencies as well as with municipal and county departments. This greatly facilitated search and rescue efforts as well as improving communication for law enforcement and other purposes.[90]

Questions did arise, as they had after the 1983 airplane rescue operation, as to the role of Navy personnel in BSP operations, operations which Director Caverly reiterated as involving the National Guard to a greater extent due to their long standing working relationship with BSP. That relationship had led to a deeper understanding of BSP operations, needs, and topography. In addition, the Guard offered a faster response time as they were closer geographically to BSP. In the past, Caverly had stated that most of BSP's backup came from the National Guard unit, and in 1987 he stated that he was most comfortable—for reasons already cited—with continuing to use the 112th for transportation and evacuation on Katahdin. The Navy, however, could provide valuable transportation of rescue personnel and back-up teams to Millinocket. The Navy had done so in a few pervious operations and during the Quiet evacuation. During the Quiet evacuation, however, more rescue workers or back-up personnel had been needed, along with the means to transport them.[91]

Other communication issues raised during the January meeting involved related aspects of field work. Suggestions were made that search and rescue members carry hand-radios, and that team members be cross-trained in rescue and evacuation procedures. The possible need for a small boat for transportation on Chimney Pond, as well as a trail around the pond, for rescue purposes was also mentioned. Certainly terrain, weather, communication, and other factors had made the Quiet evacuation a difficult one. Yet, the very topics addressed at the January meeting indicated how far search and rescue in general had progressed in recent years. Staff and rescue teams had received pertinent training, the issue was more training; trained individuals were available for operations, the issue was securing more backup individuals; communications had improved, the issue was more communication.[92] However, even the most complete search and rescue operational plan could not eliminate the potential for human beings to make unwise choices or have seemingly unpreventable accidents.

One person died and two others were injured in 1990 as a result of a lightning strike on the Knife Edge. This was not the first instance of people being struck by lightning since 1970, nor even the first such incident on the Knife Edge. In 1976, for example, four persons were injured, and another eight affected, by a lightning strike on the Knife Edge during the late summer.[93] The 1990 strike occurred at the same part of the season, on August 27. In 1990 the people involved were primarily Boy Scouts and their troop leaders. The group had almost reached Pamola Peak at the east end of the Knife Edge when a sudden storm erupted. The group tried to reach the peak and the Dudley Trail to descend to Chimney Pond, but lightning struck before they could do so. David Passalacqua, age thirteen, was killed by the strike, and fourteen year-old Fred Ulrich and troop leader Steven Sassi sustained injuries.[94]

One of the scouts reached Ranger Esther Hendrickson at Chimney Pond at 4:45 p.m. and informed her as to what had transpired. District Ranger Bob Howes happened to be at Chimney Pond and Hendrickson informed him of the lightning strike. Within fifteen minutes another five scouts arrived at the camp. While Howes communicated with headquarters, Hendrickson, at 5:25 p.m., headed up the Dudley Trail. The storm was still raging, and would soon worsen with strong winds, driven rain, and continued lightening strikes. Hendrickson intercepted two scout leaders, one scout, and a hiker at Index Rock. The troop leaders had left the deceased scout near Pamola Peak so that they might seek shelter and medical care for the injured. The day hiker was suffering from the cold, and troop leader Sassi as well as scout Ulrich appeared to be in varying stages of shock. Ulrich, the most seriously injured, needed help walking, could not hear, had a third degree burn on his neck, had had fluid running out of one ear, and had burns on his chest and feet. All of Ulrich's clothes had been "blown off" by the strike, and the entire troop had been knocked off their feet. Leader Sadowski had first administered CPR to Ulrich, who had appeared the worst hit, and then to Passalacqua. Sadowski had not been able to revive Passalacqua.[95]

Hendrickson assisted the hikers down the trail and had Ranger Howes send up people with lights as progress proved slow. By 9:00 p.m. the entire party had reached the ranger camp, and Ulrich's condition had improved to the point that Howes and Hendrickson decided to treat him overnight at Chimney Pond rather than risk having his condition deteriorate during a nighttime litter evacuation. The injured could not be airlifted that night as the storm not only made conditions impossible for helicopter flight in the Katahdin area, but also kept the National Guard grounded in Bangor and interfered with air traffic elsewhere in the state. Hendrickson checked on Ulrich's condition throughout the night, and at 5:45 a.m. the 112th National Guard Medivac Unit airlifted Sassi and Ulrich to the Millinocket Community Hospital. After receiving the appropriate legal permission, the Maine Forest Service, assisted by BSP Rangers, removed Passalacqua's remains from Pamola Peak that same day, August 28. The MFS helicopter evacuated the body.[96]

One further accidental death occurred in Baxter State Park before the close of 1994. In October 1991, seventy-six year old Robert Areson stepped onto a wet ledge on the North Slide of the OJI Trail, slipped, and fell two hundred feet to his death. The rock surface was slippery due to rain. His party of five had planned to climb Katahdin, but adverse weather caused them to change their plans and they decided to climb Mount OJI. They were debating whether or not to turn back when the accident occurred. Areson landed in a pool of water, severely broke one leg, and sustained head injuries. Areson's son, a physician, was among the hiking party and tried to revive his father through CPR, but to no avail. Ranger Mac Browning, with several volunteers, arrived first on the scene, followed by Kidney Pond Camp operator Gladys Buzzell and additional volunteers. In the meantime, Ranger Howes, serving as Duty Officer, contacted the National Guard about possible helicopter evacuation. Weather conditions precluded an immediate affirmation by the Guard, and after learning that the subject was deceased the Guard communicated that it would not respond unless a danger existed for other persons. Soon thereafter, weather conditions in the Park worsened, making air transport even more unlikely. The Park secured permission to remove the body, and Ranger Browning, Park staff, and volunteers transported the litter by hand, over extremely slippery ground, to Foster Field. From there Areson's body was transported to a funeral home.[97]

Not all falls or mishaps on Katahdin and nearby mountains resulted in fatalities. In the later 1980s and the early 1990s, as true for earlier years, BSP personnel participated in a number of searches and rescues in the area that concluded with the subjects unharmed or with non-mortal injuries. One example from the end of the twenty-five year period of 1970 through 1994 was that of Rachael Therrien. Therrien left the marked trail when hiking along the Knife Edge in 1993, realized her mistake, tried to find a route to traverse the mountain, and found herself isolated and unable to either ascend or descend the face of Katahdin. After learning of Therrien's plight that night, Park personnel initiated a rescue operation. Staff made several nighttime trips across the hazardous Knife Edge and searched from below, but could not locate the young woman. Therrien had to spend a night trapped on the mountain before Ranger Esther Hendrickson established voice contact with her in the morning. Rescuers reached Therrien in the early afternoon and lowered her off the mountain face. Medivac units from the 112th National Guard in Bangor and from the Brunswick Naval Station had responded to BSP's request for assistance, and at roughly 6:00 p.m. a rescue helicopter delivered Therrien to the Millinocket Hospital. Modern technology and the training of Park staff and rescue teams helped save Therrien's life. She also had the weather in her favor. The Therrien incident happened in the summer, not in the less forgiving months of the winter.[98]

Yet, despite the increased training of Park staff after 1970, despite greater coordination with other agencies and volunteer rescue teams, advances in technology and communications, the adoption of standard operation procedure manuals after Caverly became Director, and revised Rules and Regulations, fatalities in Baxter State Park would continue after 1994. By summer 1995, two additional deaths had occurred, one of natural causes and the other the result of a hiker becoming exhausted and disoriented. The future would no doubt bring other deaths. The numbers of fatalities averted by improvements in BSP search and rescue procedures and programs were not ascertainable during the twenty-five year period, nor would they be in the future. Those aided by Park staff and others during times of distress, danger, or injury were many, and they frequently made their appreciation known through personally delivered words of gratitude and in letters to staff members and the Authority. However, some deaths resulting from natural causes or irrevocable and instantaneously fatal accidents, could not be prevented.

In spite of the knowledge that some fatalities were bound to occur over the course of time, Park staff, the Authority and Advisory, rescue groups, volunteers and others did their best to prevent fatalities from the 1970s through the mid-1990s. Over the years Park staff developed methods of working more efficiently with one another as well as with other agencies. Rules and Regulations underwent revisions in response to actual events and in anticipation of possible occurrences. All search and rescue operations did not proceed as smoothly as possible or end as desired, but from each operation Park staff gleaned some lesson and no sad endings were forgotten.

Near the close of the period studied, BSP Ranger Ralph Heath, who had given his life in 1963 in an attempt to save that of a Park visitor, was honored as a law enforcement officer who had fallen in the line of duty. The Maine Chiefs of Police Association sponsored the Law Enforcement Officers' Memorial Project, which dedicated a monument to the state's fallen officers on Memorial Day 1990. Director Caverly had learned of the project and submitted Heath's name and history during the review process, therein securing a place for the name of his former co-worker and friend on the memorial, and a place in the annals of the state association for Heath's heroism.[99]

Chapter Six

Caribou: Twentieth-Century Dream of a Nineteenth-Century Reality

During the summer of 1977, in an interview with Alice Sproul of the Maine Attorney General's Office, Austin H. Wilkins, former Forestry Commissioner and Baxter State Park Authority member, commented that although few people realized it, caribou were once "as plentiful in Maine as [are] deer today." According to Wilkins, however, "some strange thing" happened, something which remained "a mystery to many biologists," and caribou disappeared from the state. In a 1960s attempt to "rehabilitate the caribou back in Maine," the Fish and Game Department with the approval of Governor Baxter traded fifty pairs of Maine partridges for twenty-four male and female caribou from Newfoundland. The Fish and Game Department placed the imported caribou in pen stocks at Togue Pond, just outside Baxter State Park, then used helicopters to airlift the animals to the plateau of Baxter Peak.[1]

Caribou had disappeared from what would become Baxter State Park, as well as from the rest of Maine, shortly after the turn of the twentieth century. Hunters had previously pursued caribou on Mount Katahdin, as well as moose and other game, and historian John Hakola credited Katahdin as having been "the last stronghold of the caribou in the eastern United States."[2] In 1923, Governor Baxter supported a plan to introduce "reindeer" from Lapland into the Katahdin Park Game Preserve, created in 1921 on what would later be Park land. The 1923 project did not materialize, however, seemingly due to the failure of its initiators to raise necessary funding.[3] Almost two decades later, in 1941, a research team examining the status of game birds and mammals in BSP considered the feasibility of releasing caribou in the Park. Headed by Harold Dyer, then Park Ranger and soon thereafter the first Park Supervisor, the team reported that although further study was needed before a final determination could be made, the region studied did not appear "too promising as caribou range."[4]

During the later 1950s and early 1960s, researchers apparently felt more positive about the chances for reestablishing a caribou population in or around the Park. According to wildlife biologist and project leader Francis Dunn, plans for reintroducing caribou began in 1959 "when an interested resident of Patten, Maine, asked whether or not the Inland Fisheries and Game Department would sponsor the project." The question was formally submitted to the Inland Fisheries and Game Department (IFG) in 1961 for consideration. After an evaluation of possible summer and winter ranges for caribou on and near Katahdin, four calves were airlifted from St. John's, Newfoundland, to St. John, New Brunswick. The caribou were then trucked to the Maine State Game Farm in Gray. Project members anticipated that the four caribou would become part of a proposed plan for an initial release of at least ten calves. Plans changed in 1963.[5]

In 1963 IFG learned that Newfoundland biologists would be willing to furnish adult caribou. Under a bill passed by the Maine State Legislature, IFG traded ruffed grouse for twenty-four adult caribou. The caribou were captured, tranquilized, trucked to Maine, and held in a temporary corral. Later the caribou were once again tranquilized, tagged through their ears and antlers, and had large yellow numbers painted on their backs for aerial monitoring. United States Navy helicopters then carried eighteen of the animals to the Katahdin plateau. Weather interrupted the airlift, and the remaining six caribou were transported the next day by pick-up truck to Roaring Brook and released. Park Supervisor Helon Taylor and BSP staff assisted in the airlift and in other parts of the caribou operation. Except for one caribou fatality during the airlift, the project seemed to be going well.[6]

Yet, the experiment did not progress as anticipated. The caribou released in 1963 disappeared. As Wilkins, Commissioner of the Maine Forest Service at the time of the release, subsequently explained it, although all sorts of stories had circulated about the missing animals, "it's a mystery where they are today and they [the authorities] never found them." Wilkins argued that the caribou could not have returned to Newfoundland because to do so "they'd have [had] to cross a huge lake." According to Wilkins, no one could determine if the animals had died or been killed.[7] In 1965, however, project biologist Dunn reported that although the caribou had dispersed and failed to regroup, sightings of caribou had occurred for over one year after their release. Dunn judged the outcome of the project to be still in doubt. He reportedly stated later that the dispersal of the caribou, combined with illegal killings and a brainworm parasite carried by white-tailed deer, probably accounted for the "failure" of the reintroduction attempt.[8]

In spite of the mystery—as it was so deemed by contemporaries—surrounding the 1963 release, and the mystery still surrounding the earlier disappearance of caribou from Maine, a desire to reestablish caribou in the state surfaced again in the mid-1980s. Although not focused specifically on Baxter State Park, the Park did become a central focus of the newest caribou reintroduction project. The 1980s caribou project combined a hope or dream of recreating a part of Maine's past with a twentieth-century pursuit of wildlife biology and science. As with much else in the 1970s, 1980s, and 1990s concerning BSP, public reaction was mixed and controversy ensued.

According to Park Director Irvin C. Caverly, in mid-1985 Dr. Daniel McNichol, of Bangor, Maine, spoke with a patient of his, Baxter State Park volunteer Carla Grainy, about his interest in following up the 1963 reintroduction attempt. If necessary, he would be willing to serve as a one person committee to generate funding for another attempt at reestablishing caribou in the state. Grainy told Caverly about the conversation, Caverly told Inland Fisheries and Wildlife Commissioner Glen H. Manuel about the discussion, and Manuel told Dr. Ladd Heldenbrand, who had served as veterinarian for the 1963 project, and Commissioner Richard Anderson of the Department of Conservation. Initial discussions about a possible reintroduction of caribou took place in late 1985.[9]

In early 1986, McNichol formally communicated to Caverly his willingness to serve as a fund raiser and suggested the formation of a small group of persons with expertise to study the subject. Caverly communicated with Manuel and the other Authority members about McNichol's proposals. Manuel had members of his department review the subject, and in February 1986 established a Caribou Transplant Committee "for the purpose of investigating the feasibility of another caribou transplant into the State of Maine with Baxter State Park as a possible location point."[10]

Manuel expressed a desire to avoid errors made during the 1963 project. To that end, he planned to have "a great deal of preliminary work done." His Caribou Transplant Committee was composed of several individuals including himself, Caverly, McNichol, Anderson, Heldenbrand and, also from the 1960s project, Francis Dunn. In addition, State Representatives Patrick McGowan and Paul Jacques belonged to the group, as did Chuck Hewett of the Maine Audubon Society, F. Paul Frinsko, and Chet Jordan. Wildlife biologist Frederick B. Hurley and George Matula of Inland Fisheries and Wildlife, the former the department's Director of the Bureau of Resource Management and the latter the department's supervisor of wildlife research, also served on the committee.[11]

The Caribou Transplant Committee (CTC) set to work immediately and expressed a desire to transport caribou to Katahdin by autumn 1986. The Department of Inland Fisheries and Wildlife (IFW) prepared a highly optimistic release for their *News* publication, explaining that "the dream of having woodland caribou returned to their ancestral Maine grounds where they once lived in abundance" might "be realized in a few months." The news release stated that "woodland caribou were believed to be Maine's most abundant large game animal" until the late 1800s. Their numbers had declined thereafter "as the state's northern forests were cut and developed." The release also noted that the "volunteer study group" was seeking funding from interested citizens for project financing. Seemingly "jumping the gun" once more, the IFW release identified Baxter State Park as the 1986 reintroduction site.[12]

In the meantime, Caverly wrote to Colonel Albert White of the Maine Army National Guard in March to determine if the Guard would be willing to participate in an airlift of the caribou. In addition, although no firm decision had been made by CTC about obtaining the animals by mid-April, the committee decided to send three to five individuals, including Manuel, Heldenbrand, and Dunn, to Newfoundland and Quebec to obtain firm cost figures and other specifics.[13] After the trip, Commissioner Manuel wrote to S. Frank Manuel, Deputy Minister of the Department of Cultural,

Recreation, and Youth of St. John's, Newfoundland, expressing the group's appreciation of their reception in Newfoundland. Manuel also confirmed the committee's plans to move forward with the project, and their desire to have two biologists come to Maine from Newfoundland to assess various parts of the Park and some coastal islands for possible caribou stocking.[14]

Commissioner Manuel also informed the Baxter State Park Authority of the project's status. He did so on June 18, 1986. Manuel told the Authority that his party had flown over Avalon, near St. John's, and had seen over five hundred caribou—only a fraction of the herd in the region. According to Manuel, Avalon personnel, having started with two animals in 1950 and having currently over 8,000 caribou, probably knew more about caribou than anyone else in the world.[15] Manuel would later inform the Authority that this particular herd was a non-migratory one. Along with this and other herds, Newfoundland biologists managed a herd of over one million migratory caribou. Newfoundland biologists had extensive experience in transplanting caribou, Manuel asserted, having already made twenty-three successful transplants.[16]

Furthermore, Manuel informed the Authority in June, caribou meat was available in many parts of Canada and would soon be sold in gourmet markets in western Europe, the United States, and probably Japan, at an approximate price of $8.00 per pound. Manuel made no comment on the culinary possibilities of caribou in Maine at the June meeting, although in July he did state that, as indicated by recent press interest, "from a publicity point of view, the State of Maine would have a lot to gain from this sort of a project."[17] In September, Manuel told the Authority that if the project, which he now considered a research one, was successful, "it could set an example and caribou could be reinstated in the northern tier states across the United States."[18] Clearly, in 1986, Manuel considered the caribou project to have potential benefits beyond that of reestablishing a species once native to the state.

Meanwhile, Caverly informed the public of the project at his June 23 and 24 Director's Communication Meetings,[19] and the two Newfoundland biologists previously requested by the CTC, Gene Mercer and Shawn Mahoney, arrived in Fredericton, New Brunswick, on June 23, 1986. The two biologists flew over BSP and made a land visit to the Park that afternoon. The next day they flew over designated coastal islands and met with the CTC.[20] Commissioner Manuel informed the Authority that the biologists had "no doubt that caribou can make it in Maine," that they believed the project should be an experimental one, and that Baxter State Park comprised "the most ideal place to re-stock caribou." Manuel considered the food supply to be adequate for caribou in BSP, and believed that the relative scarcity of deer in the Park, except in the northern part, would seemingly reduce the incidence of *p. tenius* (brainworm) being transmitted to caribou (as with moose) via its winter host snail.[21]

In the early summer of 1986, Manuel approached the Authority for funding for the caribou project. He explained that no money from his department was going toward the project, rather money would come from the private sector. Manuel requested $20,000 from the Authority to start the program. Attorney General James Tierney responded that numerous questions would have to be answered before such a request could be granted. The Advisory and Budget Committees would have to address a series of questions, questions they would need time to evaluate. Manuel then stated that the project's time frame was a rather tight one: October had been set as the month for acquiring caribou. Tierney reiterated his position, stating that for him, personally, it was "hard ... to spend the Park's money without at least going through some process and analysis."[22]

The mystery surrounding the 1963 caribou release surfaced in July. Walter Birt of the Advisory Committee queried Manuel about the caribou disappearance. Manuel replied that a warden serving in the area during the 1960s release had stated that he knew of at least eight caribou having been taken by poachers. In addition, bears had no doubt killed some of the caribou, and others, according to unconfirmed reports, were seen "wandering around." Manuel had earlier indicated that one Newfoundland biologist had determined that 35 percent of caribou calves fall prey to bear predation.[23] Unlike the 1963 project, caribou imported for the new reintroduction would be equipped with radio-collars and monitored as to their location and activities.[24] For a caribou transplant, Newfoundland biologists also currently tried to select an island off the coast of a region or in a large lake. Caribou were strong swimmers and could manage seven to eight miles without difficulty. Such islands could also be cleared of predators before transplanted caribou arrived. As of July, no such Maine island had been selected.[25]

Advisory member and grandnephew of Percival Baxter, Rupert White, and Jerry Bley of the Natural Resource Council of Maine, contributed other facets to consider before the Authority might take action on the proposal. Bley expressed a concern over a possible increase in Park publicity and usage resulting from the project. White stated that in addition to considering the project to be a "function of the Department of Inland Fisheries and Wildlife," one with which the Authority should cooperate but not initiate or fund, he believed firmly that Governor Baxter would not have approved the reintroduction. White said that one of the few things he had discussed at some length with Baxter was the earlier caribou project. According to White, "after the failure of the first project, he [Baxter] was very definite that there should never be another attempt." Furthermore, regarding the use of radio-collars, Baxter had stated that they absolutely should not be used. "He did not like to see collars on any animals," White asserted.[26]

Eric Baxter, great-grandnephew of Percival Baxter, agreed that the Authority should not spend money on what he considered a State project, and Attorney General Tierney concluded that as some "straight-out opposition" to funding the project existed, along with several questions about it, the proposal should be submitted to an appropriate subcommittee for consideration and a presentation made to the Authority. He would not vote on the matter that day.[27] So ended the July meeting.

Work progressed over the summer for the Caribou Transplant Committee, however, and by mid-September the project had secured $50,000 in funding from former Maine Governor Horace Hildreth. Because of their tax-exempt status, the Maine Audubon Society handled the money. Plans had tightened by autumn, with the caribou capture date planned for between October 4 and October 25. Helicopters would be used in the capture, transporting the animals—a tentative twenty-six cows and four bulls—to a holding facility. Merrill Transport had agreed to truck CTC's animals to Maine.[28] Arrangements for veterinary care of the animals were underway, including obtaining radio-collars. Chemicals might be added to the collars to kill any predators that might bite the caribou.[29] Mark McCollough of IFW had visited the University of Maine in Orono and discussed the feasibility of establishing a caribou nursery at UM. McCollough reported favorably on his discussions with Don Salinger, Director of the Maine Ungulate Research Facility, and with Ray B. Owen, Chair of the Wildlife Department.[30]

Although things seemed to be running fairly smoothly for the committee, a special CTC meeting held in September highlighted several major difficulties or questions the group had encountered. The CTC had been in contact with Mrs. Andrew Wyeth who donated her island, several buildings, and $15,000 to the project, so that the caribou might be held there. Unknown to Park Director Caverly, and perhaps to other CTC members as well, the committee had also been in contact with the Island Institute, an organization with some eight to ten years experience working with wildlife on a number of islands. The Island Institute expected to run the program while the caribou remained on Wyeth's island, Allen Island, in the Penobscot Bay. The Institute's Director, Phil Conklin, attended the September meeting and discussed the expertise the Institute could contribute to the project. He also noted, when a query arose, that he had been the person to introduce Commissioner Manuel to Wyeth.[31]

Questions arose at the September CTC meeting as to who should actually control the caribou project. The Audubon Society felt that the Island Institute was in the best position for doing so while the herd was stationed on the island. In contrast, several CTC members expressed concern over the Island Institute running the program. Representatives Jacques and McGowan agreed that eventually the project would need funding from the State Legislature, a Legislature whose members had probably never heard of the Island Institute. Jacques also asserted that IFW had statutory empowerment over the management of all wildlife and fishery resources in Maine, therefore the Commissioner's permission was required for bringing caribou into the state and the Commissioner was responsible for the management of the caribou. McGowan pointed out that although the

Island Institute might provide valuable services to the caribou project, the animals would eventually be transferred to the mainland. The Island Institute, McGowan argued, should not be given control of the project. Concerns over Wyeth withdrawing her financial support were also expressed at the meeting, and McGowan stated that if she was adamant about who ran the project then the animals should instead be placed at the University of Maine. Francis Dunn stated that the CTC had been organized to coordinate the entire project. He had been in charge of the first attempt to reintroduce caribou, and felt that Mark McCollough should be hired by the committee to fill a similar position for the second project. Concerns also arose at the meeting over the role of the Maine Audubon Society in the project, concerns which the Society shared.[32]

In addition to questions about the future management of the project, some persons expressed doubts about how the committee currently functioned. Representative McGowan argued that many people were watching the project and the committee needed to operate as a structured group, making decisions through formal motions and approving the motions through a majority vote. Representative Jacques shared this belief, as did a few other members. Dr. Heldenbrand suggested that the committee become a corporation.[33]

Those present at the September Caribou Transplant Committee meeting ultimately voted to incorporate CTC and have it function through the use of motions and popular votes. They also decided to ask Dr. McNichol to resign due to his busy schedule, to add Conklin as well as either Owen or Spalinger from UM to the committee, to place the caribou at UM, to hire McCollough as project leader through a cooperative arrangement with UM, and to transfer caribou funds to the university. Some details remained to be determined at following meetings.[34]

Commissioner Manuel gave the Baxter State Park Authority a brief update on some CTC activities when the Authority met two days later. Manuel informed those present that the University of Maine and the Wildlife Department in Orono and Bangor would be part of the caribou research project.[35] Manuel seemed pleased with the project thus far. However, Manuel was not pleased with communications with the press. At the next CTC meeting, October 8, Manuel stated that he was concerned about the media attention the project had received. Manuel voiced specific displeasure about a reporter from the *Maine Times* having telephoned him after the September CTC meeting and asking questions "as though someone had told her exactly what happened at the meeting." At Manuel's suggestion, the committee voted that all media contact would be handled by Manuel himself or by Paul Fournier, the media person for IFW.[36] This new policy may have contributed to media problems CTC later experienced.

In the meantime, a sympathetic treatment of the project appeared in the *Morning Sentinel* the following week, expressing the optimism typical of Maine newspapers and journals in the following months, and, it seems, revealing a generally successful relationship with the press during the project's early phases. The article also reflected the committee's decision to continue considering Allen Island as a holding place for caribou once they had been medicated and gone through a period of quarantine at UM. The article identified neither the island nor its owner.[37]

The *Morning Sentinel* did not mention either Wyeth's or Owen's appointment to the committee, nor discuss continued concerns over the safety of the caribou from poachers should they be placed on Allen Island. Nor did the article mention the contract drawn up with Wyeth which gave CTC full authority over the animals during their time on the island. Under the terms of the contract, the Island Institute would act as Wyeth's agent and cooperate with CTC on matters pertaining to caribou management. The committee would later sign a similar agreement with the University of Maine Wildlife Department. The UM contract outlined the obligations of each party, named CTC as the party with the overall responsibility for the project, and stated that the university would work with the committee's project leader "on all aspects of the project."[38]

One of the earliest negative reactions to the project during the autumn of 1986 came from the Maine Chapter of the Wildlife Society, Incorporated. The Maine Chapter expressed their concerns over CTC's plan to release caribou in Maine without first making long-term studies of the possible effects of reintroducing the animals. The Maine Chapter recommended that fully funded three-year studies of caribou diseases, parasites, habitats, and animal relationships be made before any caribou were released. The Maine Chapter also made a number of recommendations as to how the animals should be monitored and protected if released and expressed the organization's doubt that sufficient private donations could be raised to fund a well-researched and well-managed reintroduction. The Maine Chapter did not want IFW to have to absorb the cost of the caribou project: measures needed to be taken to ensure that the already financially stressed IFW was not further burdened. The society offered to provide the necessary "competent peer review from outside the presently involved participants." Commissioner Manuel responded to the group's report the following month, assuring the group that CTC planned to proceed in an entirely professional and scientific manner. The committee welcomed the opinions of the Maine Chapter of the Wildlife Society, and would send them a copy of a forthcoming management plan for their review.[39]

Plans advanced during the fall for capturing, transporting and tending the caribou. Plans included the travel of several committee members, at their own expense, to Newfoundland to assist in preparing the animals for transport and to otherwise help as needed. The possibility of acquiring aid from the State General Fund for research, and possibly to cover McCollough's salary, was raised, and in general the committee worked on becoming a more efficient organization.[40]

On November 4, 1986, the Secretary of the State of Maine accepted the Articles of Incorporation of CTC, now the Caribou Transplant Corporation, for filing. The Corporation elected an eleven person Board of Directors which included Park Director Caverly and had Authority member Manuel as its first president. Those elected would serve until the first annual meeting of the Board of Directors the following March.[41]

Plans for the Newfoundland trip progressed during the late autumn. The Premier of Newfoundland and Labrador, A. Brian Peckford, wrote to Maine Governor Joseph E. Brennan in mid-November expressing his pleasure in his province's participation in the project. Peckford wrote that "this international conservation measure is an example of the ongoing cooperation between our two countries, and an extension of the historic ties between Newfoundland and the New England states." Governor Brennan responded in kind, writing to Peckford: "I agree with your assessment that it will be extremely rewarding to see this project come to fruition, and I am delighted to have been a part of this fine program of international cooperation."[42]

The Director of the United States Department of the Interior, Frank Dunkle, and the Secretary of the United States Navy, John Lehman, also became involved in the project after the Caribou Transplant Corporation requested services from the Navy. The CTC identified some of its goals more specifically in its request than it had in other correspondence, stating that it wished "to restore a self-sustaining herd of woodland caribou to the State of Maine" by establishing nursery herds at the University of Maine in Orono. "Young caribou produced from the nursery herd" would "then be released annually in northern Maine to initiate a wild herd." The CTC anticipated making initial releases in summer 1988 or 1989. The Corporation designated the termination date of the project as five or six years from the current date, at which time the entire captive herd would be released. Television networks ABC, CBS, NBC, and CBC would cover the capture and transport of the animals, as would *Newsweek*, various newspapers, and local radio and television stations "from Newfoundland to Alberta, and Maine to Pennsylvania."[43]

The corporation requested that the Navy secure the truck and cattle trailer being provided by the Merrill Transport Company at their Portland terminal, and transport the truck and trailer to Argentia, Newfoundland. The corporation furthermore requested that McCollough, Heldenbrand, and Fournier be allowed to accompany the vehicles and caribou on the return trip. Before leaving Canada, the caribou would have to undergo quarantine tests for brucellosis and tuberculosis, the readings of which would require a stop at the Canadian Veterinary Laboratory in Sackville, New Brunswick. By late November 1986, both the Director of the Department of the Interior and the Secretary of the Navy had at least tentatively agreed to aid the project.[44]

Caribou Transplant Corporation members did return from their December 1986 trip with what they hoped would prove the beginnings of a Maine woodland caribou herd. The trip, however, did not go as smoothly as anticipated. Wind driven rain delayed the roundup from December 4 to December 5. The rain turned into snow in following days and, eventually, into blizzard conditions. Snow made it difficult to spot the caribou from helicopters and to shoot them with tranquilizer darts as planned, as well as to transport the sedated animals. The CTC had hoped to return to Maine with thirty caribou. But, after capturing twenty-seven caribou (eight others died during the capture), the Newfoundland Wildlife Division decided that enough caribou had been obtained for the Maine project. New herds had been successfully started elsewhere with only ten or fifteen caribou, and an estimated 80 percent of the twenty-four females just captured were pregnant. Leaving with fewer caribou than hoped was therefore not a major problem. However, once en route, a 1,200 mile trip, weather continued to cause problems. The animals spent ten hours being trucked a relatively short distance to the ferry which would transport them ninety-five miles to the Canadian mainland. The United States Government had requested a fee larger than the corporation was willing to pay for Naval transport to Maine, hence the caribou traveled the ocean via ferry.[45]

Weather continued to plague the caribou and the project. Eighty mile per hour winds—and waves reportedly forty to sixty feet high—damaged the transport ferry, necessitated the use of pumps, made the crew seasick, and caused at least one caribou to become ill. The *Bangor Daily News* quoted Ray Owen as stating that the trip had turned into one of "'survival-of-the-fittest.'" In Sackville, the animals were inoculated, tested for brucellosis—which none tested positive for—and awaited results of their tuberculosis tests. Project leaders found themselves immersed in red-tape in Sackville. Poor weather continued, and two caribou died on their three-day truck ride to Orono, a distance of just over three hundred miles. Two other caribou, does, died soon after reaching the university. A stag died a few weeks later. Project leaders attributed the deaths to the stress of capture and relocation. Drugs used in the process had also caused problems.[46]

Glen Manuel updated the Baxter State Park Authority on the trip at the Authority's December 11, 1986, meeting. He said that the project had been one of his greatest experiences since becoming Commissioner, a sentiment he had also expressed the previous day in a comment to a reporter. "'It's a great way to cap off my career,'" Manuel had stated. Manuel retired as Commissioner of Inland Fisheries and Wildlife the following month, so the caribou project was indeed an important final activity of his tenure. In terms of other shifts in personnel, the December BSP Authority meeting saw the appointment of Francis Dunn to the BSP Advisory Committee. Dunn's work on both caribou projects no doubt helped him secure his appointment, but the Authority also recognized his knowledge in general of the Park's wildlife populations, especially those of moose and ruffed grouse.[47]

Other shifts, both in personnel and in sentiments about the project, would occur in following months. Yet, for the most part, the outlook of those persons associated with the Park remained positive in late 1986 and early 1987. For example, Director Caverly noted in the "1986 Baxter State Park Annual Report" that "we all see it [the project] as a worthwhile and challenging venture and are optimistic that we will see caribou in Maine from this point on." Caverly also thanked Manuel in the report for having provided him the privilege of working on the project.[48]

The CTC as a whole entered the new year with high anticipations of success. The organization repeatedly informed the public that although scientists had learned quite a bit about caribou, their life cycles, their diseases, and about monitoring their activities in the last twenty years, the project was still an experiment. A successful reintroduction could not be guaranteed, but CTC clearly hoped it would occur.[49]

Project leader McCollough published the first "Caribou Project Newsletter" in January, briefly outlining events up to early 1987. The newsletter stated that "the future of the project lies with the calves that will be born in May." These caribou would be the first animals released, possibly in the summer of 1988. The CTC ultimately aimed to establish a self-sustaining herd of one hundred caribou in northern Maine. According to the newsletter, research would begin during summer 1987 "to investigate the suitability of several potential release sites including Baxter Park." Just how many sites the corporation would actually research became a sensitive issue that year, especially after CTC finally rejected Allen Island as a potential short term holding site. The January newsletter noted that the research involved in raising and releasing radio-tagged caribou would "provide exciting information on the adaptability of caribou to habitats in Maine and perhaps provide clues as to why caribou disappeared from Maine and across the southern portion of their range at the turn of the century."[50] Although persons involved in the project had made numerous suggestions as to how to explain the earlier disappearance of caribou—most notably logging and other forms of habitat destruction, brainworm, and predation by black bears and over-zealous hunters—the ultimate answer or answers still remained elusive for McCollough, as it did for many people interested in the project.

McCollough researched and identified potential release sites in late 1986 and early 1987. He recorded his findings, and stated the current goals of the project, in his "Management and Research Plan for the Reintroduction of Woodland Caribou to Maine." McCollough identified ten years as the time frame for establishing the one hundred member herd, and pointed out that establishing caribou as a game species in Maine was not a project objective. Field research would begin that summer, and the two best sites for a release identified by December 1988. The CTC now anticipated 1989 as the first release year.[51] McCollough communicated his preliminary findings in February 1987, identifying Katahdin and the Katahdin Ironworks Region as potentially the best of the release options, largely due to their lower densities of deer. Two weeks later, McCollough named the Katahdin and the Bigelow Mountain regions as holding the greatest caribou potential.[52]

As Baxter State Park became increasingly associated with the caribou project, especially as a, if not *the*, future release site, questions increasingly arose among Park personnel and Advisory members about the desirability of identifying the Park as the release site, and over how much thought was actually being paid alternate locations. The Advisory met a few times during spring 1987 to discuss the project and its possible effects on the Park. Owen, currently an Advisory member, attended Advisory meetings in March and April to address any questions Park personnel or Advisory members might have. McCollough likewise answered questions and gave a presentation. Some people expressed concern that spring about how the project might affect the Park's natural resources, about the possibility of an ongoing helicopter presence in the Park for tending the caribou, about the possibility that the Park might be expected to contribute financially to the project, and about potential problems with day use—particularly if the Park experienced an influx of people coming to observe the caribou. Such an influx might negatively affect both the Park and the caribou.[53]

Questions voiced in early 1987 concerned not so much the desire to have caribou in the Park, but rather on the impact of human activities in the Park and, to some extent, the impact of caribou—a species not recently native to the region—on plant life. The question of Governor Baxter's wishes also resurfaced. At the same time, tensions started to develop over concerns that the Park was not being kept informed of certain aspects of the project, and, eventually, that the Park was receiving undue negative attention in the press. Some persons, as Caverly reported to CTC in May, essentially felt that the Corporation had been negligent from the outset, having "gone ahead and made their plans to take the animals to the Park before they even brought them to Maine." The Corporation had been negligent, some people believed, "in not going to the Authority beforehand and submitting a proposal rather than ... bring[ing] the animals in and try[ing] to force a Baxter release." The Advisory did, after much discussion, recommend that the Corporation receive permission to proceed with its feasibility study as far as it concerned parasite research.[54] Yet, funding the study remained an issue for the Corporation. The CTC had had to issue a news release "appealing to Maine citizens to assist in restoring" caribou to the state. Maine citizens had responded to fund raising efforts, but financial security remained an evasive goal.[55]

The CTC presented a proposal for reintroducing caribou to Maine, written by McCollough, to BSP in late spring 1987. The proposal essentially restated objectives and techniques discussed in earlier meetings, newsletters, and press releases. The proposal also stated that based on computer survival and fecundity studies "augmenting either the first release or the nursery herd with 10 additional female calves had the greatest probability of success." Furthermore, annual releases would only be successful if "survival rates were high in the wild," and "survival of caribou in Maine may not be at the biological maximum." The CTC therefore recommended that "additional female calves or yearlings be brought to augment the first release," and that "adult male caribou from populations other than the Avalon Peninsula should be added to the nursery herd to increase the genetic diversity of offspring." This need to secure additional caribou, and caribou from a new source, had not been widely publicized before the proposal was submitted, and might be seen as an indication of future project and publicity difficulties. The CTC also proposed to make greater efforts "to promote social cohesiveness in the released herd" by keeping them together in a temporary holding enclosure for at least one month with minimal human disturbance. According to the proposal, the caribou released in 1963 probably had "had little opportunity for social bonding," as they had not been so enclosed at the release site.[56]

The 1987 proposal listed several other attempts to reintroduce caribou and reindeer into various regions in the United States, Canada, and elsewhere. In terms of establishing a wild herd, all attempts made during the 1940s through the 1970s to reintroduce the animals into regions with "high" deer density had failed. Where deer populations were low, some attempts proved successful, other had mixed results. The latest attempts had been made in the early 1980s.[57] In several ways the outlook of the project seemed more dismal than early promoters had anticipated.

Several issues remained problematic in the summer of 1987. The Authority wanted the general public to know that they had not determined the future role of BSP in the caribou project. Although Caverly and others associated with the Park had considered possible release sites in the Park should the Authority ultimately approve a release, such approval had not yet been granted and they repeatedly informed the public that such was the case. Therefore, such CTC public statements as "members of the Corporation have been working with the Baxter Park staff and the Park Advisory Committee this winter to begin plans for the reintroduction of caribou into Baxter State Park," did not rest well with some Park people. The "Caribou Project Newsletter" which carried this statement did note that a proposal for field studies had yet to be approved, but did not clearly state that the reintroduction itself had yet to be approved.[58]

The CTC's April 1987 newsletter statement quoted above did not greatly differ from the promotional brochure produced the previous summer which stated that after being held on an island, "animals will be moved to a suitable northern Maine site such as Baxter State Park."[59] An article published by McCollough in the spring and summer 1987 issue of *Maine Fish and Wildlife* likewise suggested that other sites in northern Maine might be under consideration, but mentioned only Baxter State Park by name and stated that "hand-reared" caribou might be placed in BSP within months as part of an initial study. Another article published in mid-1987 written by Herbert B. Adams, whom CTC later elected "Official Caribou Project Historian," identified BSP as the release site.[60] Although the Authority and Advisory realized that the articles had been written some time before publication, they still felt that the Park continued to receive an undue amount of attention in the media about the caribou project. Director Caverly told the Authority that he had raised this issue with the Corporation and its project leader several times, and stated that if the Authority thought that his role as Director conflicted with his membership in the Corporation, he would resign from the Corporation. The Authority agreed, however, that Caverly should continue his CTC membership.[61]

The Authority did not display animosity toward the project during this time period. However, without the project's original organizer on the Authority the project commanded less attention, and perhaps less support, than it might have otherwise. McCollough himself seems to have realized that the change in the Authority represented more than a change of people. McCollough demonstrated his frustration over the situation when he wrote to Caverly on June 1, 1987, that:

> it is unfortunate that the timing of the caribou transfer and the formation of a new Authority have occurred as they did. This is just one of many instances where I as project leader have had to try to explain to people what should have been explained to them a year ago. In light of what has transpired thus far I can appreciate

> the resentment that some people involved with the Park may feel about inferences that the Park be *THE* release site.[62]

McCollough went on to state that he had a responsibility to do everything he could to insure the success of the project and that the Park did have "many of the attributes of a good release site," but that its suitability "should be documented through facts gathered by the pre-release studies of (an)other site(s)."[63]

McCollough acknowledged to Caverly the concern some people felt about BSP's role, or perceived role, in the project, but did not state that he would try to clarify the issues publicly or otherwise deal with them in a direct manner. Similarly, McCollough had clearly stated in May that final approval for a release would only be determined by the Authority after feasibility studies had been made and presented in a final report, but he stated this in a letter to Corporation Members and Advisors, not in the CTC newsletter.[64] Both parties may have had good–and not mutually exclusive–intentions in 1987, but communications were less than ideal. Many CTC members were busy selling posters, making a video, holding public caribou viewings, caring for the newly transplanted caribou and, after May, tending the first Maine-born calves (sixteen were born in 1987, eleven survived infancy).[65] The Park and Authority, meanwhile, had a number of issues unrelated to caribou to address.

Communications slowly improved, at least for a short time. The July CTC newsletter indicated that "Baxter Park has been incorrectly mentioned as the only release site under consideration," but did not identify the number or location of other potential sites. McCollough also pointed out the site identification problem to CTC members in a July letter, and stated that "some members of the Baxter State Park Advisory and Authority ... have a valid complaint against us for continually using the Park's name when discussing release sites." McCollough later stated, in the December 1987 issue of the CTC newsletter, that "it has not been decided just where Maine's new caribou herd will be established," and informed readers that five potential release sites were under consideration, "including public lands in the Deboullie, Bigelow, and Mount Katahdin regions." The newsletter did not mention the Park specifically, nor did a short piece written by McCollough for the 1987-1988 *Maine Fish and Wildlife* winter edition.[66] From the viewpoint of several persons associated with the Park, the omission from the writings of the Park as being *the* release site must have been an accomplishment, although one several months in the making.

Still, when McCollough reported on the evaluation of potential sites in early 1988, he informed the Authority that BSP and the Bigelow area seemed the most favorable release sites. The CTC proposed a new series of studies on habitat suitability, parasites or deer density, and "social issues" which would involve local landowners, but these proposed studies did not differ greatly from those proposed a year earlier. McCollough did state that the Corporation wished to work closely with the Advisory and Authority on any pertinent issues. In response to concerns about caribou parasites or diseases spreading to other wildlife, McCollough assured those attending the meetings that, to the best of current day wildlife and veterinary science, the caribou were being closely monitored and treated, and were disease and parasite free. They would not be released unless they continued to test disease and parasite free. Other concerns about dangers to rare plants were similarly addressed that spring, with CTC representatives stating that the caribou would not further endanger any such species. McCollough and McGowan also stated that the public would be instructed to view the caribou at the University of Maine, not at release sites.[67]

Caribou Transplant Corporation workers reiterated these factors in following months, and determined BSP the superior release site due to its lower deer density, greater availability of lichens and winter food, and its greater area of protected lands, most of it closed to hunting. In November 1988, CTC submitted a revised proposal for reintroducing caribou into the Park, an earlier draft having been presented in February. The proposal, much of it more a feasibility study than an actual plan, outlined CTC's proposal to release caribou from 1989 through 1993.[68]

The November plan called for transporting caribou to BSP before peak use periods each year; for limited publicity concerning releases with set media guidelines; for attempts to minimize public viewings at the release site in favor of viewings at UM; for keeping Park personnel and IFW Wardens informed on caribou locations and on any problems that might occur; and for working with the Park Naturalist and IFW education specialists to educate the public on the project and inform them of the need to leave the caribou undisturbed by humans. A full-time wildlife biologist would be hired to monitor the radio-collared caribou and document their progress as well as record any births and deaths in the wild. The caribou would be radio-tracked from the ground (via motor vehicles, snowmobiles, or "on foot"), from aircraft, and through an automatic tracking system. Any research engaged in would be presented according to the Park's already established guidelines for scientific studies. Research and release plans would be submitted every year for approval.[69]

As far as the objectives of the project were concerned, the November proposal stated that the first objective was to determine if woodland caribou could be reintroduced in Maine and other areas of their former range and "to restore an important part of Maine's wildlife heritage for the enjoyment of future generations of Maine citizens." Two generations of Mainers had been "denied the opportunity to observe these majestic animals." "Like Governor Baxter," the proposal concluded, "the Maine Caribou Transplant Corporation intends to leave a gift for future generations of Maine citizens and trusts that the reintroduction of caribou will contribute greatly to the experience of visiting Baxter Park."[70]

At a BSP Authority meeting held in November, McCollough stated that the only reason the Newfoundland people had agreed to the project was to determine if caribou could be successfully reintroduced into a former range currently occupied by white tailed deer. The CTC had already made an agreement with IFW that all animals be radio-collared so that an animal that died could be immediately located and the cause of death determined. McCollough reiterated that caribou would be tested for disease before release. Other states and provinces, McCollough stated, were watching Maine to see how the project worked out before embarking on similar reintroduction attempts. Although some questions still remained, in general those persons attending the meeting felt comfortable with the reintroduction proposal with the stipulations that the Park and CTC agree on specific sites and release dates; that the Park, IFW, and CTC jointly decide on information to be disseminated regarding the release of caribou; and that the project be reviewed annually to determine any negative environmental, ecological, social, or economic impacts on BSP.[71]

With the initial release approved, Park employees concerned themselves with how best to handle the project in terms of publicity and resource protection in following months. In January 1989, McCollough wrote to the Park requesting permission for the distribution of pamphlets about the project. After discussion between Director Caverly, Park Naturalist Jean Hoekwater, and Assistant Attorney General Paul Stern, BSP determined that a pamphlet on caribou similar to handouts already distributed on other species could be distributed to Park visitors. This would give visitors information on the natural history of caribou and perhaps answer a few basic questions about the caribou project. The pamphlet, however, could not contain any suggestions that the Park was promoting the project or in any way asking for money. A separate pamphlet or brochure giving more details about CTC and referring the reader to the Maine reintroduction project could be given out upon request at Park Headquarters and one copy given to each BSP ranger for information.[72]

In February, Caverly resigned from the Maine Caribou Transplant Corporation. Corporation members expressed regret over Caverly's action, but had no choice but accept his resignation. Caverly's name continued to appear on the Corporation's letterhead for some time, however, as well as on CTC's list of Directors submitted with its April 1989 articles of incorporation.[73] Perhaps the Corporation felt that Caverly's name was a political or economic asset, or the continued use of his name may have been a clerical oversight.

Plans proceeded for the transport of caribou to the Park. The Authority voted to allow two members of the press as well as Paul Fournier to cover the caribou arrival. This would allow coverage by the media without gathering a large number of people at the holding site. Other members of the media as well as the general public would be encouraged to view the loading of the caribou in Orono and attend a press conference there. The transfer took place in early April, and apparently caused resentment among certain sectors of the press. One member of the Associated Press received permission to photograph the event in the Park, but as a letter from the organization indicated, not everyone felt satisfied with the arrangement. The Associated Press recommended that in the future the Maine Press Association be used as a vehicle for setting up press pools.[74]

The Corporation transferred fourteen caribou. However, problems arose with tranquilizing the animals and with the "straight jackets" used to confine them during transport, and two yearling females died. Two other yearling females escaped from the three-acre holding pen erected in the Park, but stayed in the area. The Corporation eventually released the remaining ten caribou, but only after some confusion as to the release date. The CTC informed the Park that they were moving the release back a few days, then moved the release forward and freed the caribou on May 3, 1989, only one day after notifying the Park of their intentions. Once again media coverage was limited. Director Caverly emphasized the need to restrict access to the release site to protect the road from damage and to protect the location of the site. The caribou gathered around the drop-off point in pairs and as singles in the following days. One caribou lost its collar soon after release but, after being tranquilized, had the collar replaced. Control points for monitoring caribou by the triangulation method had not yet been established, but with recently hired CTC employee Bruce Connery monitoring the animals, everything seemed to be going well when the Authority met in mid-May.[75]

After the first week of freedom, a few of the animals embarked on their own adventures. As of May 18, 1989, eleven of the caribou were still within five to six miles of the release site. By early June, one caribou had crossed the Canadian border. The other caribou remained in either the Park or the near vicinity. The caribou had separated, but project participants hoped they would regroup later in the year. One animal had already been lost—it had fallen over a cliff.[76]

Other disappointments followed. By early July two caribou had definitely developed brainworm, and CTC suspected a third of carrying the parasite. Seven caribou lingered in the Park. By October, the number of released caribou still alive had diminished to five. Two or three of them were in BSP. The nursery herd in Orono had also sustained numerous losses, and by early fall CTC considered returning to Newfoundland to acquire more

Following their transfer to Baxter State Park, caribou were acclimated in a fenced area and then released as shown here.
(Photo: *Bangor Daily News*)

caribou. The group proposed to bring the new caribou to the Park after testing them for parasites in Orono during the winter. The CTC also considered the possibility of releasing the remaining twenty-six caribou from the Orono nursery into BSP during the upcoming winter. Commissioner William Vail, who had replaced Manuel on the Authority, argued that the losses sustained in Orono were due to animal husbandry and not directly related to the scientific experiment being conducted in the Park: determining if caribou could be reestablished in Maine. Vail and the CTC representatives present at the October 1989 Authority meeting stated that the ultimate goal of releasing or establishing eighty to one hundred caribou in the Park had not changed, and they hoped that the problem in Orono—much of it thought due to bacteria carried by both humans and animals–would not discourage the Authority.[77]

By December 1989, all but one of the twelve released caribou had died. The Corporation identified predation by bears and coyotes as the key factor, but at least five of the animals had developed brainworm. A possibility existed that a second animal, one that had lost its collar, was still alive ... somewhere. The CTC had decided to abandon the nursery herd concept and instead to release captured caribou annually, an approach being used in an Idaho caribou reintroduction project. Authorities in Newfoundland had agreed to provide up to twenty-five caribou per year for the Maine project for 1990, 1991, and 1992, as well as possibly providing a few animals before the close of 1989. In spite of the difficulties experienced thus far, in November CTC requested permission to release the promised caribou in BSP. They also wanted to release caribou from the nursery herd prior to May 15, 1990. McCollough stated in writing that, "although we will be changing our reintroduction strategy radically, there will be little departure from our original plans for release activities in Baxter State Park."[78]

The CTC did wish to change the release site, however, to Rum Mountain on the south flank of Katahdin from the existing site at McCarty Field, located roughly twelve miles from the mountain. McCollough stated that white-tailed deer used McCarty Field during the winter, thus exposing caribou to the brainworm parasite. McCollough also stated that the freed caribou had stayed at the lower elevation throughout the summer and "only one caribou was able to find Katahdin." The CTC requested that a release enclosure be erected at the proposed Rum Mountain site, one which would remain there throughout the course of the project. The enclosure at McCarty Field had been dismantled after the earlier release, and was intended to be removed after every release. Assembling and disassembling such structures required too much time and labor, according to McCollough. The CTC was currently amending its memorandum of agreement with IFW to incorporate the proposed changes to the project.[79]

Baxter State Park Director Caverly had several reservations about the newest CTC proposals. In a letter to the Authority, Caverly questioned the very concept of Katahdin as the ultimate objective of the project. He also voiced reservations about constructing a holding pen and establishing a release site on Rum Mountain, an area close to the Park's high use area and a site which would require reopening a 1968 logging road which the Park wanted nature to reclaim. The CTC had earlier indicated that if caribou did not stay in the Park, the Corporation would release in the areas to which the caribou had migrated. The CTC proposals also seemed to imply that the Authority should make a four-year commitment to the project, which the Authority had previously declined to do. Approving the building of a stationary pen would imply a tacit approval of a four-year program. Caverly believed that if caribou were to be released in BSP, release in the Klondike region would have the least long-term impact on the Park. A possibility existed for airlifting the animals into the Klondike.[80]

The Maine Caribou Transplant learned of Caverly's opinion that the Klondike might prove the least disruptive place to release caribou in the Park and prepared a new proposal naming the Klondike as the release site. This time, CTC proposed to transfer the caribou from Orono to the sand pit south of Togue Pond, then transfer them by helicopter to the Klondike. The CTC planned to release the caribou in April and hoped to have calves born in the wild in May and June. The Corporation did not anticipate building a holding pen at the release site. The radio-collared caribou, both the adults and some of the calves, would be tracked by airplane, and McCollough and Connery planned to conduct studies from a base at nearby Camp Phoenix. They hoped that calves born in the vicinity of the Klondike would later return to have their own calves, and that the higher elevation of the region would segregate the caribou from deer and the brainworm parasite. The CTC requested that the Authority vote on the proposal at their January meeting and indicated that they would work with BSP staff to determine how best to approach media coverage of the release.[81]

Caverly expressed his concerns about the dangers associated with flying aircraft into and around Katahdin, as well as about other matters, in a letter to the Authority and Advisory in late December. When the Authority met in January 1990 they voted to deny CTC's request.[82] A discussion of the caribou project had been scheduled for the morning Advisory meeting, but McCollough did not make it to the meeting in time to represent the Corporation. Caverly, upon request, gave the Advisory an update on the project. Members of the Advisory raised several concerns about CTC and the caribou project in general, asserting that communications had been poor, that an anticipated report by CTC had not reached the Advisory that day as expected, that project members had not addressed problems involving the media satisfactorily, and that rules established earlier had not been followed. The Advisory thereby voted to recommend that:

> any further cooperation by Baxter State Park with the Caribou Project be clearly based on the understanding that the Caribou Project will, in the future, honor its commitments to follow specific procedures agreed upon by Baxter State Park and the Caribou Project, including following any directions issued by the Park Director, and to provide data sufficient to allow an informed evaluation of the progress of the project.[83]

McCollough reviewed the current CTC proposal at the Authority meeting that day. Advisory Member Benjamin Townsend reported the Advisory's recommendation and the reasons for it. Discussions regarding the Advisory members' concerns and other aspects of the project followed Townsend's report. Attorney General James Tierney asked McCollough if he thought the next group of caribou released would have any chance for survival in light of the fate of the first ones freed. McCollough responded that caribou could not be reestablished overnight and that twelve caribou released in the wild is not a viable number (without explaining why so few had then been released the first time), and reiterated the goal of releasing one hundred caribou. He had been to Newfoundland twice during the past year to work with biologists there, and, he asserted, those scientists were unanimous in the opinion that the Maine project still had a good chance of succeeding, although adopting the proposed changes would be of great benefit.[84]

McCollough also stated that if the results of the previous summer were repeated for the next release, "everyone would recognize that caribou couldn't survive in Maine." The CTC had already learned several things, including the fact that predation was a more serious problem than anticipated. This and other problems would be addressed through various measures. Any caribou taken from Newfoundland that year would be transported by horse trailers with individual compartments. If captured in March the animals would be taken to Orono for several weeks, if captured in November they would be taken directly to BSP for release. The Corporation proposed to airlift the caribou to the Klondike with Huey helicopters, funds for which had already been raised, and Maine Helicopter in Augusta had been contacted regarding the plan.[85]

In spite of the project leader's optimism about the potential for success in the future, other concerns surfaced during the January Authority meeting. One area of concern involved the health of the animals released. McCollough gave specific figures on the caribou whose autopsies had revealed the presence of brainworm: of the ten that had died, five had had brainworm. They had acquired the parasite in Orono. This announcement caused a bit of an upset. As Tierney expressed it, "'you mean you put animals in the Park that you knew had the brainworm?'" When McCollough answered that CTC had not known that the animals had the parasite at the time of their release, Authority and Advisory members stated that they had been informed previous to the release that the animals were parasite free. McCollough said that they had been free of a different parasite. This apparently did not reassure those persons attending the meeting. A question then arose as to the wisdom of placing the Orono nursery caribou with the new caribou from Newfoundland. McCollough assured the Authority that caribou could not directly pass the parasite from one to another. Unfortunately, the drug the CTC had treated the caribou in Orono with had proved unable to eradicate the brainworm parasite. This knowledge might well aid other wildlife biologists and constitute one benefit of the caribou study. Furthermore, Commissioner Vail assured those in attendance, white-tailed deer posed more of a problem to caribou in Maine than caribou presented to "anything else." Essentially, however, the medical situation did little to increase Park confidence about approving another release.[86]

The changes in the caribou project itself also disturbed several persons at the meeting, compounded by the continuing concern over communications between BSP and CTC. Advisory member John Loyd stated that what had concerned the Advisory most that morning was that the release currently being proposed was totally different than the one discussed eighteen months previously, and it involved the most pristine area of the Park. Although at one point some aspects of communication had improved temporarily, Park staff had frequently had to obtain their information from the CTC newsletter or from the popular media. Caverly stated that he felt that the only time CTC communicated with him "was when they wanted something." McCollough responded that Bruce Connery was the project contact in the Park, and as he understood it Connery had talked frequently with Park personnel, especially with Chris Drew. The CTC would, however, try to improve communications in the future.[87]

McCollough continued to answer questions, and Vail asserted that McCollough was not in control of the project, although he took "the heat" for its problems. After further discussion, Vail stated that the overall project had been "unnecessarily complicated" because of the caribou being released in the Park. Vail then said, "'I never imagined I would be making this motion, but I'm going to make the motion that we deny the request for the benefit of the Project as well as the continued operation of BSP—for our mutual benefit." Chair Tierney seconded the motion. McCollough asked if the CTC could later propose another operation, and Vail answered that his intentions were that CTC could do so. However, the day's discussion had revealed "a general unhappiness with the project" and concerns about its future. The project was a difficult one at best, and having it subject to the type of review it had just experienced only complicated matters. The reality of such reviews would probably not diminish in the future. Vail was, however, willing to work with CTC in finding a new location for the operation. After Vail made his opinions clear, Tierney asked John Cashwell, Director of the Maine Forest Service, if the vote to deny CTC's proposal was unanimous. Cashwell replied that it was.[88]

As indicated by a lengthy letter from McCollough to Jane Thomas, Advisory Committee Chair, both sides felt that the other had been negligent in their actions. McCollough argued that he had not known that the Advisory would be discussing the project that day; that he and the CTC had tried their best to live up to the Park and Authority's expectations as they understood them; that the process of reviewing the project had not been made clear to project members; that CTC had tried to maintain good communications with Park personnel and the Authority and Advisory; that project members had done their best to work with the Park Director on how best to handle media coverage; and, furthermore, that "intense media interest" was beyond CTC's control. McCollough outlined steps that might be taken with future research projects to avoid the problems encountered between the Park and CTC.[89]

McCollough also informed the Advisory Chair that although, "in your words we may 'no longer be having a party in your house,' we may be neighbors and like to come over for a visit now and then." Commissioner Vail and IFW had suggested that potential release sites immediately adjacent to the Park be considered, and McCollough and CTC were doing just that. According to McCollough, several landowners had already offered their property for use in the project. McCollough ended by stating that just as Governor Baxter's dream of leaving a Park to the citizens of Maine had become a reality, he hoped Baxter's dream of establishing a caribou herd in the vicinity of Mount Katahdin would also become a reality.[90] Baxter may or may not have revised his wish to have caribou reintroduced to the region; McCollough had not revised his. McCollough's communications with the popular press made his continuing determination quite evident and, one might posit, at least partially negated—as had publicity garnered from earlier CTC activities—his statement about "intense media interest" being beyond CTC's control.

Newspapers throughout the state reported on the January Authority decision, and cited many of the reasons for the decision. More than one paper quoted Caverly as telling McCollough that "'the only time communications have been good was when you wanted something from us,'"[91] and some quoted Tierney as stating that "without any exhaustive analysis ... you're simply asking us to put more animals into the wild."[92] In response, McCollough told a *Bangor Daily News* reporter that "there were expectations of me and the Caribou Project that weren't clearly enumerated." McCollough also stated that although it sounded ironic, "both ourselves and the Park Authority feel pleased with the decision." McCollough had considered tending his resignation after the meeting of the Authority, but a telephone call from Commissioner Vail had put things back into perspective for him. Richard Anderson, in a similar vein, stated he still believed that "the people of Maine feel a moral commitment to restore lost animal populations to the state."[93]

Although the *Maine Sunday Telegram* announced in late January that "Caribou Backers Vow to Continue," and project members made similar statements in following months, not all Maine citizens agreed with Anderson's assessment and assertion of their "moral commitment" to restore caribou to Maine. As the *Telegram* admitted, the deaths of caribou during the earlier capture and relocation phase of the project, the deaths of at least twelve of the caribou released in Baxter State Park, and the deaths of roughly one-third of the animals born in Orono through stillbirths, umbilical cord infections, and disease, had given rise to criticism of the project.[94] Although CTC leaders expressed high hopes for the project now that red tape had been radically decreased by removing the proposed releases from the BSP Authority and Advisory process, Maine newspapers carried numerous stories, editorials, and letters expressing concerns, and at times anger, about the project—the most common theme being the needless deaths resulting from bringing caribou to a place where "Mother Nature" no longer provided the proper environment for their survival.[95] John S. Kamanski of the Maine

Animal Coalition summarized his feelings, and perhaps those of many people in a letter to the *Portland Sunday*:

> The Maine Caribou Project should be terminated. The nursery herd has failed. The direct release is too risky to native deer and moose herds. There is little reason to traumatize another seventy-five caribou in a venture ... which has a low probability of success.[96]

Critical reviews of the caribou project continued to appear in the spring, although perhaps with less frequency, and animal rights advocates attempted to gain increased publicity and to end the project. A guest writer for the *Bangor Daily News,* Jerry Ellwell, asserted in April that CTC had made "questionable, if not false statements" in their efforts to regain public support, financial and otherwise. Entitled "Caribou Are Dying While Project Leaders Are in Over Their Heads," the article criticized project leaders for keeping the caribou in close proximity to "meningeal-worm-carrying-deer" and failing to thoroughly clear and decontaminate the Orono nursery area before bringing the caribou in; for continuing to appear "more interested in the fund-raising aspects [of the project] than in the biological and scientific; for repeatedly arguing that the state's "growing moose population is proof the caribou can also thrive and multiply while co-existing with deer," asserting—in opposition to the truth—that the parasite is just as deadly to moose as to caribou; and for a variety of other shortcomings. In spite of "public disapproval and warnings from those who have conducted in-depth studies," Elwell wrote, "the caribou experiment leaders stubbornly vow to continue the program, and let the caribou fall where they may."[97]

According to Ellwell, however, new problems might soon confront CTC leaders. State humane groups were busy circulating newsletters condemning the project, and rumor had it that "some of the national humane organizations are training their big guns Maine-ward." In addition, veterinary and biology specialists had stated that caribou from some sections of Canada carried a parasite, "one different from the brain-worm parasite and deadly to domestic livestock." In order to make it across the border, caribou from now on would have to "show squeaky clean bills of health."[98]

Park involvement with the caribou project had declined rapidly after the January 1990 Authority meeting, before much of the most vitriolic criticism of the project appeared in the press. Advisory Chair Thomas wrote a letter to McCollough in late January, in response to his earlier one, a letter which conveyed her good wishes for the caribou project, yet one which McCollough may have found rather curt. Thomas stated that she understood that McCollough was unhappy about the way the January Authority and Advisory meetings had gone. However, as she stated it, "we at Baxter Park have a different reality from yours. That's just the way the world works."[99]

McCollough amended the way he worked, in relation to the Park, and submitted a "Cooperative Research Agreement" to Director Caverly in March 1990. The purpose of the agreement was to "establish a common understanding" between the Park and CTC "for the purpose of the monitoring and study of caribou in Baxter State Park." The agreement was more specific than earlier proposals by CTC and included an agreement by CTC to submit a weekly written progress report to Director Caverly and Naturalist Jean Hoekwater beginning May 1, 1990. The weekly reports would include the number and approximate location of any caribou in the Park, and report any caribou mortalities in the Park. The CTC also agreed to forward advance copies of all press releases to Caverly; to send BSP copies of all project papers and articles which resulted from study in the Park; to submit annual summaries of the project by the November meetings; to allow Park personnel to accompany project personnel when circumstances permitted; and to meet in December 1990 to review proposed terms for research for 1991. In return, the Park agreed to provide five season passes for project vehicles; to grant project workers permission, with due notification and in accordance with existing BSP rules, "to use Park roads and trails for the purpose of monitoring caribou in the Park and retrieving dead caribou;" and to notify CTC of Authority and Advisory meetings when caribou research was a scheduled item of discussion. Caverly and McCollough signed the agreement in early April.[100] While McCollough debated whether to release caribou on the east or the west side of the Park, Caverly circulated the agreement, and reported on his meeting with McCollough. When Caverly next addressed the Advisory, member

Townsend commented—seemingly reflecting the thoughts of at least a few other people—that he supported the new agreement and "could only wish that the Caribou Project people could have been as diligent about this last year."[101]

The CTC released twenty woodland caribou on private land along the East Branch of the Penobscot River on April 23, 1990. The animals were radio-collared and appeared healthy at the time of release. They ranged in age from one through ten years, and McCollough estimated that ten or twelve of the females were pregnant. In a press release dated April 24, 1990, CTC reiterated its commitment to the project and advised its board members "to prepare themselves for serious fund-raising efforts in the months ahead."[102] The following day the Corporation wrote to BSP Director Caverly, Bob Wright of Great Northern Paper Company, and Warden Dave Sewall, informing them of CTC's plan to send them weekly updates; urging them to let CTC know if the updates were not received on time; and asking them to report any caribou sightings to McCollough or Connery. McCollough also stated that CTC would inform the media each month of the project's status, and asked the recipients of the letter to contact Richard Anderson, publicity chairman for CTC, about any questions concerning the press. McCollough thanked the letter's recipients for their aid that spring, and stated that he looked forward to working with them in the future.[103]

The Maine Caribou Transplant Corporation's future was not very lengthy after April, however. Although three of the twenty caribou released from the Orono nursery died by early July, other caribou seemed to be displaying normal wild caribou behavior and project leaders communicated their hopes for successful re-establishment for the species. If all went well, twenty-five more caribou would be brought from Newfoundland that year and released. At the same time, the Bangor-based Citizens for Animal Protection group worked to block the proposed fall or winter release and continued to try to have the project terminated. McCollough acknowledged that animal rights groups had been successful in getting their position advertised in the media, but expressed doubts as to the number of people such groups actually represented. The Maine Animal Coalition and the Humane Society of the United States had unsuccessfully petitioned the governments in Newfoundland and Maine to halt the project in the spring, and McCollough seemed little concerned about such efforts in the summer of 1990.[104]

In late January 1990, after the Authority's decision not to have caribou released in the Klondike or elsewhere that year, Commissioner Vail had stated—as other persons had stated all along—that he viewed the project as an experiment. If 1990 proved a repeat of 1989, and 80 percent of the caribou died, one obvious question would have to be asked: "Is it worth going any further?"[105] In late fall 1990, CTC members decided that it was not.

Mortality rates had once again proved high. This time all the caribou died. Project biologists decided that CTC would have to release at least one hundred caribou at a time to offset losses due to predation and other factors, and to ensure that the animals would remain in close enough proximity to one another for reproduction. Expenses had also proved substantial during 1990.[106]

In December, Park Naturalist Hoekwater reported CTC's decision to discontinue the caribou project. No caribou were located in the Park at that time, although one had entered the Klondike for a brief period after the spring release and two others had wandered elsewhere for a time. Communications, according to Hoekwater, had been "very good," that year, and the study had yielded information which would be of value to other persons.[107]

The Baxter State Park Authority and Advisory avoided much negative publicity by distancing themselves from the project when they did. The Park even received a few letters commending the Authority for its decision.[108] Yet, although negative publicity for the Park was one concern, it was not primary to the January 1990 decision. Disappointment with the project in general, particularly with what they considered a failure on the part of the project leaders to keep them up to date about day-to-day events such as the movements and deaths of caribou after their release, accounted for much of the dissatisfaction of Park staff, Advisory members, and some Authority members during the various phases of the project. Authority member and Inland Fisheries and Wildlife Commissioner Glen Manuel was instrumental in establishing the project in 1986 and his successor William Vail ultimately moved to reject the 1989-1990 CTC proposal to release additional caribou in the Park for, as he explained it, the good of both the project and the Park. Director Caverly served on the CTC Board early in the project, and like many other people had sincerely hoped that Maine would see a successful reintroduction of caribou. However, when the project seemed to go against the best interests of the Park, Caverly withdrew his support for a 1990 caribou release in BSP. Some people associated with the Park had opposed Park involvement with the project before the 1989 caribou release.

The 1980s attempt to reestablish caribou in Maine was a complicated one, one inciting both sentimental appeal and concerns over the well-being of the animals involved. The publicity generated by the caribou project captured the imaginations of young and old alike. Television, newspaper, and other media coverage brought the project to the attention of the general public more than any other wildlife study or scientific research project in Baxter State Park during 1970-1994. The project at various junctures secured national and international acclaim and scrutiny. As a cooperative wildlife endeavor, the project successfully engaged both Canadian and American governmental agencies.

Park Naturalist Jean Hoekwater wrote at the end of the project that the project had "contributed a great deal of knowledge to the science and art of large mammal reintroduction," and that as an experiment the project "will continue to offer insight to scientists in the upcoming era of wildlife restoration work."[109] Disappointing and even tragic in terms of animal fatalities, the project was still a learning experience—positive or negative—both for those persons directly involved and for the citizens of Maine and other areas. The 1980s caribou transplant project was not the first attempt to return caribou to the state, and it may well prove not to be the last. Future attempts to reintroduce caribou or other creatures to Baxter State Park, however, will no doubt face greater regimentation. Research criteria enacted after 1994 reflected some of the lessons learned from the caribou experiment. Entry to Percival Baxter's Sanctuary would not be denied, but it would be more closely regulated.

The outlet area at Lower Togue Pond (Photo: Edward Dwyer)

Sentinel Mountain, located in the southwest corner of the Park, accords the hiker outstanding panoramas such as this outlook toward Squaws Bosom and Doubletop Mountains. (Photo: Edward Dwyer)

Upper and Lower South Branch Ponds viewed from North Traveler Mountain. Katahdin dominates the distant horizon. (Photo: Ken Wadness)

Katahdin's summit cairn. The Knife Edge Trail follows the ridge line to the right, crosses South Peak and turns northeast, leading to Chimney Peak and Pamola. (Photo: Edward Dwyer)

Pamola ice cliffs as seen from the South Basin. (Photo: Jean Hoekwater)

Spring afternoon at Daicey Pond. (Photo: Edward Dwyer)

This area of Grand Lake Matagamon is known as First Lake. Matagamon Gate, the north entrance to Baxter State Park, is located on the shore of First Lake. (Photo: Edward Dwyer)

Fall sunrise, Daicey Pond. (Photo: Edward Dwyer)

Chapter Seven

Snowmobiles, Forbidden and Permitted: Continuing Challenge to Park Access and Use

Of any specific and controversial issue or user activity in Baxter State Park between Governor Baxter's death in 1969 and the mid-1990s, that of snowmobiles was without question the most persistent. The extent of snowmobile use in BSP, or whether there should be any such use, remained an issue of contention throughout the period studied. Proponents and opponents of allowing snowmobiles into BSP, in either specifically designated areas or throughout the Park, proved extremely vocal in defending their positions. They presented their opinions in the media, in letters to the Park and the Baxter State Park Authority, and in person at Authority and Advisory meetings, as well as at specially held public hearings. Although relative silence prevailed during various periods, those periods were often limited to a few months, and sometimes less.

Privately owned snowmobiles had, to some extent, been driven into BSP since the machines became popular in the early 1960s. In 1965, however, Governor Baxter wrote to Park Supervisor Helon Taylor condemning recreational snowmobiling in the Park. Baxter wrote his letter following publication in the *Bangor Daily News* of an article regarding the subject. Baxter had earlier reimbursed Taylor for his purchase of a snowmobile for staff use. By the mid-1960s, however, Baxter had decided that snowmobile use beyond that necessary for staff business should be banned. Baxter wrote to Taylor in 1965 that:

> These skis should be prohibited in the Park except for one for you as Supervisor to use in case of emergencies. I feel strongly about this for they will frighten away the wild animals ... I would be much pleased if the Authority would add this to the list of what is forbidden in their regulations ... [1]

Although Baxter's statement seems to leave little room for interpretation, such room did indeed evolve. Most of it resulted from subsequent events during Baxter's life and from Baxter's apparent struggle to keep the Park open to the public while still protecting the Park's natural resources, be they flora, fauna, or other.

The various interpretations of Baxter's actions and statements can be seen in a series of 1977 interviews by Alice Sproul of the Attorney General's Office. Helon Taylor, in his interview, asserted that Baxter had been convinced by someone from Portland that he should say that he did not want snowmobiles in the Park. The Authority then convinced Baxter that "'snowmobiles didn't do any harm—as far as access roads, the perimeter roads'" were concerned. According to Taylor, Baxter had not objected to snowmobiles in the Park as long as they did not disturb wildlife or cause other harm. Then, after Baxter's death, "'somebody else put in an oar and changed all that.'"[2]

Other Baxter contemporaries offered different interpretations. For example, Arthur Rogers, former Warden Supervisor with the Fish and Game Department, stated in 1977 that Baxter truly did fear adverse effects on wildlife due to public snowmobile use. According to Rogers, Baxter had feared that snowsled use would end the Park's ability to offer sanctuary to deer and moose in winter. Snowmobiles might frighten the animals, and possibly lead to poaching and other problems.[3] Roland Cobb, former Fish and Game Commissioner, posited another theory. Cobb stated that he believed Baxter would have been somewhere between the extremists and the moderates on various environmental issues. Cobb thought that Baxter would not have wanted either motorcycles or snowmobiles in BSP, however, Cobb continued, these were not major issues when he knew Baxter.[4] A few other persons interviewed by the Attorney General's office in 1977 were likewise vague on Baxter's views of the snowmobile issue.[5] The passage of time between Baxter's death and the interviews may explain some of discrepancy and vagueness, yet the variance in opinions is certainly not unique to the snowmobile issue. Here, as elsewhere, the Authority and Park administrators have had to base their decisions on how they thought Baxter would have acted were he still alive when a particular situation or issue arose, relying primarily upon Baxter's correspondence and the Deeds of Trust.

From the 1960s through the 1990s, the Authority consistently voted to allow BSP staff to use snowmobiles for winter duties. Decisions regarding public use, however, changed over the twenty-five years examined. In the late 1960s, during Baxter's lifetime, the Authority voted to allow the use of privately owned snowmobiles, but only in specific locations. Snowmobile riders were allowed to travel on the State maintained Perimeter Road, on roads constructed for salvage operations on Rum Mountain after the 1963 blowdown, on the trail to Chimney Pond Campground, and on the road between Avalanche Field and Katahdin Lake. Following some controversy, the Authority voted to limit snowmobile access further, allowing snowsleds only on roads maintained for regular summer traffic by the State Highway Department.[6]

The popularity of snowsleds during the late 1960s had increased concerns over their use in BSP, resulting in the changes to the 1970 Rules and Regulations. In 1971, Acting Park Supervisor Irvin Caverly wrote that 1966 through 1970 were years of "heavy usage by snowsledders." This continued, according to Caverly, "until it was necessary for the Authority to establish authorized snowsled trails and restrict ... snowsledders to these trails."[7] In an alternate or supplementary viewpoint, Forest Commissioner and BSPA Chair Austin Wilkins stated in 1970 that public pressure by persons "who felt that the Governor's wishes were being violated under the 'forever wild' concept" had had a large role in the 1969 rule revision.[8]

According to Wilkins, in reference to the earlier restriction on snowmobiles, the Governor "in his declining years [had] still understood what was meant by this snowmobile regulation." Acting on the belief that Baxter had known that further restrictions on snowmobiles might be necessary but "did not intend to prohibit people from using the Park in the wintertime," the Authority passed the snowmobile portion of the 1970 Rules and Regulations. The 1970 Rule restricted snowmobiles, but did not totally exclude them as some people had wished. As Wilkins pointed out, snowmobilers could still use the Perimeter Road to "enjoy the beauty of the Park in the wintertime ... as those who are privileged to use the Park in the summertime" might do. Based upon the evidence available thus far, the Authority did not believe that there were imminent dangers of "disturbing wildlife, causing a litter problem, destruction of any forest growth," or of a noise factor of significant "consequence." Wilkins stated that the Maine Snowmobile Law provided for the use of snowmobiles on "public roads which are unplowed and unused during the winter months," and "the Perimeter Road is a so-called public road." Wilkins considered the new regulation to be on trial in early 1970, and noted that it remained to be seen "how strongly enforcement can be carried out," a concern which remained an active one into the 1990s.[9]

John L. Baxter, Sr., later wrote that after the Authority had made its decision to allow snowmobiles on the Perimeter Road, he, his son Hartley, and Dan Drummond had met with the Authority in order to protest the decision. Baxter believed that his recently deceased uncle would not have wanted snowmobiles allowed in the Park except for official use. Attorney General James S. Erwin informed Baxter that he had voted against allowing snowmobiles Park access, but that the other Authority members had outvoted him. John Baxter also wrote that he had protested that Wilkins had, besides voting to allow the machines on the Perimeter Road, given permission for snowmobilers to use one or more side roads. Wilkins later admitted that he should not have done so, and permission to use the side roads was withdrawn.[10]

After instituting the new snowmobile rules, a question arose in February 1970 over the use of snowmobiles on Matagamon Lake. Park Supervisor Harry N. Kearney had recently given permission for public snowmobile use on the lake, something which Authority member Ronald T. Speers of the Maine Department of Inland Fisheries and Game thought violated existing rules. Park Rules and Regulations, Speers argued, superseded all other rules, and snowmobiles could thereby only be used on the Perimeter Road. However, Attorney General Erwin likened the use of snowmobiles on Matagamon to regulations allowing the use of airplanes and outboard motors there, and noted that there could be a question as to whether great ponds, of which Matagamon was one, were legally part of BSP. The Authority agreed to "watch the situation" that year.[11]

In 1971, the Authority decided to open the road from Avalanche Field to Katahdin Lake to snowmobiling once more. Although not pleasing to everyone, this extension remained in effect for some years. Later revisions allowed the public to ride snowmobiles along a stretch of land roughly one-half mile long along the west side of the East Branch of the Penobscot River in T6R8, and along a one mile stretch in T6R9 along the river. These additions were made in 1972 and 1973 to provide access from Millinocket and other locations to the Grand Lakes Matagamon.[12]

Sixty-five miles of wilderness existed in BSP for the snowmobilers' winter pleasure at the close of 1971. As Acting Supervisor Caverly wrote in December of that year, many people came to the Park to enjoy winter activities, including mountain climbing, skiing, snowshoeing, "and that new sport that makes people of all ages pray for snow—snowmobiling."[13] Yet the proportion of winter visitors who came to BSP for snowmobiling seems to have been decreasing. Caverly, as Park Supervisor, wrote in early 1973 that surprising changes had occurred during the past two years. Whereas before that time "snowsleds were the largest percent of winter use," during the previous two years the situation had changed and "we are now getting people from all over the country who come to Baxter State Park to enjoy wilderness cross-country skiing [and] winter camping in everything from snow igloos to lean-tos." A large number of people continued to use their snowsleds in BSP, however, seemingly with little conflict with other winter Park users. The Authority's actions seemed, by early 1973, to be having at least some of their desired effect, that of decreasing overall recreational snowmobiling. In early 1974, Caverly reported once again that snowsled use had dropped noticeably and had, so far that season, been minimal "with only one or two days of any activity to speak of." Snowsled use remained much the same the following year.[14]

Although indications existed that snowmobile use had decreased, the latest regulations remained unsatisfactory to many people. In the mid-1970s, the issue became a major controversy. In part, the controversy erupted over Governor Baxter's 1965 letter to Helon Taylor stating that he wished to see private snowmobiles banned from the Park, as the letter came once more to the public's attention. Prior to late 1975, except for requests or discussions involving trail maintenance and possible short trail extensions, commentary about snowmobile use was relatively minimal and non-confrontal. At the January 1976 meeting of the Authority, after the Authority's vote that the existing rule on snowmobiles remain unchanged for the 1976 Rules and Regulations, Attorney General Joseph E. Brennan indicated that his office was working on an opinion regarding the legality of snowmobile use in BSP which might affect the final adaptation of the snowmobile rule.[15] Assistant Attorney General Sarah Redfield attended the Authority meeting that day, and subsequently provided much of the research and writing that would influence the ultimate vote of the Authority on the snowmobile issue.

At a public meeting held in Orono that evening to discuss rule revisions, the snowmobile rule generated its share of conversation. Some people expressed a desire to see snowmobile access increased, some wished to have their use restricted to control and enforcement purposes. One person stated that even though Baxter's 1965 letter had indicated that only the Park Supervisor should be allowed to use a snowsled, such restrictions did not take into account changes in Park operations since 1965.[16] The lines of contention were already being drawn, and already the difficulties in determining the best course of action were becoming apparent. In addition, the Park and Authority already had their hands full with a spruce budworm problem and a controversial blowdown restoration project, and the snowmobile issue would only increase public and administrative pressures in following months.

Ongoing research by the Attorney General's office continued to delay a decision on snowmobile regulations. In April 1976, the Authority voted to exclude sections pertaining to snowmobiles from the 1976 Rules and Regulations. The remaining sections would be printed as amended.[17]

The following month Redfield submitted the requested opinion as to whether the existing rules on snowmobiles were "consistent with the Trust which created the Park."[18] As part of her research Redfield had contacted several persons who might have had information on Baxter's views on snowmobiles in BSP. Redfield had contacted the Authority members serving in the late 1960s when the first regulations were passed—Wilkins,

Speers, and Erwin—as well as Helon Taylor, Irvin Caverly, Game Warden Supervisor Rogers, Baxter's Chauffeur Joseph Lee, and Park Ranger Rodney Sargent.[19]

Erwin and Rogers had communicated to Redfield that they believed Baxter would not have wanted snowmobiles in the Park except, as Rogers worded it, for "Park Rangers and State Game Wardens." Lee indicated essentially the same opinion in his assertion that Baxter had funded the purchase of Taylor's snowmobile because "as Helon was getting along in years the Governor thought it [would] make it easier on Helon with a snowmobile." In addition, the snowmobile "had to be hid in the summer in the pole barn so no one would see it and get any ideas." Rogers stated that Baxter had been worried that snowmobilers wishing to see wintering moose and deer up close would "be charging into the deer yards with their snowmobiles, chasing, pursuing, and routing the deer and moose and where poachers are concerned—killing these animals." Baxter also, according to Rogers, feared that over enthusiastic snowmobilers might "become the victims of accidents [and] breakdowns, and [become] lost persons in a vast wilderness area." Speers, Wilkins, and Taylor, however, thought that Baxter, although changeable in his ideas, would not have objected to public use of snowsleds in the Park, and Wilkins was certain that the Authority had talked with Baxter about allowing the vehicles in the Park.[20]

None of the persons Redfield had contacted had had any strong evidence as to Baxter's views on the subject, and their "feelings" on the matter were, in Redfield's opinion, "of limited significance in comparison to Baxter's written statement precisely on point." This written statement was Baxter's letter to Taylor. Redfield also placed importance on Baxter's 1966 letter to Austin Wilkins in which Baxter stated that motorcycles, being so "noisy and numerous ... should be forbidden to go into the Park area. If unrestrained, these noisy machines would frighten the wildlife." Redfield suggested in her April report that another meeting be held to discuss the issue now that research had been completed.[21]

The Authority requested a legal opinion. Redfield submitted the opinion on May 20, 1976. Redfield stated in "The Use of Snowmobiles in Baxter State Park" that although "the Trust instruments themselves are silent on the specific subject of snowmobiles," and "some ambiguity" existed in the general Trust provisions," "analysis of the method of the creation of the Trust, the Trust instruments, and other expressions of intent," indicates that he [Baxter] did not intend the use of snowmobiles ... for purposes other than necessary use by employees of the Authority in emergency situations."[22]

Redfield discussed Baxter's 1965 letter to Taylor concerning snowmobiles, as well as his 1966 letter to Wilkins about his opposition to motorcycles in the Park, in her snowmobile opinion. She determined that "while these letters are to be accorded less weight than the formal legislative communications (and certainly less weight than the Trust documents), their significance is not to be ignored."[23]

Furthermore, according to Redfield, although snowmobiles "would, of course, provide greater access to the Park in winter," excluding them from BSP would not "'lock up the Park' but rather tend to limit its use to those 'willing to walk to get close to nature'" as Baxter had mandated. Snowmobile activities did not depend on the "unique wilderness values" Baxter had established for the Park, nor were they "compatible with those values and uses" dependent upon the Park's wilderness values, such as observing wildlife and hiking. In addition to this "potential incompatibility," Baxter had, apparently, intended to distinguish "between automobiles and snowmobiles and motorcycles." The "potential for noise and ultramobility" of the two latter types of vehicles might adversely affect wildlife ... and ... disturb those users of the Park who 'love nature' and seek the 'peace and solitude' with which Baxter was concerned."[24]

Redfield, in consideration of all these factors, concluded that:

> the use of snowmobiles as proposed by the 1976 Revision of the Rules and Regulations is not consistent with the Trust, and snowmobile use within the natural wild state areas of the Park should be limited to use by Park personnel in emergency situations.[25]

After receiving Redfield's opinion, the Baxter State Park Authority decided to consider banning recreational snowmobiling in BSP. The Park and the Authority received letters both for and against the proposed ban on snowmobiles, with much opposition expressed at the July Authority meeting held in Millinocket. About forty members of the general public attended the meeting. Attorney General Brennan informed those present that it was the job of his office to give opinions when requested, even if those opinions proved unpopular. He believed the recent opinion to be the proper legal one, based not on policy but on careful research. Authority Chair Marsh likewise stated that although the opinion was not popular with those persons present, it was the responsibility of the Authority to make regulations which the Attorney General's Office approved, and that any regulations which the Authority might make which were not approved by the Attorney General's Office were automatically null and void. The Authority gave members of the public the opportunity to voice their opinions, then moved on to other matters.[26]

Following the July meeting, correspondence concerning snowmobiles increased. Proponents of ending recreational snowmobiling wrote at least eighty letters to the Park and the Authority, either before the Authority voted or before the writers learned of the vote. Maine residents wrote the majority of the letters. So, too, did Maine residents write most of the twenty or so letters in support of recreational snowmobiling. In addition, seventeen persons from southern Maine sent a petition asking "the men of this Authority to uphold the Will and Trust of Percival P. Baxter by *banning* the use of snowmobiles from Baxter State Park."[27]

Opponents of ending private snowmobile use in BSP also sent petitions to the BSPA. One petition sent to the Attorney General contained roughly 580 signatures of persons opposed to banning snowmobiles, most of its signers from Millinocket or nearby towns. Another petition opposing the proposed ban, also sent to the Attorney General, contained seventeen signatures of East Millinocket business people who believed they stood "to be hurt financially" if snowmobiling was banned from BSP. The Board of Selectmen of East Millinocket wrote requesting that the Authority approve the use of snowmobiles on Park roads, and the Northern Maine Regional Planning Commission wrote to Governor James B. Longley that its members were "appalled by what we consider over zealous environmental concern that does not, in our opinion, seem logical," and asked the Governor to intervene in the matter. The organization also wrote to the Authority. A few people sent letters suggesting snowmobiles be allowed on a limited basis—allowed only on roads and not on any trails as was the rule for other motor vehicles—and one person wrote to suggest that all vehicles be banned.[28]

Although a few organizations, including those mentioned above, sent letters concerning the proposed ban on snowmobiles, most of the correspondence came from individuals or in some cases individual families. Opponents and proponents alike tended to argue that theirs was the stance Baxter himself would have endorsed were he still alive. Proponents of the ban argued that the machines were noisy, frightening to wildlife, and in general an "invasion" on the Park's "natural beauty," employing terms Baxter himself had used. The Authority, according to many, would only be following the mandate of Baxter in forbidding snowmobiles in BSP. Opponents of the ban argued just the opposite. According to these people, snowmobilers enjoyed their "sport" in a reasonable manner and did not threaten wildlife. They had less of an impact on the Park than did automobile users. Governor Baxter would not have wished to close the Park to them nor to end their use of Park roads to secure access to other snowmobiling localities. One person argued that snowmobilers were certainly preferable to "hippies" with their illegal "dope," and another person, concerned primarily with the possible negative effect of banning snowsleds on the local economy, foreshadowed an argument later used by those who favored allowing motorcycles into BSP by asserting that snowmobiles were much quieter than they had once been and that if Baxter were alive he would probably reconsider his position on their use.[29]

In response to a letter from John L. Baxter, Sr., who did not believe his uncle would have wanted snowmobiles in the Park, yet admitted that to date they "had not been so objectionable as many of us anticipated," Chair Marsh wrote that in spite of much opposition he believed the Authority at their next meeting would "accept the Attorney General's opinion which will mean no sleds except for official use in the Park starting next winter."[30] At the next Authority meeting, held on August 3, 1976, in Augusta, Marsh explained that the continued use of snowmobiles on the Perimeter Road had been questioned the previous year in light of Baxter's "forever wild" concept and that the Authority had therefore requested an opinion by the Attorney General. After the July 1976 meeting, the Authority had decided on a thirty day "cooling off" period, and was now ready to hear further statements for and against recreational snowmobiling. As with the July meeting, roughly forty members of the public attended the Augusta meeting.[31]

Sentiments expressed at the August meeting were much the same as those expressed in recent correspondence and at earlier meetings. Several members of the Maine Snowmobile Association (MSA) spoke in favor of allowing snowmobiles into the Park and offered to submit studies supporting the argument that snowmobiles do not adversely affect wildlife or the environment. Some individuals asserted that allowing snowmobiles was legal and not in variance with the Deeds of Trust. Opponents of the ban requested a delay on the decision so they would have time to submit legal memorandums. Proponents also spoke, some arguing that snowmobilers could go elsewhere in the state to enjoy their sport. John Baxter spoke out against the "liberalization" of Percival Baxter's original desires. He stated that although Governor Baxter had originally envisioned the Park as "being completely a backpackers' paradise" but had eventually decided to allow automobile use, snowmobiles were "more comparative to the use of outboard motors the[a]n [to] the use of automobiles." Baxter later wrote to Marsh stating that neither he nor his uncle (nor even the general public) had known about the use by the public of snowmobiles in the Park during the 1960s.[32]

Brennan acknowledged in August that the snowmobile issue was indeed a complicated one, and if it were a legislative decision it would be a difficult one to make. As a member of the Authority, however, his responsibility was to carry out Governor Baxter's intent. Brennan also stated that no decision made would be the result of political pressure, and all facts in the matter would receive due consideration. Before ending the meeting, the Authority voted that Redfield prepare snowmobile regulations consistent with the May opinion and that they be placed on the agenda for the next meeting.[33]

The Baxter State Park Authority did indeed decide to ban snowmobile use in Baxter State Park. They did so on September 7, 1976. The vote was unanimous. The adopted regulations read as follows:

> Snowmobiles are prohibited in Baxter State Park, provided, however, that snowmobiles may be used (1) for administrative purposes as authorized by the Baxter State Park Authority and (2) for emergency purposes.[34]

The Authority decided to establish guidelines for administrative use, the guidelines to be developed by the Park Director, and to consider them at the next meeting. Following the snowmobile decision, letters continued to be received by the Authority, most in support of the Authority's vote.[35]

During the spring of 1977, the snowmobile issue took a new turn. The Maine Legislature introduced Legislative Document 1387, "an act to allow snowmobiling on the entrance road of Baxter State Park." Chair Marsh reported the bill at the April 6, 1977, meeting and those present discussed its ramifications. John Baxter stated that he opposed the Legislature interfering with Authority decisions, while Attorney General Brennan stated that the act was a way of getting the Senate to request an opinion from the Maine Supreme Court about the legality of the legislation.[36]

Advisory member Winston C. Robbins wrote to the Advisory, the Park Director, and the Authority Chair the next week. What disturbed Robbins about the act was not its provision but its supersession of the Authority. The Deeds of Trust gave the BSPA the responsibility of rule making. Robbins urged a review of LD 1387 and its ramifications, as well as indicating the need to take a stance on the subject when the act reached a public hearing.[37]

When the Authority reconvened in May they discussed LD 1387 further. They decided to attend the LD 1387 hearing, and Redfield, in response to a question, stated that the Legislature could not change the terms of a Trust to the extent that the Trust is violated. In other states where this had happened, property had reverted to the family of the Trust when the Trust was similar to that left by Baxter. The Authority circulated a notice about the scheduled May 18, 1977, public hearing for LD 1387, and the following month Marsh was able to report that the act had failed to pass the State Legislature.[38] For the time being, at least, one question had been resolved.

A desire if not a demand for snowmobiling rights within Baxter State Park had been voiced by some sectors of the general public since the 1976 decision to exclude the vehicles. In mid-1979 the issue again came to the forefront when Beverly P. Rand, former president of the Maine Snowmobile Association, began circulating letters of inquiry to former BSP Authority members and Park staff concerning their positions on snowmobiles. Rand also wrote to the Park about removing the existing ban on snowsleds. A number of letters were then sent between staff and Authority members, both past and present, and a number went to Rand as well. Rand later presented those he had received which favored snowmobile use, or found it non-objectionable, to the Authority and other interested parties.[39]

Some persons made it clear in the course of events which followed that they did not necessarily think Governor Baxter had opposed recreational snowmobiling in the Park, or that he had at least remained silent on the issue at various times when he might have spoken out against their use. While not a new argument, it may well have furthered the impetus for revision. Former Supervisor Helon Taylor, for example, stated that he still believed that Baxter would not have objected to their continued use on the Perimeter Road. Taylor further stated that in 1976, when contacted by the Attorney General's Office, that interest in his, Taylor's, opinions had ended when he made them known. Former Supervisor Harry Kearney likewise submitted a notarized statement to the effect that he believed Baxter had both been aware of and pleased with snowmobile use in the Park, although the Governor had remained adamant that they be confined to the roads maintained for summer traffic.

Irvin C. Caverly, now Park Supervisor, wrote to BSPA Chair and Attorney General Richard S. Cohen in October 1979 that he had polled Park personnel about snowmobiles and a "large majority" of them felt that the vehicles should be allowed on the Perimeter Road. Furthermore, Caverly stated that Baxter had been aware of snowmobile use in BSP during 1964 through 1968, and of the five staff members who remained from the years snowmobiles had been allowed, all confirmed "that no harm was done, no problems resulted." Caverly believed in 1979 that it would be to the Park's and public's advantage to allow snowmobile use in the Park again. Caverly reiterated his position in a letter to the Natural Resources Council of Maine (NRCM) later that year, adding, however, that it was "up to the Authority and the Courts to determine if snowmobile use is consistent with the Deeds of Trust."[40]

Other persons associated with the Park also expressed a willingness to reopen the Perimeter Road to snowsleds. Former Attorney General Erwin, for example, wrote in September 1979 that although he had cast the dissenting vote in the 1969 decision to allow snowmobiles on the Perimeter Road, he had since determined that snowmobilers had not caused any harm when allowed access. In his judgment, "they earned the privilege of using the road."[41]

The "staff of the Authority" recommended that Rule 19 of the 1979 Rules and Regulations be revised to allow snowmobile use "on Webster Lake and Lake Matagamon, the boundaries of which are only partially within the Park." At the September 6, 1979, meeting of the Authority, however, the Authority determined that they could not make any such revision due to the 1976 Attorney General's opinion. The MSA also petitioned the Authority at the September meeting to allow recreational snowmobiling on the Perimeter Road system.[42]

By late October 1979, the Authority, now composed of Chair and Attorney General Cohen, Commissioner of Inland Fisheries and Wildlife Glenn H. Manuel, and Director of the Bureau of Forestry Kenneth G. Stratton, came under increasing pressure to reconsider the snowmobile issue. The *Maine Snowmobiler* wrote to Cohen about the matter. Snowmobilers and cross-country skiers were currently joining forces due to their mutual interest in outdoor recreation, Judson Roberts, the magazine's publisher, asserted. He referred to both Kearney's and Taylor's communications on snowmobiles in support of the request, and stated that "we ask only that winter use of the perimeter roads be placed on an equitable level with summer use." The *Maine Snowmobiler* had run an article in September with the headline "Baxter Authority Reconsiders Its Ban On Snowmobiles" in one inch letters. A subtitle announced that "Former Authority Member Says Ban

Decision Seems Unfair," and the article included the previously noted correspondence from Erwin as well Rand's statement as delivered to the Authority.[43]

The *Katahdin Times* also wrote to Cohen in support of snowmobiling in BSP. The letter's author, Anne R. Erickson, was a snowmobiler and had been involved in the 1976 campaign to maintain snowmobile access. Erickson stated that her family had snowsledded in BSP from 1969 to 1976, and that not only had they traveled the Perimeter Road but had also ridden on Park trails until 1969. She did not request that the trails be opened to snowmobilers, however, but did state that Baxter had known about snowmobile activity and named the Maine Snowmobile Law as her primary argument for snowmobile access. Like other arguments that would appear repeatedly in the snowmobile controversy over the years, and one which motorcycle enthusiasts would also employ, Erickson argued that her group contributed tax dollars used to maintain Park roads and should therefore have a right to use those roads via their chosen means of transportation. Erickson also stated that the people of the Katahdin region supported her position.[44]

Not only had those who supported allowing snowmobiles on the Perimeter Road become vocal, so, too, had those opposing a rule change, in particular the NRCM. The Authority subsequently decided to ask the Maine Superior Court to adjudicate the matter. On November 2, 1979, the Authority asked the Attorney General's Office for their aid in "the process of petitioning for judicial instructions on the extent of the Authority's discretion to regulate snowmobiles and other motorized vehicles in Baxter State Park." According to the Attorney General, the snowmobile issue would remain a "source of debate and uncertainty ... until judicially resolved." To this end, Assistant Attorney General Rufus Brown prepared a memorandum of law and a draft petition of instructions, the first of which Brown submitted on May 23, 1980.[45]

According to Brown's memorandum, some forty-two pages long, the Authority had the right, as determined by *Fitzgerald v. Baxter State Park Authority* (1978) to petition the Court for instructions, "even though it is a governmental entity and as such has available to it the advice of the Attorney

General." Brown advised that the Authority did not have the necessary "degree of adversariness" and "immediacy" for a petition on motor vehicles other than snowmobiles, and therefore recommended that the BSPA petition only for instructions on snowmobile use in the Park. The memorandum suggested two approaches to the petition to resolve the ambiguities on the issue inherent in the Deeds of Trust: the traditional approach, which would focus on presenting extrinsic evidence of Governor Baxter's intent such as communications accompanying the Deeds of Trust, and letters to Park personnel, relatives, and friends; and a modified approach, such as that used in *Fitzgerald v. Baxter State Park Authority*, which would focus "on whether the trustees have acted in the fashion that exceeds the limits of discretion granted by the Trust instruments." The draft petition named the Governor and legislative leadership as parties, on the theory that they represented the State of Maine (the principle trustee of the trust) more directly than the State designated Authority.[46]

Rufus Brown and the Attorney General's office later submitted a supplemental memorandum of law. They did so on September 11, 1980, in part to encompass public comments on the earlier two documents. The MSA, the NRCM, and the Appalachian Mountain Club (AMC) had sent communications regarding the issue since May 1980. The latter two opposed the Authority's petition, primarily on the grounds that the Authority should rely upon the 1976 legal opinion, or wait until someone else brought the matter to the Court. The MSA argued that the Authority should incorporate a statement of intent to reconsider the snowmobile regulations unless the Court precluded such consideration. Brown's September memorandum suggested that in order to increase the possibility of the Court's considering the petition, the Authority include such a statement of intent, but one that clearly indicated that the Authority would consider—but not necessarily make—changes in its snowmobile rules. A decision by the Court, however, would not in Brown's opinion resolve all of the Authority's concerns about snowmobile regulations.[47] When the Court made its decision it indeed did not end the debate over snowmobiles. In the meantime, and thereafter, debate continued.

The BSPA had allowed proponents and opponents of private snowmobile use in the Park to voice their opinions at Authority meetings since the MSA had presented its position in September 1979. Several persons had spoken at the November 1979 meeting, including Ethel Dyer, grandniece of Governor Baxter, who, like John Baxter, Sr., stated that Percival Baxter would not have wanted recreational snowmobiling in BSP. Moreover, John Baxter stated that his uncle had specifically asked him to "represent his interests with respect to the Park." Jon Lund, NRCM president, but speaking as a "private person," stated that he did not think that the issue could be determined once and for all. Snowmobiles might have become quieter over the years as some people argued, but if they were allowed into the Park and became noisier in the future, or if other problems arose, their presence would need to be re-evaluated. Anticipating what would later become a serious consideration, Lund, in drawing an analogy, stated that automobiles were allowed on the Perimeter Road—at least until "there were too many cars in the Park"—but in the future the Authority might have to consider group transportation and ban automobile use. As traffic conditions changed, so, too, vehicle regulations needed to change. In addition to the statements made by interested parties at the November and earlier meetings, throughout the fall letters and related correspondence continued to reach the Authority. Numerous individuals wrote to the Park and Authority both for and against snowmobile rule revisions.[48]

At the Authority's October 1980 meeting, Brown informed those attending that the petition for instructions had been filed and a deposition of Helon Taylor taken. Any intervenors in the snowmobile case needed to file prior to the end of the month. Motions to intervene were eventually made by Ethel Dyer, John Baxter, Aime Gauvin, Gerald Stelmok, Judson Roberts, the *Katahdin Times*, the NRCM, the AMC, and the MSA. The Authority had already received an MSA petition with approximately one hundred signatures requesting that if court proceedings became "bogged down" the BSPA adopt a rule allowing snowmobile use on the Perimeter Road. According to Brown, the Administrative Procedures Act did not allow "the discretion suggested by the MSA," and instead required "that the Authority begin rule making within sixty days of receipt."[49]

In January 1981, less than two weeks before the deadline for filing motions in the snowmobile case, Maine acquired a new Attorney General, James E. Tierney. The Authority had already completed its filing, however, and a hearing had been set for the week of February 23, 1981, to determine whether the BSPA could prohibit the recreational use of snowmobiles in the Park. The hearing was later moved to March.[50]

Superior Court Justice Daniel E. Wathen heard the case and rendered his decision on June 12, 1981. Wathen noted that the ambiguity in the "forever wild" language of the Trust instruments had already been determined in the *Fitzgerald* case, that snowmobiles were not mentioned in the Deeds of Trust, and that the machines were not in general use when the Trust was created. The judge had examined the available evidence, including extrinsic evidence, and pointed out that "the parties before this Court point to virtually the same items of extrinsic evidence and the same language within that evidence as supporting their respective positions."[51] Not only did ambiguity exist between the various statements of Baxter and among or between the Deeds of Trust, the individual terms or words themselves were open to widely diverse interpretations, or so, at least, the interested parties had interpreted them.

Justice Wathen quoted five pieces of extrinsic evidence as being "the most helpful in ascertaining the intent of Governor Baxter at the time of creating the Trust." Among these five were the previously discussed 1965 and 1966 Baxter letters concerning snowmobiles and motor bikes. The five items also included the often quoted 1955 Interpretation Act, in which Baxter stated that the Park was to be:

> "... maintained primarily as a wilderness, and recreational purposes are to be regarded as of secondary importance and shall not encroach upon the main objective of this area which is to be "forever wild.'"[52]

The remaining two items Wathen quoted were letters written by Baxter on January 2, 1945, and January 3, 1949. In the first of these Baxter had stated that the Park '"is for everybody,"' with '"simple forest lean-tos and small log cabins"' providing shelter '"for those who love nature and are willing to walk and make an effort to get close to nature."' In another often quoted passage, Baxter had stated that he did not want the Park "'locked up and made inaccessible,"' but rather he wanted it '"used to the fullest extent but in the right unspoiled way."' In such a park, protection of wildlife would make the animals and birds cease to '"fear man and gradually they will come out of their forest retreats and show themselves."' Baxter wanted '"hunting with cameras to take the place of hunting with guns."' That Baxter would have liked to see such changes also take place outside the Park he made clear in his statement of:

> "would that the day would come when all of Maine will become a sanctuary for the beasts and birds of the forest and field and when cruelty to the humbler orders of life no longer stalks the land."[53]

In Baxter's letter of January 3, 1949, Baxter wrote that his earlier restrictions concerning roads in BSP were '"too severe,"' which necessitated that changes be made in former Deeds of Trust. He remained adamant, however, that '"no roads or ways shall be constructed or maintained that will interfere with or detract from 'the natural wild state' of this region."' Baxter recognized that in this matter he would have to "rely upon the good faith of the State of Maine," but he was "confident that the State of Maine will live up to the terms of this TRUST and will not break faith with me."[54]

According to Wathen, testimony from witnesses as to conversations with Baxter, or about what they felt were Baxter's opinions on snowmobiles, had "value," but were "less reliable than the direct expressions of Governor Baxter" as stated in the five items discussed by the Court. Such testimony was also contradictory, and the Court concluded "that nothing can be drawn from the fact that he [Baxter] did not specifically object" to snowmobiles in the Park in the period before his death. In the opinion of the Court, it remained unclear whether Baxter actually knew about such recreational snowmobiling after 1968.[55]

Based on the evidence presented, the Court was, in sum, "unable to conclude that the Trust agreement prohibits the Authority from allowing snowmobile use within the Park as a matter of law." Although Baxter had

The Park may be accessed by snowshoe or cross country skis in winter. After much debate limited use of snowmobiles within the Park was approved by the Authority. (Photo: Edward Dwyer)

Administrative use of snowmobiles includes the hauling of building materials such as these bridge timbers. (Photo: Jean Hoekwater)

his views on snowmobiles in his 1965 letter to Taylor, he had also, in the Court's opinion, "acknowledge[d] the power of the Authority to regulate their use." Had the "terms of the Trust" been "unambiguous," Baxter would have recognized that there was "no need to submit the problem to the Authority for their consideration." Baxter's writings clearly indicated that "access should never unduly detract from the wilderness experience," but the trustees might, or might not, "authorize the limited and regulated use of snowmobiles on access roads during certain seasons without interfering with or detracting from the wilderness experience." Governor Baxter had "placed his confidence in the judgment and integrity of those high State officials guided by the terms of the Trust," and those officials had the legal right or responsibility of the decision.[56]

The Maine Superior Court having made its decision, the Authority was faced with making its own. Three days after the Justice delivered his response to the Authority's petition, the Authority met to discuss the matter. The Authority decided to take no action at that time but to meet again and discuss the issue after the appeal period had passed. The Authority developed two options which they presented at the regular public meeting in August. "Option One" maintained the snowmobile regulation as it was, confining snowmobile use to administrative and emergency purposes. "Option Two" essentially reverted the regulation to those prior to 1976, except it would include snowmobile use on Matagamon and Webster Lakes. These lakes were located only partially in BSP and were already exceptions to current aircraft and motor boat regulations. After much discussion, the Authority unanimously decided to present both options at four public hearings, the hearings to be held in Augusta, Millinocket, Orono, and Portland. All changes to the Rules and Regulations would be discussed in Augusta, the other meetings would be devoted solely to snowmobiles. The hearings were scheduled for September 1981.[57]

Ninety members of the general public attended the Augusta hearing. Attorney General Tierney told those in attendance that the Authority would stay until everyone who wished to speak had an opportunity to do so. The meeting would start, however, with presentations or testimony from the four lawyers representing the four formal organizations that had been involved with the issue from the outset. The MSA, the NRCM, the AMC, and the Maine Audubon Society comprised the four organizations.[58]

Jon Doyle, Counsel for the Maine Snowmobilers Association, initiated the snowmobile testimony. Doyle stated that as Justice Wathen had determined that the Authority was not prohibited by law from permitting the recreational use of snowmobiles in the Park, the MSA and its more than 24,000 members sought to convince the Authority to adopt Option Two and allow private snowmobiles on the Perimeter Road. Snowmobiles in the 1980s were quiet machines, machines which would not adversely affect the "grandeur and beauty of the mountains, lakes, and streams" in the Park. Nor would they frighten wildlife, a fact which, Doyle asserted, a number of studies had proven. Baxter had allowed for several public uses of BSP, recreation being one of them. Snowmobiles presented the one realistic vehicle of transportation into the Park in winter, and enough room existed for both cross-country skiers and snowmobilers to pursue their respective activities, in spite of complaints by some skiers. Allowing snowmobiles Park access would not necessitate allowing motorcycles that same access, Doyle asserted. Other types of motorized access existed for summer visitors, and motorcycles could be seen as presenting dangerous situations in the Park.[59]

Richard Trafton of the Appalachian Mountain Club's executive committee spoke next. Trafton read a prepared statement expressing the AMC's concerns over allowing snowsleds into the Park. According to Trafton, snowmobiles would indeed interrupt the wilderness experience of AMC members, and seven hundred of the organization's 25,000 members lived in Maine. Motor vehicle use in BSP needed to be kept to a minimum. The Park's emphasis should instead focus on non-motorized travel. Furthermore, the speed and mobility of snowmobiles would allow their users to enjoy "inordinate amounts of space in the Park, overtaking other users" such as skiers, snowshoers, and hikers. To permit snowmobiles, Trafton argued, would indeed violate Baxter's wishes and the AMC would rather, if it came down to it, have the roads plowed in winter to provide access via regular passenger vehicles than have such access provided by snowmobiles. Baxter State Park could and should be maintained "as a true wilderness, albeit in winter only," by prohibiting recreational snowmobiling, or snowmobiling for Park access, within BSP.[60]

The Maine Audubon Society (MAS) presented formal testimony in favor of keeping the ban on snowmobiles. William L. Plouffe presented the testimony. As Plouffe related it, the MAS's objection was not against snowmobiles per se, or against snowmobiles being allowed in some State parks, rather they objected to Option Two on the grounds that Baxter State Park was "different" from all other parks in Maine. Baxter State Park was different in that it was the location of "Katahdin—Maine's highest peak; a symbol of wilderness; an inspiration to artists and photographers; a source of recreation, relaxation, physical challenge, and spiritual renewal. Baxter is a breath-taking wilderness belonging to the people of Maine," the MAS asserted. The history of the Park and Baxter's Deeds of Trust likewise made the Park unique, with the words "'Park,' 'natural,' 'wild,' and 'sanctuary'" being "the key words used by Baxter."[61]

The MAS's members believed that to allow recreational snowmobiling would be "inconsistent with the wilderness nature of the Park and violative of the terms of the Baxter Trust." Although Maine's more than one hundred snowmobile clubs and the snowmobile industry had spent a great deal of time and money trying to change their public image, and although some improvements had been made in the machines, snowmobiles still had problems with noise, fumes, snow compaction, and off-road mobility, as well as violations by some operators, which resulted in their being unwelcome in numerous areas. Snowmobiles negatively impacted the human wilderness experience, frightened wildlife, and created conditions in which wildlife was threatened more than normally by predators such as coyotes and dogs, as compacted snow gave predators an advantage in pursuing game.

The Maine Audubon Society also voiced a number of points made by other opponents of snowsleds in BSP, and stated—in response to the argument that those who wished to ban snowmobiles were "elitist"—that snowmobiles, snowmobile trailers, and snowmobile clothing were expensive items, and "the costs alone exclude many people from snowmobiling." The term elitist might just as well be used to identify the snowmobilers as to identify those who favored keeping the machines out of the Park. As other opponents of snowmobiles in the Park would argue, and as later opponents of motorcycles would, the MAS asserted that snowmobilers had the rest of the state in which to enjoy their favored means of transportation; there was no need to open the gates of BSP to them.[62]

In opposition to the view expressed by the AMC and the MAS, Maine Senator Charles Pray from Millinocket spoke in favor of Option Two. Pray stated that he did so for a number of constituents, including members of various organizations, who had contacted him about the matter. Pray asserted that the presence of large numbers of people in some areas of the Park in the summer season already violated the wilderness principle. Showshoers and skiers only utilized a small portion of the Park in winter, and room existed for both motorized and non-motorized winter activities in BSP. Furthermore, Pray would be willing to sponsor legislation to aid in the enforcement of BSP regulations concerning snowmobiles should the Authority decide to allow them into the Park, legislation which would allow authorities to pull snowmobile registrations in the event of rule violations. (Snowmobiles in Maine at the time were registered but not licensed.)[63]

State Representatives John Masterman, Elizabeth Mitchell, Dana P. Stevenson, and Vern Austin, as well as State Senator Richard Pierce, also spoke on behalf of Option Two. Mitchell and Pierce stated that a provisional one year period would be acceptable. After these persons spoke, the Authority asked for a show of hands as to who supported which option. Nine persons indicated that they favored Option One. Seventy-four supported Option Two. When the Authority later asked for a show of hands as to how many of those in attendance were snowmobilers, eighty-five persons raised their hands.[64]

Various other persons spoke on both sides of the issue. Charles Sanders spoke on behalf of the Millinocket Town Council, which had voted unanimously in favor of supporting Option Two. As had a few people previously, and as several persons would do later, Sanders protested the common depiction of snowmobilers as being anti-environment. In addition, a few people stated (as did others at various meetings and in letters) that keeping snowmobiles out of the Park discriminated against the elderly and against anyone who due to his or her physical condition was unable to get into the Park in winter without some type of vehicular assistance.[65]

Anne Erickson stated that the Millinocket Chamber of Commerce, of which she was director, had, like the Town Council, voted unanimously in favor of Option Two. The Chamber felt that snowmobile access would have a noticeable positive economic impact on the region. Furthermore, snowmobilers asked only to use 2 percent of the Park, leaving the balance for "whomever wishes to use it." Millinocket had 742 registered snowsleds, already comprising a large business sector, and increased snowsled use by persons outside the area would help not only the local economy but "the whole of Maine as well." As publisher and editor of the *Katahdin Times,* Erickson stated that her paper had long taken a "strong position" against "discrepancies of the forever wild concept." She would go along with pulling the registrations of snowmobilers who violated regulations, but as far as a provisional period was concerned, the Park had already had a fifteen-year trial period before the ban. Erickson, as did some other speakers, also repeated statements she had made in earlier correspondence or at earlier meetings. Beverly Rand of the MSA added that many families would be interested in snowmobiling into the Park for picnics and overnight camping, as well as traveling to get high quality photographs of Katahdin and other parts of the winter landscape.[66]

Proponents of Option One other than the AMC and the MAS also voiced opinions. Whit McEvoy proposed a revised wording for Option Two. McEvoy stated that the Authority should remove all reference to locations and routes other than the Perimeter Road system as maintained by the Department of Transportation from the second option, as the Authority had probably neither the right (in the case of *Matagamon and Webster Lakes*) nor the responsibility to provide such access. As currently written, Option Two allowed, among other things, people to travel to Katahdin Lake along what was basically a foot trail, and to travel along the East Branch of the Penobscot River on a route which would be difficult to control as well as being outside of the Perimeter Road system. McEvoy favored keeping snowmobiles out of BSP entirely, but if that were not to be the final outcome the Authority should at least revise Option Two.[67]

From his perspective as both a snowmobiler and a cross country skier, former Attorney General Jon Lund testified that he believed snowmobiles would have a negative impact on the wilderness aspect of the Park and discourage foot travel. If he was still on the Authority, he would "probably vote to continue the regulation as it presently exists." When snowmobiles traveled on ski trails, and some snowmobilers did so thinking that they would improve such trails, the trail was ruined for skiing. Noise, exhaust, and the machines themselves were problems for some skiers, Lund contended. Skiers disliked using the same trails as did snowmobiles in the same way that hikers did not like to hike along automobile roads, or as canoeists did not like to boat on the same waterways as did motor boats—especially high speed motor boats. The majority public opinion, however, favored Option Two, and the Authority needed to decide how much weight to place on public opinion. The Deeds of Trust could be read in various ways depending upon one's perspective.[68]

Opinions voiced at the following three public hearings mirrored those heard in Augusta on September 21, 1981. In some cases the same individuals made essentially the same statements or added to previous statements in order to address issues raised during the hearings. Roughly 185 persons attended the Millinocket hearing. When polled by a show of hands, the majority of those present indicated that they were snowmobilers, thirty-three indicated that they skied, and not one person raised their hand in support of Option One. The Katahdin Area Jaycees, the Town of Medway Selectmen, and the Millinocket Fin and Feather Club were among those who testified in favor of Option Two, as did a few State Representatives from the region and the Speaker of the Maine House of Representatives, John L. Martin.[69] The Millinocket area community, or at least those who chose to attend the hearing, either unanimously supported Option Two or they chose, out of a sense of intimidation, solidarity, or other reason, not to vote in opposition to others in attendance.

The number of citizens attending the hearing in Orono exceeded the number attending the previous two meetings. Some 225 persons from the general public attended the Orono meeting. Both opponents and proponents of snowmobile use in the Park spoke in Orono, with more people concentrating on the possible negative impacts of the machines than was true for the other hearings. Maine State Senator and former Senate Chairman of the Natural Resources Committee, Howard Trotsky of Bangor, opened the testimony on snowmobiles. Trotsky spoke in favor of keeping the ban in place. He reviewed some of the legal background of the issue, including Senator Pray's unsuccessful sponsorship of a bill to allow snowmobiling on the Perimeter Road, and read aloud portions of Sarah Redfield's 1976 opinion. As a private citizen, Trotsky thought that the Authority's decision should not be a political one based on numbers, and he stressed his opinion that once vehicles were given access into an area it was very difficult to move them back out again.[70]

Several other persons contributed their opinions on the two options. Adrien Humphries, an opponent of snowmobiles in BSP, pointed out that "the existing policy excludes no person—it excludes only machines." Scott Mason, stating that he represented the Department of Conservation, Parks and Recreation, the Sierra Club, and the National Parks and Conservation Association, argued that the Park Management Plan, as currently written, did not accord snowmobiles a place in the Park. However, ambiguities about the Park's definition or purpose had to clarified before the Authority could make "a precise and equitable decision" on the snowmobile issue.[71] While Mason may well have had a point, the multiple use aspect of the Park, as written in the Deeds of Trust, would continue to be a major factor in controversial issues for years to come.

One proponent of allowing snowmobiles in the Park, State Senator James McBreairty, argued that if the real issue was that of protecting the environment, "it would make more sense to ban hikers and backpackers than to ban snowmobilers." Other persons likewise pointed to problems with congestion, overuse, and overabundant automobiles and other vehicles in the summer, suggesting that snowmobiles would not create any harm that did not already exist. To these types of arguments Bill Sterns of Stillwater offered the response: "it is ridiculous to argue that one problem area is reason to create another problem area." Winter was as yet unspoiled for Sterns in terms of congestion and overuse, and he wanted it to remain that way. Although opponents of Option Two were more numerous, proportionately, at the Orono public hearing than they had been at the previous two meetings, proponents of the second option still outnumbered them. When asked for a show of hands, 61 persons indicated that they favored Option One, while 148 favored Option Two. Only a few persons did not vote for one option over the other.[72]

Public participation was also high at the last of the meetings, held in Portland on September 25, 1981, which 220 private citizens attended. Once again, when asked to vote by a show of hands, Option Two received the majority vote, garnering 147 votes as opposed to 37 for Option One. At the Portland meeting, 168 persons identified themselves as snowmobilers, whereas 39 persons were "cross country skiers, etcetera." Interestingly, unless they had already left the meeting, almost twenty persons decided not to vote for either option.[73]

The range of opinions expressed in Portland, however, mirrored that heard in Augusta and Orono, with less of the solidarity heard in Millinocket. Many of the same arguments for and against allowing snowmobiles in the Park were heard in Portland as had been voiced earlier, with new facets added here and there as had been true in the previous hearings. Steve Murray, a former Assistant Attorney General and an attorney for Charles Fitzgerald and other persons who had previously brought suit against the BSPA, argued that Baxter State Park should have its name changed to Baxter Park as BSP was not a State park but a private park held for the people of Maine. Snowmobiles, furthermore, were pleasure or recreational vehicles, not means of transportation as were automobiles, and should not be allowed in BSP. Allowing snowmobiles in would make it much more difficult to keep motorcycles, all-terrain vehicles, and even airplanes out. According to Murray, those who favored keeping the ban in place were less organized and less likely to attend the hearings than were snowmobile enthusiasts, as they relied on the Authority to "do the right thing."[74]

A few persons from the AMC testified against Option Two in Portland. During the course of the hearings numerous people had spoken about Baxter and what he would have wanted, but one early AMC member had a humorous and touching story to add. Ruth Weston of Portland related a story Baxter had told her about some campers who had had their hot breakfast cereal eaten by animals. Baxter had had no concern for the people who had lost their breakfast. Baxter's concern was that the animals might have burned their tongues. To Weston, this and other things Baxter had told her twenty-five years earlier signified that Baxter would not have wanted snowmobiles in the Park "because the animals certainly wouldn't like all that noise and smell." Weston's conclusion was not unique, but her tale of Baxter's concern over hot cereal burning the tongues of foraging animals was.[75]

So, too, did Jay Madeira of Falmouth have an interesting response to the argument that to keep snowmobiles out of BSP was to deny access to the elderly or physically challenged. A few people had expressed similar sentiments earlier at the hearings, but Madeira contributed a more colorful response. He stated that he was over sixty years in age and that arthritic hips and knees had crippled him. The fact that he could no longer enjoy a wilderness experience in the Park (he did not indicate any one season) did not bother him, however. "On the contrary," he stated:

> I am uplifted, inspired by the knowledge that there are areas of wilderness of which hundreds of people can't readily penetrate at all times. I certainly feel one can enjoy the wilderness vicariously without having to stick his nose or other parts of anatomy in every area of the state of Maine.[76]

Double entendres intended or not, Madeira made his point.

A number of other people gave their opinions that night. Representatives and counsel from the MSA and local snowmobile groups spoke, as did representatives for the Pine Tree Camp for Crippled Children and the Maine Branch of the Friends of the Earth. Some people spoke as representatives from a specific organization, others, including many with group affiliations, made it clear that they spoke as private citizens. In Portland as at the other hearings, the BSPA did not attempt to reach a decision on the matter.[77] The Authority sought instead to give the public a chance to express their views.

On October 26, 1981, the Authority held a meeting at BSP headquarters to give staff members a chance to relate their experiences, their testimony not having been part of the previous hearings. The October meeting was, however, open to the public. Letters from both private citizens and public organizations had continued to arrive at Park headquarters during September, and did so into the following months.[78]

Ronald N. Wrye, Superintendent of Acadia National Park and a BSP Advisory member, had attended the October 26 meeting and wrote to express his opinion that, based largely on his former experiences as Assistant Superintendent of Yellowstone National Park, carefully regulated snowmobile use on the Perimeter Road would be "both appropriate and within the intent of former Governor Baxter." James S. Erwin, being unable to attend the hearings, wrote to restate his position in favor of snowmobiles, reiterating how snowmobilers had proven his vote of "no snowmobiles" in the 1960s to be if not wrong at least unnecessary. District Court Judge Paul MacDonald, one-time acquaintance of Baxter, wrote to say that he and his wife had described their snowmobiling activities to Baxter, that Baxter had been initially concerned about the animals, but was then reassured that the MacDonalds and their snowmobile did not scare the deer they encountered. As studies showed that modern snowmobiles did not frighten wildlife, Baxter would not, MacDonald believed, object to their use on the Perimeter Road. MacDonald also wrote that he knew Baxter had had great faith in the Authority as Baxter had spoken to him of it several times, and that Baxter had known "that he could not control the Park activities from the grave." MacDonald's letter was almost the opposite of the deposition given by Ethel Dyer earlier in the year in which she stated that her uncle had not liked the sound of snowmobiles and had once told her, "'I have seen to it that they won't be in the Park.'" Dyer stated that she had "watched him die a very unhappy man," due to his differences with the Authority at the time, primarily she thought, over the purchase of certain hunting camps and other matters.[79]

By November 19, 1981, when the Authority met to discuss the snowmobile issue at a regular Authority meeting, the Park and Authority had received 131 letters in support of allowing snowmobiles in the Park, and 90 letters opposing snowmobiles in BSP. Three petitions in favor of snowmobiles, with a total of 287 signatures, had also been received. Chair Manuel opened the discussion at the November meeting and stated that the snowmobile issue was the toughest issue he had had to face since becoming Commissioner of Fish and Wildlife. After studying the Deeds of Trust and other documents and interviewing people who knew Baxter, Manuel was positive only that Baxter had wanted all the people of Maine to use the Park. Snowmobiles were a "gray area," and Manuel had reached his decision with "a great deal of thought and consideration and a great deal of compassion." He had decided that "there is room for everyone in the Park." He had thereby identified tentative areas in the Park where snowmobilers and skiers or snowshoers could pursue their activities, either separate or alongside one another depending on their specific aims for a given trip. Manuel had earlier requested aid from Caverly, who had then devised the recreational use zones as well as creating a map for illustration purposes.[80]

Attorney General Tierney spoke next and likewise indicated a decision to vote in favor of allowing snowmobiles. He stated that he originally had felt that snowmobiles were inappropriate for BSP except for administrative use, and that his responsibility as the lawyer on the Authority would be "to analyze the Trust as a conservative legal point of view." After reading the court records and information (referring it seems to the 1976 case), he had decided that Baxter had been against snowmobiles. Additional reading and talking with people had changed his mind. Listening to the testimony of people under oath, Tierney had decided that "the truth is that Governor Baxter was like most of us, that is he said different things to different people and at different times in his life." Overall, however, "there is more evidence than not that he didn't want snowmobiles in the Park through most of his career." Yet as Justice Wathen had determined, Baxter had not "precluded this Authority from ruling to the contrary," "should we hold public hearings and feel that it is appropriate." Although contradiction existed in the testimony about snowmobiles, he "could not find one solid piece of evidence that snowmobiles or snowmobilers would injure wildlife creatures or would alter the physical stature of the Park in any way." Snowmobile advocates had not convinced him, however, that "snowmobilers and skiers share the same wilderness experience." The wilderness experience was a subjective one and the letters and statements of snowshoers and skiers were honest when they said snowmobiles negatively influenced "their experience of the wilderness." Yet Tierney did believe, after analyzing the situation and listening to staff members at their October meeting, that room could be created for both types of recreation in the Park. He was willing to give it a try, although the exact areas where snowmobiling would be allowed had to be established. If there were infringements of the Authority's rules, however, snowmobilers would not be allowed to continue using the Park. He expected to be on the Authority for some time, and planned "to exercise continued responsibility in this area."[81]

Kenneth Stratton of the Maine Forest Service spoke next and delivered the dissenting opinion. Earlier he had felt, like Tierney, that the Authority could decide to go ahead and allow "strictly Perimeter Road access for snowmobiles." But he, too, had had a change in opinion, and now felt that the Authority should retain Rule 19 in its present form. One possible exception was the Scientific Forest Management Area as it had been set up for a different purpose than the rest of the Park. Even here the area should be used, if at all, only as access, not as a thoroughfare for snowmobilers. Stratton had come to his decision after reading all of the Deeds of Trust, court and other documents, letters, and the public testimonies. Stratton did not agree with much that was said against snowmobiles at the public hearings. He did believe, however, that Baxter's letters of 1965 and 1966 had expressed the Governor's wishes clearly: Baxter knew the Authority would make the decision on snowmobiles and on motorcycles, and he was asking the Authority to vote for him to keep the vehicles out. Stratton conveyed his concerns that while the Authority had followed Baxter's wishes regarding motorcycles, they had not been consistent in the past in doing the same thing regarding snowmobiles.[82]

The Authority discussed the matter briefly, including the need to address automobile touring and overuse, the legal rights of motor boats and airplanes to land on Matagamon and Webster Lakes, and the probability that snowmobilers would be more likely to use the Perimeter Road to secure access to the Telos Gate and then to the Allagash Wilderness than to attempt crossing BSP wilderness to go from Matagamon Lakes to Webster Lake. The Authority then voted on allowing recreational snowmobiling in BSP once more. Two voted for the motion, one against. Stratton cast the dissenting vote. After the vote, Ethel Dyer and John Baxter expressed their belief that Percival Baxter would have wanted Rule 19 to stay in effect.[83] Two weeks before the meeting, Clinton Baxter Dyer had sent a letter against Option Two, including a letter from his uncle in support of his position, and, interestingly, two weeks after the meeting Lydia Baxter MacDonald, one of Governor Baxter's three living nieces, published a letter in the *Portland Press Herald* expressing her conviction that Baxter would have wanted people to have access to the Park via snowmobiles. If Baxter were still alive, MacDonald wrote, and "satisfied that the animals would not be disturbed, ... he would want to ride up to Roaring Brook Campground on a snowmobile himself."[84] Neither the Baxter family nor the Authority had been able to reach unanimity on the snowmobile issue.

In accordance with the Maine Administrative Act, the Authority prepared a snowmobile regulation and policy statement. The policy statement reviewed the history of the snowmobile issue and the major arguments voiced at the public hearings. The document also summed up the reasoning of the Authority majority. It stated, "we agree with those who argued that a denial of such access (to those who "cannot otherwise visit the Park in the summer for physical or economic reasons or recreational choice") would constitute disparate treatment for those seeking winter access to the Park in relation to access permitted in the summer." The document reiterated the Authority majority opinion that snowmobiles on the Perimeter Road would not "adversely affect wildlife or the physical status of the Park." They had also been convinced that Baxter's letters of 1965 and 1966 about snowmobile and motor bikes "were no longer valid, at least under modern day conditions."[85] In this statement the Authority opened itself to the cause of motorcycle lobbyists, although when the issue later came to the forefront the Authority's declaration was not part of the petition for motorcycle access.

The policy statement Rufus Brown prepared for the Authority also stated the Authority majority opinion that snowmobilers and cross country skiers and snowshoers could co-exist in BSP. The Authority had furthermore revised the proposed rule to provide even greater separation between the two types of activities than the draft of Option Two had already provided, mainly by excluding the roads into Roaring Brook and South Branch Pond. In addition, they had determined that in terms of enforcement, "it is difficult for snowmobiles to leave the roads, that there is no legitimate basis for assuming that snowmobilers will abuse the rule any more than others do, and that there will be selfpolicing." If snowmobilers did not follow the rule, the rule would be changed, excluding snowmobiles from the Park once more. Economic impact on the local economy was not a factor in the decision, but the "forever wild" concept had indeed been a consideration. The Authority majority believed that the new rule would not infringe upon the "forever wild" restrictions of the Deeds of Trust.[86]

Members of the Maine Snowmobile Association indicated their approval of the Authority's decision in late 1981 and volunteered to aid the Authority in making a smooth and successful transition to the new rule. All interested parties did not concur with the decision, however. Newspaper coverage of the decision was, on the whole, neither overly optimistic nor disparagingly negative. The most vitriolic protests, and in some cases praise, were lodged in the form of "letters to the editor," with the reasons for the writers' frustrations with the Authority decision being essentially those voiced in earlier correspondence and at the public hearings. An organized challenge to the decision arose in late 1981 and early 1982.[87]

In December 1981, a group of citizens, at least partially under the leadership of Charles Fitzgerald, brought suit against the BSPA. As Fitzgerald explained it in a letter written that month, in the 1970s he had carried most of the economic burden of his lawsuit with the Authority over the issues of the blowdown and spruce budworm spraying, and could not afford to bring a suit over snowmobiles without financial support from "others who love the Park and understand its intended purpose." He also found it "necessary to form a specific organization to counter a powerful and well-financed snowmobile constituency and other special interest groups who are seeking to degrade the purposes of the Park."[88]

The Northwoods Alliance (NA), the group Fitzgerald helped form in late 1981, advertised in newspapers for memberships and contributions, using a format similar to the one some of its members had employed in previous campaigns. The advertisements mentioned the previous suits and appealed for support in the new one. Full-page advertisements presented their case to the reading public, complete with quotations and illustrations.

One early Northwoods Alliance advertisement appeared in the *Maine Times* in December 1981 with the lead-in: "Is This Baxter's Vision of 'Forever Wild?'" An accompanying illustration showed one person walking and three snowmobilers cavorting in the snow with Katahdin in the background. The advertisement informed readers that as "a small group of individuals," members of the NA had in past years "fought hard to keep the Park Authority from altering the intent of Governor Baxter." The recent BSPA decision "to allow snowmobiles on forty-eight miles and two large lakes" "threatened" Baxter's "gift to the people of Maine." The decision had made them "recognize the need for a permanent membership organization ... to review the policies of the Park Authority and to prevent the gradual deterioration of those wilderness values Baxter sought to protect," and, in this case, to bring suit against the snowmobile decision. The advertisement quoted Justice William O. Douglas's statement from *My Wilderness: East to Katahdin* (1961) that, "if we are to survive, we must make Katahdin the symbol of our struggle for independence from the machines that promise to enslave us." The advertisement also quoted several writings by Baxter, including Baxter's letter to Taylor regarding snowmobiles and a quote from another Baxter letter, a fairly well known statement:

> "While I am living, I fear no encroachments on the Park, but as time passes and new men appear upon the scene there may be a tendency to overlook these restrictions and break the spirit of these gifts."[89]

In early 1982, Northwoods Alliance published another, more graphic, advertisement. The small typewritten portion of the advertisement stated the NA's intention to "do everything it can to prevent and correct violations of the Baxter Trust," in this case the snowmobile decision. The Alliance informed readers once again that they had worked to correct such "violations" in the past. It was "hard to believe," according to the group, "that the very people entrusted to uphold the will of Baxter have repeatedly failed to do so." The Authority "through the years has responded to political pressures and has gradually disregarded Baxter's fundamental intent." The advertisement carried some of the same quotations from Baxter as had the December advertisement.[90]

The typewritten portion of the 1982 advertisement was placed over a rough map of BSP, with cartoons mocking, apparently, what the Alliance saw as part of the Park's past, present, or future. For example, the SFMA portion of the map showed a clear cut area with virtually the last logs being towed away; centrally located was a truck pulling a motorboat at full speed and seemingly off the road system; and in the southwest a tanker truck sprayed the roadside with poison while a bulldozer not far behind worked on building a two-lane paved road complete with roadside electrical lines. In addition, Katahdin was pictured with a lighthouse and other ornamentation; wildlife fled to the northeast boundary of the Park as snowmobiles pursued them cross-country; a motorcycle bearing a banner stating "It's My Park Too," rushed along the Perimeter Road; and the Deeds of Trust were shown stuffed into an overflowing garbage can. Other cartoons followed the same line. In case anyone still missed the point, quotations from Baxter on the wilderness focus of the Park were printed in "hand-written" script around the outside borders of the map and a large caption read, "Forever Wild?" One corner of the outer boundary was devoted to membership and contribution forms.[91]

In addition to the threatened suit by NA, Steven Cartwright and six other individuals brought suit against the BSPA over the snowmobile decision. The individuals were Maine residents (four lived in Orono and the suit was sometimes referrd to as the "*Orono suit*") who used the Park, including during the winter, and planned to continue to do so in the future. The plaintiffs challenged Rule 19 itself and the legality of its passage. The Authority learned of the suit in late February 1982, after which time Rufus Brown began an analysis of the situation.[92] Meanwhile, in spite of opposition from the two groups and continued dissent by Stratton, snowmobilers made use of the new regulation.

By early March 1982, five hundred incidences of recreational snowmobiling had been recorded and no major problems had developed. Irvin Caverly was now serving as Acting Park Director, Lee Tibbs having resigned in late 1981. In mid-April Caverly reported that for Park day use, 838 instances of snowmobile use had been tabulated, as opposed to 241 for skiing and 48 for snowshoeing. In terms of overnight use, 506 entries for technical climbing had been tabulated, all but one party spending at least one night in BSP. Although no reliable records existed, an estimated 1000 instances of snowmobile use had been standard for previous years when snowmobiles had been allowed in the Park. Recreational snowmobiles did not seem to create any major enforcement problems in the Park during their first season "back in." They did, however, aid in some search and rescue work.[93]

The snowmobile legal suits did not garner either the Authority's or the Park's attention in 1982 or in the following few years. Charles Fitzgerald and the NA supported the Cartwright suit and withdrew their own. Fitzgerald joined the BSP Advisory in the early 1980s, working from inside the established Park system as well as continuing to battle from without when he considered it necessary. In the meantime, the Cartwright suit entered a lengthy period of preparation and litigation, and snowmobile use in BSP continued. Snowmobiles became a regular feature of the Park in winter. Tragically, the activity did have its dangers. In early 1985, a snowmobiler, Stan Sinclair, fell off his vehicle near Nesowadnehunk Lake, rolled into a tree, and received injuries from which he died several days later. In a happier, for some, vein, local snowmobilers held an Earlon B. Campbell Memorial Ride that winter in BSP with numerous riders from the 1960s participating, some riding snowmobiles of 1960s vintage.[94]

In April 1985, in the case of *Steven Cartwright, et al. v. Baxter State Park Authority*, Superior Court Justice Morton A. Brody upheld Rule 19. The Court held that the 1981 judgment that recreational use of snowmobiles was not excluded by law bared relitigation of the general proposition of such use violating the Deeds of Trust. The Court also held that the Authority had not abused its discretion in establishing Rule 19, and that "the Authority is empowered to exercise its rule-making function by majority vote." The plaintiffs had sought judicial review of Rule 19 on these three contentions. After the April ruling, the NRCM and three of the individual plaintiffs of the Orono suit–the other four members having earlier withdrawn from the suit—decided to appeal. Park Legal Council Rufus Brown and Robert J. Allen of Downeast Law Offices represented the Park during the proceedings. Barbara B. Lounsbury represented the plaintiffs.[95]

In the 1986 hearing the Maine Supreme Court determined that the "central issue on appeal ... is whether Rule 19 goes too far in allowing snowmobiles in the Park." The Court did not consider "the question whether *any* use of snowmobiles" was "barred by the Baxter State Park Trust. That question was answered in the negative, once and for all, by the 1981 judgment of the Superior Court." However, "the manner and extent to which Rule 19 allows snowmobiles in the Park exceeds the scope of the discretion" given the Authority by the Baxter Trust was under consideration, governed as it was by Maine's Administrative Procedure Act which governed rule-making procedures for all State agencies. The Superior Court in reviewing Rule 19 had determined that the rule "'greatly enhances the Park's accessibility in the wintertime without unduly infringing on the wilderness experience of other, non-mechanized, users of the Park.'" The Supreme Court, however, stated that it would "review Rule 19 independently" as the Superior Court had acted "only as an intermediate appellate tribunal."[96]

The Maine Supreme Court therefore reviewed the snowmobile regulation "independently in light of the record before the Authority." "Nonetheless," the Court stated, "we come to the same conclusion as the Superior Court." Rule 19 represented "a rational accommodation between the dual goals of the Baxter State Park Trust." It provided winter access without destroying "the public's opportunity to enjoy the wilderness experience." The rule allowed snowmobile use only in a limited area and entirely prohibited the machines from "the vast and interior two thirds of the Park," the area most favored by snowshoers and skiers who sought a wilderness experience. Baxter had entrusted the Authority "to accommodate his twin objectives" in the face of "conflicts between wilderness and access." The "keen interest" Baxter had taken "in the composition of the Authority" demonstrated the importance of the task he had given them. In the many instances where the Trust did not "resolve" an issue or controversy, or ones that required "application of specialized and technical expertise," the

Authority had to "exercise its best judgment, informed by its own careful study of the documentary evidence and by court decision and public comment, in order to discern and implement Governor Baxter's vision for the Park." In the Court's determination, "Rule 19 represents a permissible exercise of judgment by the Authority." The Authority had already committed itself to addressing any significant problems caused by snowmobiles, and thus far there was no evidence that the snowmobilers "had used the Park's Perimeter Road as a mere thoroughfare" as those who had requested the appeal argued.[97]

In addition, those who had sought the appeal had questioned the vote itself, as only two Authority members had voted to allow snowmobiles into the Park. The Supreme Court ruled that the three "joint heads" of the Authority, as with other "legislatively created commissions and similar bodies," needed only to participate in "voting on questions of the supervision and control of the Park." Unanimity was not required. Three of the justices affirmed Justice McKusick's judgment. A forth, Scolnik, dissented.[98]

Scolnik believed that recreational use of snowmobiles in BSP was "antithetical to the Trust's paramount purpose of preserving the wilderness experience." Rule 19, Scolnik argued, was intended not to "promote access" but to "allow recreational snowmobiling, which, in contrast to administrative use of the vehicles, was not in keeping with the Baxter Trust." Rule 19 threatened the wilderness experience and should thus be declared invalid. "The Trust requires nothing less," Scolnik asserted. The 1981 decision was incorrect, and a decision of the Supreme Court "that would perpetuate" the decision "would not only adversely affect the parties of record, but also the populace at large for whom the Trust was created." Scolnik, accordingly, "would vacate the judgment of the Superior Court and remand with instructions to declare Rule 19 to be invalid."[99] As with the general population and the Authority, reaching a unanimous decision proved elusive for the Maine Supreme Court. Rule 19 remained in effect, but the issue was by no means settled.

Opponents of recreational snowmobile use in BSP did make their positions known from time to time in the following years, and some violations to Rule 19 did occur. But for the most part, according to

Director Caverly, the compromise between controlled use and no use worked out fairly well from the Park's perspective. In 1992, however, a new challenge faced the Authority. The Katahdin Region Tourism Council (KRTC) contacted Caverly in November 1992 about their wish to include the Perimeter Road on their grant application to the Bureau of Parks and Recreation Snowmobile Fund for money to finance snowmobile trail maintenance. If successful in their application, the council would "drag" the trails, using "super" and "double track" sleds to even out or widen bumpy or dangerous sections of trail. They would also post signs designating twenty-five mile per hour speed limits and request that the local Sheriff's office occasionally use radar to monitor the area. The Perimeter Road section would comprise forty-six miles of the total seventy-nine miles submitted for approval, the other thirty-three miles being located outside BSP. The KRTC stated that the trail mileage in Baxter State Park would make their grant application more competitive, and the other trail mileage was crucial to keeping the region competitive with other snowmobile areas. The Park was already on their snowmobile map and listed in publications, but the council would mark it as an "unmaintained trail" so as "not to encourage more use."[100] This, it seems, would tend to defeat part of the purpose of the project.

Caverly responded to the KRTC's representative, Toni Blake, that although he understood and appreciated the council's objectives, "your objectives on this subject are totally opposite from the objectives outlined within our mandate responsibility which is "'forever wild.'" Since 1982 the Park had followed "a policy of no trail dragging as it was felt that it would lead to increased speeds and increased use." Caverly also indicated that he would advise the Authority of the council's request.[101] Although Caverly did not mention it, and it did not become part of ensuing discussions, a similar request to furnish the Park with drags for trail maintenance had been made by a member of the Bureau of Parks and Recreation in 1974, and denied on the grounds that it might increase recreational snowmobiling in the Park and make it a thoroughfare to other locations.[102]

Caverly did indeed advise the Authority of the request, and did so the same day. He wrote to the members briefly reviewing the history of snowmobiles and BSP, and stressed that James Tierney had stated the day the new snowmobile regulation was passed that as the "swing vote" he had no reservations about monitoring snowmobiles and reversing his vote should the snowmobile privilege be abused. At that time, also, Maine Snowmobile Association representatives had indicated that they were not requesting permission to develop or drag trails, as they thought doing so might increase usage, speeds, and safety problems—as well as user conflicts. Caverly since then had "remained constant in compliance with that policy statement." Although Park Rules and Regulations contained no mention of trail dragging, Caverly had, when asked, "clarified that anytime a dragged trail contributes to abuse or conflict, we would not hesitate to recommend the implementation of a rule which prohibited grooming or dragging." Rule 19 had worked thus far, the MSA had "been of significant assistance in making Rule 19 acceptable as it now is," and "a modification or change to that regulation will cause discontent and ultimately a difficult and extended controversy." Caverly sent a copy of his letter to Blake to keep her informed of his position.[103]

A number of persons became concerned over the issue of trail dragging in December 1992. Caverly outlined the KRTC's proposal at the December Director's Communication Meeting and, according to the *Katahdin Times* account of the meeting, referred to it as "a can of worms." Caverly had several problems with KRTC's request. These include the proposed twenty-five mile per hour snowmobile speed limit, as the established Park speed limit for any vehicle was twenty miles per hour; the proposed posting of signs by the council; and the communication by the council to the Bureau of Parks and Recreation that all landowners had been contacted and had agreed to the proposed trail grooming, when in fact the Park at least had not had time to respond to the request. Because of the short lead-in period and the Thanksgiving holiday, the Authority had not had a chance to make a decision within the time period (a six day period was requested for informing all Authority members) the KRTC had requested, and Caverly had contacted the Bureau to inform them that the Authority had not granted the project any form of approval.[104]

Caverly also asked Assistant Attorney General and Park Legal Counsel Paul Stern to consider the legality of snowmobiles hauling drags or grooming devices behind them when riding in the Park. Stern submitted a memorandum on the matter on December 3, 1992. Stern wrote that "generally any activities which altar any natural feature of the Park are prohibited." Without a specific regulation allowing such alteration, the activity is prohibited. And no such regulation existed which allowed "private individuals to alter the natural winter features of the Park by grooming trails." Unless the Authority specifically allowed grooming activity, "it must be deemed to be prohibited." Caverly then notified interested parties, including the Maine Snowmobile Association, of the memorandum and at their next meeting the Authority deemed the question settled.[105] Thus another Authority—William J. Vail, Authority Chair and Commissioner of Inland fisheries and Wildlife, Attorney General Michael E. Carpenter, and Maine Forest Service Director Susan J. Bell—addressed yet another facet of the snowmobile issue.

However the same Authority, with the exception of Vail's replacement by Ray B. Owen, would continue to evaluate and re-evaluate the situation until the close of 1994. Already when Caverly addressed the public on December 1, 1992, incidences of snowmobile violations had begun to increase, and problems would develop over the early 1990s, some of them involving safety risks. As Director Caverly saw the situation in mid-1995, ideally there would perhaps be no recreational snowmobiling in Baxter State Park. This opinion represented an evolution of Caverly's perceptions during the thirty-five years he had served the Park. Yet, in terms of the best interests of the Park in a practical sense, Caverly believed that providing limited access to snowmobilers still offered the best solution to the snowmobile issue. With limited snowsled travel allowed in the Park most snowmobilers obeyed regulations and did not seek further mileage. Banning snowmobiles entirely remained unenforceable and might well lead to greater transgressions against the wilderness.[106] And transgressions against the wilderness, and hence the wilderness experience, were things which Caverly as well as the various Authorities and numerous individuals on all sides of the issue had sought to avoid since snowmobiles were first officially allowed in the Park in 1968. Interpretations, both legal and personal, of how to best protect the Park changed over the years resulting in changes in policy and rules. Snowmobile use was indeed a "gray area," and promised to remain one into the near future.

Chapter Eight

Motorcycles: Public Use Challenge, Park Access Denied

At the same time as Baxter State Park personnel and Authority members continued to address other sensitive issues pertaining to public policy, including the use of motorized vehicles in the Park in general, the subject of motorcycles became a focal point for several months. Although the question of allowing motorcycles into Baxter State Park had risen from time to time over the years, proponents of motorcycle access asked the Authority to make a formal vote on the subject in the late 1980s, and in the early 1990s raised the issue once again. Motorcyclists would not have their hopes realized on either occasion, but they did make the general public well aware of their position and inadvertently brought the issue of Park overuse to the media's attention.

Baxter State Park revised its Rules and Regulations in 1970. The revised rules included a ban on the use of motorcycles in BSP. The rule which forbid motorcycle use, Rule 12, stated that:

> No person shall bring into the Park or operate within the Park, any motorcycle, trail bike or other two wheel motor-driven vehicle, or any all-terrain vehicles, so-called, which shall include without limitation, those motor-driven vehicles operating either on endless treads or wheels which are designed to operate over any terrain off the roads and highways. Nothing in this regulation shall be construed to apply to snowmobiles. This regulation does not apply to snowmobiles. This regulation does not apply to Park personnel and/or law enforcement officers while in the line of duty and in emergency cases.[1]

Rule 12, which the Authority passed during the administration of Park Supervisor Harry H. Kearney, expressly banned motorcycles while at the same time bringing up the ever controversial subject of snowmobiles. When the motorcycle issue arose in ensuing years, motorcycles and snowmobiles would remain tied to one another in both public opinion and legal documents.

Although the motorcycle rule did not raise an excessive amount of controversy in 1970, the Millinocket Fin and Feather Club did denounce it, along with other newly imposed restrictions, as being unfair. The Fin and Feather Club posted a public notice protesting the revisions in June 1970, stating that the changes, having been passed at the beginning of the summer season, were unfair to BSP users. The changes should have been made one year before going into effect, giving people a chance to learn the new regulations and make any necessary arrangements before visiting the Park. The changes, according to the club, had been imposed in a "hasty manner" in order "to void any possible organized opposition to them." The club also questioned the legality of some of the changes, inquiring, for example, as to whether "legally registered and licensed vehicles such as motorcycles and trail bikes can be denied the right to use roads within the Park, which are maintained by State highway funds and equipment?" Park users were encouraged to write accounts of their Park experiences (seemingly their negative ones) and send them to the Fin and Feather Club. The club would in turn "present them personally to our respective legislators."[2]

The 1970 motorcycle ban was not overturned. Legislation was proposed a few years later to allow the use of motorcycles within the Park, however, and to that end Attorney General Joseph E. Brennan in February 1975 requested Attorney General Staff Assistant Sarah Redfield, later Assistant Attorney General, to prepare a memorandum on the issue. Redfield responded on April 22, 1975, with a twelve page document reviewing Governor Baxter's Deeds of Trust, relevant correspondence and legal history, and assorted information on recreational vehicles. Motorcycles, according to Redfield:

> would, of course, provide greater access to the Park. However, their exclusion would not "'lock up the Park'" but rather limit its use to those "willing to walk to make an effort to get close to nature." ... Nor are they [motorcycles] compatible with ... [wilderness] ... values and the uses necessarily dependent

> thereon, e.g. hiking, wildlife observation, and camping. Because of their noise and ultra-mobility (as compared with the average automobile for example) motorcycles may adversely affect wildlife in the Park and may also disturb those users of the Park who wish to "get close to nature."[3]

After further discussion, Redfield asserted that "it is clear that Baxter intended that wilderness preservation be the primary concept governing the majority of the Park and that the allowing of motorcycles would not be consistent with this intention."[4] Nor was the use of motorcycles appropriate in the two areas of the Park in which hunting was allowed or in the "scientific forestry" section of BSP. Allowing motorcycles in the first would not "substantially affect the numbers of hunters" there, nor was it "clear that motorcycle use would in any way enhance forestry operations" in the second. Certain motorcycles might even "injure plant and tree growth" in the scientific forestry area. Redfield concluded that "it seems that allowing motorcycle use is not in keeping with the terms of the Trust for any of the area of Baxter State Park."[5]

Redfield's memorandum seemed to address the motorcycle issue both thoroughly and decisively, yet, in the mid-1980s, after Irvin C. Caverly became Park Director, the fairness of the no-motorcycle rule became an issue once again. Following a 1985 article in a motorcycle magazine which discussed the inability of motorcycle riders to enjoy the park via their chosen method of transport, United Bikers of Maine (UBM) requested a change in policy to allow motorcycles into the Park. Paul Vestal of UBM presented the organization's position to the Authority on July 9, 1986.[6]

Vestal pointed out at the July meeting that no major modifications had been made concerning motorcycles in the Park rules since 1966, even though decibel levels on the vehicles had been reduced to comply with federal regulations. In addition, motorcycles had become more popular since 1966, becoming the primary mode of transportation for many people during the summer months, and *the* method of transportation for much of the year for some individuals. Vestal claimed that United Bikers, in making the request, represented "many people who ride for the touring clubs that ride in Maine such as the Re-Treads, the Golden Hawks, the Golden Eagles." Bikers thought it unreasonable that they could not travel in Baxter State Park on their motorcycles even though a member of one group had toured the United States visiting national parks, and only in Maine been denied entrance to a public park. Vestal also related how the Illinois Supreme Court had ruled it "unreasonable and arbitrary to deny the use of public streets to motorcycles and yet allow the automobile to use those same streets," as problems with excessive noise and speed were not limited to motorcycles. The use of motorcycles in BSP, according to Vestal, would not create any new problems. Bikers wanted to use the Park for the same reasons other persons did: to camp and to hike.[7]

United Bikers of Maine did not in any way desire to have BSP disturbed by dirt bikes or other such recreational vehicles. According to Vestal, motorcycles would be used in the same manner as automobiles, trucks, and recreational vehicles (motor campers it seems he meant), and the organization would accept having just a specific area set aside where motorcycles could be brought in and parked for those persons who wished to hike. In sum, in light of these factors, UBM believed that some modification to Park rules was necessary.[8]

Terry Christensen also spoke on behalf of Maine motorcycle enthusiasts at the July 1986 Authority meeting. Christensen, United Bikers' vice-president for the southern half of Maine, had spoken with the Golden Eagles, the Sea Coast Riders, and the Gold Ring Riders Association. According to Christensen, these groups were family oriented and generally rode touring-type motorcycles. Furthermore, members of the Re-Treads, a national organization whose members ranged in age from their late thirties to their sixties and seventies, frequently traveled as many as 5,000 to 10,000 miles a year on their motorcycles, and wanted entry to BSP.[9]

A third speaker, United Bikers' vice-president for northern Maine, Harvey Starkey, likewise addressed the subject of biker stereotypes. Starkey stated that "not all bikers have long hair and wear beards." All types of people rode motorcycles, including those who belonged to the Blue Knights, a group of motorcycle-riding policemen. As he told the Authority, "don't just think of the B movies showing bikers with loud mufflers and raising hell ... most of us are family oriented."[10]

Jerry Bley of the Natural Resources Council of Maine (NRCM) then read a letter from Brownie Carson of NRCM opposing the use of motorcycles in the Park. Carson wrote that NRCM was concerned about United Bikers' request and believed that it ran counter to Governor Baxter's wishes. Baxter, Carson asserted, had wanted people to have access to the Park, but to use Park roads as a "means of transport," to "locations from where they could see the Park on foot, and not as scenic routes to view the Park by vehicle." United Bikers did, at the July meeting, indicate a willingness to park their vehicles and tour BSP by foot. However, they did not agree with Carson's assessment of the current policy providing "sufficient access for the public" wherein "anyone who would like to visit the Park can arrange to do so by car."[11]

According to Carson's letter, the NRCM recognized that many motorcycles were currently quieter than those of earlier years, and that many people toured the state on motorcycles. Nevertheless, the organization's members thought that "the dangers of allowing motorcycles in the Park far outweigh the potential benefits." Loud motorcycles still existed which might disrupt wildlife and disturb other people; irresponsible motorcycle riders might take their vehicles onto trails, old roads, and into campground areas and cause environmental damage; and motorcycles could prove dangerous on the Park's winding roads. Furthermore, allowing motorcycles in the Park might open the way for the use of all-terrain vehicles, motor homes, and motor boats. In short, NRCM strongly urged the Authority to deny UBM's request.[12]

Bley also read a letter from Barbara Lounsbury, an Auburn Attorney previously active in the snowmobile controversy, who opposed the motorcyclists' request. Lounsbury admonished Authority members to remember their duties as trustees of Governor Baxter's gift. Lounsbury quoted Maine Private and Special Laws, 1955, Chapter Two, which stated that the land was "'to be maintained primarily as a wilderness and

Until the early 1990s, the 43 mile section of Park roadway from Togue Pond Gate to Matagamon Gate was known as the Perimeter Road. The road was renamed the Tote Road to better reflect the nature of the narrow, graded gravel road. (Photo: Irvin Caverly, Jr.)

recreational purposes are to be regarded as of secondary importance.'" Recreation was not to "'encroach upon the main objective of this area which is to be "forever wild.'" Governor Baxter had not wanted the Park to be commercialized. Baxter had instead wanted it to remain a refuge from modern civilization, a refuge enjoyed by those who confronted nature on its own terms. Additionally, in terms of road safety, Lounsbury asserted that any changes to the road system–be it straightening, widening, or resurfacing—which might make it safe for motorcycle use, might also violate the Baxter Trusts. In turning to Baxter's Deeds of Trust and other writings to determine the best course of action to adopt, Lounsbury mirrored the sentiments and actions of numerous Park personnel and Authority members on this and other issues over the years. Not surprisingly, Lounsbury, like others who favored keeping motorcycles out of BSP, included Baxter's 1966 correspondence concerning motorcycles as part of her argument.[13]

In April 1966, Baxter had written to Forest Commissioner Austin Wilkins about a recent blowdown, and about the "motorscooters and motorcycles" he had heard were in Millinocket. Baxter wrote that:

> These machines are so noisy and numerous, they should be forbidden to go into the Park area. If unrestrained these noisy machines would frighten the wild life. I should like you to discuss this matter with the other members of the AUTHORITY and Helon Taylor and pass a vote putting this restriction into effect.[14]

It was this 1966 statement and the ensuing ban on motorcycles which motorcycle proponents argued was no longer valid in light of recent improvements in motorcycles.[15]

Ken Spaulding of the Sierra Club stated his organization's desire to see motorcycles kept out of the Park, both in respect to Baxter's wishes and due to the already too extensive use of the Park in the summertime. To this argument Vestal reiterated that the bikers had no desire to change or abuse the Park and that they would not impose any greater stress on the environment than other users. In addition, Vestal claimed, motorcyclists were disproportionately taxed in Maine. Motorcyclists paid money which went into the State General Fund and to the Department of Transportation—the implication being that they paid part of the money used to maintain roads in the Park and that they therefore should not be denied access to those roads. Vestal also restated that the bikers' primary intention was to walk, not ride, in BSP.[16]

Other statements followed, but in the end the Authority decided that in light of the fact that they had previously considered the matter, and that the expressed wishes of Governor Baxter were clear in his 1966 letter to Wilkins and the Authority had to honor those wishes, no changes to Park rules would be made concerning motorcycles. Changes made in motorcycle design since 1966 were not enough to necessitate a revision of the regulation. Baxter State Park did not belong to the State Park System and its situation was unique. Maine Forest Service Director Kenneth G. Stratton made a motion to deny UBM's request, Authority Chair Glenn H. Manuel seconded the motion, and Attorney General James S. Tierney's vote made the decision unanimous. After the vote, when asked how the Park responded when out-of-state persons came to BSP with motorcycles or oversized vehicles, Caverly stated that in some instances people on motorcycles had been provided with a place to leave their motorbikes, at their own risk, outside BSP and had been given rides to Roaring Brook so that they might hike. Although providing such services did not comprise official policy, Park personnel clearly tried to accommodate people when possible.[17]

The issue, of course, was not resolved "once and for all." The Park continued to receive the occasional letter inquiring about motorcycle use, then in 1993 UBM again requested a change in Park rules in favor of motorcycles. Greig Perkins, UBM president, wrote to the Authority in March asking them to change Park rules to allow motorcycle travel within Park boundaries. The request was made for only those motorcycles designed for road use, and the letter repeated many of the arguments made in 1986. United Bikers understood that Baxter had wanted some vehicles banned from BSP, however, the Authority had been invested with the power to make such changes to Park policy as it deemed necessary. Perkins wrote that existing Park rules "were quite adequate to control the use of motorcycles." He listed the pertinent regulations from the 1985 Revision and suggested that a statement to the effect that "no vehicles may be operated off of the established roadways" be added to Rule 8 which governed traffic, and that all references to motorcycles be stricken from Rule 18—the current rule forbidding motorcycle use in BSP. References in Rule 18 to all-terrain vehicles, trail bikes, and dirt bikes, however, should remain intact. United Bikers of Maine would be proud of any assistance they might provide the Authority in revising BSP Rules and Regulations.[18]

Following his March letter, Perkins sent the Authority copies of federal standards for motorcycle exhaust noise limits as set to meet the requirements of the Environmental Protection Agency.[19] Perkins attended the April 27, 1993, meeting of the BSP Park Use Committee, as did thirteen other persons, including four BSP staff members and other interested parties. Two sets of minutes, written by committee members Benjamin P. Townsend and John F. Loyd, Jr., survive and document both the specific issues discussed and the workings of the committee. At the meeting, held at the University of Maine at Augusta, Perkins reiterated the arguments set forth in his March 9 letter. Perkins also stated that reports made in the *Portland Press Herald* that either he or United Bikers of Maine would bring a lawsuit against the Authority or the Park should their request be denied were false. Perkins furthermore stated that he had read Hakola's *Legacy of a Lifetime* and reviewed Baxter's correspondence, the Deeds of Trust, and related records at the Maine State Library. Based upon these readings, he understood Baxter's concept of wilderness and, moreover, believed that the use of any vehicles within BSP "was anathema to Governor Baxter's original vision." Once Baxter allowed the use of vehicles of any type in BSP, however, "he opened the door to motorcycles."[20]

Perkins also stated at the meeting that United Bikers of Maine would agree to limiting the number of vehicles, including motorcycles, in BSP in order to help maintain the Park's wilderness character. In response to a question from Townsend, Perkins attempted to define a "touring motorcycle" as opposed to other types. Touring motorcycles were designed to be used exclusively on roads, and visual clues—such as motorcycle size, the possible presence of saddle bags or fiberglass boxes for gear, and perhaps the existence of a windshield—could help identify them. Overlap between touring and other motorcycles did exist, however, making it difficult to distinguish them completely, so the easiest solution would be to ban any motorcycle with an off-road capacity (as identified by their generally lighter weight, higher frame height, and exhaust position). When Townsend inquired as to what had changed since 1986 in either BSP or in motorcycles to support a new UBM rule change request, Perkins replied that no such changes had occurred. Rather, UBM felt that their request had been summarily rejected in 1986. They had since had time to prepare a "better proposal" and "a more thorough procedure" for making a request. The issue for them, as they saw it, was one of fairness. Perkins once again raised the issue of motorcyclists as taxpayers, taxpayers who contributed financially to the Park road system.[21]

A number of other persons addressed the Park Use Committee. Most of them expressed concerns about the possible detrimental effects of allowing motorcycles in the Park–in terms of noise, safety, and wilderness values. Perkins addressed these issues, even if he did not convince everyone there of his and other motorcyclists' positions. Both Jym St. Pierre of the Wilderness Society and BSP Park Resource Manager Jensen Bissell stated that the Deeds of Trust contained no clear answer to the issue, thus the Authority had to use its judgment in determining the matter based upon the spirit or intent of the Deeds. St. Pierre stated that the issue also had to be placed in the context of all Park traffic and the problem of increasing public use.[22]

Park Director Caverly questioned how allowing motorcycles into the Park would benefit BSP. Was it in the best interests of the Park to allow motorcycle access, Caverly queried, or was it in the best interests of a particular interest group? Caverly stated that he believed that, according to Baxter's correspondence and the Deeds of Trust, "the custodians of the Park should not act unless the proposed act or change is one which is clearly in the best interests of Baxter State Park, regardless of whether it enhances or detracts from an individual's or group's special interests." Allowing motorcycles in the Park was arguably "not in the best interests of the Park, and at best does nothing to enhance the best interests of the Park." Fairness to a specific group, furthermore, was not the issue. Regulations made in the Park's interest always adversely affected or harmed someone's interests, or could be so interpreted, such as the ban on pets and oversized vehicles, the restrictions on hunting, and so forth.[23] Chris Drew, BSP Chief Ranger, contributed the observation that even though the roads maintained by neighboring Bowater (formerly Great Northern) were better constructed and better maintained than those in BSP, Bowater, for safety reasons, prohibited motorcycle travel on its roads. In spite of UBM's argument that safety should be the concern of the individual cyclist, Drew believed that Park roads could pose serious safety hazards to motorcycle users.[24]

Having already decided to prepare a written summary of the motorcycle issue for consideration, and to adopt a recommendation in June to present the Authority in July, the Park Use Committee ended its April 1993 meeting. At the time of the April hearing, BSP and Authority and Advisory members had received roughly twenty-five letters from the public, all of which opposed allowing motorcycles in the Park, with the exception of the letters from UBM. In the following months letters continued to arrive, for a total of at least forty-two received, only two of which favored granting motorcycle access, the two sent by UBM.[25]

Some of the people who wrote to the Park about motorcycle regulations simply saw no need to allow motorcycles into BSP as motorcyclists already had the rest of the state if not the nation through which to ride. Motorcyclists also enjoyed access to the Park via other forms of transportation. Some letter writers simply found the idea of permitting motorcycle travel in the Park "appalling" or "offensive." Most of the writers considered motorcycle use to be an infringement on the wilderness, especially on wildlife, and many wrote that Baxter had clearly not wanted motorcycles or similar vehicles driven in BSP. In addition, some people seized the opportunity to suggest that snowmobiles also be totally excluded from the Park, or to assert that vehicles in general should be restricted. Writers mentioned concerns about noise levels and safety risks—to both motorcyclists and other persons. Several writers mentioned personal experiences in the Park, and discussed how motorcycles might have adversely affected those experiences or how they might negatively impact future trips to BSP. A number of writers referred specifically to the Deeds of Trust and to the responsibilities, as Park trustees, of the Authority. The correspondence ranged from handwritten messages on postcards to four or five page typed manuscripts. Previous to the April meeting, the Wilderness Society, in addition to sending a letter urging the Authority to maintain its ban on motorcycles, distributed a flier urging people to immediately write to BSP to voice their concerns and to attend the Use Committee meeting. The

Wilderness Society may have proved a catalyst for some of the letter writers, but the media had likewise played a role.[26]

The popular press, not surprisingly, followed the latest events in the continuing issue of vehicle use in BSP. One of the earliest articles about UBM's 1993 request appeared in the *Portland Press Herald* on April 8, 1993: the article which UBM said had incorrectly stated their intent to sue the Authority or the Park should the Authority vote not to revise the rule prohibiting motorcycles. The article did indeed state that the motorcycle club, 5,000 members strong, would "consider going to court, backed by the American Motorcycle Association," if their second attempt at securing entry to BSP failed. The article also quoted Greig Perkins on the motorcycle issue; stated that Authority Chair Susan Bell had said the Authority was giving the proposal serious consideration; quoted Attorney General Michael Carpenter as stating, "'I'm going to try my damnedest to adhere to what Governor Baxter wanted;'" and quoted Jym St. Pierre as stating that he considered the request "'pretty outrageous.'" The article clearly gave any interested party ammunition with which to fight, and provided the names of some of the principal participants should readers wish to make their own opinions known.[27]

The following day, April 9, 1993, the *Kennebec Journal* printed an editorial opposing the UBM request.[28] Other Maine newspapers followed suit. The *Times Record* agreed that it was unfair, but stated that "the solution is not to allow motorcycles. The solution is to ban snowmobiles, too." According to the newspaper editorial, the 1981 decision to allow snowmobiles on the Park's Perimeter Road "was a bad decision, but there's no time like the present to correct it." Motorcycles, snowmobiles, all-terrain vehicles, and any other "noisy, mechanized conveyances" should be kept out of Baxter State Park.[29] As the *Times* editorial illustrated, and as Park correspondence and Authority and Advisory minutes of the period indicated, vehicle use in general remained a controversial issue for BSP. Opening the door to discussion on one type of vehicle opened the door to debate on others.

Maine newspapers informed and queried the public about motorcycle use in BSP over the following months, while the Use Committee prepared a short legal history of the issue. The Park received additional letters—totaling fifty-one by mid-May—concerning motorcycle access. Only three of the May total supported changing the existing ban on motorcycles.[30] The Park Use Committee had formally met twice by this time, communicated by other means frequently, and made a preliminary report to the Authority in May.[31]

The Park Use Committee reconvened on June 14 in Brewer to discuss and vote on UBM's request. Park Director Caverly and Chief Ranger Drew attended the meeting, as did UBM members Joy Savoy and Darryl McTique, and Committee members John Loyd, Benjamin Townsend, John Howard, Roy Farnsworth, and Rod Hanscom. Committee member Rick Scribner voted in absentia. The Committee revisited the issues raised previously and reached six conclusions. They concluded that allowing motorcycle use in BSP might increase the total number of motor vehicles in the Park, a highly undesirable prospect as they were currently wrestling with the issue of reducing vehicle use in the Park and had been doing so since 1988. The Committee also concluded that safety hazards did indeed exist in BSP which posed greater threats to motorcycles than automobiles; that the issue of fairness was no more relevant to the motorcycle issue than it was to numerous other Park rules and users or potential user groups; that even though UBM proposed allowing only touring bikes into BSP such a distinction would be difficult to implement and would create legal and public-relation difficulties; that noise remained a concern in spite of assurances that it should not be and, again, that asking Park personnel to distinguish an allowable motorcycle from unallowable one on a case by case basis would create numerous difficulties; and that allowing motorcycles into the Park in sum would be "contrary to the wilderness character of the Park and detrimental to the resource."[32]

The Park Use Committee concluded that to grant motorcycle access privileges would be contrary to the "preservation of the resource and the wilderness as envisioned by Governor Baxter," the prime criteria for making any such decisions. The Committee reached the consensus that "the use of any additional types of vehicles within the Park, including motorcycles, is inconsistent with the preservation of the resource." After further discussion, the Committee voted against recommending the change proposed by UBM, and instead recommended that the Authority not eliminate the restrictions on motorcycles in BSP.[33] The minutes of this and other meetings, as well as various pieces of correspondence, indicate that UBM's request was seriously considered and the group's concerns and desires appreciated. The Park Use Committee, and ultimately the Authority, simply felt that allowing motorcycles into the Park would not be in the best interests of the Park.

Motorcycles comprised the first item on the agendas of the July 13, 1993, meetings of the Authority and the Advisory. Townsend, in the absence of Park Use Committee Chair Loyd, reviewed the three meetings held to discuss the request, and stated that after having considered such aspects as off-road motorcycle capacities, noise factors, Governor Baxter's vision of the Park, and the issue of cutting back on vehicle use in general in BSP, the Committee recommended that the rule prohibiting motorcycles be maintained. The Advisory then voted unanimously to make the same recommendation to the Authority. The Advisory did so that afternoon. After hearing the Advisory's report, and listening to commentary and discussion by motorcyclists, opponents of any rule change, and others, the Authority voted unanimously to deny the request by United Bikers of Maine to allow motorcycle use in Baxter State Park. United Bikers expressed their gratitude, via Director Caverly, for the openness of the process and for the opportunity they had had to have input into the process. The organization also asked to be placed on the Park's mailing list.[34]

Maine newspapers reported the Authority's vote in succeeding days. Some applauded the Authority on its decision, as did the *Lewiston Sunday Sun*. The *Sun* published a short editorial about the decision. The close of the piece simply stated that "although some concessions have been made to allow greater access to the Park—cars have been allowed since 1949—the Park Authority was wise to limit the incursion of civilization into Baxter's wilderness."[35]

What several papers highlighted in their coverage of the motorcycle decision, however, was the issue of controlling vehicle use in general in the Park. The *Bangor Daily News* (*BDN*), for example, reported that what caught many persons "off guard," was not the Authority's decision but the reasoning behind their decision and "what it portends for the future." As the newspaper interpreted it, "the press of cars, trucks, snowsleds, and people is straining capacity and a controlled quality experience at the Park." Therefore, "the Authority will consider limiting vehicular access and human congestion at Baxter before the Park chokes on its own popularity."[36]

Although the *BDN* may have used different terms in identifying certain problems which confronted the Park, the paper did communicate some of the sentiments expressed by the Authority, the Advisory, and by Park personnel during the previous meetings. The paper stated that Caverly "was convinced from the beginning" that in light of increased demand on the Park, "'this was a time for us to look for ways to reduce that traffic and not increase it.'" The paper noted that Caverly had come "away from the motorcycle deliberations with respect for the process and the quality of dialogue with UBM spokesmen." The UBM request, however, was simply not "'compatible and consistent with intent of the Park and the mandate of the Governor.'"[37]

The *BDN* also stated that Attorney General Carpenter had pointed out that different types of vehicles, be they passenger cars, vans, snowmobiles, or motorcycles, make different demands and have different impacts on Park resources and its environment. "Collectively," however, "they challenge existing management practices and issues of fairness." In regard to the specific context of the UBM request—concerning such factors as "safety, congestion, and diminishment of the Park's value as a source of solitude"—Carpenter had stated that, "'we already took a step down that slippery slope with snowmobiles,'" referring to the Authority vote to allow snowmobiles on the Perimeter Road twelve years earlier.[38]

A "slippery slope indeed." And the *BDN*'s further discussion of what it stated might well be "far tighter regulation of the flow of visitors" into BSP could easily create another slippery slope of public opinion, just as numerous media reports of vehicle and human access control, road and gate changes or reductions, the snowmobile issue, and other factors or attempts to regulate demand on the Park had created and would create slippery slopes of public opinion. The article even reported Caverly as having stated that "Park rules should be amended as a result of challenges from groups expected to demand changes in policy—an end to snowmobiling, for example." This seems to have been something of a misunderstanding, namely the omission of the crucial word "not." And it had the potential for creating greater misunderstandings. The *BDN* did, however, identify current ways the problem of Park use or overuse was being examined and possible solutions, or partial solutions, being considered, such as the consideration of adopting a shuttle service. The article rightly identified the need for the Authority and the Park to "confront and resolve the conflict inherent in enduring appeal and unlimited use."[39]

The *Maine Sunday Telegram* went further than either the *Lewiston Sunday Sun* or the *Bangor Daily News* in its coverage of, and opinions about, the Authority's decision of July 13, 1993. Five days after the decision, the *Sunday Telegram* ran an editorial entitled "Motorcycles, Snowmobiles, Don't Mix With Katahdin." In addition to congratulating the Authority on its decision, as had the *Sun*, the *Sunday Telegram* criticized the Authority for allowing snowmobiles in the Park. The Authority had done so, according to the newspaper, even after "then-Attorney General Joseph Brennan issued a 1976 opinion that their presence would violate the Baxter Trust." The paper stated that if Townsend's comment that "the noise of motorcycles alone is enough to keep them out of Baxter" was true, the same should be true for snowmobiles. The BSPA should "reconvene and finish the job of removing noise pollution from the vastnesses of Baxter" by voting to prohibit snowmobiles in the Park.[40]

In an article by Dieter Bradbury published in the *Sunday Telegram* that same day, the paper announced, in its headline, that "Motorists May Be on Way Out at Baxter." Bradbury stated that discussion at the Authority meeting had indicated that the Authority members had agreed that the time had come to address the issue of vehicle use in general in the Park and furthermore, that such discussion "could lead to a cap on vehicle numbers, the exclusion of snowmobiles—or even a ban on private vehicles altogether." Bradbury did point out that the issue of overuse was not a new one to Authority and Advisory members, and that studies in the previous five years had lead to changes in "parking spaces" and to the relocation of the Togue Pond gatehouse to "make it easier for rangers to divert vehicles away from full lots." A shuttle service had been considered, but dismissed due to a lack of money to pay for a test program and to build a lot outside of BSP for private vehicle parking. Other plans and actions involved methods of encouraging visitors to use less popular sections of the Park, areas east and north of Katahdin. Bradbury quoted Caverly and the Authority members on their opinions, and indicated that steps would no doubt be taken in the future to limit vehicle access.[41]

The Park heard more from opponents and proponents of motorcycle use in BSP in following days. The NRCM congratulated the Authority on its decision and expressed pleasure at the willingness of the Authority, as indicated by the Maine press, to re-examine the issue of snowmobile use in BSP and to consider a general limitation on vehicle use in the Park.[42] Yet, some people continued to feel that it was unfair and discriminatory to ban motorcycles. In one case, a motorcycle advocate wrote to a motorcycle enthusiast and United States Senator from Colorado, Ben Nighthorse Campbell, who then wrote to Maine United States Senator William S. Cohen, who in turn wrote to Park Director Caverly about the ban. Caverly responded by writing to the complainant, and sent copies of his letter to Cohen and other interested parties, explaining the actions and decisions surrounding the motorcycle issue.[43]

Yet, in spite of some continued controversy, the furor surrounding the motorcycle issue essentially ended in 1993, at least for the time being. As with the snowmobile issue, future Authority and Advisory members, as well as Park personnel, would no doubt have the opportunity, if it might be called that, of addressing the issue again. Unlike the snowmobile issue, however, the 1993 Authority was able to continue a consistent policy on motorcycle use in Baxter State Park: access denied.

Baxter State Park Director, Irvin C. Caverly, Jr., pictured in the Turner Deadwater. His Park career began nearby at Russell Pond.
(Photo: Edward Dwyer)

Chapter Nine

The "Staff of The Authority:" Baxter State Park Personnel

From scheduling camping reservations to participating in search and rescue operations, from harvesting trees to protecting endangered plants, Baxter State Park personnel perform a variety of duties. Some Park tasks are seasonal in nature, others require daily attention. Some operations are commonplace, others, such as rounding up caribou, have been much less so. While Park staff are assigned job categories, such categories have proved subject to revision, as have the various tasks personnel perform. In times of crisis, be it fire or fatality, the entire staff has worked together for both the good of the public and the protection of the Park. Although changes in Park staffing occurred over the years, core features of 1970 BSP jobs and personnel remained clearly recognizable in 1994.

In early 1970, Baxter State Park employed eight permanent staff members and twenty-four seasonal employees. In 1994, the Park employed seventeen year-round employees and twenty-eight seasonal workers. In early 1970, BSP daily operations were managed by the Park Supervisor, Harry Kearney, with Irvin C. Caverly, Jr. serving as Assistant Supervisor. In 1994, Irvin C. Caverly, Jr., as Park Director, managed daily operations with Chief Ranger Chris Drew filling some of the duties once assigned to the Supervisor's position. In addition to the Director's and the Chief Ranger's positions, by the close of 1994 the Park had added the positions of Park Naturalist and Resource Manager, both of them serving—as did the Chief Ranger, the Secretary to the Director, and the Reservations Clerk—immediately under the Director. Each of the five held management responsibilities for other staff members. In early 1970, the Assistant Supervisor managed all field personnel, while the Reservations Clerk and a Ranger II/Carpenter reported directly to the Supervisor.[1]

Park staff remained State employees in 1994, subject to classifications and regulations established by the Maine Department of Personnel. However, Baxter Trust Funds and other Park revenue funded their salaries. When Governor Percival P. Baxter died on June 12, 1969, he left behind combined Trust Funds of nearly seven million dollars—most of which went to Baxter State Park. Ideally, the interest on the Baxter State Park Trust Fund, as the combined Trust Fund became known, would provide sufficient funds to make the administration of BSP self-supporting. In reality, user fees and other sources of income proved necessary to supplement Trust Fund interest. In 1970, the Baxter State Park Authority voted unanimously to provide for the general operations of the Park through Baxter Trust Fund income. This became effective on July 1, 1971, and remained in effect throughout the period studied. On a practical level, it meant that additional personnel could be hired to meet the demands of Park operations, demands which a much smaller work force, generally a total of about nine individuals for a given year, had handled in the late 1960s. The increase in personnel expenses and hiring began before 1971, however, resulting in the staff structure already noted by April 1970.[2]

The change in staffing was evident in schedules prepared in 1970 to meet the new financial situation. During the 1969-1970 fiscal year, Park salaries had totaled $25,886.32. For the 1970-1971 fiscal year, the new budget allowed for salary expenses of $61,509, and estimated those for the next two years at $143,534 and $147,807 respectively, a dramatic increase for what had been a small work force. By the opening of the 1971-1972 fiscal year, the schedules anticipated modifying the work force to include fourteen permanent and twenty seasonal employees. Four new positions for Campground Ranger IIs, plus a Business Manager and a Clerk Stenographer II, would be added to the ranks of year-round employees. Changes in seasonal employees would involve Campground Ranger I positions and Campground Attendants. The 1971-1972 schedule for seasonal employees did not differentiate between personnel stationed at campgrounds and those at the four gatehouses. In 1970, four seasonal rangers were stationed at Park gatehouses. Togue Pond also had two attendants assigned, Matagamon and Nesowadnehunk each had one, while the Telos gatehouse operated with just the one Campground Ranger I officially stationed there. Personnel stationed at gatehouses worked twenty-nine weeks per year, as did one Ranger I at each of the eight campgrounds then operated by BSP. Other personnel stationed at the campgrounds, five with Campground Ranger I status and three classified as Campground Attendants, worked a fifteen-week year in 1970.[3]

Employment status and pay rates were always important in Park and personnel budgeting, but Park personnel was always more than a matter of rank and statistics. Many persons enjoyed long tenures with Baxter State Park, moving into different job classifications over the years and learning first hand both field and administrative work. Irvin "Buzz" Caverly served throughout the period studied, as did Ranger Thomas P. Chase. A number of persons worked for a majority of the period, including Rangers Barry MacArthur, Robert E. Howes, Loren Goode, Charles Kenney, and Chris M. Drew. Janice Caverly also worked for BSP for most of the period—working more of the years between 1970 and 1994 than any other female employee. She started in an official capacity as a gatehouse attendant during 1968, then counted and registered snowmobiles in 1970 and began permanent employment in the reservations department at Park Headquarters in 1972.[4]

Harry Kearney became Baxter State Park Supervisor on November 1, 1968, and served in that capacity until May 27, 1971. Kearney was the fifth person to fill the position, Harold Dyer having been the first BSP Supervisor, from 1940 to 1950, followed by Robert H. Dyer (1950), Helon Taylor (1950-1967), and Irvin C. Caverly, Jr. (1968-1969). Fred M. Pitman and Rodney Sargent had respectively served as Acting Supervisors between the tenures of Supervisors Dyer and Taylor, and Taylor and Caverly. Although the BSPA hired Kearney in November 1968 as Park Supervisor, Caverly actually remained in that position until March 1969. The years of Kearney's tenure as Park Supervisor witnessed the death of Percival Baxter, the initial expansion of Park personnel and operations following Baxter's death, and the phasing out of private leases within the Park. Questions concerning various Park operations had begun to find expression before Kearney retired in 1971—especially issues concerning leases, changing Rules and Regulations, and some forestry practices—but most of the major controversies of the twenty-five year period did not erupt until later. One major exception was that of snowmobiles, but snowmobiles would remain an issue long after Kearney departed. This does not mean that the position of

Park Supervisor proved to be an easy one for Kearney, however, as the hours were long, duties numerous, and tensions high.[5]

The Authority, specifically the Attorney General, asked Kearney to step down in early 1971 as Park administration was not operating as smoothly as anticipated. In July 1971, the Authority authorized a separation settlement with Kearney, awarding him $1,085 in salary, holiday, and vacation pay, and $2,000 "in lieu of all other rights and claims." Kearney was not the only staff member to be asked to step down in recent years. His predecessor and successor, Irvin C. Caverly, Jr., had served only ten months before stepping down, at the Authority's request, in 1969. Caverly had been only twenty-eight years old when appointed Park Supervisor in 1968. He experienced problems with under-staffing and the lack of an office and secretary, problems with Park visitors ignoring such Park regulations as the ban on pets, problems with owners of land adjacent to the Park—one issue being unauthorized wood cutting on Park lands—and a few other difficulties. He willingly handed the reins over to Kearney, who then experienced some of the same difficulties. By 1971, in addition to changes in Park funding, staffing, operations, and administration, Caverly had gained additional experience and maturity, and the Authority appointed him to the Supervisor's position once again, first on an interim basis then in 1972 on a permanent basis.[6]

From 1971 until the close of 1994, Caverly would serve as Acting Park Supervisor, Park Supervisor, Acting Park Director, and ultimately Park Director. Caverly's long tenure as a Park administrator, along with the long employment records of other staff members and Park associates, would provide continuity in Park operations and administration over the years of changing Authorities. Positive or negative, justified or unjustified, Caverly's long term association with Baxter State Park frequently resulted in his name and Park operations being viewed by the public as synonymous. Caverly did exert some influence with the various Authorities, in terms of being able to advise or update them on various issues and to make staff needs and opinions known. This was especially true as Caverly gained experience as an administrator. Yet, issues of Park policy ultimately rested with the individual members of the Baxter State Park Authority. Caverly remained an appointed official, subject to removal by the Authority should he fail to perform his duties in a satisfactory manner. And, as had been true before 1970, people associated with the Park did not always agree that Caverly was the best person available to head BSP operations. However, periods of discontent were brief, and Caverly consistently received high job evaluations from the late 1970s—the earliest years for extant records—through the mid-1990s. Caverly's job evaluations became increasingly strong from the early 1980s, when Caverly became Park Director, to the close of the period.[7]

Before offering the position of Park Supervisor to Caverly on a permanent basis, Business Manager William E. Cross, formerly of the Maine Forest Service and hired full-time in 1971 (he had previously performed some financial tasks for the Park), assembled a job description for the position. Although some items such as living arrangements might be left undefined at the current time, the basic job requirements, Cross argued, and perhaps "the conditions and terms of employment, should ... be agreed upon before the position is filled or interviews held, rather than perhaps haggle[d over] during the interview [process] or after the position is filled." Cross believed "that this should even apply to Buz[z] should he become the permanent Supervisor." The position would be advertised after the current hiring freeze ended. (Caverly, in the meantime, had been working at his old pay rate while Cross, as instructed by the Authority, determined a way to compensate him for his new responsibilities through the Personnel Board.)[8] The State listed the Supervisor's job as non-standard, meaning that Personnel had no formal description or set hours for the position. Cross determined that the job demanded at least a forty-eight hour week, and believed that it should remain a non-standard position.[9]

The Supervisor's position required that the person hired oversee "the preservation of Baxter State Park" and the "construction, operation, and maintenance of the various Park facilities" plus equipment and tools. The Supervisor was also responsible for supervising and participating in "rescue operations of lost or injured persons," enforcing recreational Rules and Regulations, maintaining "records on conditions affecting Park forest, wildlife, and winter food conditions," and "preparing preliminary budgets, requisitions for materials and supplies, etc., in conjunction with the Business Manager." The position required "extensive knowledge of professional forestry and wildlife principles and practices" and of equipment and principles used "in managing forest and recreation areas." The job also required the ability to work effectively with the public and maintain "control of the area and Park visitors" within the context of Park regulations. The desired applicant would have "considerable experience in professional management including experience in operating a major wilderness area," and a four year college or university degree "with specialization in forestry, wildlife, and outdoor recreation."[10]

Caverly, a native of Cornville, Maine, did not bring a college education to his position as Park Supervisor. The educational component desired by Cross and others in 1971 would be expressed again in the early 1980s when the Authority sought to fill a fairly new position, that of Park Director. In both instances the education Caverly had received while on the job–in some instances through formal training sessions or schools, but just as often acquired in the field and through working with the public–served to qualify him for the position. Caverly had started with the Park as a seasonal ranger in 1960, undergoing, along with other new rangers, a three day training session at the Great Northern Hotel in Millinocket. Such training sessions had been initiated by the Authority only a few years earlier, were not specific to any one location, and would be added to as time went on, some becoming increasingly specialized. Caverly attended most of the educational forums offered in subsequent years, including training programs at the Maine Criminal Justice Academy and the ten week Maine Fish and Wildlife Warden School. As a seasonal ranger Caverly worked first at Abol Campground then at Russell Pond Campground during the 1960 season; served at Russell Pond for the 1961, 1962, and 1963 seasons; then worked at Katahdin Stream Campground in 1964. Caverly became a year-round employee in 1965 and lived at Katahdin Stream until 1968, at which time he and Janice Caverly moved to Nesowadnehunk Field. The Caverlys later lived in Patten for a short time, then moved to Millinocket. By late 1971 Caverly had worked for Baxter State Park as a seasonal ranger, a Commissioned Ranger, a Supervisor, and as an Acting Supervisor. He had had sufficient time to become thoroughly acquainted with the Park, its employees, and its operations. In 1972, the Authority discussed the Supervisor's position in a closed meeting, then notified Caverly that they had elected to grant him the position on a permanent basis.[11]

While the Authority had pondered how to best fill the Supervisor's position, the increase in Park staffing and the modifications in Park administration had continued. Hiring additional rangers and campground attendants brought some problems and some advantages. Early in the period, sufficient housing had to be arranged for personnel stationed within the Park. In July 1971, shortly after he became interim or Acting Supervisor, Caverly reminded the Authority that the Park had only three year-round facilities to house the eight permanent rangers then employed. (When Caverly had ended his previous tenure as Supervisor the Park had employed only two rangers year round.) In addition, former Supervisor Kearney had told seasonal gatekeeper Homer King that he could live at Togue Pond year-round, a decision which the Authority determined unauthorized. Kearney had also promised new BSP carpenter Louis Bossey that he could have a year-round camp at Togue Pond. This likewise posed difficulties, and Caverly was instructed to look for a shop space in Patten, Bossey's current place of residence, while Cross would look for a house trailer which might be set up at Togue Pond for the carpenter and his wife. (No evidence exists, however, that the Park ever installed such a trailer.) The Authority also voted to proceed with moving and winterizing the Nesowadnehunk ranger camp for year-round use, to winterize a crew camp at the same location, and to make repairs or improvements elsewhere to meet staff housing needs. Housing for Caverly, and for Park Headquarters, was currently being leased in Millinocket at 413 Katahdin Avenue.[12]

With an increase in clerical and administrative staff, the Park experienced a shortage of work space as well as of housing. The Authority had recognized that need before 1970, and began planning for new office space in its 1971 budget. The Authority rented space for a few seasons on Aroostook Avenue (in the Gonya Building)—thus ending a long standing practice of sharing office space with the Maine Forest Service on Central Avenue—then moved to a nearby location until 1976. The Park also rented carpentry and mechanical space on Medway Road for several years. Commencing construction in the mid-1970s, the Park built a new office building and compound at 64 Balsam Drive in Millinocket. The project began with an initial purchase of three lots in 1972 for $9,500 and a final purchase of two of seven lots in 1977 for $59,730. Total cost for the grounds which would eventually house BSP Headquarters, a service station, a warehouse facility, and a home for the Director—later converted to an administrative apartment over a supply area—was $92,232. Costs for constructing the new headquarters building-which housed administrative, clerical, and reservation staff as well as a public meeting and slide show room—were just over $185,000. The Park relocated its office to the new facility in mid-1976.[13]

Other needs of the expanding work force likewise demanded attention. Park rangers had only recently received uniforms. (The Authority had approved uniforms in 1960, before that rangers purchased standard work clothing.)[14] New summer uniforms had been purchased in 1970, but additional clothing requirements still existed. In 1971 Caverly requested, and the Authority approved, the purchase of ten inch high boots which would provide rangers with necessary support and protection. The Authority likewise discussed, and reluctantly approved, the purchase of twelve, 38 caliber, revolvers for BSP Commissioned Ranger assignments. To Caverly went the task of issuing revolvers to qualified rangers. Rangers were to carry firearms only upon specific orders, or in instances of "extreme emergency." The Maine State Police would be contacted about providing training on the proper use of firearms, training which they subsequently provided at Camp Keyes, Augusta. The Fish and Game Department, which supplied some winter clothing to BSP staff, eventually agreed to provide newer serviceable used firearms and holsters. The Park and Authority continued to work on establishing comprehensive rules and regulations concerning firearm use throughout the early 1970s. In 1974, the Authority stated that in general they believed "firearms should be accessible if needed, but not worn in a conspicuous manner." They "should not be visible in the campgrounds or on patrol under normal situations." Park staff and the Authority would continue to review firearm policies in following years.[15]

In the interests of maintaining necessary communications, the Authority also approved the purchase of an AC radio unit for the Supervisor's residence as well as one for the Telos Gate, which the Authority decided needed a permanent attendant and the appropriate housing. The general Park radio system had been previously established. The Authority voted, in addition, to secure State of Maine seals, in the form of decals, to affix to BSP vehicles, boats, and equipment. After securing approval, Caverly commissioned illustrator Maurice "Jake" Day—Walt Disney "Bambi" artist—to design a unique seal for Baxter State Park. Two years later the Authority voted—after securing legislative approval—to equip BSP vehicles with blue lights to aid rangers in enforcement duties. Park vehicles themselves had been updated and upgraded after Baxter Trust Fund money had become available. By the close of 1971, Park personnel were using all 1970 and 1971 vehicles, and all Park snowsleds were of 1971 vintage.[16]

With new equipment, insignia, and relatively new uniforms to make them, at least theoretically, better prepared and easier to identify, one thing Park rangers would not have as part of their visage would be "excess hair." True to the spirit of the times, the Authority had voted in January 1971 that Kearney could advise rangers that long hair and beards would not be allowed on the job.[17] The prohibition survived, without legal challenge, for the next twenty-five years although, according to Caverly, he realized all along that such a challenge might someday arise. Caverly did meet with rangers in the early 1980s to discuss the dress code, and thereafter had the code amended to permit rangers to wear neatly groomed mustaches when they chose, and to sport beards during the winter months.[18]

Also a reflection of the times, 1970s staff training included drug education. A significant number of citations given to Park visitors in the 1970s involved illegal drug use, as recorded by rangers in their activity reports and as indicated in monthly and other reports of Park Supervisors and Acting Supervisors. Although such reports were free of the violence associated with some aspects of illegal drug use elsewhere in later decades, the concerns were significant. Staff members perceived that the potential for violence existed, and expressed concerns over possible resistance to arrests and assaults with deadly weapons. In 1972, the Authority agreed to send Ranger Thomas Chase to a drug education school if an appropriate institution could be located.[19]

Such drug education would supplement Warden School training given BSP rangers by the early 1970s. Rangers attended the Maine Department of Inland Fisheries and Game Warden School training—as they did other types of employee education in the early years such as courses offered by the New Brunswick Ranger School, the Maine Forest Service, the United States Park Service, and the United States Department of Fish and Wildlife—on a rotating basis, with an ultimate goal of having all rangers attend the school. As previously discussed, special training sessions and other educational forums were also conducted during the mid-1970s onward to meet Park needs for employees trained in search and rescue methods. Preventing illegal drug use in the Park and apprehending or fining violators of Park rules was only one sector of BSP rangers' work in the 1970s and later, and the Authority and administration attempted to keep law enforcement responsibilities to a minimum. In 1969, already concerned with an increase in "policing" duties, the Authority stated that the "main purpose" of the Authority and staff was "to preserve the integrity of the Park."[20] However, staff members did, in accordance with new State regulations, attend the Maine Criminal Justice Academy in the early 1970s (undertaking roughly one hundred hours of training). In 1974, of two BSP rangers attending the school's shorter, ten week program, Ranger Laurant Pingree became vice-president of his class while Ranger George Blackburn was co-valedictorian. Commissioned BSP Rangers also attended the academy in the 1980s, Chris Drew being the last to attend, and received in-service training elsewhere.[21] Baxter State Park employees were educated to deal with a variety of duties in a variety of ways.

After Caverly's appointment to Park Supervisor in 1972, the Park continued to seek a sufficient number of qualified employees, or those who could become qualified through standard training sessions, to meet the operational and administrative goals established at the turn of the decade. Caverly developed a new organizational chart for Park staff, proposing that eight new employees be hired for the 1973 season. The Authority approved four new positions, bringing the number of employees to forty-seven, a number raised by five the following year, then lowered to forty-eight in 1975.[22] The classifications of a few employees also changed in 1974. The

Supervisor gained a full-time secretary in 1974 after the resignation of his part-time secretary, and the Park gained a full-time mechanic. Previously local garages had serviced and repaired Park motor vehicles and the Park contracted for snowmobile maintenance. The increase and upgrading of BSP vehicles and snowsleds after 1969 made the need for a Park mechanic obvious and economically expedient. The Park attempted to have the carpenter's position reclassified in 1974 to reflect the scope of the job performed and to prevent the carpenter from resigning due to what seemed substandard wages for the job, but encountered difficulties along the way. Gerald Merry eventually replaced Bossey as carpenter. Merry later advanced to a higher ranked BSP position.[23]

During the early 1970s, the Park dealt with its increased staff size in a variety of contexts, including standardizing hiring procedures with the Maine Department of Personnel. The Authority determined that all positions should go through Personnel "in the normal method of recruitment and the establishment of an eligible register."[24] Applicants would then undergo appropriate examinations. The Supervisor could "continue the same practice as in the past" for hiring seasonal employees. He could use direct hiring—applications could be taken, screening conducted, interviews held, and decisions made at Park headquarters—until 1974. Although the Authority ultimately voted, with the Personnel Department's support, to retain direct hiring for seasonal positions, permanent or career positions were made subject to the civil service process. The initial application and screening process for permanent jobs was handled in Augusta, with successive lists of the top three candidates submitted to the Park and Authority for review until an applicant had been selected for a particular job.[25]

In late 1972, to meet administrative needs and to allow for the development of a Park Master Plan, the Authority decided to establish a new position at BSP, that of Park Director. In early 1973 the Authority voted that Chair Maynard Marsh work with Personnel to determine a job description and pay range. The Director's position, at least as initially envisioned, would in some ways overlap with or assume some of the duties of the Supervisor's position. As the Authority saw it, the position would "include Park planning, supervision, and training of all Park personnel, public relations, law enforcement, traffic control, environmental control, and liaison with the members of the Baxter State Park Authority." The successful applicant would have an educational background in "recreational and natural resource planning as well as scientific forest management."[26] With spruce-budworm infestation becoming a problem throughout the state, and with concerns over cutting rights, brush spraying, and other operations being voiced, the Authority wisely sought someone able to address these and other issues and to devote the necessary time to developing a master plan which would cover such policy matters.

The Authority approved a job description for the Director's position in late February 1973 and Personnel approved the position the following month. By late July three applicants had been screened and scheduled for interviews. The Authority held the interviews, but did not select any of the applicants for the position. The Authority did not consider the applicants suitable for the position. Those persons who discussed the matter at the BSPA meeting on July 19 generally agreed that "improper advertising/notification was the reason for the small number and type of applications."[27]

In the autumn of 1973 the Park began a new search for a Director. The Authority requested that the position's salary range be increased, but Personnel did not grant the raise. Personnel did agree to readvertise on a wider basis, however, including advertising in out-of-state publications.[28] The revised advertising strategy succeeded in drawing a larger pool of applicants, and benefits furnished the position—including housing, a vehicle, and a telephone—perhaps helped compensate for the pay range. The Personnel Department assigned a closing date of April 1, 1974, for accepting applications or letters of inquiry, sixty-nine of which were received by early March. Few if any persons applied thereafter, and an initial screening reduced the number of applicants under consideration to nine men classified as "qualified" and another nine designated as falling "in a gray area." Personnel requested that the Authority review the applications to help reduce the candidates to a number which could be reviewed by the oral board in one day. A date of May 2, 1974, was established for screening the applicants.[29]

The Authority, in October 1974, selected Arthur Lee Tibbs for the BSP Director's position, pending approval of Personnel as Tibbs held residency in another state, Pennsylvania. Personnel approved the selection, and staff and Authority worked to locate housing for Tibbs in Millinocket—where few units in the desired price range were available—prior to his starting date of March 3, 1975.[30]

With Tibbs filling the Director's position as of March 1975, the Park and Authority turned to another basic personnel need. They began to seek a full-time forester to address forestry and environmental matters, especially those concerning the 1974 blowdown and management of the northern two townships or the Scientific Forest Management Area as they were later called. The Park initially, in 1975, contracted with Kim Kolman of Kolman Land Associates of Brewer to serve as a consulting forester, his primary responsibility being that of planning and managing the blowdown salvage operation. In early 1977, the Authority hired Kolman as a temporary staff forester after personnel approved a ninety-day forester's position. As the BSP staff forester, Kolman's responsibilities included work on the Park's master plan, which was well under way by 1977, and with creating an SFMA management plan, portions of which Kolman and others had already started. In the midst of finishing the general Park plan and taking inventory in the SFMA, the fire of 1977 occurred, necessitating increased employee hours in another aspect of Park operations. Along with the general Park plan, as approved in 1978, BSP staff formulated the Park's first comprehensive fire plan.[31]

When the Maine Department of Personnel finally approved a full-time Park Forester position, and the necessary job description and classification range had been determined, the Authority hired George Ruopp in early 1979. Ruopp, like Kolman before him, had the responsibility of developing an SFMA management plan and participating in and advising about day-to-day Park forest operations. With Ruopp's guidance, Park staff and Advisory members completed the long desired and awaited SFMA management plan in December 1980. When Ruopp resigned his position in 1983, shortly after making an unsuccessful bid for the Director's position, Fred Rooney became interim Park Forester, assisted by forest technician Paul Rumney. Then, for a short period of time in the mid-1980s, the Maine Forest Service guided SFMA operations with Dennis Brennan serving as the assigned Baxter State Park Forester.[32] The Authority eventually authorized the hiring of a Natural Resource Manager to manage the SFMA. In the meantime, other personnel issues had to be addressed.

Just as the mid- to late-1970s had witnessed difficulties in getting a Park Forester hired and silvicultural operations under way in the SFMA, other problems affecting Park operations and personnel surfaced. Some of the difficulties involved basic adjustments to changes in Park management and operations resulting from the shift to Baxter Trust Fund based finances and the increased interactions with the Maine Department of Personnel. Issues such as Collective Bargaining, Workmen's Compensation (later renamed Workers' Compensation), the Maine Fair Employment Act, and related measures had to be addressed. So, too, did the Park and Authority have to acknowledge the fact that Trust Fund income, although ample, had to be carefully managed if the Park was to meet staffing and other needs without securing compensation from the State General Fund. Part of the difficulty arose from the simple increase in the number of persons employed by Baxter State Park by the mid-1970s, employees hired largely to meet the ever increasing demands on the Park for public recreational opportunities and to meet staffing shortages experienced in the 1960s and earlier. Environmental, recreational, and forestry related issues all created increased demands on Park personnel.

Requests for job reclassifications continued in the mid-1970s, as numerous Park employees still believed that they were doing more work, or more types of work, than their current salaries or titles indicated. Authority members sometimes found themselves in the frustrating position of trying to reconcile employee perceptions that the Authority could make any necessary decisions to meet employee requests, while in reality the Authority and the Park "by law had to abide by most of the same rules" established for other State departments, regardless of funding sources. This conflict of perception and reality was apparent at a May 1976 Authority meeting at which a group of employees presented their stances on various issues. Ranger Chris Drew spoke for the rangers present, stating that the rangers had to deal with a variety of matters including management, public relations, and law enforcement, and do so while dwelling in primitive living conditions. The rangers believed that they should be considered "law enforcement oriented, and as such [they] were not getting equal pay for equal work."[33]

Drew's comments led to a discussion as to whether rangers served primarily as law enforcement officers or as conservation oriented personnel. Attorney General Joseph Brennan stated that the rangers' first need was for higher salaries and that the issue of their primary role fell second to that need. Fred Holt, Advisory member and former Director of the Bureau of Forestry, stated that if the Authority did not establish a policy which placed less emphasis on law enforcement and more on public relations the Park would suffer, and suggested that Tibb's staff reorganization plans be carried out with "the idea of rangers being primarily recreational and not law enforcement" personnel.[34]

Park employees had concerns over fringe benefits as well as job classifications and pay rates. Business Manager William Cross was able to inform the staff at the May 1976 meeting that a new Workmen's Compensation Insurance policy had become effective as of that April. In addition, the State and the Personnel Department, especially through the Hay Associates Study, were currently examining some of the same issues as interested Park employees, and the Authority in following months tried to work out the best solution to such issues as subsidized housing and utilities. Employees also inquired about—if they had to pay for it at all—purchasing propane gas at the State's price, which Cross agreed to look into, and about securing a food or gas allowance, or both.[35]

The Hay Study, initiated by Governor James Longley to evaluate State employee pay rates, benefits, performance, and so forth, did establish new pay rates for State employees as of November 1, 1976. The Park, however, was exempt from the new regulations governing pay and housing (the State regulations did not allow for employer paid housing unless an employee was required to live in State furnished facilities as a requirement of employment). Yet, Baxter State Park employees would receive a pay increase in November, and those who worked non-standard work weeks would receive an additional 10 percent pay increase as of October 19, 1976. The Authority voted to give

BSP workers pay increases because they wanted the staff to retain salaries equitable to those of other State employees.[36]

The issue of how to handle the housing situation remained unresolved in November. Numerous staff members lived in Park housing. Several rangers maintained residences inside BSP for work purposes and homes outside the Park to provide for their children's schooling needs. In addition to facilities within Park boundaries, the Park also maintained housing outside BSP for administrative staff. Those employees furnished Park housing did not pay rent or utilities. Inequities existed in that all employees did not receive Park housing (the growth of personnel had continued to exceed the availability of Park housing), nor were all Park facilities, even those within the Park, considered equally desirable. Another problem, one which Ranger Charles Kenny voiced in October, was that any rent or utilities charged rangers for Park housing, rangers who maintained additional housing outside the Park, would place such a burden on them that perhaps no such rangers would be able to afford living in the Park. The housing situation caused sufficient problems as to necessitate immediate attention. With the Park currently facing budgeting problems, and with salaries comprising 65 percent of the annual budget, constructing additional housing so that all permanent employees could live in Park housing was suggested but not a real option. The Authority also considered the options of adopting the State policy, establishing a living allowance, or initiating a combination of several options.[37]

The Advisory subcommittee established to study the issue of housing and fringe benefits reported their findings in early December 1976. Tibbs and Caverly had already recommended that no charges be levied for Park facilities, as living in the Park was a condition of employment for those who did so. If the Authority made any policy changes they should not initiate them until at least April of the following year so that employees would have time to budget. The committee supported the first portion of this recommendation, that such Park housing was a condition of employment, but believed that the employees should still pay for their utilities (propane gas as well as any gasoline burned in generators). After some discussion, the

Authority voted unanimously that as of January 1, 1977, personnel living in housing within the Park would pay for utilities.[38]

The Advisory subcommittee recommended that staff members living in Park owned housing in Millinocket pay both rent and utility expenses. They also recommended that at some time in the future the house currently occupied by the Director be sold and Park property consolidated. Director Tibbs stated that although the housing allotted him had been a condition of his employment, in light of current budgetary problems "he would have no problem with paying rent should the Authority so vote—provided all employees were treated in the same manner." Although the Park had traditionally furnished housing for the Park Supervisor, Caverly indicated that he agreed with Authority Chair Maynard Marsh that benefits enjoyed in the past by some Park employees could not be expected to continue. John Walker, Bureau of Forestry Director, concurred. After further discussion, Attorney General Joseph Brennan moved "that the Authority continue to follow through on commitments of previous Authorities on housing in Millinocket with the understanding that when a change in personnel is made, a new policy be adopted." Walker seconded the motion, Marsh opposed. The Authority then voted, unanimously, that all Park employees who lived in Park owned housing, including those in Millinocket, pay for all personal utilities. The rent issue for Park facilities would become active once again the following year due to action by the State Budget Office, and Tibbs, on his own initiative, moved out of his Millinocket home. The Authority subsequently voted to sell the house.[39]

A few additional personnel matters remained to be settled in late 1977. At that time, Assistant Park Supervisor Philip McLaughlin was earning less money, at pay range 17, than were the rangers he supervised, who were classified at ranges 18 and 20. At the December Authority meeting, Chair Marsh stated that as he understood it the Personnel Department would resolve the matter after December 20, 1976. The pay adjustment did not come through, however, until May 2, 1977, at which time the Baxter State Park Assistant Supervisor's position was classified at range 21. William Cross negotiated with Personnel to have the classification become retroactive to October 17, 1976.[40]

In spite of financial problems, and having to temporarily place everyone on a forty-hour work week to maintain costs, Park administrators believed that there existed a strong need for a Park information/education or ranger/naturalist position which, along with a forester if hired, would be used to fill current vacancies. The 1977 organization chart reduced the Park's administration districts from eight to six, and the two positions thus freed would, under the proposal, be replaced by a northern area supervising ranger and a naturalist.[41]

The desired positions of naturalist and forester were not filled in early 1977 due to continued financial problems. In addition, Director Tibbs recommended that the Park maintain a forty-hour work week for field personnel due to increased costs for non-standard work hours resulting from a recent Personnel decision, although, Tibbs acknowledged, the forty hour week would probably result in a reduction of field personnel availability to the public. The Authority unanimously voted to adopt the plan. The Authority also recognized another change in BSP staff, the establishment of five collective bargaining units: Law Enforcement; Administrative Services; Operations, Maintenance, and Support Services; Supervisory Services; and Professional and Technical The units resulted from processes initiated the previous year. Certain personnel were exempt.[42]

While the Park and Authority labored to settle lingering personnel and financial problems, Cross retired as Business Manager in early autumn 1977. Until a replacement could be hired, the Park planned to use an Account Clerk II and a part-time Clerk in Augusta to fill administrative needs. The Authority and Park staff also discussed the possibility of closing the Augusta office at which Cross had been based but which the Authority now considered a nonessential operation. The Authority ultimately voted to close the office before July 1, 1978, or within two months of hiring a new Business Manager, or upon the resignation of the one staff member still working there. The Park did eventually secure another Business Manager, Peter J. Maderia, Jr., in the summer of 1978. The following two years proved relatively peaceful, in terms of personnel issues, except for changes in SFMA management. However, although not a controversial or disruptive event, long time reservations clerk Helen Gifford retired in mid-1979.[43]

Throughout the studied period men outnumbered women in the staffing of BSP. The first female staff member, as well as the Park's first clerical worker, had been Helen Gifford. Gifford began work as a summer employee in 1957, charged with handling Park reservations and correspondence. Gifford started working part-time during the winter months, as well as full-time for the summer season, in the early 1960s, and in 1969 became a full-time year-round employee. By January 1970, the Park employed three other women on a contractual basis: part-time secretary to the Supervisor, Joyce Givens, and Janice Caverly and Jeanette York, both of whom contracted with the Park for snowmobile counts in BSP.[44] Several women had been hired to work for the Park by the late 1970s, yet when Gifford retired after twenty-two years with the Park in 1979 she left her position as both the longest employed Park female to date and as the employee of either gender with the longest, currently active, work record. Gifford's successor would also, in the mid-1990s, be the longest employed BSP female staff member.

Wives of BSP rangers, whether officially on the payroll or not, provided numerous services during the 1960s and 1970s to Park visitors, such as distributing information and advice (and sometimes comfort or aid), and handling reservations and Park radio communications. The Park permitted the women to maintain small stores on the porches of the rangers' camps and to retain the profits as a form of compensation. Once Baxter Trust Fund money became available, these women were often hired as assistant rangers or campground attendants or in various other capacities.[45] Such employment comprised a formal recognition of services long provided. The woman who replaced Helon Gifford as Reservations Clerk in 1979, Janice Caverly, had a similar background as a former ranger's wife. She had married Ranger Irvin C. Caverly, Jr. in 1963, and in the years since had worked for the Park in a variety of positions, including running a campground store for four years. By the time of her appointment as head reservations clerk, Caverly had worked in reservations under Gifford for seven years.[46]

Women would continue to make inroads in Park personnel in the future, both at Park Headquarters and in the field. In the meantime, two other important changes occurred in BSP staffing due to 1981 resignations. In 1981, A. Lee Tibbs resigned his position as Director and Peter Maderia left his job as Business Manager. Tibbs tendered his resignation on September 17. It became effective on October 27. He wrote to the Park staff and the Advisory that he felt that after almost seven years as Director of the Park the time had come to pursue other interests. His years with the Park had been "challenging, interesting, and rewarding," and his experiences with staff, Authority, and Advisory members "interesting, rewarding, and, at times, frustrating, but overall of immense personal benefit, adding a dimension to [his] life that would have been difficult to obtain otherwise." Tibbs would be entering private business in the Lincoln area and continue to live in the home in Chester which he had purchased when he moved from Park housing in Millinocket. He hoped to see everyone again in the future.[47]

Caverly, as Park Supervisor, stepped into the void left by Tibbs. Although some dislocation was no doubt experienced in Park operations and administration, Caverly kept the Park operating smoothly enough that several months passed before the Authority made any extensive effort to secure a new Director. The Authority discussed the situation in December 1981, noting that Caverly "had been carrying the entire load," but held off making any decisions while a committee established by Authority Chair Glenn Manuel reviewed the two personnel vacancies.[48]

When the committee–composed of Walter Birt, William Cross, Paul Firlotte, Whit McEvoy, and Winston Robbins–reported in January 1982, they had several observations to make along with some specific recommendations. The committee recommended that the position of Director be left unfilled at the present time and that "the Supervisor be authorized to operate the Park under the direction of the Authority." They pointed out that Caverly had had twenty-three years of experience with BSP, that he was familiar with the staff–having been one of the persons to put it together–as well as with the Park and its growth. Caverly was well versed in the Deeds of Trust and in the Park's master plan. The Supervisor's salary should be adjusted to meet the increased responsibilities. The committee also recommended that a person with a strong business background and familiarity with State procedures be hired to fill the Business Manager position. The Park had been in a planning phase for several years and the time had arrived to pursue a more positive and productive course. Their recommendations, they believed, would contribute to this change and save the Park money in the process.[49]

Discussion of the committee's recommendations centered on questions about the feasibility of some of the suggestions, including that of hiring a Business Manager at the present State classification and that of combining the positions of Supervisor and Director. After hearing comments, the Authority voted to go into Executive Session. When the meeting reconvened Chair Manuel announced that the Authority had decided to hire a Business Manager as soon as possible and to make Caverly Acting Director. The Authority had not voted on the proposed staff reorganization. Further decisions on the two personnel positions would be made in the future.[50]

Caverly hired a new Business Manager in early 1982, Robert J. Williams. Selecting a Director took longer. The Authority decided in March to have the Maine Department of Personnel establish a register for the Director's position, and to leave the Supervisor's position vacant for the time being. Personnel established the requested register for the Director's position, and following initial screening nine candidates were assigned interviews with the Authority and with an oral review board. The Authority sought input from the Advisory and other interested parties, and a committee so formed participated in the interview process.[51]

The person selected for the Director's position ultimately underwent seven separate formal interviews: interviews with the Authority members (together and separately), with Advisory members, and with environmental groups or their representatives. Some persons opposed the candidate's selection as he did not bring an academic background to the position. He countered with the argument that twenty-three years as a dedicated Baxter State Park employee, more than ten of them spent as Park Supervisor, should count for something. After a long and sometimes painful process, the Authority appointed Irvin C. Caverly, Jr. Director of Baxter State Park.[52]

Caverly did indeed bring a unique training to the Director's position. He had undergone virtually all of the same training as did the rangers under him, as well as that of some other Park personnel. More than a decade of supervisory experience had taught him the basics of administration and employee relations. And perhaps just as important if not more so, in the early 1960s Caverly had undergone an education that few staff members still working for the Park after 1969 had had, and one which none would be able to obtain thereafter; he had known Governor Baxter personally, and had trained under the man who had supervised the Park during much of its formative period, Helon N. Taylor. Both men exerted a continuing influence over Caverly, and Caverly's respect and admiration for both would be apparent in his words and actions in ensuing years.[53]

More than three decades after his initiation as a Park ranger, Caverly would retain and retell stories of his first years at Baxter State Park. His favorite stories about Percival Baxter and Helon Taylor reveal as much about the perceptions, values, and humor of Caverly as they do those of the other two men. Three such stories might serve as illustrations: one a story about a bashful young man's visit to a Governor's office, one about a postage stamp and a steam kettle, and one about two poachers and a bag of peanuts.[54]

Caverly worked on a seasonal basis during his first four years at Baxter State Park in the early 1960s. This necessitated his finding another job for the winter months, a task which sometimes led him to southern Maine. Governor Baxter had invited Caverly to stop by his Portland office sometime to say hello. One day Caverly decided to take the afternoon off from his job searching and do just that.

Caverly found Baxter's Congress Street office, entered the front door which was situated almost on the sidewalk, and began to climb the stairs to Baxter's office. About halfway up the stairwell was a landing. The set-up reminded Caverly of the stairway at his childhood dentist's office, a place Caverly had not been eager to visit. He had always procrastinated on his way up the stairs. Facing Baxter's stairway, Caverly wondered what he would find at the top. Would Baxter be in? Would he want to talk to Caverly? Would Caverly be imposing on Baxter's time?

Gathering up his courage, Caverly climbed the rest of the stairs. At the top of the stairway Caverly found one large room, and seated at a desk he thought must be at least one hundred years old was Baxter's long-time secretary. She reminded Caverly of one of his grade school teachers. Caverly timidly asked her if the Governor was in. She answered, "Good

Lord lad, of course he is. Can't you see him sitting over there?" Sitting on the left, in a side room, seated at the biggest desk Caverly had ever seen, was Governor Baxter.

Baxter welcomed Caverly and invited him to sit down. For the next hour and a half Baxter talked to Caverly about his plans for the Park, his trips to the Park, and about Helon Taylor and his respect and admiration for him. Baxter gave Caverly a wealth of information which Caverly could not have received from anyone else.

As Caverly was preparing to leave the following exchange occurred: "Mr. Caverly?" "Yes, Sir?" "Do you need any money?" "No, I've got all I need." "All right, Good Day."

Caverly left Baxter's office upset and furious thinking that Baxter had thought that he had stopped by to ask for money. When Caverly saw Helon Taylor again he told Taylor what had happened. Taylor told Caverly not to worry about what had transpired, explaining that most people who went to see Baxter asked for some sort of contribution. "But he won't forget that about you," Taylor stated, the former Governor would remember that Caverly had not wanted anything material from him. Taylor told Caverly that the experience would make his relationship with Baxter a more meaningful one, and help him to understand the problems Baxter had faced.

Caverly stated more than thirty-years later that that one hour and a half in Baxter's office probably had been his most meaningful experience with Baxter. When Caverly first started with the Park (and quite likely for the decades that followed), he felt that Baxter was probably the most important man in the world. Even the animals seemed to recognize the importance of Baxter and his work. Not everyone who came to the Park to see animals went away satisfied, but Baxter always encountered wildlife. As Caverly explained it, "no matter the season, Baxter would see his critters, almost as if they were there to thank him." Caverly's first introduction to the Governor had occurred in 1960. He met him yearly thereafter until 1967, when Baxter made his last trip to the Park. In between visits, Caverly had Helon Taylor to inform him of the Baxter-correct way to do things.

When Buzz and Jan Caverly planned their wedding in early 1963 they sent Governor Baxter an invitation. Although Baxter was unable to attend the ceremony he sent the young couple a check for fifty dollars as a wedding gift. Caverly was stationed at Russell Pond at the time. On his first off-duty day he wrote Baxter a thank-you note, addressed an envelope, and enclosed the letter. Not having a three cent stamp—all that was currently needed for a one ounce letter—Caverly placed a six cent stamp on the envelope. He then walked out to Taylor's cabin at Togue Pond and asked Taylor if he would mail the letter when he went to town. Taylor said he would mail the letter, but looking closely at it through his thick glasses noticed the six cent stamp and said, "Oh my, this will never do."

Taylor then started a steam kettle heating, steamed off the six cent stamp, walked to his desk, placed the six cent stamp in it, and placed a three cent stamp on the envelope. "You know," he said to Caverly, "Governor Baxter would give away thousands, but if he thought you were giving away a single cent to the federal government he'd never speak to you again." Generally a frugal man, Caverly seems to have learned his lesson.

Taylor had taught Caverly a somewhat different lesson on another day during the same era, this one concerning perhaps the most efficient and enjoyable way to catch a villain or two. Caverly had been stationed at Abol Campground at the time, and was rather inexperienced in rangers' work. Two bear hunters came to the Park and decided to do some hunting even though they were not in an area which permitted hunting. When Caverly informed them of the situation they asked Caverly what he planned to do to stop them, then proceeded to head up the trail in search of game. Caverly radioed Taylor, and Taylor told Caverly not to worry about the situation, that he would handle it himself.

Taylor then gathered his necessary equipment and headed off to enforce Park regulations. Taylor knew that the men would not find the bear they sought. Not willing to waste energy where he deemed it unnecessary, Taylor selected an appropriate position along the trail, sat down, and pulled out two of his favorite things: a bag of peanuts and a Zane Gray novel. When the bear hunters returned along the trail empty handed some time later, they found what seemed to be a harmless old gentlemen eating peanuts and reading. They walked up to Taylor to say hello, at which time Taylor unfolded his 6'4" frame, asked for their guns, and informed them that they were under arrest.

Such lessons, and the many others he received, gave Caverly an appreciation of the Park and human nature which he believed served him well as a ranger and as a supervisor. He would not, he stated in the mid-1990s, have traded that education for any other one. Caverly had learned additional lessons since the 1960s in dealing with staff, the public, and the media, and would continue to do so in the years to come.

In addition to his on-the-job training, both standard and unique, Director Caverly had, as numerous persons pointed out during the hiring process, a thorough knowledge of the Park staff and how it functioned. Caverly had been involved in the hiring process of many BSP employees over the years, and as Supervisor had held staff meetings to both communicate changing policies and operational needs to personnel and to secure input from Park personnel. He did so before and during Tibbs' years as Park Director.

The staff composition had continued to evolve in the late 1970s and early 1980s. Not only had a Park Forester and Forest Technician been hired to manage SFMA planning and operations by mid-1981, but the position of Park Naturalist had been filled by Gerald Merry, previously Park Carpenter and a "born naturalist" as Caverly—who had encouraged Merry to apply to the position—later called him. Merry, as Park Naturalist, in addition to identifying Critical Areas as part of a state-wide program and inventorying Park flora and fauna, served as a liaison with the public in identifying Park policies and providing public education on BSP natural resources. During 1982, for example, Merry traveled around the state speaking to about forty-eight different groups as well as developing a new educational slide show for Park Headquarters and assembling various displays and other interpretive information at Park Headquarters and at the various ranger stations. Furthermore, Merry served as Caverly's administrative assistant in 1982. As such, he screened winter reservation requests, helped formulate revisions to the "Baxter State Park Standard Operating Procedures" which Caverly had developed early in his tenure as Park Director, and generally supervised the Park's Duty Officer program. (Duty Officers were personnel assigned, on a rotating basis, with assuring that all was well in the Park during weekends and other times when Headquarters was closed; handling any problems which might occur during these times and contacting the proper personnel or authorities to resolve any given situation; and with collecting fees from the various stations as gathered by Park personnel.) Merry also volunteered to serve as volunteer coordinator for the 1983 summer season. As Caverly described Merry in January 1983, "a forty-hour week means nothing to him."[55]

The Park had been divided into two major administrative districts by the early 1980s, with Chris Drew serving as North District Ranger and Robert Howes serving as South District Ranger. Both Drew and Howes reported to Caverly in his roles of Supervisor then Director, and each supervised two fully commissioned BSP Rangers as well as a number of Campground Rangers, Assistant Campground Rangers, and Gatehouse attendants.[56] Drew, hired in 1973, was the last person hired who became a Commissioned BSP Ranger during the period studied. During the 1980s through the mid-1990s, six commissioned Baxter State Park Rangers served the public and the Authority: Chris M. Drew (later Chief Ranger), Robert E. Howes, Thomas P. Chase, Loren C. Goode, Barry K. MacArthur, and Charles Kenney. Bernard Crabtree, although not commissioned, also served as a Ranger I throughout much of the period. At the close of the period new State regulations mandated that the Park Director have commissions renewed on an annual basis, thereby ensuring that such personnel kept up-to-date on all pertinent training and educational requirements as well as maintain solid work records.[57]

In addition to the hiring of rangers of various rank, SFMA personnel, and the Park Naturalist, the Park's maintenance division had developed such that in 1981 the Park employed a Maintenance Supervisor (a position filled by Philip McGlauflin, previous Assistant Supervisor), an Auto Mechanic, Maintenance Mechanic, and a four person, seasonal, Trail Crew. The BSP Business Manager supervised a Storekeeper (charged with maintaining clothing and other supplies), and six administrative or clerical workers. In March 1981, the Park employed forty-seven people, nineteen of them year-round personnel.[58] Under Caverly's tenure the staff composition would continue to evolve, but the numbers of persons employed would not change significantly. In 1984, for example, the Park employed eighteen year-round personnel and thirty seasonal workers, and in 1994 BSP employed seventeen year-round employees and twenty-eight seasonal personnel.[59]

Caverly held a workshop for Park personnel soon after assuming his new position as Director of Baxter State Park to identify any major concerns of year-round and seasonal employees. The workshop, held in Millinocket in October 1982, proved productive and Caverly would hold similar workshops in the future. Such workshops frequently included discussion on how to best increase Park revenue and decrease operational expenses. Operating expenses approached or nearly equaled income during the early and mid-1980s, and budgeting remained a problem. In 1983, citing employee workshop discussions, Caverly sent all employees a memorandum concerning some of the suggestions which would be implemented during the coming season. These included shortening by two to four weeks the time worked by gatekeepers, campground rangers, and one Park receptionist. The new work periods remained approximately the same throughout the period studied, with minor adjustment made to maintain employee benefits under State regulations.[60]

Another suggestion, one discussed at the February 1983 Authority meeting, involved the Collective Bargaining contracts covering BSP workers which Park finances, it seemed, could not afford. Suggestions raised at the meeting involved the possibility of BSP employees forming a separate bargaining unit, or Park personnel in one way or another separating from other State personnel. Such measures might be obtained by an employee vote. Winston Robbins of the Advisory posited that Park personnel might follow the example of the staff of the Maine Turnpike Authority, as those workers fell under auspices of the Maine Municipal Association. The primary issue was that of maintaining autonomy over Park finances and keeping the operating budget within total Park income. Another issue surfaced at a latter, 1984, Advisory meeting which concerned State regulations: the duties, including attending meetings in Augusta, required of BSP's Affirmative Action Officer, Shirley Brewster, had become too time consuming. Although not as crucial a matter, the complaint indicated continued tensions between perceived Park needs and existing State regulations.[61]

Park personnel underwent a reorganization during the mid-1980s which addressed some of the financial and administrative concerns of the era. Upon recommendation by Caverly and the Advisory in June 1983, the Authority voted to review the efficiency of Park operations and consider a reorganization. Caverly would draft a study or program and give it to an Advisory sub-committee for review. After committee review, any findings or proposals would be submitted to the Authority.[62]

The BSP organizational review was completed by January 1985 and the resulting proposal for reorganization submitted to the Maine State Employees Association for consideration. In March 1985, Caverly presented the proposal to the Authority. Some personnel reclassifications were necessary, Caverly explained, due to changes in the Park's administration. Some employees had taken on different or additional duties than they had had in earlier years. The recommendations included changing the Business Manager I position to a Business Manager II, the Reservation Clerk (currently ranked a Clerk III) to a Reservation Supervisor, the Park Naturalist to an Administrative Assistant, and the Maintenance Supervisor to a Park Specialist. The proposal also recommended moving the Trail Crew Leader from Park Headquarters to Roaring Brook, and eliminating the fifty-two week Maintenance Supervisor position in lieu of two twenty-six week Maintenance Rangers, one for each district. All Park positions would be classified as standard as it was currently less expensive to pay any necessary overtime than to pay nonstandard classification rates. The proposal eliminated three of the Park's year-round positions. Park receptionists had already requested that the State Personnel Department conduct an audit of their jobs, and an additional gatekeeper for Nesowadnehunk Field had recently been approved. The proposal was expected to save money and increase productivity. The Authority voted unanimously to adopt the reorganization proposal.[63]

The Park underwent not only a personnel reorganization but also a personnel change in following months. The Business Manager I position was not reclassified as Robert Williams left the Park for another position and

Elizabeth Gray, previously employed by Thomaston State Prison and understandably having less experience with BSP, replaced him. Gerald Merry's position did get reclassified, to that of Interpretive Specialist, but Merry fell ill in 1985 and had to leave his job in the spring of the year. Merry died in late 1985 and his position remained unfilled for sometime thereafter. Maintenance Mechanic Donald J. McKenna left the Park and two seasonal Maintenance Rangers replaced him. Maine Forest Service Forester Dennis Brennan replaced, for a short time, Fred H. Rooney as SFMA Forester under a contract with the MFS. Forest Technician Paul E. Rumney left the SFMA and his position remained unfilled. Chris M. Drew became BSP Chief Ranger, assuming many of the duties once performed by the Park Supervisor (and some of which Merry had earlier assumed), that position having been unfilled since Caverly vacated it to become Park Director. Barry MacArthur replaced Drew as North District Ranger. Bernard Crabtree became a BSP Ranger for the South District. Tim Sides replaced Edwin N. Jandreau, who was suffering from health problems, as Park Auto Mechanic.[64]

In addition to the above changes, which occurred in 1985 and 1986, changes occurred in the reservations and clerical staff, then supervised by the Business Manager. (The Business Manager also served as a contract manager or administrator, helping formulate and administer Park contracts for such services as janitorial work for Park Headquarters, latrine vault pumping, and running the Kidney Pond Campground.) Although Shirley Brewster secured a reclassification from Clerk Typist II to Clerk Typist III, Janice Caverly did not receive the reclassification recommended in March 1985. A few turnovers occurred among the personnel the two women supervised, with Judith A. Hafford being the one person hired at the time who would stay with the Park through the close of 1994. The reservation and clerical staff remained female in following years, and by the close of 1987 the staff employed in late 1994 were all in place. S. Jean Howes joined the staff as a Clerk Typist II, Rosemary K. James as a Clerk Typist I, and Roxanna F. McLean as Secretary (working for the Director). Hafford later became an Accounting Clerk II in charge of payroll and other accounts, and

James became BSP Stores Clerk, working directly under McLean, Secretary to the Director. Brewster, meanwhile, retired from the Park.[65]

While the Authority, Caverly, and the Maine Department of Personnel worked to secure the best candidates for year-round staff positions, the mid-1980s also saw a relatively large turnover in seasonal staff. The turnover caused a minimal amount of difficulty, however, and apparently did not significantly interfere with public services provided. Caverly held annual training workshops to educate new personnel on Park policies and operations. The workshops, along with help given by more senior workers, both year-round and seasonal, no doubt helped create smoother transitions.[66]

Keeping personnel costs within the Park's budget remained a challenge throughout the decade. The provisions of the Fair Employment Act covering pay rates for hours worked per week in excess of forty continued to pose difficulties. In earlier decades staff had been expected, whether they liked it or not, to work for as long a time as it required to accomplish a given task. Those in non-standard job categories were essentially employed not by the hour, but by the tasks to be performed. In some cases the practical difference was small, in other cases it was not.[67] One example of where overtime pay became a crucial issue and an operational deficit was that of Chimney Pond.

With an increase in winter activities, especially that of technical climbing, in the 1970s and thereafter it became important to maintain personnel at Chimney Pond Campground throughout the winter season. For a time the Park had assigned one ranger to the camp for the winter season. However, some rangers felt that it was too difficult for one person to be so assigned and submitted a formal protest. Upon losing their Personnel hearing, the rangers had essentially agreed to rotate the assignment among the six Commissioned BSP Rangers, each being stationed at Chimney Pond for about two, one-week shifts each winter. Later, in 1986, a ranger requested compensation for his time beyond the standard eight hour day, and filed an official grievance over the matter. Apparently more than one ranger believed that they should receive time-and-one-half pay for each hour spent at Chimney Pond over eight hours per day, ultimately receiving pay on a per hour basis for all twenty-four hours. Yet, as Caverly stated at the March

1986 Authority meeting, "three-quarters of the justification of their position in the winter time is to cover Chimney Pond."[68]

Members of the Authority, while noting that the basic issue of duty stations versus pay rates also confronted the Maine Forest Service and Inland Fisheries and Wildlife in terms of their firefighters and wardens, discussed whether rangers who refused to accept Chimney Pond as their duty station might be given seasonal status and the winter work at Chimney Pond handled on a contract basis. Attorney General James Tierney made a suggestion which had been voiced before 1986 and would be heard again in the future: that winter campers pay a larger fee than that currently charged in order to help defray personnel costs.[69]

One temporary solution which the Park used to maintain a presence at Chimney Pond, and which helped meet Park needs elsewhere, was the service of volunteers. The Park used volunteer help extensively at Chimney Pond during the winter of 1987-1988, but gave rangers first priority. Stationing a ranger at the campgrounds in winter cost the Park approximately $120 per day, while users fees—at $10 per person in 1988 with a minimum number of four persons per party–might total only $40 per day. In 1988 the prospect of raising user fees for Chimney Pond became a topic once again.[70]

While the Park struggled to find ways to keep down personnel costs—most of them mandated by employment laws and union contracts and therefore not realistically reducible[71]—volunteers filled an important role in providing needed labor. Volunteers had long contributed to the Park, especially in the areas of trail maintenance and search and rescue operations. There was a marked increase in the total volunteer hours worked in the 1980s and their contributions became more extensive. At the Authority's behest, the Park initiated an overall volunteer program in 1982, extending the types of volunteer jobs available, drawing up various job descriptions, and sending pertinent information to interested parties. During the 1982 summer season the Park drew thirty-two volunteers. The level of volunteer participation rose thereafter. Park records identified almost 4,000 work hours contributed by 85 volunteers in 1985; 7,148 hours of volunteer service for 1986; 9,158 hours for 1987; 10,963 hours for 1988; and 11,244 volunteer hours for 1989. Volunteers continued to contribute significantly to the Park in the early 1990s. The actual number of hours donated decreased somewhat, but the number of volunteers rose to over two hundred per year.[72]

Volunteers worked throughout the Park in the 1980s and 1990s, as well as in Millinocket. They generally worked in the area of greatest need, contributing their time as both private citizens and as members of various organizations. After Caverly became Park Director in 1982 he had "Annual Reports" compiled each year. The reports identified work performed, financial affairs, personnel organization, statistics on Park use, and so forth. The reports became more inclusive over the years, and they consistently recognized the work contributions of volunteers.[73]

With a marked increase in volunteer labor in the mid-1980s onward, during which time Chief Ranger Drew began supervising the program, some BSP staff members became concerned about the possibility of personnel positions being lost to volunteers. The use of volunteers during the winter season at Chimney Pond did not cause undue consternation, but their use elsewhere sometimes did. Park administration did indeed come to rely on voluntary labor to fill certain needs as hiring personnel to perform all necessary work was not a viable option. Caverly stated at an Authority meeting in May 1988 that volunteer efforts had made it possible for the Park to function with fewer personnel hours per year than it had twelve to fifteen years previously. Projected increases in staffing after the Fair Labor Standards Act became effective had not become a reality.[74] Yet, as early as 1986 when staff had raised questions about personnel cutbacks, Caverly had assured them in writing that the purpose of the volunteer program was to augment not replace Park staff: "these positions have not been used to replace employees but rather [to] supplement employees." However, Caverly continued, "in all [honesty] I told you when a position was vacated, it is my policy to review that position carefully to consider the job standards of the position, our financial resources available, and the best options available to us to accomplish the functions of the position." The contract recently issued for the Daicey Pond Campground operation was one example of a labor option utilized for the best interests of the Park.[75]

Two years later, when questions arose concerning the necessity of hiring a full-time Park Naturalist once again, and about the possibility of reducing hours worked by personnel, Caverly stated that it would be "hard to convince him" that the Park should reduce the number of BSP employees. With the hiring of a Park Naturalist the year-round staff would number nineteen, and the seasonal workers twenty-nine to thirty. Not only did the Park need a naturalist in spite of recent volunteer help in that area, it would also probably need a back-up team to cover Park needs in the future. Nor—in light of current and eminent projects involving SFMA operations and major repairs and renovations at Togue Pond and at Kidney Pond Campground, and with the need to maintain a strong presence at the gatehouses to control vehicle access—would it be wise to consider reducing seasonal staff without close study.[76]

Caverly had recently, in late 1986, hired Jensen Bissell as Baxter State Park Resource Manager, and plans for the SFMA, as well as for work elsewhere in the Park, were important concerns in the late 1980s. The process of hiring Bissell had been a long and extensive one, and the position had in part been budgeted with money previously used to fund a Park Naturalist with the understanding that the Resource Manager would initially devote a portion of his time to the Naturalist's duties. A full-time Park Naturalist would be hired a year or so later.[77] By mid-1988 that time had arrived.

After discussing the need for a Park Naturalist and the possibility of using volunteer or part-time workers, the Authority and the State Personnel Department authorized Caverly to proceed with the process of hiring a naturalist. Caverly did so with an appointed interview committee, one similar to that employed when he had hired Jensen Bissell as Park Resource Manager, and ultimately selected Jean Hoekwater from the register of eligible candidates.[78] Hoekwater started work in early September 1988, amidst a wave of controversy. One of the three top candidates for the position, Keith Smith, was already employed by BSP. Smith felt that Hoekwater had been unfairly hired, primarily due to her gender and the personal caprice of the Park Director, and that he, having seniority and being equally qualified for the job, should have been selected. Smith and the Maine

State Employees Association filed an arbitration suit against the Park and Authority. The arbitrator for the Maine State Employees Association and the Governor's Office of Employee Relations rendered its decision on May 6, 1991, ruling that "the State did not violate the seniority responsibilities of the parties or the non-discrimination article of the 1987-1989 Professional and Technical Services Bargaining Unit Contract" when it hired Hoekwater for the position of Park Naturalist. The arbitrator refuted all charges made by the plaintiffs and stated that the interviewing panel had found Hoekwater the "superior" candidate, especially in terms of being better prepared for the interview and, they thought, better able to deal with the divergent groups and types of people which performing the job would entail.[79]

The plaintiffs in the arbitration hearing concerning Hoekwater's appointment had also asserted that the Baxter State Park Authority was the "appointing authority" for the Park Naturalist position, as they had also interviewed the candidates, and should therefore have made the final selection in the hiring process. The arbitrator, however, determined that Caverly had "asserted his appointment authority" at all times, and that the Authority had interviewed the final candidates only as a familiarization procedure at Caverly's request. Caverly had in no way given up his responsibilities as the Park's appointing authority. In this instance, as in all others except for his own, the Director of Baxter State Park maintained the right—subject to governmental regulations—to fill all BSP personnel positions.[80]

Hoekwater found the Park Naturalist position somewhat changed since Merry had first filled it and since she had performed work for the Park several years previously as a Youth Conservation Corps Crew Chief, a volunteer then grant supported intern, and as a gatekeeper during one season. Before Caverly had hired Hoekwater he had informed her that the job would be different. Merry had personally compiled an extensive photograph collection during his years at the Park, and Hoekwater would initially spend a good deal of time developing a new and Park owned photograph collection. Hoekwater also helped develop an updated Park slide show. Merry had spent a significant portion of his time in the field, establishing an inventory of plant and animal species and investigating possible Critical Areas. Another major component of his job had involved traveling throughout the state in a public relations capacity, both expounding the beauty of the Park and educating the public about its purpose and operations. Hoekwater would spend less time in the field taking inventories, instead devoting more field work to monitoring the effects of public use and various research studies, and spend less time traveling for public relations activities. Hoekwater's travel activities generally involved attending various meetings and conferences instead of presenting papers or educational materials. (During the studied period Drew and Caverly also spent extensive hours at various meetings, as did Bissell after his appointment, and Caverly maintained a continual schedule of public appearances as a Park representative.) Like Merry, Drew, Bissell, and Caverly, Hoekwater would also spend time at Park Headquarters performing administrative work.[81]

While Bissell and Hoekwater settled into their relatively new positions in the late 1980s, BSP staff continued to feel concern over how their job classifications compared to those of employees doing similar work for other State agencies, and the Park administration considered the necessity of securing higher pay rates to ensure a supply of good workers, especially in seasonal and SFMA positions. Employees also expressed concern in the late 1980s over the use of contract services, particularly those at Daicey and Kidney Ponds. The contract system as used at Daicey Pond had replaced positions previously held by rangers, rangers who had left the Park staff. Some employees expressed, albeit indirectly, concerns that as the contract operations were less expensive to the Park and required no overtime pay, they might pose a threat to the job security of other Park personnel were the contract system to spread. The SFMA currently contracted for the services of two consulting foresters on an as-needed basis, as well as contracting for various operations over the next few years, but Park personnel seemed to have less concern over those contracts. In view of the various personnel costs, the Park included projected wage increases for the first time in its 1990 budget, using national inflation averages for a basis. The Park also planned for increased expenses based on expected reclassifications.[82]

Elizabeth Gray played an important role in meeting with collective bargaining units, drawing up BSP budgets, and overseeing the reservations operation in the late-1980s. In 1990, however, Gray (now using the surname

Austin) resigned her position as Business Manager. Caverly, with general Advisory support and Authority approval, elected not to fill the position in the near future. Under Personnel regulations, the position could be held for up to three years, as had happened with the naturalist position following Merry's resignation. The Park made the decision not to hire a Business Manager in order to ensure that further cuts would not be necessary in field personnel, and because the staff had agreed to having many of her responsibilities delegated to them. The Park had also secured assurances from Inland Fisheries and Wildlife and the State of Maine Bureau of the Budget in Augusta, as well as from the Advisory Committee, that they would provide aid in developing Park budgets, and had set aside funds for contracting for a financial consultant if needed. The BSPA Finance Committee did indeed play a significant role in developing Park budgets in following years. From 1990 through 1994 the committee maintained a consistent and financially astute membership consisting of Steve Crockett (Chair), William Cross, Jim Garland, Rupert White, John Howard, and, from 1992 onward, John Bibber. Natural Resource Manager Jensen Bissell also came to play a key role in developing the Park's annual Work Program Budgets and the Biennial Budgets, and Judith Hafford, performing accounting and payroll duties, came under Bissell's supervision. The Park also instituted a budget tracking system which allowed transfer between two of the Park's budget categories, "Capital" and "All Others"—the third category, "Personnel," according to law and sound business practices could not be modified during the course of a budget period—in order to meet changing budgetary situations and keep the Park operating "in the black" throughout any given year. The budget tracking system allowed the Park a more practical and efficient method of meeting financial and budgeting needs. Greater autonomy was also realized when changes in the purchasing process no longer required that all goods be obtained through the State of Maine Bureau of Purchases. The Park did not elect to fill the Business Manager's position during the period it remained open. Nevertheless, Baxter State Park entered the mid-1990s financially sound.[83]

Upon Director Caverly's request, the Park Naturalist agreed to oversee the reservations staff following Business Manager Gray's departure.

Hoekwater did so until 1994, at which time Janice Caverly became the supervisor of reservations, rated in turn by the Park Naturalist. The methods of taking reservations—in person and via the telephone and mail—did not change significantly from 1970 through 1994. Reservations taken in person at Park Headquarters, initially in rented quarters and later on Balsam Drive in Millinocket, were recorded in ledgers according to the month and days of the reservation and the location reserved. Near the close of the period the Park, to facilitate the reservation process and to meet Maine fire code regulations, rented space at a nearby hotel to handle part of the reservation process on opening day—the first day reservations are taken for the upcoming summer season—and to keep Park visitors out of the frigid January weather. So popular remained the Park, however, that many people continued to stand in line in the middle of the night–lining up long before Park and hotel accommodations opened for the day—in order to ensure that they would be able to reserve their favorite campsite for a preferred date.[84]

New procedural methods aided the reservation process in the 1990s, but crowds still seemed formidable at times. Even with fewer Park visitors in the early 1970s, however, reservations personnel, fewer in number then, had had a difficult task keeping up with both opening day and year-round reservation requests, correspondence, and billings—responsibilities they managed while also spending a considerable amount of time answering the public's questions about BSP. The Park and the Authority discussed the possibility of adopting a computer based reservations system numerous times in the 1980s and early 1990s, but for various reasons chose not to do so. Yet, the eventual transition to a computer system seemed inevitable during the mid-1990s. In the meantime, long time Reservations Clerk Janice Caverly assumed administrative responsibility for the department assisted by two forty-week Clerk II employees, Joan King and Gladys Hanson, and a fourteen week Park Receptionist, Mary Ellen Bell.[85]

A few changes made elsewhere in operations at the end of the period promised to aid Park services in following years. The Park gained a year-round Carpenter again in 1992, Albert Rickards. Rickards would do for Park facilities what Lester Kenway, Trail Crew Supervisor, had been doing for Park trails for years: helping to protect natural resources and to ensure the safety, and to some degree the comfort, of Park visitors. In 1994, Mac Browning, formerly a BSP Campground Ranger, was hired as a year-round Forest Technician to help with SFMA operations, operations which by 1994 were well under way and seemingly free from the controversy of earlier years. An important 1994 project, a project in which the Advisory played a key role, was the building of the Visitor Information Center at Togue Pond. Designed to function as an educational and informational center and to help free the nearby gatehouse from vehicle congestion, the Visitor Information Center gave the Park Naturalist another opportunity to use her primary skills at the same time as she turned over her supervisory role in reservations. The seasonal Clerk II assigned to the Visitor's Center worked under Naturalist Hoekwater.[86]

Baxter State Park employees, "the Staff of the Authority," performed a variety of duties and contributed to the preservation of the Park and its resources in countless ways. Working under the Park Director, who in turn served directly under the Authority, BSP staff implemented the policies established by the Authority in accordance with the mandates of Percival P. Baxter. Baxter State Park personnel helped ensure visitor safety and served as law enforcement officers when necessary. Staff training continued through the 1980s and the 1990s, helping to ensure that all personnel—from seasonal workers to administrative staff—were better able to serve the needs of the public and the Park. All personnel issues were not resolved by 1990 or during the following years, no more than they were in work places outside BSP. As with other work places, personnel conflicts arose and the administration sought the best methods to resolve them. In spite of the various personnel issues which surfaced over the years, the longevity of numerous careers with the Park, and the commitment of the vast majority of Park workers to their jobs, remained central to Baxter State Park operations and the successes—immediate or eventual—therein.

Chapter Ten

Conclusion: Baxter State Park in the 1990s

A visitor to Baxter State Park in the early 1990s would have seen fewer changes than one might expect after the passage of twenty-five years. Roads remained largely the same in 1994 as they had been in 1970. Some buildings had been removed and a few others simply moved. In the summer season, motorcycles and all terrain vehicles remained taboo, and motor boats or boats with outboard motors remained limited to Matagamon and Webster Lakes until after 1992, when two ponds newly under the jurisdiction of the Baxter State Park Authority were allowed to retain limited motor boat usage. Bicycles continued to be welcome in the BSP, but only along roads open to regular vehicular use. In winter, snowmobiles traveled only along the Perimeter Road and on a few other designated trails for access purposes. Moose, deer, and other animals continued to enchant visitors, and the Park's scenery remained primarily pristine. However, additional numbers of people did visit the Park; the Park's work force had grown and evolved; public relations had become a matter of continual consideration if not continual concern; forest operations had become more sophisticated; and, by mid-1992, along with other changes, the physical size of the Park had grown.

In late 1992 the Park purchased some 1,046 acres from the Georgia-Pacific (Great Northern Nekoosa) Corporation for $200,000. Such a purchase was in keeping with Governor Percival P. Baxter's correspondence and his will. Funding for the purchase came from the BSP Land Acquisition Account, which over the years had grown to $500,000. The Togue Pond Purchase, as the purchase became known, comprised land situated at the former southeastern boundary of the Park, property around Upper and Lower Togue Ponds. The Park currently held a lease to some of the property. Outgoing Authority Chair John H. Cashwell proved instrumental in securing the land for BSP. Cashwell had previously worked for the company and used his personal contacts to bring three executive officers to the Park for several days. Cashwell, Caverly, and Park staff gave the company officers an in-depth tour of the Park and explained the Park's history and goals. At the end of the officers' visit Caverly and Cashwell showed the men the Togue

Pond area, pointed out improvements already made on the leased property, and stated that BSP would like to buy the land. Senior officer John Razer then turned to his less senior coworkers and stated that "the right thing to do is to see that the Park has all of this property, including the two ponds." The offer Georgia-Pacific subsequently extended to the Park was deemed generous, and Baxter's grandnephew Rupert White stated that his family "felt it was the most important development that [had] come along since his uncle's death." Caverly had alerted the Authority of the offer and urged them to vote for the purchase. Then composed of Authority Chair and Commissioner of Inland Fisheries and Wildlife William J. Vail, Attorney General Michael E. Carpenter, and Susan J. Bell, who had recently replaced Cashwell as Director of the Maine Forest Service, the Authority did indeed vote to purchase the Togue Pond property. They did so unanimously on December 16, 1992.[1]

As purchased, the Togue Pond property included two inholdings–Clark Island (privately owned) and Girl Scout Camp Natarswi–as well as four family camps on leased land. The Park anticipated some camp owners selling their holdings while others would remain and enjoy their rights as lease holders. In addition, at the time of sale the Georgia-Pacific Company conveyed a parcel of land to the Millinocket School Department. The conveyed land, already leased to the school department, was not to exceed two and one-half acres, was to be used only for educational and municipal recreation purposes, and its title would pass to the Baxter State Park Authority should the property cease to be used for the stated purposes.[2]

Soon after making the Togue Pond Purchase, the Park made a few alterations and, with the help of an Advisory committee established for the purpose, began work on a five year management plan for the area. The Park and the committee sought to create a management plan in keeping with the Baxter-based philosophy governing the rest of the Park while still considering traditional uses of the area. The Park began physical work on the purchased property by renovating buildings located on the former public beach on Upper Togue Pond, making changes primarily to bring the buildings into parity with those located elsewhere in the Park and to remove features considered unsightly or not in keeping with the Park's wilderness focus. The Park also undertook measures to combat erosion along the waterfront. Some of these renovations and improvements had been initiated before the land purchase during the decade that BSP leased the property, the 1980s in particular had seen Volunteers for Peace aid in shore stabilization and the removal of a number of dilapidated buildings. Changes in beach rules and regulations would be included in the area plan being developed. In the meantime, the beach continued to be popular with the general public who enjoyed the beach free of charge. In 1993, the Park moved the Togue Pond Gatehouse (the control booth only, the gatehouse living quarters remained at the original location) several hundred feet north to the junction of Roaring Brook access road and the main Perimeter or Tote Road. The Park did so to control access to Roaring Brook and other Park locations, particularly for day use traffic. The gatehouse move accomplished and deemed successful in its objectives, the Park turned to the idea—first voiced in 1970 during the initial budget process following the receipt of Baxter Trust Fund income—of establishing an information center for BSP visitors. The Park and Advisory also worked to secure approval of its management plan for the area, a revised draft of which was ultimately included as part of a new Baxter State Park Management Plan issued in 1994.[3]

In 1994, the Park held public hearings in Millinocket and Augusta to present its newly completed plan and to receive public commentary. By 1994 the Park had also purchased the Robert Shinners cabin located on Lower Togue Pond, converting it for administrative use. Alterations included replacing the flush toilet with a vault toilet and designating the septic system for gray water use only. Access to this property, along with that to other camps within the purchased land, would need to be controlled, and the Park proposed a uniform gate system for doing so. The "Togue Pond Management Plan," as revised after the public meetings, also established regulations for the public beach—ruling it closed between the hours of 10:00 p.m. and 6:00 a.m., and prohibiting pets. The plan recommended placing a sign at the new southern boundary line; established criteria for any generators and septic systems used in the area, as well as setting standards for any building construction; and noted that the Park would establish and maintain any hiking trails deemed appropriate, and that the Department of

Transportation would maintain the paved road leading to the Togue Pond Beach area.[4]

Much of the discussion at the public meetings had centered on the proposed information center and the use of snowmobiles, watercraft, and aircraft. Motorized vehicle issues drew the largest response, not a surprising occurrence in light of the Park's history. After the meetings, the planning committee recommended that the Authority vote to allow snowmobiles only on the existing Park entrance road through the land purchase. The original draft had been more liberal, proposing that at least initially snowmobile use be permitted on the new purchase, judging such use minimal and non-problematic. However, the Clark family, owners of Clark Island in Lower Togue Pond, testified at the second meeting that snowmobiles did cause problems in the area. Yet, the Clark family did favor allowing small aircraft to continue to land on the ponds as a few family members occasionally gained access to their camps through this means. Here the committee rejected the Clarks' request, recommending that aircraft be forbidden from both Upper and Lower Togue Ponds except for emergency and administrative purposes. After much deliberation, the committee revised its earlier draft and recommended that boats with outboard motors of 10 HP or less be allowed on the two ponds as motor boats had been used there in the past, their use was minimal, and they would provide access to Clark Island. Should any problems arise from their use, the issue would be revisited. Supply access could be gained in winter to Clark Island and other camps by the use of snowmobiles, such use granted only on a permit basis, the permits to be secured from the Park Director on a seasonal basis. The Baxter State Park Authority voted unanimously in May 1994 to accept the Togue Pond Management Plan. Authority member Ray B. Owen, who had replaced William Vail as Commissioner of Inland Fisheries and Wildlife in 1993, expressed concern about motor boats being allowed on the ponds, but decided that as long as the issue would be reviewed should any abuses occur he could accept the plan as submitted.[5]

By May work had begun on the Visitor Information Center. The inside renovations necessary to create the Information Center in an extant building on the 1992 land purchase had been approved in April for an estimated cost of $26,781. The project almost faltered due to funding problems, but after Visitor Information Committee Chair Edward Dwyer made a persuasive presentation to the Authority the Authority reconsidered and voted its unanimous approval. Renovations to the building would create not only the Information Center, but also a smaller conference room and a storage area. Handicap access to educational areas and to new rest room facilities had been provided for. (The Park attempted to meet handicap needs whenever possible during the studied period. Renovations to Headquarters during and after the close of the period included providing improved building and rest room access and facilities. In the Park itself, the Park installed handicap accessible latrines and BSP personnel provided ramps and other basic aids upon request where possible. However, the Park would not, and was not so required by law, violate the Deeds of Trust in order to ensure that everyone could go everywhere in BSP. Requests to allow helicopters to land on Katahdin carrying ill or handicapped persons, for example, had to be denied.) Improvements to the old building would ultimately include its exterior. In addition to producing a more functional facility, immediate and future renovations would result in a more rustic facility, one in keeping with other Park buildings.[6]

Renovations on the old block house proceeded quickly and the Visitor Information Center opened for the 1994 Memorial Day weekend. The first summer season proved the facility a success in reducing lines at the Togue Pond control booth and in providing an additional forum for educating Park visitors. The new Administrative Camp at Togue Pond also opened during 1994, in time to house the October Authority and Advisory meetings. The Administrative Camp promised, like the Information Center, to prove multi-functional in the future, providing space for meetings, housing for staff for short-term needs, and offering secure shelter near the Park entrance for any emergency situation which might arise. The Park also worked to make any further renovations considered necessary in the Togue Pond area at the close of the period, while at the same time making repairs at the Kidney Pond Camps.[7]

The changes made at Togue Pond did not end all concerns regarding Park property and lands. As discussed previously, changes made at Kidney

Pond Camps remained a subject of public scrutiny at the close of the period as did the matter of the holdings included in the Togue Pond Purchase. According to the 1992 sale contract with Georgia-Pacific, the four lease holders concerned—three with one-half acre, and one with one acre, holdings—had the right to purchase their lands at a fair market value as determined by an independent real estate appraiser or in accordance with an appraisal made for the Georgia-Pacific Company in 1992. The lease holders had until the expiration of their current leases to purchase their holdings. Any purchases made were restricted in several matters: the land could not be used for commercial purposes, no new buildings could be erected without Park permission, the land could only be conveyed to immediate family members, and the Park held the right of first refusal should the lessee or the lessee's heirs seek to sell the property to someone outside of the immediate family—the immediate family being defined as the "direct lineal descendants" of the lessee. The family of Robert Shinners, as noted earlier, elected to sell their cabin to the Authority. The family of Helen Lewis purchased their lease. As of early 1996, talks between the families of Raymond Corrigan and Frederick Lewis and Baxter State Park over the settlement of their two leases were still in progress. The two families had until later that year to make a decision, after which time both their leases and their purchase options would expire.[8]

The Park and Authority also had concerns in the 1990s about certain property outside Park boundaries such as the Harpswell or Austin Carey Lot. Formerly managed by the Maine Forest Service, and before that by the Maine Forest Authority, the land came under BSP's jurisdiction in 1978, along with the Mt. Chase Lot. Purchased in 1973 and 1972 respectively, the lots each contained two hundred acres. The first is located just north of Portland in the town of Harpswell on the Maine coast and the second is located approximately twenty miles east of BSP in Mount Chase Plantation. The lots being non-contiguous with the Park, the BSPA needed a way to manage and protect the lands without maintaining a constant presence. When acquired by BSP, the Mt. Chase property had a ten year plan in place covering 1974 to 1983, but operations had not yet started. The Harpswell Lot had had only a vague management plan in place, and had almost nonexistant boundary markings. The Maine Forest Authority had, it seemed, not even met between 1973 and 1976. The Baxter State Park Authority and the Park would essentially be starting from scratch in managing the lots, but in the late 1970s the Authority and Park staff had work enough to do within the Park. Indeed, in 1980 the Authority voted to return the lots to the supervision of the Maine Forest Service. Management responsibilities ultimately stayed with BSP, however. In 1985, the Harpswell Lot garnered attention as the site of a Department of Conservation biomass harvest demonstration, as approved by the BSP, and subsequent thinnings were made in a separate section of the property. At the close of the period, beginning with an initial lease proposal in 1986, the Park and the town of Harpswell worked on a plan to have the town look after the Harpswell property in exchange for the use of a small segment of the land for an overflow parking area for the local school. Plans were being finalized in late 1995. The Mt. Chase land was treated similarly with management somewhat less distant, small harvests made occasionally, and a plan for the land being developed largely under the guidance of Resource Manager Jensen Bissell.[9]

In addition, the close of the studied period witnessed what would hopefully be the conclusion of a lengthy boundary dispute with the privately owned Camp Phoenix and associated Daicey Camp along the northwestern perimeter of the Park on Nesowadnehunk Lake. Both Park and private land owners claimed title to a portion of land in T5R10—the dispute partially resting on a 1942 land survey made by Sewall Company. The ownership of Camp Phoenix and contiguous private lands changed a number of times over the years, complicating settlement procedures. Members of the Daicey family owned Camp Phoenix as well as Camp Daicey during much of 1930s, 1940s, and 1950s. The family eventually divided their total holdings and sold one portion, that which included Camp Phoenix, outside the family. The boundary dispute had started before 1970. A new round of contention began in 1971, however, after George and Beryl Emerson, who had received the property from Arnold Daicey in 1956, conveyed Camp Phoenix to Irving and Claire Salley. The Daiceys retained ownership of Camp Daicey. Thereafter, the Authority worked to settle the dispute.[10]

By 1977 the Park had reached a tentative settlement with its western neighbors. After making a few modifications, the Attorney General's Office filed a Petition for Instructions in 1978 for the proposed settlement. After the Court hearing in December, negotiations on the settlement continued into the 1980s. The settlement would convey a contested lot of roughly twenty acres to the Phoenix property owners in exchange for a scenic easement protecting the bordering Park road from "esthetic disruption" and for a smaller contested piece of property contiguous to the Park which would place the Perimeter Road in the area clearly within Park boundaries, a portion of it currently being outside BSP. The Attorney General's Office deemed the settlement more consistent with existing property deeds than previous proposals. A revision as prepared in 1982 reflected the conveyance of portions of Arnold Daicey's land to William L. Daicey and James A. Daicey in 1971 and his remaining land to Ruth Daicey in 1979, as well as Harold Burbank's purchase of Camp Phoenix in the late 1970s. Burbank would grant the Authority the scenic easement while the Authority would issue the quit-claim deed to Ruth Daicey. Although IFW marked the new boundary and the Park expected the matter to be settled post haste, new problems arose and one year later the Authority expressed concerns over the lack of a finalized agreement with the Daiceys.[11]

After a new round of proposals, which the Attorney General's office deemed not in the best interests of the Park, the case reached court again in the lawsuit *State of Maine, et al. v. Ruth A. Daicey, et al.* Under the newest settlement, the Park granted the Daiseys a quit-claim deed to the property noted above, and the Daiceys granted a scenic easement to the Park as well as a quit-claim deed to contested property lying east of the westerly boundary of the old Nesowadnehunk Road. Following the opening of a new road west of the Park by Great Northern Company, the Park began relocating the Perimeter Road in the Nesowadnehunk region, establishing the road totally within firmly established Park boundaries. In 1988, the Park would close old access points at Nesowadnehunk Field and Telos Road and open a new West Gate.[12] Dick LeDuc, former Camp Phoenix owner, was included in the suit and would sign the settlement papers. Both parties would pay for a boundary survey. Sometimes extremely heated in the 1970s and 1980s, by the 1990s, after lengthy legal action, the dispute had settled substantially. In addition to basic concerns over land titles, the Park had had specific concerns over the years concerning construction along the boundary and Park road, dumping of private goods, hunting in the game preserve, and unauthorized trail construction in BSP. At the close of the 1980s, Camp Phoenix was sold to the TM Corporation, and in the 1990s the corporation divided the land into separate holdings—the various cabins being sold to individual owners. The new Camp Phoenix Owners Association communicated their desire to establish good relations with the Park. Thereafter, relations remained essentially cordial.[13]

Boundary disputes such as that with Camp Phoenix highlighted the need to keep Park boundaries clearly defined. The Park with the aid of the Maine Forest Service had conducted a boundary survey and marking operation between October 1970 and February 1971, traversing the entire perimeter with the exception of two miles buried under snow, two miles which although not painted were chained and marked. The survey crew made an impressive showing as the terrain is alternately—and sometimes simultaneously—difficult, heavily forested, rocky, and, in winter, frigid. A previous survey had been made, but the need for a new survey arose in 1970 following concerns that Great Northern Paper Company might be cutting wood on Park property. In the years succeeding the 1970-1971 survey, the boundary would need further attention. In the 1980s the Park determined that a ten year cycle of surveying, clearing, and marking would be optimal. More than ten miles of the boundary might be covered in a given year, but with BSP staff working as time and events allowed, ten miles per year would achieve the ten year renewal goal.[14]

Even as the late 1980s survey continued, other neighbors also concerned Director Caverly, his staff, and the Authority and Advisory at the close of the period. In 1990, the Park worked out a quit-claim agreement with Gary Merrill of Sports Real Estate, Incorporated, for nearby land in T4R10 and T5R10. In this instance the company retained only a small section of contested land off the Nesowadnehunk Road, as well as travel rights along the road and the right to carry guns as allowed by State law.[15] Other challenges late in the period included that of jurisdiction over the management of the Webster Stream Canoe Touring Route and its operation in T6 R9, the latter designated primarily for Maine Warden Service use but located in BSP with occasional BSP personnel use. In both instances the Park gained some influence over sites concerning BSP. In the first instance, the Director of the Maine Bureau of Public Lands and the Park Director reached an agreement wherein BSP would manage lands under the Bureau's jurisdiction just to the west of the Park boundaries around Webster Lake and Webster Stream. In the second instance, the Park and the Chief Warden of the Department of Inland Fisheries and Wildlife signed an agreement as to their respective duties and rights concerning Camp Davigneau.[16]

The Park faced other challenges along its borders at the close of the period, including the creation of a proposed sixty-one site campground at Pockwockamus Pond by Northern Outfitters, Incorporated, on land leased from Great Northern Company. The site for the proposed campground was located only one-half mile off the Park access road near the southern end of BSP. The Maine Land Use Regulation Commission (LURC) granted permission for the facility—which would focus on white water rafting, canoeing, and kayaking—in 1986 with certain restrictions. The company built fifty-six camping sites in following years plus a lodge and a few other structures. In 1993, the Penobscot Outdoor Center, Incorporated, new owner of the facility, proposed that the camping area be enlarged. The company requested LURC's permission to build facilities to accommodate not only the initial 1980s proposal of 160 to 180 persons per night, but facilities with a 252 persons per night capacity. The same request had been made a few years earlier, but LURC had denied it after determining that it would negatively affect BSP, Pockwockamus Pond, and surrounding wilderness areas. The company had, however, secured permission in 1990 to have non-rafters camp at their facilities.[17]

On July 6, 1993, LURC held a public hearing on the newest proposal. Numerous persons testified. Those who expressed opposition to the proposed expansion included Park Director Caverly, SFMA Advisory member and long-time wilderness advocate Charles Fitzgerald, the Natural Resources Council of Maine, the Wilderness Society, local camp owners Peter Pray and Charles Theriault, and LURC's Planning and Zoning

Division. One major argument opponents voiced, in addition to stressing anticipated negative effects to the local environment as a whole, was that the peak period of camping at the facility corresponded with peak use periods for Baxter State Park. The Park was already trying to deal with day use concerns in the southern portion of the Park and did not want to see day use there increase during the summer season. After the hearing, the rafting company revised its application to state that it would deny camping privileges to non-rafters during Friday and Saturday nights in the peak months of July and August. Critics rebutted and argued that the amendment was only a symbolic one, and would not eliminate the adverse affects of any facility enlargement. In view of the evidence presented as to potential adverse effects resulting from any expansion, and the failure of the applicant to demonstrate through substantial evidence that BSP and the surrounding areas would not be adversely affected, LURC denied Penobscot Outdoor Center, Incorporated's request. Those who had resisted the proposal in the mid-1980s, and there had been others besides the Park, had not been able to halt the campground's construction. Opponents were, however, able to check its expansion in the 1990s.[18]

After the public hearing held by LURC in 1993, Director Caverly had written a follow-up letter to LURC Director David Boulter. In his letter Caverly stated: "the record will reflect that I am always conservative when issues arise that I believe have a potential impact to our Park and its operation."[19] Additional demands by day users on BSP had been one of Caverly's major concerns regarding the new campground. Caverly's record over the preceding decade had indeed shown him increasingly conservative about Park resources, sometimes to the dismay of other individuals or groups, and the issue of day use levels had become one of prime focus for the Park by the early 1990s.

Much of the day use in BSP centered on the southern portion of the Park, the area that contained Katahdin, surrounding peaks, and numerous bodies of water. While the Park wished to limit the numbers of persons and vehicles which entered BSP and therein placed demands on resources and potentially threatened the wilderness experience throughout the Park, the ever popular southern region presented a particular challenge. Most people entered the

Park through the southern entrance, and a majority of hikers wished to hike Katahdin or its environs. Baxter himself had considered Katahdin the jewel of the state, and visitors to the Park wished to get as close to the jewel as possible.[20]

The relocation of the Togue Pond Gatehouse, the creation of the Visitor Information Center, and the tensions over the Pockwockamus camping area all reflected increasing concerns over day use in the southern portion of BSP. Such actions, however, did not result from a sudden awareness of extensive use of the Katahdin area. The Park had studied the problem throughout the 1980s and sought ways to divert people to other regions of the Park, regions also rich in beauty yet less extensively explored by Park visitors. Increased education on offerings throughout the Park marked the 1980s as well as the 1990s. The Park also conducted, largely under the guidance of Park Naturalist Jean Hoekwater, visitor surveys late in the period to obtain pertinent information. Day use issues, although not primary to the Park's decisions, had surfaced during the discussions of extended snowmobile use in BSP and of permitting motorcycle access to the Park. Late in the period, the Park set quotas on the number of motor vehicles allowed to enter the Park, and especially endeavored to control the number of vehicles going to the Roaring Brook parking and recreation area. Parking space at Roaring Brook and other high use areas quickly filled during the high peak usage times, especially summer weekends. This did not eliminate the need for regulating traffic, however, as some Park goers simply pulled to the side of the road, especially where turnouts existed, to secure parking even though Park rules prohibited it. Although the topic of increasing parking capacity arose several times, Caverly and other persons demonstrated that "always conservative" philosophy and argued that it would be difficult to remove additional parking once it had been established, and that such additions would only create increased demands on the southern region.[21]

In a related matter, in May 1990, the Authority voted to close the recently opened West Gate, as statistics indicated that 95 percent of Park visitors entered through the Togue Pond and Matagamon entrances. The West Gate also, due to its low usage, exerted a financial drain on the Park. The Park initially tried leaving the gate unstaffed but with a self-registration system. Many people failed to participate in the honor system, and the Park decided to close the gate, not just shut down gatehouse operations. Some local fishermen, property owners, and other persons did protest the decision. When the Park had earlier closed the Nesowadnehunk Gate due to a State mandate that expenses be cut and to the lack of State authorization to spend money to keep the gate open, property owners on Nesowadnehunk Lake petitioned Great Northern for a new access road from the company's Golden Road. The company complied and the Park then closed the Harrington Lake Road which had served the area and connected with the already closed Nesowadnehunk Gate. Property owners and others then requested a new gate leading to BSP. The West Gate had served this purpose, hence the protest over its closing. In view of financial factors and the difficulty of monitoring gate traffic and therefore overall Park traffic, as well as indications that some peple used the gate primarily as a means to access neighboring Georgia-Pacific lands without paying the company's use fees—thereby increasing Park traffic for no valid reason, the Authority, at the request of Director Caverly, elected to close the gate permanently. Park staff removed the buildings from the West Gate in 1991, relocating them to other portions of the Park, and landscaped and reseeded the grounds.[22]

The Park Rules and Park Use Committees of the Advisory increasingly addressed day use concerns in the early 1990s. In addition to examining the day use issues above, in autumn 1993 the committee agreed with Caverly that the gradual widening of the Perimeter Road, now referred to as the Tote Road in recognition of its origins as a tote route for transporting lumber and supplies and its still primitive condition, needed attention. The committee stated that it would also examine day use at Chimney Pond, where the high volume of hikers was taxing both the campground area and Park staff. So, too, would they examine hiker impacts on surrounding alpine and sub-alpine areas. Regarding an issue previously raised, the committee stated that they hoped the Authority would hire an historian to update the Park history, thereby creating a new resource tool for evaluating various Park issues. Caverly also discussed with the Advisory the possibility of closing a portion of the Perimeter or Tote Road thereby separating the northern and southern portions of the Park in terms of motor vehicle access. Another possibility examined in detail by the Advisory at the end of the period, and one which the media discussed during the motorcycle access controversy, involved the use of small vans or busses to transport visitors from Togue Pond to Roaring Brook and other areas. The Park Use committee obtained as much information as possible at the close of the period on a shuttle system, with hopes of testing a system in the near future. Finances had thus far precluded a trail period[23]

The new gatehouse location at Togue Pond facilitated vehicle control for Roaring Brook. During peak user periods the area might be closed during portions of a majority of days. Those who planned to hike Katahdin or nearby trails from Roaring Brook might well find their plans in need of revision if they failed to arrive early enough in the day. As the hike up Katahdin took several hours each way, some feeling existed that decreased access during afternoon hours might actually serve the public well by lessening the possibility of people starting a mountain climb with insufficient time to return to their cars, or to make it to an overnight camping destination, before nightfall. Trail relocations, increased use of rocks on trails and other means of surface hardening, and signs denoting the presence of endangered flora and instructing hikers to keep to the trails, helped lessen impacts in alpine and sub-alpine regions. Lester Kenway and the BSP Trail Crew labored seemingly endlessly throughout the Park to make such improvements, and created, among other things, a myriad of non-obtrusive stone stairways, wooden bridges, and plank walkways. Some immediate results were realized in terms of erosion control, flora protection, and other concerns through day use reforms. Yet, here as elsewhere, study on how to best protect the environment long-term extended beyond 1994. Some of the proposed measures would no doubt stir great controversy if implemented. This is especially true for the idea of closing a portion of the Perimeter Road, which met with resistance as soon as Caverly mentioned it at a 1993 Director's Communication meeting. Using a shuttle system which would prohibit private vehicular travel to Roaring Brook might likewise be expected to encounter opposition. Virtually all access decisions made during 1970-1994 encountered both public opposition and public support, and no reason exists to posit any radical changes in that pattern for the near future. (One access issue that gathered little anti-BSP policy protest involved the use of air space over the Park for missile testing by the United States Air Force, as well as numerous instances of Air Force pilots flying dangerously—and irritatingly—low over BSP. Caverly addressed these issues over the course of many years, securing reforms by the 1990s including an Air Force regulation prohibiting aircraft from below 2000 feet from any point in BSP.)[24]

As evinced in day use issues, the Baxter State Park Advisory Committee had become increasingly specialized during the 1980s and early 1990s. A source of valuable insight and advice since 1970, by the 1990s the Advisory had become involved in virtually all issues of Park policy and operations. Separate committees or sub-committees had formed to address such issues as SFMA operations, rules and regulations, personnel, financing, investments, capital equipment, Park management plans, and scientific research in the Park, as well as visitor use. Some committees, such as those dealing with personnel and capital equipment, lasted for only a relatively short time, served a specific purpose, and were then abolished. Others, such as the Liaison Committee which served as an intermediary body between the Park and the State Legislature and the State government in general, gained in importance during the 1990s. Although most committees were composed of Advisory members, members of the Scientific Study Review Committee and the SFMA Advisory Committee did not all hold Advisory or Ad Hoc Advisory positions, but had instead been selected by the Authority for the special professional expertise which they could bring to SFMA or scientific research discussions and decisions.[25]

The original seven person membership of the Advisory in 1970 included Robert Ohler, Paul Knaut, Daniel Drummond, Bud Leavitt, State Representative Walter Birt, Alonzo Garcelon, and John Baxter. The Authority appointed Ohler "permanent chairman of the Baxter State Park Authority Advisory" in May 1970. However, other persons would serve as Advisory Chair in succeeding years. Under the Baxter State Park Advisory Statement of Purpose as formulated in 1990, the Advisory would consist of fifteen persons appointed in staggered three year terms. The staggered terms would help provide continuity, one of the original purposes of the group in

1970; 1970, for example, would see, along with other developments, turnover in all three Authority positions. In addition to Ad Hoc members "appointed at the pleasure of the Authority as an entryway to the Advisory" and subject to annual review, and Emeritus members chosen by the Authority, the Director of the Park or his designee enjoyed Ex Officio membership in the Advisory. The Park Director as well as staff members including the Chief Ranger, Park Naturalist, and Park Resource Manager—depending on the specific subject or committee—worked closely with the Advisory. Ad Hoc members attended Authority and Advisory meetings, and partook in discussions and research as did Advisory members. After demonstrating their commitment to the Park, they could be elected to the Advisory at the discretion of the Authority. The Authority remained the appointing body for the Advisory and, in spite of some conflict over the issue, could reappoint standing Advisory members or not as it deemed appropriate. Indeed, in the early 1970s Attorney General Jon Lund, who disagreed with the principle of having an active Advisory as he considered it too legislative, was essentially able to disband the Advisory for a few years. This did not happen again, and the development of the Advisory from the mid-1980s would make a reoccurrence extremely unlikely.[26]

At the close of the period, the Authority decided to make official a long standing practice of reserving a seat on the Advisory for a member of Governor Baxter's family. Baxter family members had served on the Advisory since 1970, including John, Hartley, and Eric Baxter—son, grandson, and great-grandson of Percival Baxter's brother Hartley; Rupert White—grandson of Percival Baxter's brother Rupert; and Ethel Dyer—grandniece of Governor Baxter, granddaughter of Percival Baxter's brother Clinton. The Park also reserved a seat, as generally filled in previous years, for the Superintendent of Acadia National Park with whom the Park and Authority felt valuable information and insight could be exchanged. In the matter of appointments and reappointments, the Authority voted to have "increase of diversity and talent," as the first criteria for selections.[27]

The issues of appointment and reappointment were sensitive ones, as almost everyone who served on the Advisory showed commitment to the Park and many, if not most, wished to continue to serve on the Advisory for as long as possible. So, too, might an Ad Hoc member who had regularly attended meetings and had taken an active role anticipate securing an appointment as a full member of the Advisory when an opening occurred, and be disappointed if he or she were not selected. A similar situation could occur with a person who had demonstrated an active interest in becoming an Ad Hoc member. Discussion of appointments could be both emotional and heated, which proved to be the case when appointments were made in May 1994, at which time the Authority was revising the "Advisory Statement of Purpose." Several persons present in May 1994 did not agree with the Authority's decision not to reappoint a member of the Advisory, Philip Ahrens, a person deemed more than worthy of reappointment by his peers. The following year he secured reappointment. Another matter raised during the May 1994 meeting involved establishing a procedure which would allow potential Advisory members to secure leave of absences from employers to attend Advisory and Authority meetings. An official policy was not formulated on this issue by the close of the period, although the Authority addressed individual cases.[28]

Although individual difficulties or grievances had occurred over the years, the Advisory as well as the Park staff and the functioning of the Authority had evolved to meet the many challenges which faced the great gift of Percival Baxter. The natural environment of the Park remained largely unchanged in the 1990s due to the mandates of the Deeds of Trust and the vigilance of Park staff and Authority and Advisory members. Some aspects of Park operations had changed over the years, however. Many of the changes occurred as those persons involved with BSP became more experienced with various technical issues and with public affairs. Numerous issues, many of them controversial, challenged the Park during the period and resulted in various policy decisions. While painful at the time to some people, controversies surrounding such matters as forest management, snowmobile and motorcycle access, and caribou reintroduction forced the Park to make long reaching policy decisions. Other issues, such as search and rescue, resulted in a series of operational decisions throughout the period, some with more immediate results than others. Both the very controversial and the less controversial issues and events culminated in a more educated work force, a better informed public, and a more clearly stated set of policies than had been true in 1970. Although the Authority, Advisory, and Park staff made decisions which resolved countless issues, or at least granted a temporary reprieve, other issues, such as the basic level of public use allowable in a wilderness area, remained unresolved and a continual challenge in the mid-1990s.[29]

One of the areas with the clearest, most visible, progression was that of forest management. In addition to a more conservative approach to resource management throughout the Park over the period, developments in the Scientific Forest Management Area continued after the close of the 1980s. The SFMA in the 1990s differed significantly from that of the 1970s through the mid-1980s. In addition to the 1980s hiring of Resource Manager Jensen Bissell, the development of a comprehensive SFMA Management Plan, a resumption of cutting operations, and other events discussed in an earlier chapter, the 1990s saw further changes.[30]

The SFMA Advisory continued to meet in the 1990s, although its membership did change. Road construction continued early in the decade—but with modifications—as did access and use monitoring. The SFMA contractor's crews settled into the newly constructed camps at Coffeelos, where improvements and additions were made in following years. People involved in forest management from different parts of the country and from different parts of the world visited the SFMA in the late 1980s into the 1990s, exchanging information which the Resource Manager and other members of the BSP staff found valuable if not directly applicable to BSP operations. As SFMA operations progressed, requests for visits by and information from the Resource Manager increased. In 1993, the Resource Manager attended a silvicultural tour of Germany and Switzerland, homes to the forest operations Governor Baxter had so admired. As Park Director, Caverly continued overall supervision of the SFMA, but Bissell remained in charge of day-to-day operations through the close of the period and his appointment has been labeled a "turning point" for the SFMA. As initiated in 1987, a one-day-per-week consulting forester, John Mills, aided Bissell, and after 1993 a Forest Technician/Roving Ranger, Mac Browning, would also provide assistance in the SFMA as well as provide support as needed throughout the Park. Although the SFMA generally operated on a June to March basis, Bissell filed reports on a calendar year basis in accordance with recent Maine regulations.

Due to the relatively large size of the SFMA and the comparatively small work force in place, all acres did not receive attention every year. Projections called for roughly three to four hundred acres to receive some form of stand treatment annually, although more acreage did in fact undergo treatment during some years. Roughly three hundred acres received treatment in 1990, most of it being some form of shelterwood or selective cutting, a labor intensive approach in which a forester examines every tree in a stand and evaluates potential growth and resource value increase. Not only do economic considerations figure into the decision of whether or not to harvest a tree, so, too, are wildlife, stand stability, and forest diversity considered. By the close of the period, almost 100 percent of the trees harvested, be they destined for Park use or the commercial market, were marked by SFMA personnel. Not only did the Resource Manager and staff hand select timber for harvesting, the marketing of SFMA products also became a responsibility of the Resource Manager, ensuring that tree selections would be made consistent with Park policy. All harvesting contracts became service based.

In 1990, the SFMA witnessed a Swedish Rottne Harvester demonstration. Supplied by the company's U.S. division, Blondin, Incorporated, two machines performed all aspects of harvesting. One machine grasped the tree and severed the bole close to the ground, delimbed the bole, and cut it to specified lengths. A second machine then loaded the logs or pulpwood—depending on tree size and quality—and transported it to the roadside. The machine harvested an eight acre section in the SFMA that August, providing Bissell, contractor Randy Cyr, and others an opportunity to evaluate its performance. Before the operation Bissell established sample plots so that silvicultural evaluations could be made. The system proved more promising for SFMA work than other systems tested, and in 1991 another eighty acres underwent such harvesting. The following year Cyr purchased a Rottne "single grip cut-to-length" system and employed it in the

SFMA thereafter. A more conventional harvesting crew using chain saws and a skidder continued to work in the SFMA as well.[31]

Bissell utilized computer systems in SFMA management. He had done so since he arrived at the Park and would do so increasingly in the 1990s. In 1993, a University of Maine graduate student proposed using the SFMA for a project base for a Master of Forestry degree Geographic Information System (GIS) project, a project which would aid the Park in utilizing a variety of mapping and informational services. The student, Andy Goodwin, toured the SFMA with Bissell, established GIS points and entered them into the GIS digital system. The Park later purchased a computer and digitizer for running GIS computer software, thereby increasing Park mapping and management capabilities.[32]

During the 1990s the SFMA remained free of the controversies prevalent in the mid-1980s and earlier. Although not everyone expressed complete satisfaction with SFMA operations, most apparently agreed that the land was under sound management and no legal suits were filled over forest operations. In spite of a depressed market during some years, the SFMA by the close of the period was operating at a profit and predictions for the future were positive. Some of the work accomplished in the 1990s was preliminary in nature, and future operations were expected to bring the SFMA ever closer to Baxter's ideals of an area which could serve as a showcase of forest practices.

Work in the SFMA and elsewhere progressed in the 1990s. So, too, did scientific research continue. Scientists had engaged in research in Baxter State Park long before 1970 and they continued to do so into the 1990s, yet in the early 1990s numerous people—including some members of the Authority and Advisory as well as individuals seeking research permits—felt that research parameters had still not been clearly defined. The Park and Authority struggled to define such parameters in the late 1980s to mid-1990s. Most research in the Park resulted in furthering staff and public (or at least the pertinent scientific community's) knowledge of a given plant or animal species, a geological process, or other natural event or system. Examples from the later 1980s to the early 1990s include: a 1986 survey of Katahdin area spiders (at least forty-one species were collected); a 1987 survey of birds north of Nesowadnehunk Field to determine long-term changes in bird populations resulting from the spruce budworm infestations of the 1970s, and compared to a study made in 1982 to assess early changes; a 1987 study of the effects of land use patterns (harvested versus unharvested) on woodland hawks with the BSP supplying the basis for unharvested data gathering; a 1987 study of water acidity and separate study of a beetle species that year; a 1989 study of loon behavior at Kidney Pond; an extensive study of pine martens which included capturing, radio collaring, and monitoring the animals which began in 1989 and extended past the close of the period; a 1990 study of alpine vegetation conducted above the tree line on Katahdin; a mushroom collection and classification project (sixty-two species were found) in 1991; and a 1993 survey of Bicknell's Thrush (a threatened songbird) on eleven peaks in the Park. Such studies yielded a wealth of information and can be considered, where results were indicated by the close of the period, "successful" by most criteria.[33]

Most scientific study applications and projects proceeded smoothly during the 1980s and 1990s. Some studies, or portions of studies, did not. Although the caribou reintroduction project of the late 1980s through 1990 had yielded information deemed valuable to the scientific community, it also left portions of the public, the Park staff, and some of the researchers frustrated. Other projects raised similar questions about what types of research should be allowed in Baxter State Park or about which procedures should be followed in certain types of research. The issue would not be resolved during the period studied, although lessons learned from caribou and other research clearly tempered decisions made in the early 1990s.[34]

At the same time as the Park and Authority worked to resolve research issues, an issue came to the forefront which in some ways resembled a research request and which brought the treatment of natural systems in BSP into sharper focus. The operation or request proved as important for what did not occur as for what did occur. Although not approached as a research request, predator control raised some of the same questions or concerns as were currently surfacing in the area of scientific study, namely: what degree of human interaction with wildlife is acceptable in an area devoted to the ideal of animal sanctuary?

Baxter State Park Director Caverly only learned that predator control measures had been taken against coyotes within Park boundaries after the fact. A few citizens had inquired as to whether coyotes were being trapped in the Park, and staff members had replied that they were not. However, Caverly and Park staff learned soon thereafter that the IFW District Warden had found evidence of what he considered high deer predation in BSP in T6R9 during the 1991-1992 winter and had directed licensed coyote trappers to the area. Under Maine law, licensed trappers could set snares for coyotes in the unorganized townships of Maine where coyote predation had been identified by wardens and biologists. Besides proving embarrassing to staff members, the 1991-1992 trapping in BSP can also be viewed as a failure in communications as the Commissioner of the Department of Inland Fisheries and Wildlife is a member of the Baxter State Park Authority. After learning of the coyote trapping, Caverly wrote to Henry Hilton of IFW's Game Management and stated that the Park wanted to be informed before any such activity occurred. The Park operated as much as possible within a public forum, "evaluating all information prior to implementation." The Park wanted to be part of any proposals or decisions for future trapping. Hilton responded promptly, explaining the course of events and stating that IFG would make every effort to inform the Park Director before future control activities were undertaken.[35]

The IFW Warden Service indicated a desire to implement further coyote snaring the following winter and on January 11, 1993, Caverly convened a meeting with Warden Service personnel, Henry Hilton of IFG's Game Management, Joe Wiley also from Game Management and an SFMA Advisory member, Dan Harrison of the University of Maine's Department of Wildlife, predator control agent Don Dudley (coyote trapper), and BSP personnel. Hilton stated that any future IFW initiated coyote snaring would have to be requested by the Park and that any "recreational" snaring, which any further snaring in BSP probably would be, would be subject to control agents securing BSP permission. Meeting participants discussed the coyote presence in the Park, the number of deer killed, baiting and snaring techniques, and predator and predator control impacts on hunters. Caverly concluded that more scientific information was needed before an informed

The Pine Marten was the focus of a long term scientific field study conducted in Baxter State Park. (Photo: Bill Silliker)

decision as to the appropriateness of coyote snaring could be made. He was therefore unwilling to authorize such control for the current season. The subject needed to be reviewed in regards to the Deeds of Trust and the best interests of the Park.[36]

As some members of the public, of the Park staff, and of the Warden Service continued to desire some degree of predator control in the hunting zone in the northern portion of BSP, the Advisory formed, at the request of the Director, an Ad Hoc committee to examine the issue. Chaired by Ray B. Owen of the Department of Wildlife of the University of Maine, the group held discussions and deliberations in late winter and early spring 1993. Scientific and philosophical considerations received attention. According to Chair Owen, several members believed that if other forms of hunting or wildlife management activities were allowed in BSP, IFW endorsed predator management or control should also be allowed. Some committee members felt that substantial justifications and clearly defined objectives had to be demonstrated before any control measures were taken, some believed that snaring should be prohibited, and at least one person remained undecided. Most members, Owen reported, believed that "social pressures" on the Authority and Director would probably "make predator control untenable from a public policy point of view." However, allowing snaring as a recreational activity without formal IFW or BSP involvement "may be considered an acceptable policy by the public."[37]

Caverly, who had earlier requested that IFW Commissioner William Vail allow him to make the decision as Vail "wore two hats in the matter," considered the committee's response. He communicated with Vail again, then issued a memorandum stating the Park policy that "predator control by a technique of snaring will not be conducted until such time as is requested by the Director of BSP to the Commissioner of Inland Fisheries and Wildlife." The following year Caverly reported that no known negative impact on Park resources had resulted from the policy, and conveyed his apparent pleasure in having been able to follow Baxter's Deeds of Trust mandate that the Park be a place where animals could "live, grow, flourish, and die in nature's endless cycle."[38]

Caverly would follow a similar line of reasoning after the close of the studied period when participants in the ongoing pine marten study requested permission to trap small mammals—voles and shrews—as part of their prey availability research. With anticipated shrew mortality in the sanctuary portion of the Park, the request demanded careful consideration, but the timing of the request allowed for only a short lead time before the anticipated trapping would occur. This once again gave rise to numerous questions about the purpose and requirements of scientific research in BSP. After lengthy consideration (and a denial—which Caverly urged—of the prey trapping request), the Authority issued revised scientific research guidelines in early 1996.[39]

The "Guidelines for Scientific Study in Baxter State Park" as issued in January 1996 more clearly defined in general the types of research allowed in Baxter State Park, and identified the types of research which might be conducted in various parts of the Park. In the largest portion of the Park, the Sanctuary, research opportunities were most limited. There the Park aimed to allow flora and fauna to, as quoted from Baxter once again, "live, flourish and die in nature's endless cycle." In the Sanctuary, as Baxter had envisioned it, "the hunting of animals [would] be done with cameras rather than guns." Under the terms of the new guidelines, a researcher should not expect to have studies predicting resultant mortality approved for the Sanctuary. Studies not approved for the Sanctuary, however, might be approved for the SFMA, where hunting was allowed and Baxter had specifically allowed for scientific forestry. Approval still necessitated that no long-term effects be made on the natural systems of the environment. Researchers seeking a less managed area than the SFMA to conduct studies might be allowed to pursue them in the third area of the Park: the 22,906 acres outside of the SFMA where Baxter had allowed hunting and trapping. Although the criteria for study in that area would be less severe than that for the Sanctuary, it would be more stringent than that for the SFMA.[40]

Under the new guidelines, research applications fell into one of three categories. The first category required only short term approval and requests could be made within about two weeks of an anticipated study date. The second category required a six month lead time for approval by the Park Director and review by the new Director's Research Committee. Category III, the third and most involved, necessitated a nine month lead time to allow the Director, the Director's Research Committee, and the Authority sufficient time to make a thorough inquiry and informed decision. All requests involving reintroductions, collecting specimens, of research of a nature deemed controversial enough to require a lengthy lead time fell into the third category. No research request was guaranteed acceptance. Failure to follow category lead time requirements was sufficient reason to deny a request. Applications had to follow specific rules, and written reports of research were required by December 31 of the year of research.[41]

The new guidelines established additional research regulations and requirements over those listed in previous years, and removed the emphasis on studies being welcomed which led to "a greater understanding and appreciation of the natural systems of northern Maine" as stated in guidelines of the 1980s. The new guidelines continued to stress the desirability of studies which contributed to an understanding of the Park's natural systems, but added that such studies "may also provide a basis for comparison with other natural systems," without mention of the possible locality of such studies. The new guidelines did not clarify some questions raised during the preceding years, such as Baxter State Park's role in or obligation to—or the lack of the same—the broader scientific community and thereby the wider public, but did clarify several Park expectations of researchers, which would hopefully lessen frustrations encountered by parties on both sides of the application and research process.[42]

The Park also established a new policy on donations near the close of the studied period. Visitors and others had inquired frequently about donating money to the Park, and the Park had investigated the possibility of accepting donations. In 1990, following research by Legal Council Paul Stern, BSP adopted a donations policy. Under the terms of the new policy all gifts had to be "unrestricted regarding their use;" could not "be in the nature of a public memorial" (no statues, plaques, or named structúres); gifts under $500 could be accepted by the Director but the Director had to account for them annually to the Authority, whereas those valued over $500 could only be accepted by vote of the Authority; and no persons associated with the Park could solicit donations—they could, however, answer any queries initiated by potential donors. The Authority and Park would not accept any gift which would overshadow the great gifts of Governor Percival Baxter to the citizens of the state of Maine in his creation of Baxter State Park.[43]

During the years of 1970 through 1994, members of the Baxter State Park work force tended, with the exception of some seasonal staff, to have long tenures as BSP employees. They provided continuity, and the Park benefited from their increased experience in addressing BSP needs as their years with the Park progressed. Other people associated with Baxter State Park likewise stayed involved with the Park for lengthy periods. Various members of the Advisory served for numerous years, often, but not always, consecutively. Some of the longest periods of tenure on the Advisory included Robert Ohler who served on the Advisory from its 1970 establishment through 1995 and secured emeritus status in 1992, sharing emeritus status after 1991 with former Business Manager William Cross. Winston Robbins belonged to the Advisory committee for most of the period, and held emeritus status from 1991 until his death in 1993.[44]

So, too, did some individuals serve the Park in a variety of capacities. Benjamin Townsend, for example, worked for Baxter State Park during the years of 1979 to 1984 serving as an Assistant Campground Ranger, a Campground Attendant, and eventually a Campground Ranger at Chimney Pond; wrote about the legal history of the Park during his years in law school; and served on the Advisory and a number of its committees during the 1980s through the close of the period. Charles Fitzgerald followed a more circuitous route to the Advisory: he fought against BSP forest and other practices in the media and in the courtroom in the 1970s and early 1980s, then joined the Advisory. Although Fitzgerald did not serve consecutively through all subsequent years, he remained on the SFMA Advisory at the close of the studied period. Ray B. Owen, Jr., a wildlife professor for the University of Maine, had some type of working relationship with BSP throughout the period, from requesting a study of black bear in BSP in 1972 (the request was tabled by the Authority); to hiking with members of the AMC in late 1974 and reviewing the blowdown area; to sitting on the Department of Conservation's Review Board following the 1977 BSP fire; to holding university classes in the Park; to becoming involved with the caribou reintroduction project in the 1980s and subsequently serving on the Advisory; to, upon his appointment as Commissioner of Inland Fisheries and Wildlife in late 1993, becoming an

Authority member and serving as such until after the close of the period. In addition, by 1994 Owen had spent thirty years celebrating New Years Day either in BSP or just outside its borders. Other Authority members also served on the Advisory. Most of them joined the Advisory after their Authority tenures, but some like Owen (and after the close of the period Charles Gadzik), served on the Advisory or in an advising capacity before they sat on the Authority.[45] Clearly Baxter State Park exerted a pull on many persons besides casual visitors, a pull that lasted year after year, decade after decade.

Not only did numerous employees and Advisory and Authority members have long relationships with the Park. Press coverage of Park affairs occupied a significant amount of work time for some individuals over the years. Phyllis Austin, who covered events for the *Maine Times* from the 1970s to the close of the period, provides one example. Bud Leavitt, former *Bangor Daily News* sports writer, provides a second example. Leavitt served on the first Advisory, covered BSP affairs for the *BDN*, discussed Park issues in such other forums as his television programs until his death in 1994, and, among other things, narrated most of the 1989 slide show as shown at Park Headquarters in following years until a new show was developed at the close of the period. Like the *Bangor Daily News*, the *Maine Times*, and other Maine newspapers, the Millinocket area local weekly, the *Katahdin Times*, devoted a great deal of attention to the Park over the years, with Anne Erickson and later Barbara Waters providing much of the coverage. Photographing Baxter State Park occupied some individuals. Paul Knaut, member of the first Advisory, visited the Park through much of the period and produced a volume of BSP photographs. Other photographers produced books centered on BSP, and in the 1990s photographer Bill Silliker, Jr. spent much time photographing the Park's beauty, produced an annual Park calendar, and contributed landscape photographs to the new Visitors Information Center in 1994.[46] Such photography was of course superseded numerically by the sum of photographs taken by average Park visitors, newspaper writers and photographers, and BSP staff, Authority, and Advisory members.

The first Baxter State Park Advisory Committee members wrote, soon after assuming their duties in 1970, a "Statement of Purpose" for Baxter State Park which incorporated many statements from Baxter's Deeds of Trust and attempted to define the objectives of the Baxter State Park Authority. Written largely by Robert Ohler of Winthrop and Norman Minskey of Bangor, and introduced into the State Legislature by Advisory member and State Representative Walter Birt of East Millinocket, the Legislature passed the bill in 1971. The first paragraph of the "Statement of Purpose" read as follows:

> Seldom has a more generous gift been presented to a people than has been given by Percival Proctor Baxter to the people of the State of Maine. It is incumbent upon them, the recipients, to preserve the trust impressed upon them, to ensure for themselves and for future generations the fullest use of Baxter State Park consistent with the desires of the donor.[47]

The recipients of Baxter's great gift have endeavored to do just that. From newspaper editorials to letters to the editor, from legal suits against the Authority to legal suits by the Authority, the citizens of Maine have struggled to preserve Baxter's gift in the manner they considered most appropriate and in keeping with the Deeds of Trust as they interpreted them. The Deeds of Trust do not purvey final answers to all questions, and the very vagueness and inconsistencies found among some of the Deeds and Baxter's correspondence and actions have made for a dynamic Park history and will, no doubt, continue to do so.

Several years before his death, Percival Baxter wrote to Maine Governor John Reed of his anxieties concerning his beloved Park. "While I am living, I fear no encroachments on the Park," Baxter wrote, "but as time passes and new men appear upon the scene there may be a tendency to overlook these restrictions and break the spirit of the gifts."[48] Humanity by its very existence encroaches upon the wilderness. Yet, in the years since Baxter's death in 1969, the Baxter State Park Authority, the Baxter State Park Authority Advisory as established in 1970, and Baxter State Park personnel

Toll Dam on Nesowadnehunk Stream, 1987. The spring thaw once facilitated transport of logs south of this point to the waters of the West Branch of the Penobscot River. Mount OJI can be seen in the distance. (Photo: *Bangor Daily News*)

have worked to the best of their abilities to protect Baxter State Park and its wilderness from human encroachment.

To ensure the protection of Park resources, successive Park administrators have worked to develop increasingly comprehensive management strategies. Under Supervisor Harry Kearney the Park developed its first published Park Plan, only a few pages in length but stating basic policies; under Director Arthur Lee Tibbs BSP formulated its first comprehensive "Baxter State Park Policies and Concepts Plan;" and during Irvin C. Caverly's tenure as Director, Baxter State Park continued to update and refine its management goals, particularly in the area of forest practices and visitor information. So, too, did such areas as search and rescue techniques and organization, fire management, and scientific research policies undergo revision after Caverly became Director. In addition, challenges concerning Park visitor access such as motorcycle and snowmobile use, as well as those involving Park property and leases, forced ongoing evaluations of Park policy and administration. Serving as a Park administrator from 1971, and as chief supervisor of many sectors of Park operations for the entire studied period, Irvin C. Caverly participated in the formulations of all Park Management Plans from 1970 through 1994 and beyond. He also played an instrumental role in the 1992 purchase of over one thousand acres of land on the southeastern boundary of BSP, thereby enlarging Percival Baxter's gift through revenue produced by the Baxter State Park Trust Fund which, carefully managed, had grown substantially since 1970 and promised to ensure BSP's financial independence into the foreseeable future.

Various awards and formal recognitions have been given the Park in recent years in acknowledgment of the struggles and triumphs of the Park in preserving the gifts of Governor Baxter to Maine citizens and to the natural environment. These have ranged from certificates presented by local fraternal and other clubs to ceremonies by, and plaques from, national organizations. Two notable awards include one from the Humane Society of the United States and from the Wilderness Society.

Director Irvin C. Caverly, Jr. received the Olaus and Margaret Murie Award from the Wilderness Society on July 12, 1991. The Wilderness

Society presented Caverly with the award in recognition of his "more than three decades, from [his] first stint in the field at Russell Pond in 1960 to [his] ongoing duties ... as Director." Caverly, the award stated, had "embraced, nurtured, and protected the living integrity of the oldest and most beautiful natural reserves in the United States—the state of Maine's Baxter State Park, whose treasure of wilderness and wildlife enriches us all."[49]

The Olaus and Margaret Murie award recognized Baxter's work as well as Caverly's. The Humane Society of America gave a perhaps more formal recognition to Baxter as well as to the citizens of Maine in its 1994 award, and recognized Caverly's efforts on behalf of Baxter State Park by asking Caverly to accept the award in Boston. The Humane Society invited the existing Governor of Maine and the current Authority to attend the ceremony, but wanted Caverly to be the person to accept the plaque given BSP. The award was given on October 14, 1994, "in honor of Sir Percival Baxter for his precious gift of land, and in recognition of the citizens of Maine for their commitment to the preservation of Baxter State Park."[50]

User demands have created a continual challenge to Baxter State Park resources, and Park stewards have struggled to keep the great gift of Governor Percival Proctor Baxter as he wanted it: "a sanctuary and home for the creatures of the wild," a place where "hunting with cameras will take the place of hunting with guns," a place where "those who love nature and who are willing to walk and make an effort to be close to nature" can enjoy all the beauty Katahdin and Baxter State Park have to offer.[51] Baxter also wanted to create a "showcase of forestry" in the northern two townships, and in this, too, have the Authority, Advisory, and staff labored to fulfill Baxter's mandates. Controversies have arisen over uncountable issues since Baxter's death, and will continue to do so. As the Park struggles to reconcile the many demands of a multiple use mandate, the Deeds of Trust provide substantive guidance but not ultimate solutions. Baxter left his Park to the people of Maine in Trust, and it is in Baxter's Deeds that those who seek to protect the Park in turn place their trust. Some of their work and actions may prove short lived, others may be of lasting duration, but, as Baxter wrote, "Katahdin in all its glory forever shall remain the mountain of the people of Maine." With Katahdin and its surrounding glory largely

Katahdin, viewed from Abol Deadwater on the West Branch of the Penobscot River (Photo: *Bangor Daily News*)

unchanged since 1969, in spite of numerous struggles along the way, Governor Percival Proctor Baxter's trust was wisely placed.

KATAHDIN

You love it and you fear it
It is big and harsh and high
A mass of ancient granite
Towering into the sky
From the Indians who revered it
To the climber of today
A symbol of a spirit
That can never pass away

Earl Victor Shaffer

In 1948 Earl Victor Shaffer became the first person to "through hike" the entire Appalachian Trail. Fifty years later on October 22, 1998 the 79-year-old hiking pioneer completed his third and final through hike on the AT and wrote this poem.

Winter shadows, Katahdin's South Basin. (Photo: Irvin Caverly, Jr.)

Endnotes

Chapter One: An Introduction to Baxter State Park

1. Taken from the Deeds of Trust and general records of Baxter State Park and the State of Maine. For further information see the Deeds of Trust of Governor Percival Proctor Baxter to the State of Maine, as well as other legal documents, on file at BSP. The Maine State Library with its Percival Proctor Baxter Collection supplies a wealth of material on Baxter and the history of BSP. For coverage of the Park from the nineteenth century to the close of Baxter's death, as well as material on certain aspects of the Park's history for a few years thereafter, see Dr. John H. Hakola, *Legacy of a Lifetime, the Story of Baxter State Park*, TBW Books; Woolwich, Maine, 1981.
2. Specifics taken from Hakola, *Legacy of a Lifetime*, 288-295. The Baxter State Park Authority, particularly its representative and employee, the Park Director, would later become involved with the school's Board of Trustees.
3. Ibid. pp. 298-301. Quote taken from Baxter's will.
4. Taken from general Park records for the period. Following information is taken from the Deeds of Trust and general Park records unless otherwise indicated. Much of the information is addressed further in following chapters.
5. General Park records. See Minutes of the Baxter State Park Authority Meetings (Hereafter BSPAMs) for 1990-1994 and 1981 for information on the guide dogs. Information on Mike Perry supplied also by Irvin C. Caverly (Hereafter ICC), 6 January 1996. Information on Irwin from telephone interview with Bill Irwin, 6 March 1995.
6. See 1980, 1986, and 1994 Baxter State Park Annual Reports (Herafter *AR*s) and Hakola, *Legacy*, p. 254 for 1970 and 1971 figures.
7. Hakola, *Legacy*, pp. 215-216. Quote from Baxter and the Authority p. 216.
8. Hakola covered the termination of the leases discussed in this section, as well as others which occurred before 1970. See Hakola, *Legacy*, pp. 215-227 for further background information. Also see materials on file at Baxter State Park covering property sales, lease negotiations, and related materials, as well as BSPAMs for the years covered and other sources as noted.
9. Ibid. Also see James S. Erwin to Henry Cranshaw, 13 March 1968, and Austin Wilkins to Walter L. Cook, 6 September 1968. Property in T3 R10.

10. Ibid. See also Austin H. Wilkins to Earl W. York, Jr., 17 July 1970 and attachments, and Wilkins to Mr. and Mrs. E. W. York, Jr., 24 July 1967. Property in T3 R10. Interview with Irvin C. Caverly, Jr. (Hereafter ICC), 6 January 1996 on decision to convert Daicey Pond Camps to single cabin rental facility.
11. Ibid.
12. Ibid. Property in T2 R9.
13. Hakola, *Legacy*, p. 227. Property in T2 R9.
14. Ibid. See also Justice Thomas E. Delahanty, *Baxter State Park Authority v. The Fin and Feather Club, et al*, Law Docket No. Ken-73-8; and *BDN*, 13 March 1974. Property in T2 R9.
15. William E. Cross (then in Forestry Department) to Austin H. Wilkins, undated but circa late 1967-early 1968.
16. Appraisal of Marshall and Stevens Incorporated, 28 December 1967, sent with letter to Wilkins. Property inspected 10 September 1967.
17. Contracts on file at BSP; also, William Cross to BSPA, 11 May 1972; and ICC to Charles Norris, 23 May 1972.
18. Cross to Maynard F. Marsh, 6 June 1974.
19. Robert Williams to Whit McEvoy, 24 June 1982. BSP Advisory Meeting (Hereafter BSP AdvM) on Kidney Pond, 30 June 1982.
20. Robert Williams to ICC, 21 March 1984.
21. Cross to ICC, 4 October 1986; KPC Advisory Subcommittee Meeting 15 July 1986; Elizabeth Gray to Cross, 15 July 1986; Cross to KPC Subcommittee, 5 October 1986 and 8 April 1987.
22. BSP AdvM, 30 June 1987; BSPAM, 18 September 1987.
23. BSPAM, 17 December 1987. Also see BSP AdvM of same day, and related correspondence on file at BSP. Park Resource Manager Jensen Bissell recalls an Advisory member stating at a different time that he favored removing all buildings, but he did not attend the December meetings or make his opinion made at that time through other means.
24. BSPAM, 17 December 1987.
25. Ibid.
26. ICC to Charles Fitzgerald, 18 February 1988, "Baxter State Park Operational Plan, Kidney Pond Camps," 9 March 1988; and BSPAM, 23 September 1988.
27. Kirk P. Mahoney, Maine Historic Preservation Commission to William [sic] Robbins, 16 November 1987.

28. George Kerivan to ICC, received 10 October 1988; ICC to Kerivan, 18 October 1988; Kerivan to ICC, received 30 November 1989; copy of Kerivan's 1988 letter to *Yankee* on file at BSP; ICC to Kerivan, 1 December 1988; and Kerivan to ICC, received 27 September 1989.
29. Mahoney to ICC, 29 March 1991.
30. ICC to Mahoney, 12 April 1991.
31. *Katahdin Times*, 17 March 1992.
32. Joint Resolution 0395W-LR3870(01), 25 March 1992.
33. Earle J. Shettleworth, Jr. to Jensen Bissell, 28 April 1992.
34. Paul Stern, Memorandum on National Register of Historic Sites, sent to BSPA members and ICC, 30 April 1992; BSPAMs 2 June 1992.
35. See BSPAMs, 1995, or *Katahdin Times*.
36. See BSPAMs and *AR*s, 1990-1996.
37. See general BSP records for period, especially BSPAMs and *AR*s for 1981-1996.

Chapter Two:
Wood, Wind, and Fire: Challenges to Baxter State Park Forest Policy and Protection

1. Deeds of Trust; Legislative Records of 1955, Chapter 3, and of 1963, Chapter 1. Also see Hakola, pp. 73-79 for a history of BSP land acquisitions. Although newspaper coverage of the cutting controversy is relatively extensive, Park documentation of the events is less extensive than with other controversial issues during the examined years.
2. For an examination of the legal issues surrounding the controversy, and a review of its events, see Benjamin P. Townsend, "Jurisdiction of the Land Use Regulation Commission Within Baxter State Park," *Maine Law Review*, Volume 42, Number 2, 1990, pp. 515-552.
3. William E. Cross to BSPA, 19 September 1972.
4. Ibid.
5. *BDN*, 22 November 1972.
6. William E. Cross to BSPA, 19 September 1972.
7. BSPAM, 23 January 1973; *BDN*, 16 November 1972; 22 November 1972; 18-19 November 1972; *PPH*, 20 and 21 November 1972.
8. IDM, Lee M. Schepps to Jon A. Lund, "Baxter Park Authority Contract with Great Northern Paper Company," 12 January 1973.
9. *PPH*, 23 November 1972; *BDN*, 24 November 1972; *PPH*, 26 October 1972.

10. *PPH*, 15 November 1972.
11. BSPAM, 22 January 1973.
12. Quoted from George C. West to John L. Martin, "Baxter State Park Has Control and Management of Baxter State Park Paramount to Another State Agency," 2 January 1973. Also see newspapers for the period, and Townsend, "Jurisdiction of the Land Use Regulation Commission," for an interpretation of the Opinion which was, according to Townsend, erroneous.
13. Ibid.
14. BSPAM, 23 January 1972.
15. BSPAM, 23 January 1973.
16. BSPAM, 13 February 1973. Also see *PPH*, 4 January 1973.
17. IDM, Lee M. Schepps to Jon A. Lund, "Baxter Park Authority Contract with Great Northern Company," 12 January 1973.
18. Circa 6 February 1973, as determined from Park records.
19. BSPAMs, 13 and 21 March 1973.
20. IDM, John H. Benoit to Maynard F. Marsh, "Baxter State Park Trust Fund; Purchase of Rights to Cut and Remove Timber," 8 March 1973.
21. Ibid. In an autumn 1994 discussion with former Business Manager Bill Cross, Cross stated that the decision was made in Augusta and without his foreknowledge.
22. A general overview taken from BSP records for 1969-1974.
23. Jon A. Lund to Governor Kenneth M. Curtis, 13 April 1973.
24. Ibid.
25. BSPAM, 6 December 1974; *Kennebunk Journal*, 4 December 1974 and 7 December 1974; *BDN*, 5 December 1974; 1 & 9; *Katahdin Journal*, 11 December 1974; *PPH*, 21 December 1974; IDM, ICC to Maynard Marsh, 2 December 1974.
26. Irvin C. Caverly, Sr., "Baxter State Park Storm Observation," 12 December 1974.
27. Ibid.
28. See note 24.
29. See note 26.
30. BSPAMs, 9 and 19 December 1975; Fred E. Holt to James W. Sewall Company, 9 December 1974.
31. Andrew B. Berry, Maine Helicopters, Inc., to Fred Holt, 10 December 1974; BSPAM, 19 December 1974.
32. ICC, Monthly Report for December 1974, dated 7 January 1975; A. Lee Tibbs, Monthly Report for April 1975, dated 9 May 1975. Also see

reports for intervening months and for autumn 1975.

33. BSPAM, 16 January 1975; *Maine Sunday Telegram*, 29 December 1974.
34. Clifford H. Goodall to BSPA, 15 January 1975.
35. Ibid.
36. Maynard F. Marsh to Clifford H. Goodall, 17 January 1975; BSPM, 16 January 1975.
37. John Neff to ICC, January 1975; John Neff to BSPA and MATC, undated, 1975; John Jay Maderia to BSPA, 12 February 1975.
38. ICC to Fred Holt, 23 January 1975; BSPAM, 28 January 1975. Also see Fred Holt to ICC, 30 January 1975, and Minutes of 11 March 1975 Forestry Meeting, Old Town.
39. George H. Bourassa, Department of Conservation, to BSPA, 10 January 1975. Also see related BSP correspondence for January and February, and BSPAM, 28 January 1975.
40. ICC to ICC, Sr., 29 January 1975; ICC to John Neff, 29 January 1975; BSPAM, 28 January 1975.
41. IDMs: Bill Cross to Keith Percival, 13 February 1975; Bill Cross to ICC, 20 February 1975; and Lee Tibbs to BSPA, 14 March 1975. Also see summary of Bid 75-339 in Court Records, *Fitzgerald v. BSPA*, BSP files.
42. IDMs: Tibbs to BSPA, 21 May 1975; Marsh to Purchasing Agent, June 2, or 27 1975. Quote from first source, second source contains same information in paraphrased form. Also see bids on file at BSP and related materials.
43. Summation of Bid 75-457, contained in Court Records, *Fitzgerald v. BSPA,* BSP files. Also see BSPAMs, 2 and 9 September 1975; minutes of the Public Hearing on 9 September 1975, and ICC to Francis____ (Last name not indicated), 15 September 1975.
44. Kolman Land Consultants, Inc., "Baxter State Park Blowdown–1974," August 1975. Kolman's salvage proposal and its addendum later became BSPA's "Exhibit 6" in *Fitzgerald v. BSPA*.
45. Ibid.
46. Ibid.
47. BSPAMs, 9 and 29 September 1975; 24 and 29 October 1975. Also see "Fire Hazard Restrictions–1975 Season–Blowdown Area of Park," and various news releases for June and July 1975, in BSP *Fitzgerald v. BSPA* file; IDM, ICC to George Blackburn 23 June 1975; and "Minutes of Meeting With Vladik Kolman," 28 July 1975.

48. BSPAM, 29 September 1975, BSPM, 25 November 1975.
49. IDM, Bill Cross to Majorie Dudley; BSPAMs, 25 November 1975 and 10 December 1975; IDM, Lee Tibbs to K. Damborg, 23 December 1975. "Timber Sales Agreement, Baxter State Park Restoration," 7 January 1976, this became exhibit 10 in the legal suit.
50. For examples see: IDM, George Bourassa to Fred Holt, 2 July 1975; and IDM, Lee Tibbs to BSPA, 11 July 1975. Also see BSPAMs from 19 December 1974 on.
51. Joseph Brennan to Maynard Marsh and Fred Holt, 16 July 1975.
52. Minutes of Public Hearing, 9 September 1975.
53. Jon Lund to Fred Holt, 15 September 1975.
54. E. Stephen Murray to Maynard Marsh, 4 September 1975.
55. Maynard Marsh to E. Stephen Murray, 16, September 1975.
56. *BDN*, 22-23 November 1975 and December/end November 1975 article by Cummings; P. Stephen Murray and John C. Lightbody, "Complaint for Declaratory Judgment, for Review of Governmental Action, and for Injunctive Relief," 20 November 1972; Sarah Redfield and John Patterson, "Answer to Complaint," 9 December 1975.
57. Ibid.
58. Sarah Redfield and John Patterson, "Answer to Complaint," 9 December 1975.
59. For examples of public reaction see: *BDN* 2, 4, 10, 12, 13, 17, and 22 December 1975. Gauvin's column appeared in the *BDN* on September 17, 1975. Also see his letters in *BDN*, 9 and 22 December 1975. Davis' column appeared in the newspaper on 9 December 1975.
60. Phyllis Austin, "Why Charles Fitzgerald is So Angry About the Blowdown in Baxter State Park," *Maine Times*, 6 February 1976, pp.2-3.
61. *BDN*, 22 December 1975.
62. Maynard F. Marsh to Ronald B. Davis, 24 December 1975. See BSPMs for 1976 for Gauvin's attendence.
63. BSPAMs, winter and spring 1976.
64. See BSPAMs for 1976, also see Chapter Six on the snowmobile issue.
65. For information on 1975 spraying, see spring 1975 BSPAMs and Maynard Marsh to Richard F. Brooks, 3 June 1975.
66. Two samples of Ronald Davis's letter are on file at BSP, one being a slightly revised version of the other, the first complete with notes from the person to whom Davis had sent the letter.
67. Ibid.

68. As tabulated from letters on file at BSP Headquarters.
69. Ibid.
70. Ibid.
71. Ibid.
72. BSPMs, 7 January , 3 February, and 2 March 1976.
73. BSPAM, 3 February 1975; Memo from Bill Cross to BSPA, 23 February 1976; and BSPAM, 2 March 1976.
74. BSPAMs, 2 and 12 March 1976.
75. BSPAMs, 12 March and 6 April 1976.
76. BSPAM, 12 March 1976.
77. BSPAM 8 June 1976.
78. Ibid.
79. BSPAM, 7 September 1976.
80. Justice Lewis I. Naiman, "Findings and Order for Injunctive Relief," *Charles Fitzgerald, et al v. Baxter State Park Authority, et al*, Superior Court Civil Action, Docket No. 751110, 24 August 1976.
81. Ibid.
82. Ibid.
83. Ibid.
84. Ibid.
85. Percival Baxter to Helon Taylor, 23 April 1964.
86. See BSPAMs, autumn 1976 through spring 1978.
87. See BSP records for 1976 and 1977, and LT to John Patterson, 6 October 1976.
88. BSPAMs, 19 October and 9 November 1976.
89. See BSPAMs, autumn 1976 through spring 1977.
90. Ibid.
91. Ibid.
92. BSPAMs, 7 June and 6 July 1977.
93. BSPAMs, 2 August and 13 September 1977. Also see Radio Log of the fire at BSP Headquarters, and William G. Herbolsheimeb, "Principal Advisor's Report, Suppression of Forest and Grassland Fires, Section 417, PL 93-288," 25 July 1977.
94. "Baxter Fire Review," Meeting, Bangor, 14 September 1977.
95. Ibid.
96. IDM, ICC to All Concerned Persons, 18 July 1977; "BSP Sector Assignments," 25 July 1977; IDM, LT to Bill Cross, 27 July 1977; LT to John Walker, 28 July 1977; IDM, LT to BSP Employees Working on Fire, 27 July 1977; A. Temple Bowen, Jr. to Maynard Marsh, 21

November 1977; "BSP Cost and Damage Report as of 25 July 1977," Bob Umberger for Director Earle Williams.

97. Ibid. Also see IDM, ICC to All BSP Employees and Family Members, 2 August 1977.
98. IDM, "Fire Reclamation Project," Kim Kolman to LT, 12 August 1977; IDM LT to Kenneth Henderson, 15 August 1977.
99. A. Temple Bowen, Jr., to LT, 30 August 1977; Roger Milligan to LT, 17 August 1977.
100. See note 2.
101. "Baxter State Park Forest Fire Rehabilitation Project," submitted by LT, 1 February 1978.
102. Ibid. Also see IDM of same date, LT to Kenneth Henderson; Henderson to LT, 31 May 1978; and Vladek Kolman to LT, 1 April 1978.
103. Tibbs to "interested parties," 13 April 1978. Also see BSP Fire Plans of 1975 and 1978, and BSPAMs for the period.
104. Tibbs to the eight person "Review Committee," 10 May 1995; Charles P. Williams to Tibbs, 17 April 1978.
105. Holt to Tibbs, 22 April 1978.
106. Ibid.
107. Bart Harvey to Tibbs, 24 April 1978.
108. "Baxter State Park Fire Plan," Revised June 1978.
109. Ibid.
110. Ibid.
111. "Baxter State Park Management Objectives," Revised 3 June 1976. Also see "Baxter State Park Policies and Concepts," August 1978, for fire management policies.
112. BSPAMs, July to December 1977. See especially 2 August, 13 September, and 6 December 1977.
113. BSPAMs, winter and spring 1978. See especially 3 May 1978 and 3 January 1978 meeting of Planning Task Force.
114. BSPAM, 3 May 1978.
115. Ibid.
116. BSPAM, 12 September 1978.
117. "Baxter State Park, Policies and Concepts," August 1978.
118. Ibid.
119. Ibid.
120. Ibid.
121. Ibid.

Chapter Three:
The Scientific Forest Management Area: Development and Progress in the "Northern Townships"

1. An overview. See previous pages and BSPAMs for the indicated years for further information.
2. Ibid.
3. BSPAM, 27 April 1979, and 7 March 1980. Quote and following statement taken from: IDM, George M. Ruopp to ICC, 16 December 1982. Ruopp was stating the purpose of spraying in the SFMA as identified in the 1979 "Spruce Budworm and Protection Recommendation," no copy of which is available.
4. BSPAM, 6 September 1979.
5. BSPAM, 31 July 1980.
6. BSPAM, 20 August 1980.
7. BSPAM, 21, August 1980. See following BSPAMs for contributions by Robbins. The exact degree of aid he offered is, however, not ascertainable.
8. Ibid.
9. Ibid.
10. BSPAM, 22 October 1980.
11. "Baxter State Park Authority Scientific Forest Management Area, A Forest Management Plan for the Initial Ten Year Operational Period," December 1980, p. vi.
12. Ibid.
13. Ibid, Quote p.1.
14. Ibid, pp. 8 and 23.
15. Ibid. Percentages p. 20, rotations p. 26.
16. Ibid, pp. 40-84, quote p. 41.
17. BSPAMs, 26 January and 24 February 1981.
18. BSP AdvM, 30 March 1981.
19. BSPAMs, 13 July, 4 August, 18 August, and 26 October 1981.
20. BSPAMs, 19 November 1981, 12 January, 5 March, 16 March, and 13 April 1982.
21. BSPAM, 14 December 1982. Also see "Baxter State Park 1992 Annual Report" (1982 *AR*), pp. 4-5. The 1982 *AR* dates the harvest operation to July, but without identifying the specific activity which began then.
22. Ibid. Also see IDMs, G. M. Ruopp to ICC, 15 November and 16 December 1982.
23. Ibid.

24. See BSPAM, 9 August 1993, for information on Ruopp's resignation. Also see BSPAMs for era for following information, which was verified in an interview with ICC on 4 October 1995. ICC provided the information on Kolman and Ruopp following their departure from BSP.
25. BSPAMs, 8 February and 12 April 1983.
26. BSPAMs, 7 June and 15 November 1983.
27. BSPAM, 15 November 1983. See BSPAM, 10 January 1984, for the revised figures and also 1984 *AR*, p. 7.
28. Ibid. Also see BSPAM, 10 January 1994, for stumpage figures.
29. See 1984 *AR*, pp. 7-8, for road information, most of which was also discussed at BSPA meetings.
30. Ibid.
31. BSP AdvM, 23 April 1984; BSPAM, 24 April 1984; BSP AdvM, 11 June 1984.
32. BSPAM, 25 September 1984.
33. BSPAM, 11 December 1984.
34. BSPAM, 8 January 1985.
35. 1984 *AR*, pp. 22-23.
36. Ibid.
37. Ibid.
38. BSPAM, 12 March 1985. Information on wood, some 2,000 cords, being piled up taken from 1985 *AR*, Section C.
39. BSPAM, 10 September 1985. Names of the two contractors and their districts taken from 1985 *AR*, Section C.
40. BSPAM, 21 November 1985.
41. *Maine Times*, 4 October 1985.
42. Ibid.
43. Ibid.
44. Ibid.
45. *BDN*, 21 November 1985.
46. BSPAM, 21 November 1985.
47. Ibid.
48. Ibid.
49. Ibid.
50. Ibid.
51. Ibid.
52. Ibid.
53. Ibid.
54. BSPAM, 26 November 1985.

55. Ibid. Also see *BDN*, 28 November 1985.
56. Ibid.
57. BSPAM, 21 January 1986.
58. BSPA Special Meeting, 21 January 1986.
59. Ibid.
60. Ibid. Also see: SFMA Advisory Committee, "Recommended Actions After February 1, 1986, on the Baxter State Park Scientific Forest Management Area," undated.
61. Ibid.
62. BSPA Special Meeting. Also see *BDN*, 30 January 1986; and author's interview with Charles Fitzgerald, 30 December 1996.
63. Ibid.
64. Ibid. The "untainted" and "white washed" quotes taken from Fitzgerald, "Serious Omissions in the Committee's Recommended Actions," 29 January 1986. Also see *BDN*, 30 January 1986; interview with Charles Fitzgerald, 30 December 1986.
65. BSPA Special Meeting. Also see *BDN* 30 January 1986.
66. Ibid.
67. Ibid. Also see NRC to BSPA, 29 January 1986, as presented to the Authority at the Special Meeting.
68. BSPAM, 11 March 1986.
69. BSPAM, 8 May 1986.
70. BSPAM, 6 June 1986. Also see: SFMA Standing Advisory Committee, "Baxter State Park Scientific Forest Management Area Revised Staffing and Budget Proposal," 28 May 1986, reprinted in the 1986 *AR*, pp. 20-26.
71. Ibid.
72. Ibid.
73. BSPAM, 18 June 1986.
74. Ibid.
75. Ibid. Also see BSPAM, 9 September 1986.
76. BSPAM, 11 December 1986; 1986 *AR*, p. 19.
77. BSPAM, 11 December 1986.
78. Ibid.
79. Ibid.
80. Ibid.
81. See general Park records.
82. SFMA Advisory Meeting, 21 May 1987.

83. Director's Communication Meeting, 11 December 1987; 1987 *AR*, p. 40.
84. BSP AdvM, 10 May 1988. See BSPAM, 9 March 1988, for mention of the budget, and 1987 *AR*, p. 40, for more information on contract process.
85. BSPAM, 11 May 1988.
86. See BSPA & AdvMs for the time period as well as *AR*s.
87. BSPA & AdvMs, 23 September 1988; 1988 *AR*, pp. 43-44. Also see BSP records in general for these years for an overview of Park personnel and Advisory members participating in public and/or educational forums.
88. Composite taken from BSPA & AdvMs, for 1989, and from 1989 *AR*, pp. 41-49.
89. Ibid.
90. For information on the court case see preceding note. Balance of paragraph and the following one is an overview taken from BSPA records.

<u>Chapter Four: Native Americans: A Demand for Unequal Access</u>

1. ICC, "Monthly Report for April and May 1976;" ICC, "Special Activity Report, Indian Affairs, Spring 1976;" *PPH*, 17 April 1976. The *Kennebec Journal* and other Maine newspapers carried the same AP and UPI Bulletin as did the *PPH*, as they did on following days. Also see the *Maine Sunday Telegram*, 18 April 1976, on the Park being closed to public during this time.
2. *PPH*, 17 April 1976; *BDN*, 17 and 18 April 1976.
3. ICC, "Special Activity Report, Indian Affairs, Spring 1976;" *PPH*, 17 April 1976.
4. ICC, "Special Report;" *PPH*, 17 April 1976; *BDN*, 20 April 1976.
5. Ibid.
6. Ibid.
7. Ibid. Also see *BDN*, 17-18 April 1996. For an example of the former type of editorial see *BDN*, 22 April 1976. For an example of the second see *PPH*, 22 April 1976.
8. ICC, "Special Report."
9. Ibid.
10. Ibid. See *BDN*, 20 April 1976, for information on Sockabasion's statements and *PPH*, 19 April 1976 on Deputy Attorney General Donald Alexander's statements.

11. Ibid.
12. ICC, "Special Report;" *PPH*, 21 April 1976; *BDN*, 21 April 1976.
13. ICC, "Special Report." See *PPH*, 21 April 1976 and *BDN*, 21 April 1976 on the charges.
14. ICC, "Special Report."
15. Ibid.
16. *PPH*, 21 April 1976 and *BDN*, 21 April 1976.
17. *PPH,* 22 April 1976; *Kennebec Journal*, 22 April 1976.
18. ICC, "Special Report." Also see *BDN*, 23 April 1976 and *PPH*, 23 April 1976, for further information.
19. Ibid.
20. ICC, "Special Report;" *PPH*, 23 April 1976.
21. ICC, "Special Report."
22. Ibid.
23. Ibid.
24. Ibid.
25. Ibid.
26. Ibid.
27. Ibid.
28. *PPH*, 23 April 1976.
29. Ibid.
30. *BDN*, 28 April 1976. Also see BSPAMs for 1976 through 1978.
31. BSPAM, 4 May 1976.
32. BSPAM, 2 August 1977.
33. BSPAMs, 13 September 1977; 12 September 1978; and 17 October 1978.
34. BSPAM, 15 November 1978.
35. Ibid.

Chapter Five: Search and Rescue: Visitor Protection in Baxter State Park

1. Hakola, *Legacy*, p.311.
2. The author was fortunate in being able to hike several of the trails in the Katahdin area, as well as in other parts of the Park, while working on the Park history, which allowed her to experience and view many of the beauties and the hazards of the area. Other hazards were revealed through researching search and rescue and related documents.
3. Hakola, *Legacy*, p. 311.
4. Compiled from general Park records for the era. See especially: BSP, "Summary of Deaths in Baxter State Park."

5. Ibid.
6. BSP 1970 and 1973 Rules and Regulations, also see later years.
7. Ibid. See Park records for the incident referred to here and those mentioned above.
8. BSPAM, 16 December 1969. See following meetings for information on the building of radio towers and later years for changes to the system.
9. Austin Wilkins, "For the Record," 5 Dec. 1969.
10. ICC, "1971-1972 Report for Commissioners Biennial," circa 1972.
11. ICC, "Report of the Month of October 1972," 8 November 1972.
12. ICC to BSPA, 28 May 1971.
13. ICC to BSPA, 2 June 1971.
14. ICC to BSPA, 6 June 1971.
15. ICC to BSPA, 2 July 1971.
16. ICC, "1971-1972 Report for Commissioners Biennial."
17. Tibbs, "Monthly Report for June and July 1976", undated.
18. "Minutes, Rules, and By-Laws of Baxter State Park Mountain Rescue Team," 26 March 1973; IDM, ICC to BSP, 28 March 1973; and IDM, George L. Smith to Maynard Marsh, 5 April 1973.
19. Ibid.
20. For statistics see BSP "Summary of Deaths," or *BDN*, 5 February 1974.
21. "The Katahdin Tragedy: A Report to the Baxter State Park Authority," 6 March 1974. Prepared by team leader Robert Proudman with help from the four other survivors: Mike Cohen, Doug George, Page Dinsmore, and Paul DiBello.
22. Ibid.
23. Ibid. Also see ICC to BSPA, 7 February 1974 for information he received from the survivors. ICC informed the author that he had not granted permission for the group to spend any night away from any camp, 24 February 1996.
24. Proudman, "The Katahdin Tragedy."
25. Ibid.
26. Ibid.
27. Ibid. See ICC to BSPA, 7 February 1974 and related records for Cohen's separation from George.
28. Ibid.
29. Ibid.
30. An overview taken from testimony presented to the BSPA in March

1974, as well as from Park correspondence and contemporary newspaper accounts.

31. Ibid.
32. ICC to BSPA, 7 February 1974.
33. An overview of testimony presented to the BSPA. For wind chill estimate and Army National Guard information see *BDN*, 4 February 1974.
34. Ibid. For the initial decision for a night ascent see Rick Wilcox, "Mount Katahdin Rescue," undated but part of the testimony presented to BSPA. Ross and Wilcox were both members of the EMS team. The team had flown in from North Conway, NH. Also see: Danny Watson, IFG Warden, "Report to Inquiry Committee on Proudman Party Accident, 1974," undated but part of the BSPA inquiry testimony.
35. George L. Smith to BSPA, 5 March 1974. Information on the condition of the party supplied by ICC.
36. Ibid.
37. See note 30.
38. Wilcox, "Mount Katahdin Rescue." Also see note 30.
39. Taken primarily from George L. Smith to BSPA, 5 March 1974.
40. General information taken from Park records. Also see: *BDN*, 5 February 1974; *Kennebec Journal (KJ)*, 7 March 1974; Proudman, "The Katahdin Tragedy;" and Robert Dinsmore to BSPA, 3 March 1974.
41. *BDN*, 7 March 1974; *KJ*, 7 March 1974. Quote from Wilcox, "Mount Katahdin Rescue."
42. Eric T. Wight, "Proudman Party Rescue," undated but included in BSPA hearing testimony.
43. William G. Kittredge to BSPA, undated but part of hearing testimony.
44. Proudman, "The Katahdin Tragedy."
45. Ibid.
46. Ibid. Also ICC to BSPA, 7 February 1974.
47. Proudman, "The Katahdin Tragedy."
48. See especially Wilcox, "Mount Katahdin Rescue," and BSPA, "Recommendations, March 6, 1974, Inquiry."
49. BSPA, "Recommendations," and related Park records.
50. Ibid. Also see BSPAMs for 1974.
51. Ibid. Also see BSP Rules and Regulations, 1974 and 1975 Revisions, BSP Winter Rules and Regulations, 1975 Revision.
52. Taken from ICC to BSPA, 15 July 1974, and Loren Goode, "Augustus

Aldrich, Lost Persons Report," undated but attached to ICC's report to the Authority.

53. Ibid.
54. Ibid.
55. Ibid.
56. Ibid. Also see BSP, "Summary of Deaths," and BSPM, 9 July 1974.
57. BSPAMs for period. See BSPAM, 27 April 1979 for disbanding of BSP Mountain Rescue Team.
58. BSP "Summary of Deaths."
59. "State of Maine Report of Investigation by Medical Examiner" as completed by Dr. H. C. Gilman on 20 February 1980.
60. Ibid. Also taken from Thomas Chase, "Rangers Report," 19 February 1980. For an example of press coverage, see *KJ*, 26 February 1980.
61. Ibid. Quote from Gilman, "Report of the Investigation."
62. ICC to Tibbs, 21 February 1980. Also see *KJ*, 26 February 1980.
63. ICC to Tibbs, 21 February 1980.
64. See general Park records for 1970's and 1980's. Also see ICC to BSPA, 22 January 1982, reprinted in 1982 *AR*.
65. ICC to BSPA, 22 January 1982.
66. Ibid.
67. Ibid. Also see BSPAM, 9 February 1982.
68. Ibid. Also see BSP Administrative Procedures Governing Winter Activities, 1982 Revision.
69. BSP, "Summary of Deaths," and BSPAMs for era.
70. ICC to BSPA, 11 August 1983, "Critique Meeting, BSP Plane Crash," 18 September 1982, presided over by Al Martin of Dirigo Search and Rescue. Also see the *Lewiston Daily Sun* (*LDS*), 8 August 1983, AP Release, and the *Katahdin Times* (*KT*), 9 August 1983, for press coverage examples.
71. Ibid.
72. Ibid.
73. Ibid. Quotes from *LDS*, 8 August 1983.
74. Ibid. ICC to U.S. Aviation Underwriter, Inc., 20 September 1983; ICC to David Martin, 13 October 1983; ICC to BSPA, 1 September 1983; and Ben Breithaupt to ICC, 1 December 1983.
75. ICC to BSPA, 13 February 1984.
76. Ibid.
77. Ibid.

78. Ibid and BSP radio log of the operation as recorded on 8 February 1984.
79. Ibid.
80. Ibid. Also see two BSP press releases for 8 February 1984.
81. Ibid.
82. Ibid. See Lyn Schriner to ICC, 22 June 1984, about the status of the survivors in June. The men and/or their families wrote the Park to thank the staff for the rescue work and their kindnesses, letters on file at BSP. The BSPA and Park later awarded Kenney a certificate of recognition for his role in the rescue.
83. ICC to BSPA, 13 February 1984, Kevin Slater, "Baxter Park Avalanche Analysis," undated, submitted in February 1984.
84. 1985 *AR*, p. 7, and BSP "Summary of Deaths."
85. ICC to BSPA, 14 August 1986, Reproduced in the 1986 AR; Esther Hendrickson to Robert E. Howes, 20 August 1986.
86. Ibid. Quote from Hendrickson's report.
87. Ibid.
88. Ibid.
89. Ibid.
90. Ibid; "BSP Critique-Quiet Evacuation," 14 January 1987. Also see notes for airplane search and review meeting. Information on radio from ICC, 28 December 1986.
91. "BSP Critique-Quiet Evacuation," 14 January 1987, and a general overview of the era.
92. Ibid.
93. BSPAM, 7 September 1976.
94. Esther Hendrickson to ICC and Bob Howes, 31 August 1990; Barry MacArthur to ICC, 5 September 1990; *BDN*, 29 August 1990.
95. Ibid.
96. Ibid.
97. IDM, Mac Browning to Chris Drew and Bob Howes, 12 October 1991; Robert Howes, "Complaint and Investigation Report," for 12 October 1991; ICC to BSPA, 15 October 1991. Other related reports on file at BSP.
98. ICC to BSPA, 17 June 1993; Guay Stewart, "Complaint and Investigation Report" with attachments.
99. See 1990 *AR* for copies of numerous letters pertaining to the memorial.

Chapter 6:
Caribou: Twentieth-Century Dream of a Nineteenth-Century Reality

1. Austin Wilkins interview with Alice Sproul, summer 1977, Maine State Archives (Herafter MSA). Number of caribou taken from BSPAM, 18 June 1986. Manual also stated that 300 grouse had been traded.
2. Hakola, *Legacy*, p. 173. Also see pp. 41 and 48 and pertinent endnotes.
3. Ibid, pp. 61-62.
4. Ibid, pp. 172-73; report cited p. 173; McCollough stated that Dyer reached a favorable decision in 1948, and did not mention the 1941 skepticism. Dyer, 1948 M.S. thesis, "Preliminary Plan for Wildlife Management" for BSP, UM.
5. Francis D. Dunn, "Reintroduction of Woodland Caribou to Mt. Katahdin, Maine," Northeast Fish and Wildlife Conference, 17-20 January 1965. Also see ICC to Col. Albert White, Maine National Guard, 26 March 1986.
6. Ibid.
7. Wilkins interview with Sproul, summer 1977.
8. Dunn, "Reintroduction;" McCollough, November 88, pp. 1-2.
9. ICC interview with author, 30 January 1995. See endnote 10 for further information.
10. IDM, ICC to Glen H. Manuel, 4 February 1986; Manual and Fred Hurley to ICC, DM, Francis Dunn, and George Matula, 10 February 1986. Quote from the letter of 10 February 1986.
11. Letter of 10 February 1986, see note 10. Also see *News* release, IFW, March 1986.
12. *News* release, IFW, March 1986.
13. ICC to Albert White, 26 March 1986. Minutes of Caribou Transplant Committee (CTC) Meeting, 15 April 1986; also see IFW *News*, March 1986 for related information.
14. Manuel to McCollough, 16 May 1986.
15. BSPAM, 18 June 1986.
16. BSPAMs, 18 June and 9 July 1986.
17. Ibid. Quote: BSPAM, 9 July 1986.
18. BSPAM, 24 September 1986.
19. Directors Communication Meetings, 23 & 24 June 1986.
20. IDM, Manuel to Caribou Transplant Committee (CTC), 18 June 1986.
21. BSPAM, 9 July 1986.
22. Ibid.
23. Ibid. Also see BSPAM, 18 June 1986. At the June meeting Manuel

gave the figure for both caribou and moose, with no specification as to their age, which might have been more correct as the 1963 imported caribou had been adults.

24. BSPAM, 9 July 1986.
25. Ibid. Also see BSPAM, 18 June 1986.
26. BSPAM, 9 July 1986.
27. Ibid.
28. BSPAM, 24 September 1986.
29. Ibid. Also see: IDM, Mark McCollough (MM) of IFW to George Matula and Ladd Heldenbrand of IFW, 17 September 1986.
30. IDM, MM to Matula and Manuel, 20 September 1986.
31. CTC Meeting (CTCM), 22 September 1986. Also see CTCM, 8 October 1986.
32. CTCM, 22 September 1986.
33. Ibid.
34. Ibid. Also see CTCM, 8 October 1986.
35. BSPAM, 24 September 1986.
36. CTCM, 8 October 1986.
37. *The Morning Sentinel*, 18 October 1986.
38. See CTCM, 8 October 1986, for details on these and other decisions. Contract with Wyeth signed by Manuel on 10 October 1986. Contract with University of Maine ran from 1 November 1986 to 31 June 1987, signed by Ray B. Owen and GHM, approved by CTC on 15 November 1986.
39. Ungulate Committee Report, The Maine Chapter of The Wildlife Society (Hereafter MC, TWS), 9 October 1986; Manuel to Eugene Dumont, president of The Maine Chapter of The Wildlife Society (Hereafter MC, TWS), 12 November 1986.
40. CTCM, 15 October 1986; IDM, MM to CTC, 14 October 1986.
41. Martin L. Wilk to Manuel, 4 November 1986, CTC By-Laws, 3 November 1986.
42. BH to GJB, 17 November 1986; JB to BP, 1 December 1986.
43. Fred Dunkle, United States Department of the Interior, to John Lehman, Secretary of the United States Navy, 18 November 1986, and attached Service Request.
44. Ibid.
45. *BDN*, AP Releases, 8 and 9 December 1986; *BDN*, 11 December 1986. Also see *BDN* coverage of 5-7 December 1986 and *Newsweek*, 15 December 1986, pp. 92-93.

46. *BDN*, 10, 11, 13-14, and 15 December 1986.
47. BSPAM, 11 December 1986; *BDN*, 11 December 1986.
48. 1986 *AR*, p.2.
49. Composite for November 1986-summer 1987.
50. CTC Newsletter, January 1987.
51. MM, "Maine Caribou Transplant Corporation, A Management and Release Plan for the Reintroduction of Woodland Caribou to Maine," undated. McCollough revised this a few times.
52. MM to CTC Technical Advisory Committee, 4 February 1987; MM to BSPA and Advisory, 21 February 1987.
53. See BSP AdvMs, spring 1987.
54. BSP AdvM, 10 March and 28 April 1987; Winston Robbins to ICC, 22 April 1987; ICC to RBO, 23 April 1987; BSP AdvM, 12 May 1987; quotes from CTC Meeting, 22 May 1987.
55. CTC News Release, 3 February 1987. Also see: CTC, News Release, 25 February 1987; MM, "Emergency Financial Report" to CTC Members, 15 February 1987; MM to CTC Members, 20 February 1987.
56. MM, "Maine Caribou Transplant Corporation, A Management and Release Plan for the Reintroduction of Woodland Caribou to Maine," undated, circa late spring 1987.
57. Ibid.
58. Quote: CTC Newsletter, April 1987. See BSPAMs, spring 1987, for general information.
59. CTC, "Caribou for Maine, An Informational Brochure," summer 1986.
60. MM, "Return of the Native II," *Maine Fish and Wildlife*, spring/summer 1987, pp. 2-5; Herbert Adams, "Return of the Native," *Habitat: The Journal of the Maine Audubon Society*, July 1987, pp. 26-31; CTC Newsletter, December 1987.
61. BSPAM, 14 July 1987.
62. MM to ICC, 1 July 1987.
63. Ibid.
64. Ibid; MM to CTC Members and Advisors, 11 May 1987.
65. Ibid; CTC Newsletter, July 1987; MM to CTC Members, 20 July 1987; and composite of records for this period.
66. CTC Newsletter, July 1987; MM to CTC Members, 20 July 1987; CPN, December 1987; *MF&W*, winter 1987-88, pp.6-7.
67. BSPA and AdvMs, 9 March 1989; BSPAM, 11 May 1988.
68. See note 55. Also see his final revision of 25 February 1988.
69. Ibid.

70. Ibid.
71. BSPAM, 16 November 1988. Also see minutes of the Advisory meeting of the same day, and the Special Advisory Meeting of 10 November 1988.
72. MM to ICC and JH, 10 January 1989; JH to PS, 30 January 1989; JH to MM 31 January 1989; and MM to ICC and JH, 7 February 1989.
73. Richard B. Anderson to ICC, 21 February 1989; Letter and attached Articles of Incorporation, Timothy P. Benoit to Richard Anderson, 20 April 1989. ICC was not listed in the body of the incorporation material.
74. BSPAM, 31 March 1989; Larry Laughlin to James Tierney, 13 April 1989; Tierney to ICC, 24 April 1989. Also see MM to ICC, 14 April 1989.
75. CTC Director's Report, 19 May 1989; BSPA & AdvMs, 12 May 1989; ICC to BSPA, 2 May 1989.
76. CTC Director's Report, 19 May 1989. BSPAM, 9 June 1989.
77. BSP AdvM, 7 July 1989; BSPAM, 13 October 1989.
78. BSP Director's Communication Meeting, 5 December 1989; Also see general press coverage of the project for 1990. MM to BSPA, 6 November 1989.
79. Ibid.
80. ICC to BSPA, 16 November 1989.
81. CTC to BSPA, 21 December 1989.
82. ICC to BSPA & Adv, 29 December 1989. Also see notes attached to BSP copy of CTC to BSPA, 21 December 1989.
83. BSP AdvM, 9 January 1990; MM to Tierney, 15 January 1990.
84. BSPAM, 9 January 1990.
85. Ibid.
86. Ibid.
87. Ibid.
88. Ibid.
89. MM to Jane Thomas, 15 January 1990.
90. Ibid.
91. For examples see: *Portland Press Herald*, 10 January 1990; *Katahdin Times*, 17 January 1990; *BDN*, 11 January 1990.
92. For examples see: *PPH*, 10 January 1990; *Portland Sunday*, 14 January 1990.
93. *BDN*, 11 January 1990.
94. *Maine Sunday Telegram*, 28 January 1990.

95. For examples in one paper see: *BDN*, 15 and 16 January, 9 February, and 6 March 1990.
96. *Portland Sunday*, 14 January 1990.
97. *BDN*, April 1990.
98. Ibid.
99. Thomas to MM, 25 January 1990.
100. MM to ICC, 29 March 1990; "Cooperative Research Agreement," signed 4 April 1990.
101. BSP AdvM, 20 April 1990.
102. CTC Press Release, 24 April 1990.
103. MM to ICC, Bob Wright, and Dave Sewell, 25 April 1990.
104. *BDN*, articles, 6 July 1990.
105. *Maine Sunday Telegram*, 28 January 1990.
106. 1990 *AR*, Part B, p.2 and Part D, p. 6.
107. BSP Director's Communication Meeting, 4 December 1990.
108. See BSP files for examples.
109. 1990 *AR*, p. 6.

<u>Chapter Seven</u>:
<u>Snowmobiles, Forbidden And Permitted: Continuing Challenge to Park Access and Use</u>

1. Governor Baxter to Helon Taylor, 11 May 1965; original on file at MSL. Also see Hakola, *Legacy*, for general information on the subject of early use of snowmobiles in BSP, especially pp. 122-23, and 240-41. Hakola does not cover all aspects of the issue, however.
2. Alice Sproul interview with Helon Taylor, summer 1977, MSL.
3. Sproul interview with Arthur Rogers, summer 1977, MSL.
4. Sproul interview with Roland Cobb, summer 1977, MSL.
5. Sproul interview collection, summer 1977, MSL. Hakola included other statements dealing with the issue which might be of value to the reader.
6. See BSP Rules and Regulations for the included years.
7. ICC to Maine Forestry Department, 3 December 1971, in Supervisor's Yearly Reports File, BSP.
8. Austin H. Wilkins to Edmund S. Muskie, 15 January 1970.
9. Ibid.
10. John L. Baxter, Sr. to Maynard F. Marsh, 7 July 1976.
11. BSPAM, 3 February 1970.
12. See Park Rules and Regulations, 1970-1975.

13. ICC to Maine Forestry Department, 3 December 1971.
14. "1971-1972 Report for Commissioners Biennial," ICC, 16 February 1973; ICC, Monthly Report to BSPA, 10 February 1974 and 12 March 1975.
15. BSPAM, 7 January 1976.
16. BSPA Public Hearing, 7 January 1976.
17. BSPAM, 6 April 1976.
18. Assistant Attorney General Sarah Redfield, "The Use of Snowmobiles Within Baxter Park as Contemplated by the 1976 Revision of the Rules and Regulations," 20 May 1976.
19. Redfield to Joseph E. Brennan, 1 April 1976, succeeding quotations taken from material included with Redfield's letter.
20. Ibid.
21. Ibid. Also see Baxter to Wilkins, 18 April 1966.
22. Redfield, "The Use of Snowmobiles."
23. Ibid.
24. Ibid.
25. Ibid.
26. BSPAM, 6 July 1976.
27. Tabulated and quoted from letters and petitions on file at BSP, most dated July to early August 1976.
28. Ibid.
29. Ibid.
30. John L Baxter, Sr. to Maynard F. Marsh, 7 July 1976; Marsh to John Baxter, 8 July 1976.
31. BSPAM, 3 August 1976.
32. Ibid. Also see John Baxter to Marsh, 9 August 1976.
33. BSPAM, 3 August 1976.
34. BSPAM, 7 September 1976.
35. Ibid. Also, see note 27; Alfred and Susan Cooper to BSPA, 31 July 1976; and ICC to BSPA, 10 November 1976. The administrative use of snowsleds and such regulations were discussed in following meetings as planned, and Katahdin Lake Campgrounds, whose owners had protested the ban, were given permission to use snowsleds in BSP to supply the camps and for emergency purposes.
36. "Notice of Public Hearing, BSPA," 12 May 1977; BSPAM, 6 April 1977.
37. BSPAM, 6 April 1977; Winston C. Robbins to Maynard F. Marsh, A. Lee Tibbs, and Advisory Committee, 12 April 1977.

38. BSPAM, 10 May and 7 June 1977; "Notice of Public Hearing, BSPA," 12 May 1977.
39. Compiled from BSP files for 1979. Also see BSPAM, 6 September 1979.
40. Ibid. Also see ICC to Richard S. Cohen, 4 October 1979, and ICC to Robert H. Gardiner, 29 November 1979, for quoted materials.
41. Ibid. Quoted material from James S. Erwin to Beverly Rand, 5 September 1979.
42. Attorney General, "Petition for Instructions," 11 September 1980.
43. Jud Roberts to Richard S. Cohen, 29 October 1979; *Maine Snowmobiler*, September 1979.
44. Anne R. Erickson to Richard S. Cohen, 31 October 1979. Erickson also asserted that she had helped submit a petition several years before with 120 signatures in support of snowmobiles. The petition referred to seems to have been the 1976 one which, as far as can be determined, contained roughly 580 signatures.
45. AG's Office, "Memorandum of 23 May 1980," to BSPA. See BSPA minutes for spring 1980 for further information.
46. Ibid.
47. Rufus Brown, AG's Office, "Supplemental Memorandum of Law," 11 September 1980. Also see BSPAMs for these months.
48. BSPAM, 2 November 1979. For Lund's statements see the more detailed draft of the meeting minutes.
49. BSPAM, 22 October and 2 November 1980. For names of interveners see Justice Daniel E. Wathen, Superior Court Civil Action, Docket No. CV80515, 12 June 1981.
50. BSPAMs, 26 January and 24 February 1981.
51. Justice Daniel E. Wathen, Superior Court Civil Action, Docket No. CV80515, 12 June 1981.
52. Taken from direct quotations in the decision, see previous note.
53. Ibid.
54. Ibid.
55. Ibid.
56. Ibid.
57. BSPAMs, 15 June and 8 August 1981; IDM, Lee Tibbs to BSPA & Adv. 26 August 1981.
58. Ibid.
59. Ibid.
60. Ibid.

61. Maine Audubon Society Testimony before the Baxter State Park Authority, William L. Plouffe, 21 September 1981. This testimony later became Exhibit Two in the snowmobile trial.
62. Ibid.
63. See note 57.
64. Ibid.
65. Ibid.
66. Ibid.
67. Ibid.
68. Ibid.
69. BSPA Public Hearing, Millinocket, 23 September 1981.
70. BSPA Public Hearing, Maine, 24 September 1995.
71. Ibid.
72. Ibid.
73. BSPA Public Hearing, Portland, 24 September 1981.
74. Ibid.
75. Ibid.
76. Ibid.
77. Ibid.
78. See BSP files, September through November 1981.
79. Ibid. Also see Ronald N. Wyre to Glenn H. Manuel, 29 October 1981; James S. Erwin to BSPA, 22 September 1981; Paul A. MacDonald to BSPA, 18 September 1981; and Deposition of Ethel Dyer, Civil Action Docket No. CV80515, 3 February 1981.
80. BSPAM, 19 November 1981; also see his interview with Helon Taylor, autumn 1981, exact date unknown. Information on staff meeting supplied by ICC, 1995.
81. Ibid.
82. Ibid.
83. Ibid.
84. Clinton Baxter Dyer to Glenn Manuel, 5 November 1981; *Portland Press Herald*, 30 November 1981; also see Rufus Brown, "Baxter State Park Authority Factual and Policy Statement for Rule 19," Draft, 15 December 1981, for further information on the vote.
85. Brown, "Factual and Policy Statement."
86. Ibid.
87. See BSP files for letters from snowmobile organizations and members during late 1981, and general Maine newspapers for the same period for editorials and news items.

88. Charles Fitzgerald to Ralph Palmer, 26 December 1981. The letter, with Palmer's name handwritten and the balance typed, seems to have been a form letter sent to those who had earlier contributed to the other lawsuits and who might be willing to contribute to the present one.
89. *Maine Times*, 4 December 1981, p. 14. The quotation from Baxter, as it appeared in the advertisement, was taken from Baxter's letter to Governor Reed, 20 May 1960.
90. For an example see the *Ellsworth American*, 18 February 1982, section 2, p. 8.
91. Ibid.
92. Memorandum, Rufus Brown to Glenn Manuel, 23 February 1982, copy of snowmobile suit attached.
93. BSPAMs, 12 January, 9 March, 16 March, 13 April, and 17 June 1982.
94. See BSPAMs for these years. Also see Communication Committee Meeting Minutes, 6 and 7 June 1985.
95. See BSP files for these years. Ruling for 1985 taken from *Roger Norman et al v. Baxter State Park Authority*, Argued 15 January 1986, Decided 6 May 1986, Decision No. 4115, Law Docket No. Ken-85-175, McKusick, C.J., and Nichols, Roberts, Glassman, and Scolnik, JJ.
96. Ibid.
97. Ibid.
98. Ibid.
99. Ibid. Also see BSPAM, 8 May 1986, for a brief discussion of the matter.
100. ICC to Toni Blake, 24 November 1992; Toni Blake to ICC, 25 November 1992. First contact made by telephone on November 24, 1995.
101. ICC to Toni Blake, 24 November 1992.
102. BSPAM, 6 December 1974.
103. ICC to BSPA, 25 November 1992.
104. Director's Communication Meeting, 1 December 1992; *Katahdin Times*, 8 December 1992.
105. Memorandum, "Suspension of Snowmobiling in Baxter State Park." Paul Stern to ICC, 3 December 1992. In spite of the memorandum's title, it contained no reference to ending snowmobile use in the Park. Alse see ICC to Scott Ramsey (Department of Conservation), 3 December 1992; ICC to William Vail, 3 December 1992; ICC to Howard Hannon (MSA), 4 December 1992; and BSPAM, 12 January 1993.

106. See Director's Communication Meeting, 1 December 1992 as well as the BSPAMs for the 1990s. Caverly's 1995 opinions were given in an interview with the author on 21 July 1995.

Chapter Eight:
Motorcycles: Public Use Challenge, Park Access Denied

1. "Notification of Changes in Rules and Regulations, Baxter State Park, Revision 1970."
2. Public Notice by the Millinocket Fin and Feather Club, June 1970.
3. IDM, Sarah Redfield to Joseph E. Brennan, April 22, 1975.
4. Ibid.
5. Ibid.
6. Dick Parker, "Mt. Katahdin," *Northeast Riding*, May 1985, pp. 40-42, BSPAM, 9 July 1986.
7. BSPAM, 9 July 1986.
8. Ibid.
9. Ibid.
10. Ibid
11. Ibid.
12. Brownie Carson, NRC, to BSPA, 9 July 1986.
13. Barbara B. Lounsbury to BSPA, 9 July 1986. See Chapter Seven for Lounsbury's involvement in the snowmobiling controversy.
14. Percival B. Baxter to Austin H. Wilkins, 18 April 1966.
15. See note 13.
16. BSPAM, 9 July 1986.
17. Ibid.
18. Greig Perkins, United Bikers of Maine, to BSPA, 9 March 1993.
19. Perkins to ICC, 18 April 1993.
20. Quotes taken from 27 April 1993 minutes by John F. Loyd, Jr. Also see notes of same date by Benjamin P. Townsend.
21. Compiled from note 16 sources. Quotes from B. Townsend
22. Ibid.
23. See note 20.
24. Ibid.
25. Letters on file at BSP. Also see Jym St. Pierre to BSPA, 16 April 1993.
26 Ibid.
27. *Portland Press Herald* (*PPH*), 8 April 1993.
28. *Kennebec Journal* (*KJ*), 8 April 1993.
29. *Times Record* (*TR*), 12 March 1993.

30. Memo, J. Loyd, 13 May 1993; Memorandum, B. Townsend, 4 May 1993.
31. BSPAM, 12 May 1993.
32. Public Use Committee Meeting, 14 June 1993.
33. Ibid.
34. BSPA & AdvMs, 13 July 1993.
35. *Lewiston Sunday Sun*, 18 July 1993.
36. *BDN*, 17-18 July 1993.
37. Ibid.
38. Ibid.
39. Ibid.
40. *Maine Sunday Telegram*, 18 July 1993.
41. Ibid.
42. Catherine Johnson, NRCM, to Sue Bell, 27 July 1993.
43. Robert Martin to Ben Nighthorse Campbell, 23 September 1993; Campbell to William Cohen, 27 October 1993; Cohen to ICC, 3 December 1993; ICC to Martin, 16 December 1993.

Chapter Nine: The "Staff of the Authority:" Baxter State Park Personnel

1. Information on personnel taken from the April 1970 "Baxter State Park Organization Chart and Attached Schedules," and from comparable information published in the 1994 *AR*. For a review of Park Personnel and administration before 1970, see Hakola, *Legacy*, pp. 207-214 and related sections.
2. Information on personnel taken from the April 1970 Baxter State Park Organization Chart and Attached Schedules, and from comparable information published in the 1994 AR.
3. April 1970 Baxter State Park Organization Chart and Attached Schedules.
4. Taken from general Park records for the era, plus information on Janice Caverly taken from interview with Janice Caverly on 12 January 1996.
5. Taken from general Park records for the era. For years of the Park Supervisors and Acting Supervisors, as well as Authority members, see Hakola, *Legacy*, pp. 319-322.
6. Interview with ICC, 2 October 1994. Information on Kearny's settlement with BSPA taken from BSPAM, 9 July 1971. Information on job evaluations taken from personnel records for 1977-1994 as supplied by ICC.

7. General overview of the era.
8. BSPAM, 9 July 1971, also see 1970 Organizational Chart for Business Manager's data, and earlier Park records for related information.
9. William Cross to BSPA, undated but intrinsic evidence suggests a date of early to mid-1971.
10. Ibid.
11. See general Park records. Information on Caverly's notification taken from an inverview with him on 6 January 1996, and some of the career information from an interview with ICC on 14 November 1995 and 12 January 1996. For a brief coverage of early BSP ranger training see Hakola, *Legacy*, 211-212.
12. ICC to Maine Forestry Department, Supervisor's Report, 3 December 1971. BSPAM, 9 July 1971.
13. Information taken from deeds and contracts on file at BSP.
14. Lee brand work clothing had been used in 1960 and for some time previous, according to an interview with ICC on 6 January 1996. Also see Hakola, *Legacy* on 1960 approval as well as ICC interview.
15. BSPAMs, 9 July 1971; 23 January 1973 and, long quote, 21 May 1996. Also see general Park records for the 1970's.
16. BSPAMs, 9 July 1971; 13 January 1970; and 23 January 1973.
17. BSPAM, 19 January 1971.
18. Interview with ICC, 6 January 1996.
19. BSPAM, 1 March 1972. See general Park records for coverage of illegal drug use in the 1970s and later.
20. BSPAM, 16 December 1969. The particular instance of drug education was for a special Warden School held 6-8 January 1970 by Inland Fisheries and Game. Information on New Brunswick Ranger School and the United States Park Service taken from the interview with ICC, 6 January 1996, and information on other training appears in the general Park records for the era. See Chapter Four for information on related training in the 1970's. Quote from BSPAM, 20 February 1973.
21. 24 April 1974.
22. BSPAM, 20 and 27 February 1973; 17 January 1974; 16 January 1975.
23. BSPAM, 21 May 1974, and 6 November 1973. Information on servicing of Park vehicles and snowmobiles taken from interview with ICC, 6 January 1996.
24. BSPAM, 23 January 1973.
25. BSPAM, 13 February 1973; interview with ICC, 6 January 1996.
26. BSPAM, 29 January 1973.

27. BSPAMs, 27 February, 21 March, 5 July, and 19 July 1973.
28. BSPAMs, 6 and 28 November 1973.
29. BSPAMs, 12 March and 24 April 1974.
30. BSPAMs, 24 October and 6 and 24 December 1974.
31. See BSPAMs, May 1975 to August 1978, and Chapter Two for additional information.
32. See Chapter Three for further information as well as BSPAMs for the period.
33. BSPAM, 4 May 1976.
34. Ibid.
35. Ibid.
36. BSPAM, 19 October 1976. Additional information on Hay Study provided by ICC, 24 February 1996.
37. BSPAMs, 19 October and 9 November 1976.
38. BSPAMs, 9 November and 7 December 1976.
39. BSPAMs, 7 December 1976 and 2 August 1977.
40. BSPAMs, 19 October, 9 November, and 7 December 1976; 10 May 1977.
41. BSPAMs, 19 October, 9 November, and 7 December 1976.
42. BSPAMs, 6 April 1977.
43. BSPAMs, 13 October and 16 December 1977; 6 June 1978, BSPAMs, mid 1979.
44. See Hakola, *Legacy*, p. 210 on Gifford, and for a record of the women contractors see BSPAM, 13 January 1970.
45. The efforts of the women are evident in accounts of rescue and other operations for the era. See Hakola, *Legacy*, p. 207 for the connection between Trust money and employment of rangers' wives, and interview with ICC, 6 January 1996, for the camp stores.
46. Interview with Janice Caverly, 12 January 1996.
47. A. Lee Tibbs to "Staff and Members, Advisory Committee," 29 September 1981, reprinted in 1981 *AR*.
48. BSPAMs, 21 and 22 December 1981; 12 January 1982.
49. BSPAM, 12 January 1982.
50. Ibid.
51. BSPAM, 16 March 1982.
52. Interview with ICC, 6 September 1994.
53. Information and observations based on numerous conversations with Caverly during the writing of *In the Deeds We Trust*, and from Park documents from throughout the period studied.

54. The following stories were told by Caverly in 1995 during an interview with the author. Caverly had previously told her the stories, and she had heard parts of two of them at other times. Caverly has a supply of numerous other such tales which he occasionally recites at the many functions he attends in his role of Park Director—several of which the author attended while conducting research. In all honesty, the three stories which follow are perhaps as much the favorites of the author as they are of Caverly.
55. Initial comments on Merry taken from interview with ICC, 6 January 1996; information on his 1982 work taken from the 1982 *AR*.
56. "Baxter State Park Organizational Chart, April 1982," and related documents, reprinted in 1981 *AR*.
57. General Park records and interview with ICC, 6 January 1996.
58. "Baxter State Park Organizational Chart, April 1982," and related documents, reprinted in 1981 *AR*.
59. Numbers taken from 1984 and 1994 *AR*s. See *AR*s for other years during the 1980's and 1990's for further information.
60. BSPAMs, 15 October and (draft) 14 December 1982; ICC to BSP Employees, 23 February 1983. See *AR*s for rest of period for length of seasonal employment for various workers.
61. BSPAM, 8 February 1983 and BSP AdvM, 24 September 1984.
62. BSPAM, (draft) 7 June 1993.
63. 1984 *AR*; BSPAM, 12 March 1985.
64. Taken from organizational charts and related material printed in the 1984, 1985, and 1986 *AR*s. See previous and subsequent *AR*s for comparative purposes, and BSPAMs, 13 May and 10 September 1995.
65. Taken from 1984-1994 *AR*s.
66. General overview taken from Park records for 1984 through 1987. See *AR*s and BSPAMs for further information.
67. Ibid.
68. BSPAM, 11 March 1986. See other records of the period for further information.
69. Ibid. The Park did later raise winter camping rates.
70. BSP AdvM, 10 May 1988; BSPAM, 11 May 1988.
71. BSPAM, 5 May 1987 and others for mid-1980s.
72. 1982, and 1984 to 1994 *AR*s.
73. See 1982-1994 *AR*s. The 1981 report, compiled after Caverly became Director, was more primitive than later issues and did not include information on volunteer activity.

74. BSPAM, 11 May 1988.
75. ICC to staff, 1986.
76. BSP AdvM, 10 May 1988; BSPAM, 11 May 1988. Also see Director's Meeting, 12 June 1987.
77. See Chapter Three for information on hiring of Bissell and related SFMA information.
78. See BSPAMs of spring and summer 1988 for general information.
79. Case Number 11-390 0014189, *State of Maine Employees Association-Keith Smith v. Baxter State Park Hiring of Jean Hoekwater*, decision 6 May 1991 by John Burgess.
80. Ibid.
81. Taken primarily from an interview with Hoekwater, 15 November 1995, see general Park records for further information.
82. See BSP AdvM, 12 May 1989, on reclassification of Gatekeepers from Clerical to Field Personnel and the resulting pay increase, as well as information on possible need for higher wages for other seasonal and SFMA workers and concern over contracts. Also see BSPAMs, 12 May and 5 December 1989.
83. BSPAM, 14 September 1990. Also see minutes of Advisory meeting the same day, and interview with ICC, 10 January 1996. Benjamin Townsend objected, at the September meeting, to leaving the position unfunded in the Park's budget as an unfunded position was not an available one regardless of whether or not personnel continued to hold the position open. Information on budget tracking taken from general Park records.
84. See general Park records for the era. Opening day was also a popular one with the media late in the era, and newspapers and radio stations frequently provided brief coverage of the event. The author was also fortunate to attend opening day 1995 as well as observing staff and asking questions of them on numerous dates.
85. Ibid.
86. See 1992-1994 *AR*s and BSPAMs for same years for further information.

<u>Chapter Ten: Conclusion: Baxter State Park in the 1990's</u>

1. Contract of Sale between BSP and the Great Northern Nekoosa Corporation (Georgia-Pacific), dated 16 December 1992; and BSPAM, 16 December 1992. Also see "Togue Pond Plan," Revision of 12 May 1994, a map prepared of purchse in 1993; and BSPAM, 16 December

1992. Information on Cashwell's role from ICC, 7 August 1996.

2. Ibid.
3. "Togue Pond Plan," Revision of 12 May 1994, and map prepared of purchase in 1993. Also see "Baxter State Park Management Plan," original date January 1994, Chapter Three; and "Togue Pond Gatehouse Relocation, Draft Technical Summary," 30 March 1993; BSPAM, 12 April 1994, on committee; and BSPAM, 8 October 1970 on discussion of a visitors information center.
4. Ibid.
5. "Togue Pond Plan," May revision; ICC to BSPA, 21 April 1994; Togue Pond Plan Public Meeting, 15 April 1994; and BSPAM, 12 May 1994.
6. BSPAMS, 12 May and 14 April 1994. Information on Advisory role from Edward Dwyer, 7 August 1996.
7. See 1994 *AR* and BSPAMs for further information on Togue Pond, and Chapter One for information on the Kidney Pond Camps.
8. Contract of Sale, by Great Northern Nekoosa Corporation, for Togue Pond Purchase, dated 16 December 1992. Information on the purchase options of the Lewises and Corrigans taken from discussion with ICC, 21 February 1996. See BSPAMs for pertinent years for further information. See Paul Stern to Darrell Morrow, 2 June 1993, regarding a complaint over how Park management of leases on Togue Pond Purchase compared to earlier leases.
9. BSPAMs, 6 June and 17 October 1978; BSPAM, 7 March 1980 as well as other for the rest of the year; IDM, Sarah Redfield to Joseph E Brennan, 23 April 1976; Memorandum, attachments included, Paul Stern to BSPA, 1 October 1985; BSPAMs 1994-1995; Malcolm B. Whidden, Jr. (chairman, Board of Selectmen, Town of Harpswell), to Vladek Kolman, (then with the Bureau of Forestry), 6 February 1986.
10. See general Park records for the era. See especially records dated 1975-1977; Allan A. Toubman, Assistant Attorney General, to BSPA, 12 September 1977; Toubman to Wakine G. Tanous (Attorney for Arnold R. Daicey, William L. Daicey, and James A. Daicey), 29 December 1977.

11. Allan A. Toubman, Assistant Attorney General, to BSPA, 23 September 1977; Touman to Wakine G. Tanous (Attorney for Arnold R. Daicey, William L. Daicey, and James A. Daicey), 29 December 1977; BSPAMs, 1 February, 6 April, 10 May, 2 August, 13 September, 13 October, and 6 December 1977; BSPAMs, 12 September and 19 December 1978; Sarah Redfield, Assistant Attorney General, to Tanous, 30 July 1979; Redfield to Tanous, 24 August 1979; Redfield to Harold Burbank (new Camp Phoenix property owner), 24 August 1979; Rufus E. Brown, Deputy Attorney General, to Tanous, 20 October 1982; Brown to ICC, 20 October 1982; BSPAMs, 14 December 1982 and 15 November 1983.
12. 1987 *AR*.
13. Paul Stern, Assistant Attorney General, to James Austin, Attorney for the Daiceys, letter with Draft Degree, 13 October 1988; BSPA & AdvMs, 31 March 1989; BSPAM, 13 October 1989; and Camp Phoenix Owners Association to ICC, 23 June 1992.
14. See BSPAM, 3 February 1970, on the need for a new survey and Hakola, *Legacy*, pp. 315-318 for further information of the 1970-1971 survey as conducted. See 1988 *AR* on the ten year survey cycle goal.
15. See general records for the period, and Paul Stern to Gary Merrill, 5 February 1990, concerning boundary dispute on Nesowadnehunk Lake.
16. "Memorandum of Understanding Between the Maine Bureau of Public Lands and Baxter State Park," signed 5 and 6 April 1992; Agreement between BSP and Inland Fisheries and Wildlife, signed 10 and 14 1989.
17. Maine Land Use Regulation Commission, Department of Conservation, "Commission Decision in the Matter of Penobscot Outdoor Center, Inc., Findings of Fact and Decision," 18 November 1993. Also see: ICC, "Events and Considerations Regarding the Pockwockamus Project," circa 1986 and LURC, Amendment D to Development Permit DP 3669, EC 89-156, applicant James P. Mahoney, signed 2 December 1992.
18. Ibid. Park records also include correspondence on the issue and a copy of testimony given by Caverly on the expansion proposal.
19. ICC to David Boulter, 22 July 1993.
20. Taken from general Park records from 1980's and 1990's.
21. Ibid.
22. BSPAMs, 1990, especially 27 November; ICC to BSPA, 13 November 1990; and 1991 *AR*.

23. BSPAM, 15 October 1993; and Director's Communication Meeting, 15 December 1993.
24. General Park records for 1992-1995.
25. See general Park records for the 1990's; BSP AdvM, 14 July 1992, for the indicated changes in committees.
26. See BSPAM, 11 May 1970, for Ohler's appointment as permanent Chair. See 1990 *AR* for a printing of the Advisory Statement of Purpose. The basic functioning of the Advisory and associated members had been the same for quite some time, however. The Authority reviewed the Statement of Purpose in 1994, but the changes were more a matter of clarification or addition than of transformation. Information on Lund from ICC, 7 August 1996.
27. BSPAM, 12 May 1994.
28. Ibid. The May 1995 Authority meeting was the first attended by the author, and her notes are more extensive concerning certain portions of the meeting than are the official minutes, which are generally abbreviated due to the length of the meetings.
29. General overview of the period. See preceding chapters and BSP records for further information.
30. See general Park records for the late 1980s through the mid-1990s for this and following information unless otherwise noted. See especially Bissell's reports in the *AR*s.
31. 1991-1993 *AR*s.
32. 1993 *AR*.
33. See *AR*s and BSPAMs for these years for further information.
34. See Chapter Five for information on caribou reintroduction, and following pages for more information on the pine martin study. The predator control issue also provides a glimpse into methods or questions which played a role in scientific research of wildlife treatment in BSP during these years.
35. ICC to Henry Hilton, 29 April 1992; Hilton to ICC, 4 May 1992.
36. ICC to BSP Administrative Staff, 21 January 1993.
37. Ray B. Owen to Committee, 5 February 1993; Owen to ICC, 2 June 1993.
38. First quote: IDM, ICC to BSP Administrative Staff, 6 June 1993. Second quote and related material: 1993 *AR*.
39. General Park records for 1994-1995.
40. "Guidelines for Scientific Studies in Baxter State Park," January 1996 Revision.

41. Ibid.
42. Ibid. Also see 1980's guidelines and BSPAMs, 1994-1995.
43. Paul Stern to ICC, 1 May 1990, "RE: Donations to BSP," and "Donations Policy as Approved 4 April 1990." Also see general Park records.
44. List of Advisory members attached to letter Austin H. Wilkins to Dr. Alonso Garcelon, 9 April 1970.
45. BSPAM, 1 March 1972; discussion with Owen, October 1995. See BSPAMs and *AR*s for other information.
46. List of Advisory members attached to letter of Austin H. Wilkins to Dr. Alonso Garcelon, 9 April 1970; *BDN, Maine Times, Katahdin Times* for period; and 1989 and 1994 *AR*s on slide shows.
47. Quoted from the "Statement of Purpose" as recorded in *Public Laws of Maine*, 11971, Chapter 477. Also see BSPAM, 3 December 1978.
48. Percival Baxter to Governor John Reed, 20 May 1960.
49. Taken from award.
50. Ibid.
51. These and following quotations from Baxter's Deeds of Trust and Communications.

Annotated Bibliography

Numerous books have been written concerning Baxter State Park, works discussing both the early, or pre-1970, history of the region and works illustrating the beauty Katahdin and the surrounding area offer the naturalist and the outdoors person. In terms of the development of BSP, the most comprehensive and scholarly historical monograph for Baxter State Park before 1970 remains John Hakola's *Legacy of a Lifetime, The Story of Baxter State Park* (1981). The reader is encouraged to consult Hakola on developments concerning BSP in general for early Park history, and as noted in the body of *In The Deeds We Trust: Baxter State Park, 1970-1994. Legacy of a Lifetime* is currently available at Baxter State Park Headquarters in Millinocket and at various Maine libraries.

The Maine State Library in Augusta with its Percival Proctor Baxter Collection, as well as other Maine archives, contain various works pertaining to Governor Baxter and Baxter State Park. The time period covered by *In The Deeds We Trust*, and the book's emphasis on the various challenges facing Baxter State Park and the development of Park policy, necessitated that most research involved primary sources—particularly minutes of various meetings, Park and Authority correspondence, and legal decisions—a majority of which are on file at Park Headquarters. Some of the primary documents are also on file at the Maine State Library.

The primary documents consulted in writing *In The Deeds We Trust* are too numerous to list individually, but citations for the sources are provided in the Endnotes. Numerous newspaper and journal clippings are on file at Park Headquarters, and the Raymond H. Fogler Library at the University of Maine at Orono contains most of these as well as other newspaper and journal sources. The Bangor Public Library likewise holds a number of pertinent newspaper and journal sources. The Maine State Library as well as the Attorney General's Office houses legal documents used in this work, the vast majority of which are also available at Park Headquarters. One collection not available in Millinocket is a series of interviews conducted in 1977 by Alice Sproul of the Attorney General's Office which the Attorney General's Office made available to the author. The reader can locate many of the laws concerning Baxter State Park in the *Laws of Maine* and the *Legislative Journal*.

Oral interviews played a less extensive role in this work than the author initially anticipated. Noting the effect on Hakola's research of the loss of Park records in a 1967 fire at the home of Park Supervisor Helon Taylor, and in consideration of Park histories yet to be written, Irvin C. Caverly, Jr. as Park Supervisor and Park Director maintained extensive files of Park documents of which the author enjoyed the full use. The Park maintained files encompassing numerous aspects of policy issues, including correspondence to and from members of the general public and numerous organizations, petitions, and other records involving opposition to, or concern with, Authority and Park decisions. Supplemented by other sources as noted above and in the Endnotes, a wealth of primary documentation existed which provided ample coverage of most issues. Park staff and others provided answers to many questions posed by the author, but in general these questions involved general processes concerning Park operations or, in some cases, personal viewpoints. One exception to this is information on various subjects provided by Director Caverly. Where used as historical sources in *In The Deeds We Trust*, information from Caverly or other persons has been so identified in the Endnotes.

BAXTER STATE PARK AUTHORITY AND CHIEF ADMINISTRATORS 1970-1994

1970 Chair: Austin H. Wilkins, Commissioner, Forestry Department
Members: James S. Erwin, Attorney General
Ronald R. Speers/George W. Buckman,
Commissioners, Inland Fish and Game Department
Harry Kearney, Supervisor BSP

1971 Chairs: Austin Wilkins/James Erwin, Comm'r, FD & AG
Members: George Buckman/Maynard F. Marsh, Comm'rs, IFG
Harry Kearney/Irvin Caverly, Supervisors, BSP

1972 Chair: James S. Erwin, Attorney General
Members: Austin Wilkins, Comm'r, Forestry Department
Maynard F. Marsh, Comm'r, Inland Fish and Game
Irvin C. Caverly, Supervisor BSP

1973 Chair: Maynard F. Marsh, Comm'r, Inland Fish and Game
Members: Fred E. Holt, Director, Bureau of Forestry
Jon A. Lund, Attorney General
Irvin C. Caverly, Supervisor BSP

1974 Chair: Maynard F. Marsh, Comm'r, Inland Fish and Game
Members: Fred E. Holt, Director, Bureau of Forestry
Jon A. Lund, Attorney General
Irvin C. Caverly, Supervisor BSP

1975 Chair: Maynard F. Marsh, Comm'r, Inland Fish and Game
Members: Fred E. Holt, Director, Bureau of Forestry
Joseph E. Brennan, Attorney General
Irvin C. Caverly, Supervisor BSP
Arthur Lee Tibbs, Director BSP (as of March)

1976 Chair: Maynard Marsh, Comm'r, Inland Fisheries & Wildlife
Members: Joseph E. Brennan, Attorney General
John S. Walker, Bureau of Forestry
A. Lee Tibbs, Director BSP
Irvin C. Caverly, Supervisor BSP

1977 Chair: Maynard Marsh, Comm'r, Inland Fisheries & Wildlife
Members: Joseph E. Brennan, Attorney General
John S. Walker, Bureau of Forestry
A. Lee Tibbs, Director BSP
Irvin C. Caverly, Supervisor BSP

1978 Chair: Maynard Marsh, Comm'r, Inland Fisheries & Wildlife
Members: Joseph E. Brennan, Attorney General
John S. Walker, Bureau of Forestry
A. Lee Tibbs, Director BSP
Irvin C. Caverly, Supervisor BSP

1979 Chair: Maynard Marsh/Richard S. Cohen, Comm'r IFW & AG
Members: J. William Peppard/Glenn Manuel, Acting Commissioner
& Commissioner, IFW
A. Temple Bowen/Kenneth G. Stratton, Director & Acting Director, Bureau of Forestry
A. Lee Tibbs, Director BSP
Irvin C. Caverly, Supervisor BSP

1980 Chair: Richard S. Cohen, Attorney General
Members: Glenn Manuel, Comm'r, Inland Fisheries & Wildlife
Kenneth G. Stratton, Dir., Bureau of Forestry
A. Lee Tibbs, Director BSP
Irvin C. Caverly, Supervisor BSP

1981 Chair: Glenn H. Manuel, Comm'r, Inland Fisheries & Wildlife
Members: Kenneth G. Stratton, Dir., Maine Forest Service
James E. Tierney, Attorney General
A. Lee Tibbs, Director BSP (until October)
Irvin C. Caverly, Supervisor BSP

1982 Chair: Glenn H. Manuel, Comm'r, Inland Fisheries & Wildlife
Members: Kenneth G. Stratton, Dir., Maine Forest Service
James E. Tierney, Attorney General
Irvin C. Caverly, Acting Dir./Director BSP

1983 Chair: Glenn H. Manuel, Comm'r, Inland Fisheries & Wildlife
Members: Kenneth G. Stratton, Dir., Maine Forest Service
James E. Tierney, Attorney General
Irvin C. Caverly, Director BSP1984

1984 Chair: Glenn H. Manuel, Comm'r, Inland Fisheries & Wildlife
Members: Kenneth G. Stratton, Dir., Maine Forest Service
James E. Tierney, Attorney General
Irvin C. Caverly, Director BSP

1985 Chair: Glenn H. Manuel, Comm'r, Inland Fisheries & Wildlife
Members: Kenneth G. Stratton, Dir., Maine Forest Service
James E. Tierney, Attorney General
Irvin C. Caverly, Director BSP

1986 Chair: Glenn H. Manuel, Comm'r, Inland Fisheries & Wildlife
Members: Kenneth G. Stratton, Dir., Maine Forest Service
James E. Tierney, Attorney General
Irvin C. Caverly, Director BSP

1987 Chair: Glenn ManueVJames Tierney Comm'r, IFW & AG
Members: Kenneth Stratton/Thomas Rumpf, Dir. & Acting Dir.,
Maine Forest Service

William J. Vail, Comm'r, IFW (from mid-year)
Irvin C. Caverly, Director BSP

1988 Chair: James E. Tierney, Attorney General
Members: William J. Vail, Comm'r, Inland Fisheries & Wildlife
John H. Cashwell, Director, Maine Forest Service
Irvin C. Caverly, Director BSP

1989 Chair: James E. Tierney, Attorney General
Members: William Vail, Comm'r, Inland Fisheries & Wildlife
John H. Cashwell, Director, Maine Forest Service
Irvin C. Caverly, Director BSP

1990 Chair: James E. Tierney, Attorney General
Members: William Vail, Comm'r, Inland Fisheries & Wildlife
John H. Cashwell, Director, Maine Forest Service
Irvin C. Caverly, Director BSP

1991 Chair: John H. Cashwell, Director, Maine Forest Service
Members: William Vail, Comm'r, Inland Fisheries & Wildlife
Michael E. Carpenter, Attorney General
Irvin C. Caverly, Director BSP

1992 Chair: John Cashwell/William Vail, Dir. Maine Forest Service & Comm'r Inland Fisheries and Wildlife
Members: Michael E. Carpenter, Attorney General
Susan J. Bell, Dir. Maine Forest Service (after autumn)
Irvin C. Caverly, Director BSP

1993 Chair: William Vail/Susan Bell, Comm'r, Inland Fisheries &Wildlife
and Dir. Maine Forest Service
Members: Michael E. Carpenter, Attorney General

Norman Trask/Ray B. Owen, Acting Comm'r and Comm'r, Inland Fisheries & Wildlife
Irvin C. Caverly, Director BSP

1994 Chair: Susan J. Bell, Dir., Maine Forest Service
Members: Michael E. Carpenter, Attorney General
Ray B. Owen, Comm'r Inland Fisheries & Wildlife
Irvin C. Caverly, Director BSP

BAXTER STATE PARK ADVISORY MEMBERS 1970-1995*

Robert Ohler, MD (C)	1970-1995
John Baxter, Sr.	1970-1984
John Cole	1970
Bud Leavitt	1970-1972
Walter Birt (C)	1970-1987
Horace Hildreth	1970
Norman Minsky	1970-1972
Alonzo Garcelon	1970-1972
Daniel Drummond	1970-1972
Paul Knaut, Jr.	1970-1972
Winston C. Robbins (C)	1971-1991
George Buckman	1971-1972
Clifford Goodall	1973-1975
Fred Knight	1973-1981
Sam Butcher	1973
Keith Miller	1973-1977
Stephen Clark	1974-1981
Chris Herter	1975-1979
John Jay Madeira	1975-1979
Paul Firlotte	1976-1989
Fred Holt	1976-1978
Ethel Dyer	1976-1985
Charles Pray	1976-1978
William Cross, Jr.	1978-1994
W. Lowell White	1978-1979
Malcolm Coulter	1978-1979
Charles Bolte	1978-1979
Walter Anderson	1978-1981
Maynard Marsh	1979
Robert Gardiner, Jr.	1979-1986
Whit McEvoy	1979-1984

Hartley Baxter	1979-1981
James Erwin	1979-1981
Michael Pearson	1979-1981
Ronald Wyre	1981-1986
Eric Baxter	1982-1995
Jane Thomas (C)	1982-1995
Jud Roberts	1982-1989
Stephen Crockett	1982-1995
David Redmond	1984-1985
Everett Carson	1984
Rupert White	1984-1995
Jack Hauptman	1987-1990
Benjamin Townsend	1987-1995
Frank Clukey	1987-1995
Francis Dunn	1987-1989
Roy Farnsworth (C)	1988-1995
John F. Loyd, Jr.	1989-1995
Ray B. Owen	1990-1991
John Howard	1989-1995
James Garland	1990-1995
Rick Scribner	1993-1995
John Bibber	1991-1995
Philip Ahrens	1991-1995
Robert Reynolds	1991-1993
Shirley Burke Thaxter	1994-1995
Rodney Hanscom	1994-1995
Paul Haertel	1994-1995
Edward Dwyer	1995

*List includes full Advisory Members, assembled primarily by Bill Cross
(C) Chair

Index

Roy,

Thanks for the help. This is for the memories. Enjoy!

Roy,

You have gone above and beyond the call of duty in earning this complimentary copy. We are pleased with the end result and thank you sincerely. Enjoy! Buzz